BORDER CROSSINGS
Then and Now in the Welsh Marches

Richard Dobson

Grosvenor House
Publishing Limited

The right of Richard Dobson to be identified as the author of this
work has been asserted in accordance with Section 78
of the Copyright, Designs and Patents Act 1988

The book cover is copyright to Richard Dobson
Front cover painting Shelton Oak, Shrewsbury by D. Parkes
With kind permission of Shropshire Council, Shropshire Museums

This book is published by
Grosvenor House Publishing Ltd
Link House
140 The Broadway, Tolworth, Surrey, KT6 7HT.
www.grosvenorhousepublishing.co.uk

A CIP record for this book
is available from the British Library

ISBN 978-1-83975-198-1

To Linda for her precious love and limitless patience

WALES

14TH CENTURY

KEY

PURA WALLIA
(PRINCIPALITY OF WALES)

MARCHIA WALLIA
(WELSH MARCHES)

COUNTY PALATINE
LORDSHIP
LORDSHIP
Lordship

COUNTY
Commote
CANTREF
SENESCHALRY

CL   CLIFFORD
HU   HUNTINGDON
RC   RICHARD'S CASTLE
ST   STAPLETON
Bu   Burford
De   Deugleddy
Gr   Grosmont
Kn   Knighton
Ld   Llanddewror
No   Norton
Pr   Presthesmede
Sk   Skenfrith
Wa   Walwyn's Castle
Wc   White Castle

Talybolion   Twrcelyn
ANGLESEY   Dindaett
Llifon
Malltreath   Menai

Is
Gwyrfo

CAERN
Uwch
Gwyrfai
Eifionyc

Dinllaen

Cafflogion

Cymydmaen

IS AERON

CEMAIS   CILGERRAN   EMLYN

CANTRE

PEBIDIOG

Elfaed
De
LLAWHADEN   ST CLEARS   CARMARTHE
PEMBROKE   YSTLWYF
HAVERFORD   NARBERTH   Ld   LLANSTEFFAN   IS
Wa   LAUGHARNE   CYDWELI
Wa
CARNWYLLION

PEMBROKE

CA

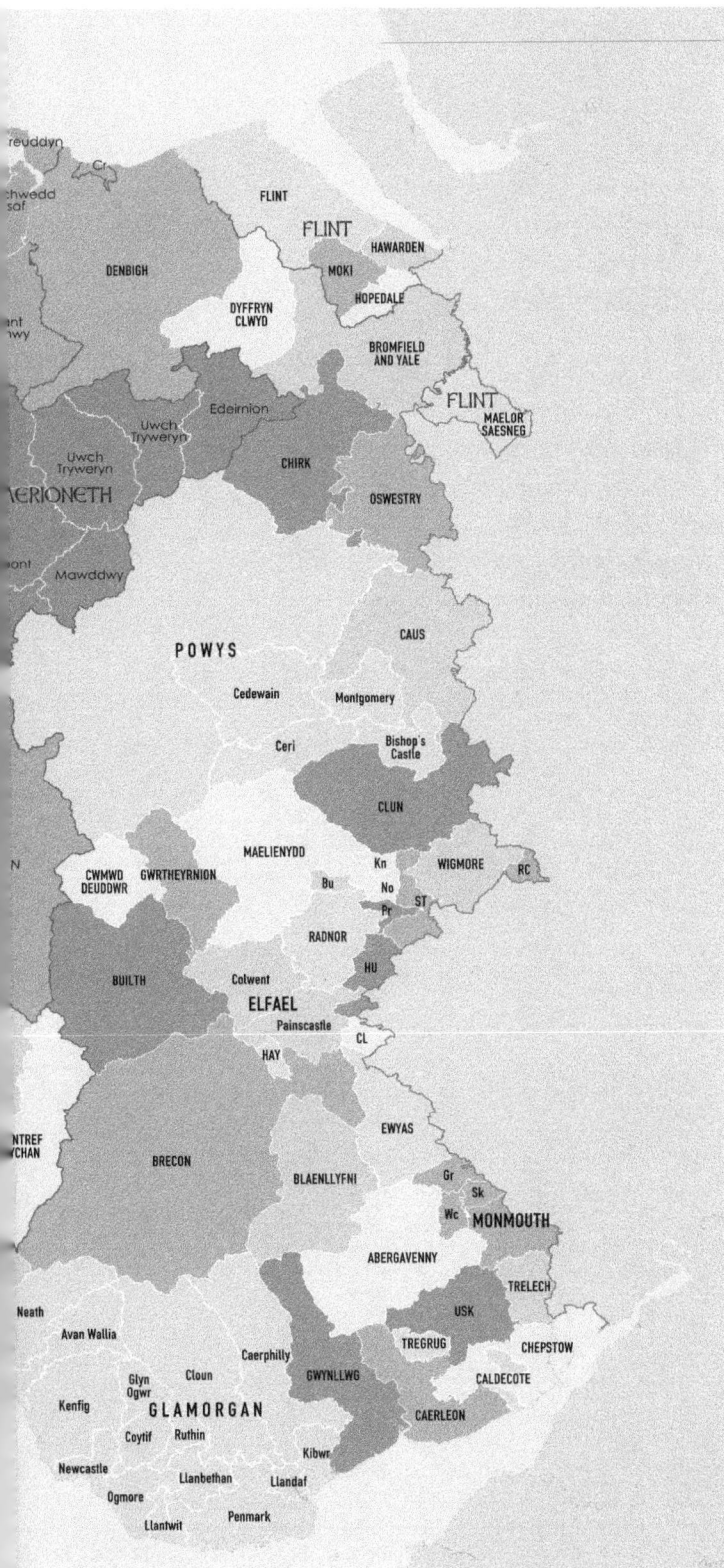

reuddyn

Cr

chwedd
saf

FLINT

FLINT

HAWARDEN

DENBIGH

MOKI

nt
wy

DYFFRYN
CLWYD

HOPEDALE

BROMFIELD
AND YALE

Uwch
Tryweryn

Edeirnion

FLINT

MAELOR
SAESNEG

Uwch
Tryweryn

CHIRK

ERIONETH

OSWESTRY

ont

Mawddwy

CAUS

POWYS

Cedewain

Montgomery

Ceri

Bishop's
Castle

CLUN

MAELIENYDD

Kn

WIGMORE

RC

CWMWD
DEUDDWR

GWRTHEYRNION

Bu

No

ST

Pr

N

RADNOR

HU

BUILTH

Colwent

ELFAEL

Painscastle

CL

HAY

EWYAS

NTREF
CHAN

BRECON

BLAENLLYFNI

Gr

Sk

Wc

MONMOUTH

ABERGAVENNY

TRELECH

Neath

USK

Avan Wallia

Caerphilly

TREGRUG

CHEPSTOW

Glyn
Ogwr

Cloun

GWYNLLWG

CALDECOTE

Kenfig

GLAMORGAN

CAERLEON

Coytif

Ruthin

Newcastle

Kibwr

Llanbethan

Llandaf

Ogmore

Llantwit

Penmark

From high Pumlumon's shaggy side
Three streams in three directions glide;
To thousands at their mouth who tarry,
Honey, gold, and mead they carry.
Flow also from Pumlumon's high
Three streams of generosity;
The first a noble stream indeed
Like rills of Mona runs with mead,
The second bears from vineyards thick
Wine to feeble and the sick;
The third till time shall be no more
Mingled with gold shall silver pour.

Lewis Glyn Cothi 1420 – 1490

Contents

Illustrations

Foreword

There have been many books about the Welsh Marches – but none quite like the present volume. The Marchland is perhaps one of the most enigmatic regions of the British Isles, a land which promotes itself as a magnet for tourists, but at the same time contrives to retain its essential mystery as a place of secrets, sometimes from past millennia, sometimes more immediate. This enigmatic quality, amongst the many others which characterise the Marches, is captured by Richard Dobson in his book. This is not a uniform land – it is one of very varying landscapes, from the flat lands of the Dee estuary and the Gwent levels to the hilly terrain of the middle March. It is full of massive contrasts, from distinctly urban centres at Wrexham, Newtown and Newport, old and stately county towns at Chester, Shrewsbury, Hereford, and Monmouth, market towns of great quality and picturesqueness, such as Welshpool, Builth Wells, Brecon, Abergavenny, Hay on Wye and Chepstow, to rural landscapes characterised by villages and mere hamlets. And then there are the lost towns exemplified by Trellech, symbolic of the shifting quality of the Marches.

Contrasts have always characterised the region. In medieval times the landscape combined burgeoning urban environments with territories which were amongst the least populated in Britain. In more recent centuries the Marches have become a destination for tourists, attracted by the spectacular views of mountain ranges like the Black Mountains of the south and the Berwyn mountains of the north, the great rivers, Severn, Wye, Usk and Dee, and the opportunities for walking – classically along Offa's Dyke Path, the very spine of the Marchland. But they have also been home to pockets of significant manufacturing development and major centres of extractive industry. The Marches have seen, notoriously, conflict between peoples, Welsh and English, and their princes and kings. But they have also been a land of the meeting of peoples and cultures. In places the national boundary twists and turns through landscapes, institutions of church and chapel, even accents, which are much the same on either side of it. For the border is often of little account, except as an administrative marker, in a zone in which peoples of different backgrounds have been thrown together and have learned to co-exist. While many of the towns and regions on the Welsh side of the Marches betray signs of profound Anglicisation, places like Oswestry, standing within Shropshire, are culturally and linguistically as much Welsh as English. All this complexity and all the underlying elusive quality of this rich and varied borderland is brought out in Richard Dobson's book. It is indeed a splendid collection of the reactions of the many peoples who have made their mark on this land from prehistoric times to the present day, and a rich tapestry woven from the commentaries of the visitors, illustrious and humble, who have encountered it on their travels, from medieval observers such as Gerald of Wales, through the accounts of the travellers of the age of romantic tourism, to the wanderings and observations of the author himself.

Dr David Stephenson,
Honorary Research Fellow in Welsh History,
Bangor University

February 2019.

Acknowledgements

Writing such a book as this requires help and collaboration, for which I am grateful to the following.

Dr David Stephenson for taking time off writing his own books on medieval Wales to write the foreword for mine.

The Society of Authors for giving me licence to use H.J. Massingham's wonderful descriptive prose from his own 1952 work *The Southern March*.

My good friend Charles Boase who came up with the idea for the title of this book.

Gordon Dickins for his excellent camera work.

Author and historian Keith Pybus for his generous help with all things Shropshire.

Tim Ryan owner of the Severn Princess, for providing a history of the last ferry boat to operate between Aust and Beachley and for allowing me to take photographs of her in retirement on the Wye bank.

Thanks to Michael Senior for his invaluable assistance identifying crucial landmarks around North Wales. As well as writing several books on subjects of mythology, literature and history, Michael is the author of more than twenty books and booklets dealing with areas and subjects concerned with the history, topography and legends of Wales.

Fellow adventurer and author Chris Barber, protector of Frederick Hando's legacy, who agreed that Fred's descriptions of the Gwent countryside deserved to be re-aired.

Harriet Harvey of Halston Hall for allowing me to visit the chapel in the grounds of her home where centuries of Myttons were laid to rest, including Jack Mytton, the maddest of them all.

Thanks to Ceri Payne for permitting me to quote his father Ffrancis Payne from his *Exploring Radnorshire* and to Peter J Conradi for introducing me to the excellent Transactions of the Radnorshire Society.

Richard Watts for agreeing that Ernest Elliot-Stock's *Land of the Lords Marcher* was worthy of being praised for its unique bicycle ride around Monmouthshire.

Sheila Hooper for graciously agreeing to snippets from her ancestor Francis Kilvert's diary being brought back to life.

Steve Rudd of the King's England Press who liked the idea of reminding followers, if they are still about, of SPB Mais's *Highways & Byways of the Welsh Marches* which he published in 1939 and can see titbits here.

Mark O'Hanlon of the Malcolm Saville Society who have done excellent work to keep Magdalene Weale's memory alive.

Mark and Nicky Bell, owners of the Daisy Bank Caravan Park who looked after my caravan where I did most of the research for the North Wales section of my book.

And finally, a grateful thanks to the locals of the Miners Arms pub in the Border village of Priest Weston, where I spent many contented evenings after long days typing my work, and for making me feel at home.

An Introduction

The Welsh Marches, the name for the area of border lands between England and Wales, are neither England nor Wales but an entity of their own creation, absorbing into their own separate identity the very different characteristics of both countries. The border runs for 257km (160mi) between two great river estuaries, the Severn in the south and the Dee in the north. It has followed broadly that same line since the 8th century when the West Mercian leader Offa built his famous Dyke to hold back the ambitions of the Welsh princes. The Saxon West Mercians never succeeded in conquering Wales, nor did they get much beyond the established border which exists today, more or less. Following the Norman invasion in 1066 a grateful Duke William rewarded his closest followers with land in the area known to be disputed by Welsh tribal chiefs and left them to conquer and rule as they had in their Norman homelands. They became lords again in their Welsh border territories.

The origins of the word 'mearc', or 'march', meaning border or boundary, are both Frankish and Saxon. The northern march was ruled from Chester by Hugh d'Avranches, Duke William's nephew, the middle march was administered from Shrewsbury by Roger de Montgomerie and the southern march from Hereford by William FitzOsbern, perhaps the Conqueror's most intimate ally. During the early years of the marches, control was contested by the English king, the Norman marcher lords, and the Welsh princes. There were numerous combinations of alliances and at the centre of most of them were the self-interest ambitions of the marcher lords, long established as a law unto themselves, even as far as granting life or death. In later years middle ranking lords also established territories - Bernard de Neufmarché at Brecon, Robert Fitz Hamon at Cardiff, and Ranulf de Mortimer at Montgomery. Eventually, more areas came under Norman control as subordinate lordships. There were 141 of these, so says S.P.B Mais in his 1939 publication of *Highways and Byways in the Welsh Marches*.

In 1231 the Welsh prince Llywelyn ap Iorwerth, Llywelyn the Great, incensed by the growing influence and Welsh land grabbing of Henry III.'s justiciar, Henry de Burgh, gathered a large army and sacked marcher strongholds at Montgomery, Brecon and Hay-on-Wye and eventually took the 'Arthurian' Gwent stronghold of Caerleon. At this time Llywelyn was being supported by the young Earl of Pembroke, Richard Marshall, who had seen a chance to challenge King Henry's weakness of controlling border instability. Together Llywelyn and Marshall took control of much of the southern march lands. King Henry was unable to prevent the rebels' advances and after Shrewsbury was taken in the early part of 1234 the King reluctantly agreed to a treaty with Llywelyn, leaving him in control of much of Welsh border territory. Towards the end of the 13th century, Edward I had seen enough of marcher power and troublesome Welsh princes, and decided the English Crown needed to take more control of its own territories. The Statute of Rhuddlan in 1284, carved up Wales into shires subject to English law and prevented any further marcher expansion. The national border was fixed in 1536 by Henry VIII, when the marcher lordships were abolished altogether, and new county boundaries were created. The administrative boundary of Wales was confirmed further in the Local Government Act 1972, and that settled the perennial argument that Monmouthshire was part of Wales and no longer an English county treated for most purposes as though it were Welsh.

The custom of touring in England and Wales began in the sixteenth century and gained momentum when turmoil in Europe during the 18th century interrupted the traditions of the Grand Tours. Gentlemen of leisure took to travelling the highways and byways for weeks or even months to discover hitherto undiscovered home territory. Professional travel guides were made available at Posthouses, but travellers were often dependent on local men, who might have been expected to recognise any diversions or danger points *en route*. The terrible conditions of the roads up to the nineteenth century were a constant theme of the writings of Sir Richard Colt Hoare and his erstwhile travelling companion Archdeacon William Coxe. Another, Arthur Young, was so appalled at the state of the roads in Wales during his tour in 1768, he wrote accusingly about turnpikes being of little use:

> What am I to say of the roads in this country! From Chepstow to the half-way house between Newport and Cardiff they continue mere rocky lanes, full of hugeous stones as big as one's horse, and abominable holes. The first six miles from Newport were so detestable, and without either direction posts or milestones so that I could not persuade myself I was on the turnpike.

In 17th century John Ogilby, a Scottish cartographer best known for publishing the first British road atlas was appointed by James II of England as His Majesty's Cosmographer and Geographic Printer. His Britannia atlas of 1675 set the standard for all the road maps that followed. During that period some of the minor roads used the local mile of 2,428 yards and known as long miles rather than the standard mile of 1,760 standard yards which Ogilby had adopted. Celia Fiennes frequently noted that the roads she followed during her tour of England and Wales in 1685 were measured in those local long miles. Milestones and signposts were rare in the 17th century and where they were found travellers complained about their inaccuracy. It remained like this until the introduction of turnpike trusts.

The birth of British tourism occurred in 1745 with the introduction by the Rev John Egerton of river tours down the Wye from Ross on the Herefordshire border. But it wasn't until after the industrial revolution that there was an effective tourist industry advising the services of suitable inns to satisfy a gentlemen's culinary and comfort needs, or those of his servants or horses. William Cobbett lived simply, not to say austerely, on his travels. He told his readers with no little complacency after covering 965km (600mi) in the early autumn of 1826 that:

> During the whole of this ride, I have very rarely been a-bed after daylight, I have drunk neither wine nor spirits. I have eaten no vegetables, and only a very moderate quantity of meat; and, it may be useful for my readers to know, that the riding of twenty miles

was not so fatiguing to me at the end of my tour as the riding of ten miles at the beginning of it.

Celia Fiennes observed with a woman's eye and noted intimate details that she witnessed. She wrote enthusiastically of the fine furnishing of country houses she visited. She was aroused though by matters of sanitation and living conditions of people in the towns. In the countryside, the landscapes of the farmers were regarded by the followers of William Gilpin's Picturesque movement with disapproval and contempt. And so, while the likes of Young and Cobbett, Colt Hoare and Coxe, strode and rode the countryside for practical results, Gilpin's disciples were setting out on expeditions of a more aesthetic purpose: The search for ideal material for an artist's palette. The Victorian traveller, author, and self-illustrator, Charles George Harper, published a record of a visit to the Welsh border, *The Marches of Wales,* in 1894. Harper's journey had begun a year or two before at Chepstow and followed the more regular pattern of south to north and had the time and energy to travel mostly on foot. Interestingly, he was prepared for his journey to progress, not without annoyances of travel and even wrote in the preface of his book:

> I cannot understand why it should be an accepted convention with the writers of touring works that they should ever be in a steadfastly good humour through all the mishaps of their touring, as though they relish their trials and inconveniences.

Because of his own misgivings, Harper warned that his record:

> Should be seen in spectacles both rose coloured and neutral tinted; nor blame him for the skies that are sometimes dark and himself footsore, and therefore in an unreceptive frame of mind.

It can be said that the first tour of the Welsh borderlands was in 1188 when Giraldus Cambrensis, Gerald of Wales, in accompaniment with Archbishop Baldwin, set out on a Crusade to enlist fighters to defend Jerusalem against Saladin. In a convoluted journey, they covered their entire distance to St David's in west Wales, through South Wales as far as Caerleon, then north to Basingwerk Abbey on the Dee estuary, and finally to Hereford. Quite a haul. They met to begin with at Hereford on Friday 4th March and left immediately for New Radnor over the border in Powys, riding horseback for the best part of that day. According to Lewis Thorpe's translation of Gerald's *Journey Through Wales* they stayed for two nights at Castle Crugerydd, Cruker Castle, before moving on to Hay on Wye. Thorpe put Cruker Castle near Old Radnor whereas the OS map places it at Fronddyrys further west along the modern A44. It is not entirely clear why the Crusaders went to New Radnor in the first instant when they could have gone to Hay straight from Hereford, only a half day's journey, then called at New Radnor later in their schedule. No converts are recorded at Hay, or Brecon, where they stayed the following night at Gerald's own Bishop's Palace. (Are you still following?)

Celia Fiennes became the first woman traveller and by 1705 had covered nearly the whole country on horseback, 'to regain my health by variety and change of air and exercise'. She wrote vivid day-to-day accounts of her travels, allowing her readers to follow her into all the varied adventures in which she continually found herself. She wrote purely for pleasure, and apart from one passing reference to William Camden, she was oblivious to any other travel writings. In 1932 Magdalene Weale, a teacher from London, spent the summer break touring on horseback in the Shropshire hills. It was a brave move for her, too, as she only had a hired racing pony for company, an unlikely alliance, and used lonely inns in which to stay each night. Another unlikely alliance was Dr Samuel Johnson and Mrs Hester Thrale who toured together in 1774. Johnson was a close friend of Hester's husband, Henry Thrale, at that time the Member of Parliament for Southwark. Hester was herself a descendant of the wealthy Salusbury clan of North Wales and had inherited property there which she wished to visit. Henry thought it a good idea if Dr Johnson should accompany his wife and have a look around the area in the process. They both kept diaries of the adventure each offering different opinions of where they went and who they met. One person they didn't meet was the naturalist, writer and antiquarian, Thomas Pennant. Though his home was at Downing Hall, close to the Dee estuary, around the time Johnson and Thrale were calling on landed residents of North Wales, Pennant was compiling his own *Tours in Wales* and most likely on his travels, paradoxically never crossing their path.

The Colt Hoare banking family's wealth had provided for the construction in the 18th century of Stourhead House in Wiltshire, the home of Sir Richard Colt Hoare. He had inherited the estate through his mother in 1785 but took to travelling around Europe after the tragic death of his wife in the same year. He particularly enjoyed touring Italy but when war intervened, he turned his thoughts to Wales and spent the next twenty summers touring the Principality either by himself, or with Archdeacon William Coxe, or the Welsh topographer, Richard Fenton. Colt Hoare was a trained artist and in 1798 and 1799 he contributed to Coxe's subsequent book *An Historical Tour Through Monmouthshire* with many fine drawings. His own Welsh plans were influenced by Henry Penruddocke Wyndham, another Wiltshire man and friend, and it seems that both used the route taken by Gerald of Wales as a guide for their own separate 18th century tours. Both chose to ride horseback, though Colt Hoare called often on the more leisurely use of a post chaise.

Another challenge in travelling was in the use of the bicycle for lengthy and often uncomfortable journeys. Victorian author, Arthur Granville Bradley, wrote at least three volumes between 1898 and 1911 after exploring Wales, and was surprisingly very much in favour of this chosen method of transport:

A cycle is of course the ideal method by which to see the countryside for the man or woman who is on terms of intimacy with that modest and serviceable machine. The automobile has no doubt immense fascinations as well as utility, but as at present used does not suggest itself as a good vehicle for leisurely exploration or the enjoyment of the scenery. A horse and trap are the obvious alternative for numbers of persons, but your slug of a horse is a trying companion on the road, and with anything better you cannot look about you as freely as when rolling slowly along on a cycle.

Ernest Elliot-Stock, writer and publisher and a man of the old Home county of Middlesex, also chose the bicycle to tour around the southern march in the summer of 1908. He even took with him an early model camera complete with heavy glass plates, the only capture medium available at the time, and relied to a great degree on dry and bright weather for his photography. Later, he drew thirty-six sketches from the photos he'd taken to include in the resulting book which he titled rather grandly *The Land of the Lords Marcher* and subtitled rather confusingly, *being a record of six vagabond days among the peaks and rivers of the West Country*. Perhaps the least popular transport of our time, but not of his, was the charabanc. Journalist and broadcaster, S.P.B Mais, did the whole trip from London by bus in 1937! He started the border tour at Chester, staying at hotels from Monday to Friday, returning by bus to London for the weekend, then beginning again in whichever part of Wales he had left off, until he had completed his journey in Chepstow in South Wales, though why he chose the most crowded method of completing his task, heaven knows.

George Henry Borrow didn't need transport of any kind. In 1854 he set out from Chester to walk through Wales and later wrote *Wild Wales* having completed the task before the year was out. Borrow was a big man, broad shouldered, and had immense stamina. He was often seen in his native Norfolk countryside riding bareback on his black Arab stallion, a speedy high-spirited breed cherished by ancient desert warriors. A big horse for a big man. He also had a large ego and many prejudices which alienated him wherever he went. In writing about North Wales in particular, it is impossible to escape the companionship of the incomparable Borrow. He was equipped for his exploration of the Principality by a knowledge of the Welsh language. During his many attempts to air his accomplishment he had frequent opportunities of proving the hybrid character of those he chanced to meet in the borderlands but was often at a loss whether to address them in Welsh or English.

One man who could neither ride a horse, or a bicycle, nor walk for long stretches, was the leading writer of country matters and agriculture, Harold John Massingham. His best-known book was *World Without End* which he wrote in 1932, reflecting his experiences living in Chipping Campden in the Cotswolds. In 1937, he injured his leg in a serious accident leading to a two-year period of regular hospital visits. Tragically, he hurt the same leg again in a second accident and it had to be amputated. Forced to stop travelling as frequently as he had been doing, he settled down to writing some thirty more books. One such was *The Southern Marches,* which he wrote in 1949 as a contribution for the Country Books Series. That meant at times further difficult travelling and even the occasional feigned climb. It was reading that book which persuaded me to take my own grand tour of the Welsh Marches, beginning on Severn side and ending by the shores of Dee, recalling as I journeyed the experiences of travellers who had gone before me, pedestrians, pedalists, horse and pony riders, stagecoach and carriage users, charabanc or motor coach passengers, and in my case, a camper van. I had just completed *In My Own Time,* my own journey on foot through the beautiful county of Herefordshire, itself a part of the marches, so I had already had a taste of what might be to come.

Part One

The Southern March

Estuary

From the windswept Welsh bank of the Severn Estuary, I looked out onto a modern scene. It was November 2015 and in front of me the massive Second Severn Crossing arched away, carrying the M4 motorway towards the English shore. The sea had retreated earlier that day and was not yet ready to return, leaving vast areas of mud flats glistening in the afternoon sun. Somewhere out there may still be scant remains of the eastern section of Sudbrook Iron Age fort swallowed by centuries of rising waters, tidal advances, and coastal erosion. The western section lies behind me, high and dry clear of the Severn tides. It is a forlorn sight. Although the huge earthworks remain intact, they are choked now by many years' growth of brambles and ivy. On its northern side, the fort has lost two sections of ramparts and ditches to accommodate the gardens of a row of old railway workers' cottages, built in 1877 to accommodate the labour forces constructing the Severn rail tunnel, and a football pitch – complete with twisted rusting goalposts – now forms part of the grassy central plateau. If the picture is not depressing enough, a thirteenth century chapel, built bizarrely within the grounds of the fort, has been allowed to fall into terminal decay – a thick coat of ivy covering the last of the fabric of the building in a ghoulish fashion. It has not been used for worship since 1790. In this place two-and-a-half millennia ago, the Silures people lived in their roundhouses, farmed the surrounding fields, fished in the young Severn river, and worshipped their gods until the Romans arrived and enslaved them. When Archdeacon William Coxe saw the site for the first time in 1798, he observed:

> Heaps of stones and rubbish, which seem to be the remains of ancient buildings. The picturesque ruins of a chapel lie at the distance of half a mile from any habitation but was probably in former times the chapel to a great mansion, for we find that in the 12th century, John Southbroke is mentioned for his house at Southbroke.

3

According to interpreters of the medieval writer, Walter Map, the promontory of Beachley where Wye rejoins Severn at the end of a long journey from their Pumlumon Fawr twin birth in west Wales, was the site of a meeting around 1056 between the unchallenged ruler of Wales, Gruffydd ap Llywelyn, and the King of England, Edward the Confessor, to establish the disputed national boundary between England and Wales. Map's only surviving writing is a collection of anecdotes and trivia containing court gossip and a little history written in a satirical vein, which hasn't enriched his authority on the accuracy of this royal 11th century conference. But it did bring Beachley into the public eye for the first time.

The first regular crossing of the Severn between here and the Gloucestershire shore was by 12th century monks of Tintern Abbey. A ferry of a kind had existed for centuries, since it has always been the narrowest crossing point. The old passage from Aust on the English bank to Beachley was much used in the 15th century by pilgrims to Chapel Rock, lying just off the southern tip of the peninsular. This tiny island, with room only for a small stone cell, was once home to St Tecla – a 4th century anchoress who abandoned her Roman father's home of splendour to live a Christian life. The 16th century antiquarian, William Camden, records the rock as being the home of St Teigyl, while the 15th century chronicler William of Worcester, referred to it amusingly, if not insultingly, as that of St Treacle.

Sadly, Tecla's life of isolation didn't last. She was murdered when her hideaway was discovered by pirate raiders. At some stage in the 6th or 7th century, Tecla's lonely hermitage was taken over by another hermit, Twrog, a Celtic missionary from North Wales who converted Tecla's old cell into a chapel. It is by his name that the current Ordnance Survey map labels this small tidal rocky outcrop. There is little left today of the ancient chapel, but it was used for services when the tide was out, up until the mid-16th century.

On the English shore, Aust is the place from where St Augustine is said to have crossed into Wales during his unsuccessful attempt to bring the Celtic bishops into line with the rituals of Rome. At this point in the river, the tides run swiftly and have always been dangerous, particularly for small boats. That reputation deterred many travellers, one of whom was Daniel Defoe in 1720. As he viewed the crossing from the Aust side, he did not trust the ferry to survive the weather on that day and so, elected to continue on horseback via Gloucester instead, extending his journey by 105km (65m).[1] He did not have the sea legs of Alexander Selkirk, Defoe's Robinson Crusoe, whom he had just left at the Llandoger Trow Inn on Bristol's dockside. Charles Wesley, the English leader of the Methodist movement, was less concerned when he used the ferry in 1743 yet had a lucky escape when his ship almost foundered in a storm.

Figure 1 The Severn Princess Ferryboat in retirement on the Wye bank at Chepstow in in 2016

Travellers have crossed the Severn to Wales since before the 17th century by another crossing. That was from Redwick, a few miles south of Aust on the English side of the estuary (not to be confused with another Redwick on the Caldicot levels) to a landing stage at

---

[1] That journey remained the sole alternative to large vehicles and late arrivals for the modern ferry boats until the opening of the First Seven Crossing in 1966.

Black Rock on the Welsh side, immediately south east of the village of Portskewett. It, too, has been an important crossing point for many centuries. Coins found in the mud along the shoreline, possibly discarded as offerings for a safe crossing, show that it was in constant use throughout the Roman period on their route between Aquae Sulis (Bath) in North Somerset and Venta Silurum (Caerwent) in Monmouthshire. In later years, apart from foot passengers, the ferry boats carried cattle from the Monmouthshire flat lands and wire products from the Angidy iron furnaces at Tintern.

There are dangers along this part of the river, too, though of a different kind. A story that has never been proven but remains a thoroughly acceptable truth tells that during the English Civil War, a troop of Cromwell's Roundheads were drowned off the English Stones rocks while pursuing Prince Rupert across the river. After being assured that they had reached the opposite shore, the cunning ferryman – a Royalist sympathizer – left them significantly short of safety and to a watery fate. In 1715, a new ferry service given the name New Passage was developed by the Lewis family of St. Pierre Park, operating from English Redwick, allowing it to be used by mail and passenger coaches between Bristol and South Wales. At the same time as the New Passage Hotel was being built on the Gloucester shore, an inn at Black Rock was being constructed to serve travellers entering and leaving Wales. These two ferry services, the Old and the New Passages, were the status quo for travellers for the next one hundred years.

In 1798, Archdeacon William Coxe and his friend and fellow traveller, Sir Richard Colt Hoare of Stourhead House, crossed the River Severn from New Passage on the Gloucestershire coast and landed at Black Rock on the Welsh side. They had embarked together on a journey around Monmouthshire. Unlike Colt Hoare, who used his own post chaise and driver, Coxe chose to travel on horseback. At first, they would take the ferry the short distance across the river to the Black Rock Inn and ride from there each day until they had found another convenient base. The Archdeacon's intention on this trip was to travel only through Monmouthshire, while Sir Richard would continue his journey through the marches towards Denbighshire and North Wales, as he had done times before. It had become a welcome relief from the tiresome work on his house and estates in Wiltshire. Until he bought Fach Ddeilliog, his retreat at Bala, he often travelled from Wiltshire, covering predetermined stretches of country and staying at an inn, or as a guest of a distinguished estate owner acquaintance before returning to Stourhead. Invariably, he would sleep at the New Passage Inn before taking the Black Rock ferry. On a previous trip in 1793, he had written in his diary:

> After a rough and tedious passage of two hours and a half, I landed on the opposite side of the channel. I never would recommend anyone to go over in the large New Passage boat, as I did, but to take a small one, as the former is generally much loaded with cattle and horses, which are not the pleasantest companions in a rough sea.

Coxe's account of 1798 was more matter of fact:

> We crossed into Monmouthshire by the New Passage ferry. The breadth of the Severn from shore to shore, at high water, is three miles and a quarter, from the inn on one side to that on the other, three and a half. The shores of Gloucestershire are quite flat at the place of embarkation; higher up stream, near the Old Passage, the cliffs are rocky and steep.

After starting his Welsh adventure from Chepstow in 1892, Charles George Harper, headed west on foot and, after stumbling along stony lanes near Portskewett, sought night shelter at the Black Rock Inn. Following the opening of the Severn Tunnel for rail passengers in 1886, the last ferry to the Gloucester shore had long since left and the inn was about to close. Harper would become its final customer.

From Black Rock, the Wales Coastal Path follows the riverbank north eastwards towards St Pierre Pill – now a quiet anchorage for the Chepstow and District Yacht Club, but as recently as 1860, the harbour for 70-ton barges from Bristol. Writing in *An Historical Tour Through Monmouthshire in 1801*, Coxe described:

> A pleasant walk across the fields, by the side of the Severn, leads to St. Pierre Manor, the residence of the ancient family of Lewis. It is an ancient structure, much altered and modernised with sash windows. The present proprietor, Mr Lewis, was so obliging as to accompany me through the apartments; the frieze of the dining-room is ornamented with coats of arms, carved and emblazoned, among which are the arms of the present family, which they bear from their ancestor Cadivor the Great, who died in 1084. The great Morgan family are descended from the same stock.

The origin of the name St Pierre is contentious. I have read that it might be derived from 'Pyr' and could be either Welsh or Norman. However, the name is clearly French for St Peter, and in the chancel of the church on the estate are two ancient slabs bearing an inscription in Norman French to Urien de St Pierre, lord of this manor until his death in 1293. The origin of the name Lewis is easier to explain. In the 14th century, this was the home of Dafydd ap Philip, and the name of his son, Lewis, was adopted by his descendants as the family surname. Lewis's remained here at St Pierre until 1925, when the estate was sold out of the family. Nevertheless, the Lewis family lineage remains one of the oldest in the UK. In 1960 the great house of Lewis became a hotel and the grounds converted into a golf course.

The nearby village of Mathern, in an older form Merthyr Tewdrig, is now bisected by the M48 motorway which passes over the village's main street. In the church, a stone slab fixed to a wall in the chancel records the demise and burial of Tewdrig, King of Glywysing (Glamorgan), at the end of the 6th century. At some point in his reign, Tewdrig had abdicated in favour of his son, Meurig, in order to live the life of a hermit at Tintern in the lower Wye Valley. When a threat to the kingdom emerged from the advancing Saxons, he swapped his hermit clothing for strong leather and helmet to assist his son in defence of their territory. In the skirmish that followed, Tewdrig was mortally wounded.

He had asked that if he did not recover he was to be taken for burial to Ynys Echni (Flat Holm) in the Bristol Channel. Tragically, he got no further than Mathern Pill by the river when he died, and to satisfy his father's wish Meurig built a church near that spot and buried his father's body there. Such events throughout history have usually carried a legacy, and so it was that the dead king was revered long after as martyr and saint. St Tewdrig's church has been rebuilt several times but today outside the church yard walls stands a wooden statue of the martyred king, splendidly carved in blue cedar by Neil Gow in 2011. The subject is bare-legged and Viking-like, but one wonders whether the old king may have looked saintlier in a longer shirt!

On one of his many 20th century travels around his beloved Gwent, schoolteacher and later reporter for the *South Wales Argos*, Fred Hando recounted the story told to him by an old lady who had lived in Mathern. She claimed to have seen for herself in 1881 the stone coffin bearing Tewdrig's remains with his mortal wound – a hole still visible in the skull made by a spear point. Hando was a little sceptical about her story, but in spite of his doubts, he knew that old ladies should always be believed!

Chepstow

Except for the suburbs of Sedbury and Tutshill, the town of Chepstow sits on the western bank of the River Wye, in Monmouthshire and Wales. In Norman times, it was the centre of the marcher lordship called Striguil, though the origins of that name are confusing and might derive from a Welsh word *ystraigyl*, meaning 'a bend in the river'. Chepstow's imposing castle was begun in 1071 by the Norman lord William FitzOsbern, the Conqueror's closest ally. FitzOsbern cleverly chose to build on tall cliffs above the river – a natural defensive position – and used stone rather than the usual Norman method of turf and timber. It was the first post-Roman construction of its kind, and it was the southernmost of a chain of fortifications that FitzOsbern built along the English-Welsh border of the southern march. It dominated the medieval town which developed at its foot, and even after centuries of growth, still does. Ironically, FitzOsbern did not live long enough to see his new stone home on the clifftops completed; he died in battle in Flanders, pursuing a more personal act of expansionism. But before he left for his date with destiny in northern France, FitzOsbern founded a Benedictine monastery in the town, which, along with stone castles, is another integral sign of the Norman psyche. Monks were brought from his home monastery of Cormeilles in Normandy as its community, and by the early 12th century the monastic establishment overlooking the river about 300 metres from the castle had developed the status of an autonomous religious house in its own right, though it probably never held more than a dozen monks at any one time. St Mary's church and its impressively ornate west doorway are all that remains of the priory.

The Normans weren't the first to pitch camp here. In earlier times, the Celtic Silures people occupied an Iron Age fort south of the town at what is now the suburb of Bulwark, before they were driven away by the invading Romans. The most southerly point of the great dyke built by the Saxon Offa begins on Sedbury cliffs, overlooking the Severn but soon to join and stretch along the east bank of the Wye beyond the castle. The dyke was the original 'march' boundary and was constructed to separate Saxon Mercia from the Welsh Kingdom of Gwent. Its position meant that Offa had intended to include the river as an extension of the dividing line, but it also gave the Welsh continuous access to fishing along the Severn shore and the Wye as far as Monmouth, a generous but still preventative measure by the Mercian chief. The popular national trail that follows the dyke, begins or ends at this point, too, although the various guides indicate that the south to north route ending at Prestatyn by the Irish sea seems to be the preferred option for long-distance walkers.

The first mention of a river bridge at Chepstow dates from 1228. Records later described it as 'feeble and ruinous' and a replacement bridge had also 'fallen into great ruin and decay and likely to fall' less than thirty years after it was built in 1546. Tudor antiquarian, John Leland, wrote:

The town of Chepstow hath been very strongly walled as yet well doth appear. The walls began at the end of the great bridge over the Wye, and so came to the castle, the which yet standeth fair and strong not far from the ruin of the bridge.

Sir Richard Colt Hoare later gave the 19th century picturesque view of the bridge:

The bridge is of great length and from the variety of its architecture affords a fine object for the pencil. The piers on the Monmouth side are of stone, those on the Gloucester side are of wood. One of the great beauties of this scenery is owing to the harmonious and mellow tints with which the stone is coloured and the variety of herbage which overhangs them and grows amongst their fissures. A variety of shipping animates the scene and nothing, but a clearer stream is wanting to render the landscape perfect.

In 1793 an artist of greater reputation, J M Turner, painted a famous view from the opposite bank of the river, of the town, the castle, and a timber-decked bridge. Today, an elegant cast iron bridge – opened in 1816 – has replaced Turner's earlier timber-topped version and continues to hold against Wye's extreme tides. On Colt Hoare's visit, he recorded in his diary of lunching at the Beaufort Arms, now the Beaufort Hotel, before moving on to Abergavenny where he stayed the night at the Angel Hotel. Both these hotels remain in business and still carrying their flags for highly rated accommodation. Coxe has left us a good recommendation for Chepstow itself:

The appearance of the town is cheerful and animated, the inhabitants seem active and industrious. I have seldom visited any town whose picturesque situation surpasses that of Chepstow.

Not so for the Rt. Hon. John Byng, the 5th Viscount Torrington, on tour a few years beforehand in 1774. He expressed in his diary a strong displeasure:

At the inn door of The Three Cranes where I stopped, was a bevy of Welsh squires intoxicating themselves. Of the inn, nothing could be worse or more imposing. The stables were a wretched dungeon; everything was bad and charged high, and this arises from it being the only inn.[2]

Charles Harper and his travelling companion (who he referred to occasionally as 'the other man') had begun their journey to Wales at Temple Meads railway station in Bristol. In the third-class carriage were two other passengers – the Vicar of Chepstow and the resident engineer at the Severn Tunnel Pumping Station on his way to his Sudbrook office. After passing through Pilning on the western outskirts of Bristol, the train plunged into the darkness of the lengthy tunnel, emerging as the night closed into the windy platforms dimly lit with oil-lamps of the Severn Tunnel Junction. Knowing nothing about Chepstow where they would stay the night, the Vicar 'charged himself with advising their wandering steps, in so far as the choice of accommodation lay'. As with Sir Richard Colt Hoare, their choice would be the Beaufort Arms. After breakfast in the clearness of the day, Harper formed an early opinion of the town:

Modern Chepstow is merely sordid. The lapse of ages and changed conditions of life and travel have rendered it into a mere nothingness. If ever a place lived upon romantic history or existed by reason of its situation amid lovely scenery, Chepstow is that place in excelsis. Town and Castle touch two extremes; the town is poor and with a shabbiness that can never wear the interest of the delightfully ruinated castle, perched beside the Wye.

William Makepeace Thackeray's misfortune with his visit to Chepstow in 1842 was with the weather. The rain had poured heavily during the first day of his arrival and it was hard going to

[2] Three Cranes Inn was in Hocker Hill Street off Beaufort Square. While visiting Chepstow in 1802, Lord Nelson and his party stayed there, too. It was demolished and replaced by two houses in 1809.

see any of the beauties of the place. Having indiscreetly scrambled up Beachley Road from the ferry landing slip, he sat obscured under a thick-set hedge for a full hour and a half while the rain poured down:

> Presently afterward, this celebrated literally man, rising from his shelter as there was nothing else for it, had the good luck to find, (though, to be sure the good luck might have come a little earlier) that there was refuge hard by in a little ale-house that goes by the pretty name of The Bonny Thatch[3]. I should have passed the day there with pleasure.

That 'celebrated literary man' chose a more appropriate town hostelry for his night stay, the George Inn, by the old West Gate, which he decided to enthusiastically recommend as one of the 'cleanest, neatest, cheerfullest, freshest salmon' inns to be found anywhere. The 'Gate' through which a single carriageway enters the Chepstow town centre is a 15th century section of the town's port wall and was once the only point of entrance other than the bridge below the castle. It is a feature now of Chepstow tourism, and as such its narrow width will probably remain a restriction for traffic passing into and through the centre for a long time to come.

Chepstow has been a market town since the beginning of the fourteenth century, and for seven hundred years the people had to endure the filth and odours of street livestock. Cattle could wander freely in the town square until required by the butcher, and carcasses were afterwards hung in the streets to drip blood. Farmers conducted sales by private agreement from street pens, but in 1873 auctions were introduced, followed by a decision to find land away from the centre for a new livestock market. A site was chosen between town and river and, though twenty years late, opened in December 1893. In his 1952 book, *About Chepstow*,

---

[3] The Bonny Thatch Inn stood close to the junction of Beachley Road and Sedbury Lane and was conveniently placed for travellers on the way from the Beachley Ferry into Chepstow.

local historian Ivor Waters wrote a *resume* of modern-day urban life there:

> To-day goods are brought to the shops by train or lorry, not made behind the counters of the tradesmen. Articles from abroad are supplied according to the purchasing power of central government, not brought to the Wye side quays in local ships. Customers from the villages around travel comfortably in cars or buses, not along rocky lanes of "huge stones as big as one's horse". But the main features of local trade have not changed essentially, and after nine hundred years of existence, Chepstow is still a market town.

In the Middle Ages, the Port of Chepstow was a major exporting centre for timber from the forests of the Wye Valley and Dean and was the largest port in Wales before the nineteenth century. The exceptional high Severn tides – the river has a 15m (50ft) fall from high tide water levels and is one of the highest tide ranges in the world – enabled large ships to dock there. However, Thackeray was not impressed with the port area:

> There is a suburb along the river with little quays and old faded storehouses, and a dry dock, and a few small craft on the river, and here you see a few sailors lounging about with the fair companions of their leisure hours, and a few tradesmen smoking pipes at little inns.

Years before, he might have seen large numbers of men in full employment as shipwrights and sailmakers, cable makers and pump makers, makers of ropes and masts, and there were customs officers, pilots, and dock porters, too. Foreign tongues would be heard on the quays and in the taverns, and the talk was of quick passages and shipwrecks on the seven seas. The ships have long gone and in recent times a major clearance of the port area has begun to remove redundant factory buildings to create a housing estate. Chepstow is left primarily as a centre for service industries. Its location at the southern end of the Wye Valley, together with its own attractions including its castle and internationally known racecourse, have contributed to its development as a major tourist centre for South Wales.

The Levels of Gwent

The modern westbound A48 road from Chepstow roughly follows the old Roman road to Newport and beyond. Via Julia – so named in tribute to Sextus Julius Frontinus, the Roman governor of Britain from AD 74 to 78 – began at Aquae Sulis (Bath) in Somerset, reached to the shore of the Severn near Aust, continued by use of a ferry to the Welsh bank, then extended to Venta Silurum (Caerwent) and Isca (Caerleon). From there, it became the Via Julia Maritima as it proceeded westward towards Moridunum (Carmarthen) and far West Wales. Edwardian author, photographer, publisher and keen cyclist, Ernest Elliot-Stock and his companion on their cycling tour of Monmouthshire in 1911 found Chepstow momentarily uninviting under leaden skies where photograph subjects showed them 'flat grey pictures, badly lit, and difficult of composition'. However:

> With the old West Gate behind us, our damp spirits rose considerably, though the open country and a good level road may have been the direct cause. And here the landscape is open indeed. Between the old Roman road and the river, the country slopes away upon a carpet of rich pasture to meet the Nedern Brook and the marshes of the Severn shore. Another half-mile of distinctly poor surface, and we had crossed the brook to the marshland around Caldicot.

Impressions of Caldicot struck them even more adversely than had Chepstow as wind and rain swept in across the flat marsh from the Bristol Channel. But then, even a Dutch landscape painting can be easily rendered dour and cheerless beneath a grey pall of cloud, and they were being treated to a particularly unforgiving one that day. In the mid-19th century, Caldicot was still a small farming village. After the opening of the South Wales Railway brought London and Cardiff within easy reach, it inevitably led to the introduction of new industries, and with the beginning of work on the Severn Tunnel, Caldicot's population doubled. When the completed tunnel opened, the community continued to grow, and to increase even more rapidly with the opening of the first Severn Motorway Crossing in 1966. Now Caldicot has become part of the M4 motorway corridor and the population is around 11,500 and counting. But even with a mediaeval castle, the town was and is still not on anyone's touring map. For them, the Via Julia led only to Venta Silurium (Caerwent). When William Coxe and Sir Richard Colt Hoare left Chepstow to continue their Monmouthshire tour, Coxe wrote in recognition of the road's origins:

> In a little more than a mile, we passed through the neat village of Crick, from which place the road continues in a strait direction to Caerwent, and was undoubtedly the site of a Roman way. The foundations of the causeway are yet visible; and I am informed that this part is uncommonly compact and dry. I observed on the sides of the road in several places, large hewn stones, overgrown with the moss of centuries, which were probably employed in the construction of the old causeway.

The previous tribal home of the local Silures is thought to have been the substantial fort on Llanmelin Hill, looking out over the Caldicot levels and the Bristol Channel and within sight of Caerwent. Geographically, Llanmelin was ideally positioned for the Silures to control the seaport by their previous tribal base at Sudbrook. In due course, the defeated tribe accepted the Roman way of life under the rule of the Second Augustan Legion and were eventually given their own form of local government based in the plains below, astride the Via Julia at Venta Silurum, 'the market town of the Silures'. Whether Llanmelin was the tribe's original main home in Gwent is open to speculation. It isn't a huge fort and could not have housed more than a few hundred people and their animals at the most. The Silures were not thought to have lived in multi-tribal communes, but it is fair to assume that when the Romans built Venta, the town would have been open to all Silurians in the wider territory of South Wales. The Romans established Venta Silurum[4] as a civil control centre for the defeated Silures but at first they did not include any notable defences due to the mistaken belief that there would be no tribal revolts which the army couldn't deal with. Nevertheless, the process of complete subjugation was slower than expected, so earth ramparts went up around AD 130 and, as the still reluctant population grew, these were followed in the 4th century by substantial stone walls. Much of these walls survive – rising spectacularly in places to 5m (16.5ft) – and they have been described as the most impressive of Roman town defences anywhere in Britain, or indeed Northern Europe. Certainly, anyone who sees this great structure in situ, or walks the 1.6km (1 mile) distance around it, could do little other than stare in awe and wonder at how it has survived for so long.

Venta was in easy reach of the Romans' Welsh river port at Sudbrook, which then gave them access to the English coast at Abonae (Sea Mills). Sometime before the third century, Venta had become a wealthy town, and suggested it had attracted veterans of the Second Augustan Legion from Isca (Caerleon) as their place of retirement. However, back home in Italy, civil war was brewing. The Roman military force's general for Wales, Magnus Maximus – known to the Welsh as Macsen Wledig – had become a favourite with the Britannia-based army and took many of his troops over to Gaul. There, he defeated the Emperor Gratian in battle, and for a time had control of Roman matters in both Britain and Gaul.

From the fifteenth century onwards, various travellers wrote in their day of the old Roman town. One of the first to do so was John Leland, who described it as 'sometime a fair and large city'. Another visitor was William Camden. In 1565, he wrote, 'Venta is a very ancient city, whose name neither the rage of men nor time has yet extinguished'. But even by then, much of the old place had already been pulled apart and robbed of its stone to build the new town of

---

[4] The name Venta Silurum meaning 'market town of the Silures' was probably the origin of the later Welsh Kingdom of Guenta, which eventually became Gwent.

Caerwent. When Whig MP, Henry Penruddocke Wyndham, arrived in 1774, he expressed with some regret that:

> This was a considerable station in the time of the Romans. It stands on a gentle elevation and was fortified by that people with a strong wall inclosing a large square. At present it is a miserable village and had nothing till lately to manifest its former greatness, excepting here and there some long fragments of the ancient walls.

By a coincidence of timing, the Rt. Hon. John Byng was touring the marches during the same year as Wyndham, and Caerwent was also on his route. He noted the beginnings of the new town:

> Within the walls, a church and a small village have been built. In an orchard, near the southern wall, has lately been discovered the most perfect and beautiful mosaic pavement of the size and pattern of a modern carpet of three colours. It belongs to Mr Lewis of St Pierre, who has been prevailed upon to erect a building over it with a locked door; so though it has suffered already, as it must from being walked upon, it should be considered a most wonderful curiosity and a drawing ought instantly to be taken, to perpetuate the workmanship.

Ernest Elliot-Stock first saw the town in 1911 as nothing more than a pleasant little collection of small farms and cottages dotted about amongst orchards along the straight stretch of road that cuts it so neatly in half from East to West. Whilst there, he heard a farmer argue that 'tessellated' paving made indifferent cattle food and preferred that the re-discovered ancient stones be covered up again! Might it have been the latest owner of the barn that was standing four-square on the site of the Basilica's official department, and a pig sty where togas of councillors once swept? One wonders if Elliot-Stock's response to the farmer's outburst might have been "Tempora mutantur, et Venta Silurum mutatur in illis." Times change, and Venta Silurum changes with them. Writing later about Caerwent's basilica, he reflected:

18

How easily imagination can picture the busy shop surrounded Forum; the crowded steps leading to the paved south aisle of the Basilica with its lofty nave, and roof carried on massive columns, each with its Corinthian capital. Within, a discreetly screened chamber for the judges, and, at the farther end, the row of subordinate offices opening outward upon another flight of steps to the northern streets and walls of the city. But all we are allowed to see today are the rough foundations that carried those massive columns, and a few broken fragments of their capitals, and even these were only brought to light in the year of 1900!

The first archaeological excavations of any significance at Caerwent began in 1855 by Octavius Morgan, Member of Parliament for Monmouthshire and a notable antiquarian but his discoveries were limited and the work was not followed up for many years. In fact, it was more than forty years later before any further serious explorations took place. The modern town has continued to grow on top of the Roman one, and half of the ancient settlement still remains to be uncovered. Today, however, the A48 traffic passes by on its northern side and leaves Caerwent to its ghosts and as yet still buried tessellated cattle food.

Opposite the site of the Venta's north gate, on the far side of the A48, is a second Caerwent – a vast 20th century military area partly hidden behind tall bordering trees and shrubs. In 1939 farmland here and the nearby village of Dinham were requisitioned by the Government, and a huge factory complex was built over them to produce explosives materials and the storage of ammunition for use in World War 2. The subsequent complex had its own standard gauge railway system linked to the national network, an enormous range of buildings – over four hundred of them with connecting roads and communication structures – all encompassed by an 11km (7 miles) perimeter road and security fence. On completion, the site covered six hundred hectares (1,490 acres). It was assigned at first as the Royal Navy Propellant Factory (RNPF) and later re-assigned and renamed RAF Caerwent.

In 1967, Charles De Gaulle fell out with the United States, having decided he could no longer tolerate their military presence in Europe. Consequently, when the UK Government transferred the site to US administration, Caerwent was once again occupied by a foreign force. That side of the A48 road became a storage depot for part of the US Army European Theatre reserve stocks. The RAF Caerwent signs came down and were replaced by USADA Caerwent (United States Arms Depot Activity) with a Royal Air Force liaison team present as guests. At its height the USADA base was among the largest ammunition supply depots in Western Europe, storing over 80,000 tonnes of conventional munitions – a substantial part of the US Army's European stocks. 11,000 tonnes of ammunition were shipped from here to the Middle East in 1990 and played a critical part in Operation Desert Shield and Desert Storm. The US occupation of Caerwent came to an end in June 1992, by which time the climate in Europe and Asia had quietened down and the US Army announced it was to close their storage operations in the UK. Over 60,000 tonnes of munitions were moved out over a period of less than ten months; the last batch removed by train in July 1993. By the end of August that year, they had all gone home.

Down the western side of the vast area left vacant after the US withdrawal, flows a little-known brook some nine miles long known as the Castrogi Brook[5]. It moves northeast and then southeast around the Great Went Wood (Wentwood), penetrating a romantic combe and emerging under the prehistoric Llanmelin hilltop fort before skirting Roman Caerwent, Caldicot Castle and emptying into the Severn estuary. What other stream barely nine miles long includes in its itinerary so much of modern and pre-history? Indeed, what other brook waters a more exquisite valley than the one in these parts called the Cwm? Local author Fred Hando knew it well:

As we made our enchanted way that day between those forest slopes, we realised that the birds seemed to be answering the

---

[5] Castrogi Brook becomes the Neddern Brook after the A48, before continuing its journey to the Severn.

brook, whose varying music of faint tinkles and deep rushing notes, called them all. Not a movement of air stirred twig or grass, greener now than in any other season and jeweled with spring flowers. The stems of willows flushed with new life, the tiny leaf-green points of tree buds, the scent of primroses, violets and the damp earth. Together with the music of birds and brook, all captivated us.

In another time, Sir Richard Colt Hoare in his one-horse chaise, and Archdeacon William Coxe on horseback, raced along the Newport road for a moment of friendly challenge, after which they found a quiet comfortable inn, the Rock and Fountain. Sir Richard was familiar both with the terrain and the inn and had occasionally stayed the night on his way north from where he had made excursions into the neighbouring parts. Here the road runs in a valley bounded by ridges of wooded hills which converge near Penhow and forms a narrow pass. Poised on the northern point of Salisbury Hill and overlooking the inn, Penhow Castle is a fine fortified manor house, developed from a heavily built Norman keep. It started life as a stone pele tower belonging to a local Welsh prince but following the Norman invasion and the construction of Chepstow Castle, Penhow was given to one, Roger de St Maur. In return, he had the task of controlling local Welsh resistance, providing a quota of men for guard duty at Chepstow every month, and – possibly inexplicable for the modern accounting man – for supplying one man mounted on a horse in times of war. It was the first home in Britain of a family destined to become one of the greatest in the land. The family name St Maur eventually changed to Seymour, the origin of all Seymours; just off the A48 here is a hamlet that bears their name, Parc-Seymour, the site of their earliest known head house.

In 1973, Penhow Castle stood roofless, but film maker Stephen Weeks fell in love with the place, bought it, and embarked on an ambitious programme of restoration and landscaping. He turned Penhow into an award-winning tourist attraction, but after thirty years of spending all his time and most of his money to keep his venture going, he sold up and moved to the Czech Republic.

In contrast, the new owners have returned the castle once again to being an exceptional, though strictly private family home.

The Rt. Hon. John Byng travelled this road on his tour through South Wales and he, too, stopped at the Rock and Fountain. Later, he wrote of it agreeably in his diary:

> After our observations at Caerwent and another three miles of riding, we stopped at a small public house, the Rock and Fountain, near Penhow. Our dinner consisted of beans and bacon and mutton chops, in a parlour and house of my sort for a summer noon stop!

For over 300 years, the inn has been a popular stopping-off point for travellers along what many described as 'the London road'. It ceased trading in 2009 – a rare event – but its popularity and convenience meant it would not remain closed for long. And so, it was that a new owner and a £1m renovation and redevelopment breathed new life into this historic watering hole. Modernisation appears to have been kept to a minimum, and accommodation is still available for those on the move.

Four miles west of Caerwent and nearing Penhow, our intrepid cyclists, Ernest Elliot-Stock and friend, as if in ridicule of their labouring efforts, were passed by an old man in a donkey cart, his seating a bench of new-mown hay, his smile a mixture of indulgent contempt and utter contentment, and his pace far above the legal limit for a donkey. After which experience, a beer or two may have been sorely needed at the R & F!

In this land of castles, a short distance from that at Penhow is another, more heavily-constructed and more castle-like at Pencoed – a partially ruinous, three-storied Tudor mansion hidden in quiet countryside. It was once owned by the great Morgan family but was derelict by the early part of the 18th century and being used as a farmhouse. There were ambitious plans, first mooted in 1989, to use the site as part of a golf and hotel complex, but Sir Terry Matthews had already put forward a similar idea for Celtic Manor a few miles down the road. More proposals came forward to build a large theme park around the

Pencoed ruins, which would have been known as Legend Court, but the promoters failed to obtain planning permission. It was too late, anyway; by then, Sir Terry's grand golf resort was well underway. Since then, the present owner of Pencoed has repaired the roof and reglazed some of the windows to prevent further rain damage, but the prospects of actually doing something with it look decidedly uncertain.*[6] When Colt Hoare and Coxe discovered Pencoed, it struck the pair more forcibly than they expected, as it had been little mentioned in their researches:

> Here however we are agreeably surprised in finding a most beautiful pile of building. The gateway is perfect, one tower like that of Raglan and Caldicot completely covered with ivy. A round tower adjoining has good effect. The outward walls being broken down admit a view of the old mansion behind which is well built of grey stones and well varied with ivy. The windows are particularly picturesque, as also is the porch.

Nearing the end of his walk around *Wild Wales* in 1854, George Borrow left Newport on the 16th of November, heading for Chepstow. At the time, the roads were wet and muddy following a night of heavy rain, and the sky dull and gloomy. Curious to discover where Welsh speaking ceased east of Newport, he engaged in conversation in Welsh with several people along the way. After eight miles, he was still receiving replies in the native tongue, but it was another familiar sound that stopped him in his tracks:

> At Llanvaches, a pretty little village, I was about in the middle of this place when I heard an odd sound something like a note of recognition, which attracted my attention to an object very near to me from which it seemed to proceed, and which was coming from the direction in which I was going. It was the figure of a female

---

[6] Property developer, Peter Morgan, bought the castle in 2003 and received planning permission in 2007 to convert the ruin into offices and build twelve houses in the grounds. In 2016, Mr Morgan was given a life sentence in prison, so any further work is unlikely now to go ahead.

wrapped in a coarse blue cloak, the feet bare and the legs bare also nearly up to the knee, both terribly splashed with the slush of the road. The head was surmounted by a hood which just permitted me to see red hair, broad face, grey eyes, a snubbed nose, blubber lips and great white teeth - the eyes were staring intently at me. I stopped and stared too and thought I recognised the features of the uncouth girl I had seen on the green near Chester with the Irish tinkers.

Amazingly, it seems this girl had somehow walked for over 209km (130mi) as far as Chepstow and was now on her way to Newport to sell her needles. In conversation, the girl told Borrow she had been on the road for a week, and this without shoes or stockings. He had invited her to the nearby inn (yes, it was the Rock and Fountain), and there bought her food and drink. She confirmed to him that she was indeed Irish. Her father and mother had both died, and the tinkers of Chester had been her guardians for a while. She could not read or write but Borrow found in her vulnerability a toughness and resilience and determination to stay alive. When they came to part, Borrow gave her some advice. "Whether you learn to read or not, eschew striopachas (prostitution), don't steal, don't deceive, and worship God in spirit, not in image. That's the best counsel I can give you."

> In the middle of the road, we shook hands and parted, she going towards Newport and I towards Chepstow. After a few yards, I turned and looked after her. There she was in the damp lowering afternoon wending her way slowly through the mud, her upper form huddled in the rough mantle, and her coarse legs bare to the top of her calves. "Surely," said I to myself "there never was an object less promising in appearance. Who would think that there could be all the good sense and proper feeling in that uncouth girl, which there really is."

Westbound from Chepstow, and lying between the A48 and the Severn mudflats, is an area of lush farmland criss-crossed by reens, the type of drainage channels so familiar in western flat lands. For centuries, this landscape has been at the mercy of flooding from the unpredictable rise and falls in the estuary. These levels are part of a greater expanse spreading beyond the mouth of the River Usk in the direction of Cardiff Bay, and recognised accumulatively as the Gwent Levels. But it's not all level. There are occasional hidden rises topped by an occasional tidy, if not pretty, village. Llanwern village is one of the prettier ones and defies the ugly vast areas of derelict steelworks now lying at its feet. It is a typical Gwent village on the moors. The ancient church sleeps amidst rich meadows, and with the inn and neat cottages, the wooded slopes and the barns, remains as the local poet, W.H. Davies, once knew it. Fred Hando spent much of his time, in all weathers, wandering these quiet agricultural flatlands. It was one of his favourite haunts:

> I have known the Levels in the depths of winter, when the high winds whistle through the reeds; I have seen, on a still summer's evening, a heron, unaware of my presence for minutes, standing as if in meditation in the cool water; but for magical loveliness give me the banks of the Monks-ditch[7] near Great Barn in February, when the snowdrops nod to their silver reflections.

On the cliff tops at Goldcliff, overlooking the Bristol Channel, a priory was founded in 1113 by Robert de Chandos, whose father, Robert senior, was companion-in-arms to William the Conqueror in 1066 and earned lands in South Wales as his reward. Robert junior returned that compliment by granting the priory to the abbey of Our Lady of Bec in Normandy. Goldcliff eventually became the largest and richest monastic centre in Wales but exists now only in the stones of Hill Farm perched on the headland overlooking the sea. The name 'Goldcliff' is said to have originated from the assumed silica influence in the limestone cliffs standing about 18m (60 feet) high. They have

---

[7] The Monks Ditch is a drain constructed by the monks of Goldcliff Priory to provide them with fresh water. They made the facility available to inhabitants of the levels who lived close to the priory

been seen by seamen on passing ships in the Bristol Channel to reflect 'jewel-like' in sunshine. Gerald of Wales, referred to the location as "Gouldclyffe" and described it as "...glittering with a wonderful brightness". William Camden described it with even greater conviction:

> A Golden Cliff, so called, because the stones there, of a golden colour, by reverberation of the Sun shining full upon them, glitter with a wonderful brightness: neither can I be easily persuaded that Nature hath given this brightness in veins unto the stones, and that there should be a flower here without fruit, were there any man that would search into the veins there, and using the direction of Art enter in the inmost and secretest bowels of the Earth.

In 1878, a large flat stone was discovered here in the mud of the River Severn beyond the sea wall. Carved into it seems to be a record of the efforts made by soldiers from the Second Augustan Legion, that they constructed 33.5 paces of some form of structure, presumably the first sea wall. The Romans of Caerleon recognised the potential of the fertile alluvial soil of the Levels and enclosed the land behind the wall, then dug a series of ditches to drain it and turn it into a rich meadow. By the time the Benedictine monks arrived in the 12th century, the Romans' wall was in ruins, so under their guidance the stretch closest to their abbey was rebuilt. On 30 January, 1607, the coasts of the Bristol Channel suffered from an unexpectedly high tide that broke the old monks' walls and further coastal defences in several places. The devastation was particularly severe on the Welsh side, extending from Laugharne in Carmarthenshire to Chepstow in Monmouthshire – a distance of 193km (120 mi) – Cardiff being the most badly affected town. More than 2,000 people were drowned, houses and villages were swept away, farmland swamped, and livestock destroyed. Today, the repaired wall stretches along the shore for several miles from Caldicot, again protecting the marsh from the constant threat of the Severn's unpredictability. A number of commemorative plaques can be seen on surviving church walls showing how high the waters rose; the best example being inside on the north wall of

St Mary's church at Goldcliff. The plaque records the year as 1606 because, under the Julian calendar in use at that time, the new year did not start until March 25th.

As backdrop to the Caldicot Levels, Wentwood is a forested area of high hills rising to 309 m (1,014ft) at Pen-y-Cae-mawr. Historically known as the Great Forest of the Kings, it is the largest site of ancient woodland in Wales and the ninth largest in the UK, 1,000 acres in all, most of which has been owned since 2006 by the Woodland Trust. Once it stretched between the rivers Wye and Usk, and was a hunting preserve of the lords of Chepstow Castle. This huge arboreal landscape was renowned for its many native trees, but in particular two species which are represented by areas of the wood known as Cadeira Beeches and Foresters Oak. Often viewed in the past as the Great Gwent Wood, it also contains bronze age burial mounds, a stone circle, and a Megalithic alignment on Gray Hill. During World War 1, part of the forest was cleared to provide timber for trench-building, and the devastation left had lasting consequences. Visiting the wood in 1949, traveller and writer on country affairs, H.J. Massingham, described the landscape in gloomy tones:

> Everywhere I saw the void where trees once stood, filled in with a litter of bramble, will-herb and tussocky white grass. The haughty woodland nymph intoxicating in her wild ways has become a raddled cast-off slut. The whole area is a dismal derelict waste, an upland hell and the bleakest of monuments to man's suicidal policy and cupidity.

On a bright summer's day in 2015 I climbed to the summit of Pen-y-cae-mawr where, from the midst of forest scenery, I looked down on a rich vale of Monmouthshire, watered by a calm and winding Usk, randomly dotted with villages and bounded to the west by the long chain of hills which stretch from Pontypool to the mass of mountains above Abergavenny. In this diverse landscape I caught the first glimpse of the Sugar Loaf and Skirrid, the Holy Mountain, which form the principal features of this glorious valley. From Kemeys Graig the forest descends to the road and begins to close about the traveller, forming a delightful avenue through which he is given occasional glimpses of the Usk, now a very pastoral stream fifty feet below. In days gone by, the valley road passed a little church buried in the sloping woodland – a solitary cell that was full of charm and beauty but lacked a congregation. All Saints was at one time for the sole use of the residents of Kemeys House, the summerhouse on the brow of the hillside erected by George Kemeys in the 18th century. Boasting one day to his uncle that he had constructed a building from which eleven counties could be seen, the uncle replied, "I am sorry, nephew, that eleven counties can also see thy folly."

On reaching the village of Llanbeder in the district of Langstone, the Via Julia separates itself from the A48 and continues westward over Chepstow Hill towards Isca Caerleon. Soon, a turning to the left leads to the entrance to a rich man's dream. The Celtic Manor Resort is a golf and leisure complex of considerable size. It has three championship golf courses and three hotels. The largest of them, the Resort Hotel, is a four hundred-room mammoth looking down from the heights of Coldra Woods over junction 24 of the M4 motorway with an in-your-face appearance. It is all the invention of Sir Terry Matthews, Wales' first billionaire, who was born in the Manor House – later a maternity hospital for the local health authority, but eventually becoming the first of the resort's hotels.

Matthews grew up in the town of Newbridge, ten miles north west of Newport, but left Britain to seek his fortune in Canada, which he duly found. Driving along the M4 one day on a rare visit to relatives, he saw the old hospital boarded up and left to fall into ruin. It was another defining moment for the lad from Newbridge, and from then on, his life was never going to be the same. He embarked on a journey spanning 30 years and spending more than £100m of his personal fortune to develop the landmark golf and country estate. For Sir Terry, the crowning glory for his investment was surely its choice of venue in 2010 for the Ryder Cup – the first to be held in Wales – followed four years later by the bonus of hosting a NATO summit.

Beyond Celtic Manor, the Via Julia passes through the village of Christchurch, whose church steeple has for centuries been a beacon for travellers in the Usk valley far below. According to Fred Hando, the Normans built Holy Trinity on Mount St Albans, a hill which had been treated as holy ground by ancient Britons. It has long been thought that there was once an ancient chapel on the Mount, which is mentioned by William Coxe as the traditional burial site of Alban – the saint after whom the Hertfordshire Roman town of Verulamium would be re-named.

Figure 2 Frederick James Hando

If he is indeed buried there, Alban may be not alone, because Julian and Aaron, Roman martyrs of Caerleon, are also said to be have been interred in the same chapel. Nothing remains of the chapel above the surface, but recent excavations by Cardiff University discovered east/west aligned walls signifying a building, yet unidentified. Looking out across the vale from this same hill one day, Fred Hando recalled:

> My father took me there on one of our earliest walks and showed me a hilltop gate overlooking Caerleon. "I used to see a tall, bearded gentleman leaning on this gate, smoking a pipe, and watching the sunset. He told me his name was Alfred Tennyson."

In later years, Hando often visited the Hanbury Arms in Caerleon where the friendly innkeeper once showed him the 'Magistrates Room', in which Tennyson stayed in 1833 and where he mused and planned his *Idylls of the King*, his well-read poem of King Arthur and Camelot.

Newport: No Time to Stand and Stare

Located on the River Usk close to its confluence with the Severn estuary, the old industrial town of Newport has recently evolved as a cathedral and university unitary authority area within South Wales. It is also now the third largest city in the whole of Wales. Originally translated straightforwardly from the Welsh Cas Newydd as New Castle, the name is probably a mark of distinction from Caerleon, which, in early times, was the old port with the old castle. Gerald of Wales mentioned Newport in 1188 as being a new burgh or new port by a little river named Nant Pencarn:

> Which cannot be waded and passed over but at certain fords, not so much for any depth that the water is of, as for the hollowness of the channel, and the easy mud in the bottom: and it had of old a ford named Rydpencarn, that is, the ford under the top of a rock.[8]

William Camden also mentions the New Port in 1577 and later wrote:

> At the mouth of Usk, grew up the new port, a town of later time built, and not unknown, by reason of the castle and commodious-ness of the harbour: in which place there was in times past one of these Roman high ways or streets, whereof Alexander Necham hath made mention in these Verses: "Usk into Severn headlong runs and makes his stream to swell / Witness with me is Julia Street, that knoweth it full well."

The first castle at Newport was a motte-and-bailey type, built on Stow Hill high above the modern city at the time of William Rufus, around 1075. The stone replacement was built in a new place by Hugh de Audley, 1st Earl of Gloucester, in the style befitting a great, great grandson of Henry II. The new castle's

---

[8] Possibly a settlement below Stow Hill where St Woolos built his church, now Newport's cathedral.

position by the river allowed its southern marcher occupants to control the river crossing and upstream trade, but often it was vulnerable to any determined attacker. Owain Glyndŵr found it an easy target as he marauded his way around South Wales in the 15th century, as did Oliver Cromwell's forces during the Civil War two hundred years later, and its use continued to decline further in later centuries. By 1743, the castle was in a state of ruin, and to add insult to injury, 19th century town building projects and the later addition of the inner ring road resulted in further reductions to the castle site, including the destruction of most of the inner bailey and the removal of the moat. Notwithstanding the only part of the castle to survive is a section by the riverbank, it was given a Grade II listing in 1951.

Newport has been a port since medieval times. It outgrew the earlier Roman town of Caerleon downstream and in the 19th century increased considerably when its port became the focus of coal exports from the eastern valleys of South Wales. Until the rise of Cardiff from the 1850s, Newport was Wales's largest coal-exporting port. The wharves along the stretch of river immediately in front of the town were hugely important in creating Wales as the world's first industrialised nation. They linked the valleys with their coal and iron via canals and railways to the ships which transported their products to the rest of the world.

The Newport townscape has become populated in recent times by a series of modern sculptures that haven't always been appreciated nor welcome and have provoked controversy as the new city has attempted to gain a reputation for itself in the world of the arts. *Stand and Stare* by Paul Bothwell Kincaid is a puzzling, almost sinister, veiled statue on Commercial Street and celebrates W.H. Davies's best-known poem, *Leisure* – though how, only the sculptor would know. At the other end of the same street, *Chartist Suffrage*, created by Christopher Kelly, is placed by the old Westgate Hotel building, commemorating the Chartist uprising of 1839. *The Bell Carrier*, Sebastian Boyesen's sculpture of a huge bronze ox with a bell on its back, was inspired by the tale of St Gwynllyw's conversion to Christianity. Legend has it that an angel appeared to him in a dream, telling him to seek out a white ox and build a church where he found it. You'll find the ox now outside Debenhams store, but Gwynllyw allegedly saw it first at the top of Stow Hill and his church has become the city's cathedral, named after him in the anglicised form of St Woolo's.

Another difficult piece to fathom, *Archform* by Harvey Hood, has been standing next to the taxi ranks outside Newport's railway station since 1981. It was made from steel and commissioned by the old British Rail company, with support from the Welsh Arts Council. Local MP, Paul Flynn, once claimed that he saw it "fall off the back of a lorry", and poet and author of *Real Newport*, Ann Drysdale, thought it "looked like an air conditioning vent". The official clarification states 'the sculptural form explores the engineering processes and structures fundamental to the building of Britain's railway system'. Personally, I think Drysdale's description is nearer the mark. By far the most remarkable and visual art form is Peter Fink's tribute to Newport's steel industry. *Steel Wave* is a 14m (45ft) high and over 35m (115ft) long sculpture, painted in Welsh rugby red. This monster is the centrepiece of a riverside promenade space where once commercial and passenger ships berthed during the town's industrial heyday.

Figure 3 Peter Fink's 'Steel Wave' at Newport, South Wales

On the ridge of Stowe Hill above the new city, St Woolos isn't the most attractive of Welsh cathedrals, certainly not on a par with that of Llandaff or even Brecon, and seems to have been chosen over Monmouth, Abergavenny or Chepstow as an appropriate throne for the diocese's bishops, primarily due to it being in the centre of the episcopal see. A 1963 extension of the chancel made use of stones from the tragically demolished All Saints church of Kemeys Inferior which used to grace the east banks of the Usk but has warranted only the briefest of mentions in the cathedral's guidebook. There are a few striking features, not least in St Mary's Chapel where the magnificent Norman arch rests on Roman pillars said to have been rescued from Caerleon. The view through this archway centres on the east end creation by John Piper of a circular window of stained glass above a painted canvas. As my reader will know, I have previously doubted the reasoning behind mixing ancient and modern, as in All Saints church in Hereford, and here again the one doesn't enthrall me with the other. Piper's marbled effect is clever and beautiful but does not compare, with the work of an eleventh century master mason, the arch-maker. Outside the cathedral, in the corner of a wall of the burial ground, is a plaque with the statement:

ON NOVEMBER 4TH 1839 MORE THAN TWENTY SUPPORTERS OF THE CHARTIST MOVEMENT, WHICH SOUGHT TO ESTABLISH DEMOCRATIC RIGHTS FOR ALL MEN, DIED IN AN EXCHANGE OF SHOTS AT THE WESTGATE HOTEL NEWPORT. TEN WERE BURIED IN THIS CHURCHYARD IN UNMARKED GRAVES. THIS STONE IS DEDICATED TO THEIR MEMORY.

In 1839, the heavy industrial areas of the South Wales valleys were seen as a hot bed of resentment towards their employers, in particular the wealthy iron masters of Nantyglo and Blaenavon. Inevitably, there was talk of strikes and even rebellion. Anger went deep, and there were underground preparations for a rising, but what followed was tragic and farcical. On November 9th that year, several thousand men – mostly miners and iron workers – led by John Frost, a Justice of the Peace and former mayor, marched on Newport. It rained heavily that night and the poor weather was critical and inevitably led to a low concentration among the rioters. The organisers had expected 20,000 men to join within an hour's march. As it turned out, their ammunition was useless in the conditions, and many were spiritless and hungry as they sought shelter, many in St Woolos church. When the main body of men finally arrived outside the Westgate Hotel in the centre of the town, their revolt was met by local militia who fired on them. Twenty-two marchers were killed and the leaders arrested. John Frost was sentenced to death for treason, but his sentence was later commuted to transportation to Tasmania. He was allowed later to return to Britain, but not to Newport.

Had he been living at the time I have no doubt poet and writer William Henry Davies would have stood with the marchers. He was born not far from the Westgate Hotel in 1871 in Portland Street, and much of his later work grew from observations about life's hardships born from his own disparate childhood in and around Newport Docks. He spent a significant part of his life as a rootless drifter in North America, but for all that, he became one of the most popular poets of his time. After badly damaging a foot jumping from a train in Canada, he ended up with a wooden leg and the sense that, 'all the wildness had been taken out of me.' He eventually returned to Wales to write, sleeping rough and, on good days, living in a poorhouse. His attention to the ways in which the human condition is reflected in nature was highlighted in his classic poem, *Leisure*, written in 1911.

What is this life if, full of care?
We have no time to stand and stare.
No time to stand beneath the boughs
And stare as long as sheep or cows.
No time to see, when woods we pass,
Where squirrels hide their nuts in grass.
No time to see, in broad daylight,
Streams full of stars, like skies at night.
No time to turn at Beauty's glance,
And watch her feet, how they can dance.
No time to wait till her mouth can
Enrich that smile her eyes began.
A poor life this if, full of care,
We have no time to stand and stare.

I have had those lines encased in a glassed frame hanging on my bedroom wall for many years, and Davies's words have become my eternal epitaph as I grow old and slow, while life about me gathers pace towards who knows what end.

On the outskirts of Newport is Tredegar House, the stronghold of the great Morgan dynasty since the earliest days of the 15th century. For over five hundred years it was home to one of the greatest of Welsh families until they left in 1951. Morgans' mansion once stood at the centre of a 1,000-acre estate but has been whittled down to its present ninety acres by urban development and the M4 motorway. The house itself became an addition to the estates of the National Trust in 2012. To Leland in the 16th century, it was a familiar setting when he wrote the condensed words:

> At Tredegar park, Mr William Morgan hath a very fair place of stone. It is a mile and a half from Newport south west on the hither side of the Ebbw river. Newport is a big town whereof that part where the parish church is standeth on a hill. The church is St Gwynlliw (St Woolos). The fairest of the town is all in one street.

That street is Stow Hill and it ends by the old Westgate Hotel, scene of Newport's most tragic rebellion.

Theatre of Idylls and Legends

> *Land of lore in song oft told;*
> *Another Eden, heaven sent,*
> *That faultless Arthur fought to hold;*
> *Peaceful 'smiling land' of Gwent.*

Isca Silurum, later becoming Caerleon, was the Roman garrison of Legio Secunda Augusta, the Second Augustan Legion, named after its founder, Emperor Augustus. It was built around the same time as Venta Silurum (Caerwent) as a base from which Governor Sextus Julian Fontinus began the conquest of Wales, and became their headquarters acting as a control centre in the south, similar to that at Deva Victrix (Chester) in the north. As with Caerwent and the hilltop fort at Llanmellin, Isca was built in the river plain below an abandoned Iron Age fort crowning Lodge Hill, more than likely vacated by the local Silurian tribe when the Romans arrived. The garrison housed the 5,500 heavily armed infantry troops that made up part of the Legion of the original invasion force of Britain in AD 43. It had served with distinction under its previous commander, Titus Flavius Vespasianus stationed at Exeter in Devon. After Vespasian became Emperor of Rome in AD 69, and it was he who appointed Frontinus to finish the job of defeating the Silures tribe in Wales. Nine hundred years ago, Gerald of Wales, saw in Isca a place of unquestioned antiquity. In his *Itinerary Through Wales* he has left us an account of the Roman ruins:

> You can still see many vestiges of its one-time splendour. There are immense palaces, which, with the gilded gables of their roofs, once rivalled the magnificence of Rome. Many remains of its former magnificence are still visible for it was originally built by the Roman princes, and adorned with stately edifices; a gigantic tower, numerous baths, ruins of temples, and a theatre, the walls of which are partly standing.

Gerald would have seen too, the remains of much of the amphitheatre exposed outside the walls. In the 9th century, a monk from the Celtic monastic community at Bangor on Dee wrote *Historia Brittonum, History of the Brittons,* which included many references to a great leader called Arthur. Later, another monk, one of Gerald's contemporaries, Geoffrey of Monmouth, used it as his source to write at length of a King Arthur in his own work, *Historia Regum Britanniæ, History of the Kings of Britain,* in which Geoffrey puts Arthur's capital at Caerleon. Even Sir Thomas Malory in *Morte d'Arthur* has Arthur re-crowned here. In Geoffrey's time, the just visible amphitheatre was associated with the round table element of Arthurian legends, and as has already been mentioned Tennyson got a good feel for his *Idylls of the King* while staying at the Hanbury Arms in 1856. Another believer was the Elizabethan poet, Thomas Churchyard, who wrote about him in *The Worthiness of Wales* in 1587:

> *In Arthur's tyme, a table round,*
> *Was there whereat he sate,*
> *As yet a plot of goodly ground,*
> *Sets forth that rare estate.*

From the 18th century onwards, more travellers appeared on the scene who had read or heard of this historic entity in South Wales and would not disregard an opportunity to visit. Henry Wyndham saw Caerleon for the first time while touring Wales in 1774:

The present Caerleon is a melancholy contrast to the ancient, and scarcely a decent house is now to be seen in its streets. Near the centre of a field adjoining the west wall of the town is an amphitheatre. The form of it, which is oval, now only remains, all traces of its walls being lost. The diameter of the area is very large and is bounded with an intrenchment of earth which surrounds it.[9]

The Rt. Hon. John Byng arrived later the same year and wasted no time in climbing Caerleon's castle keep which was covered by brushwood and other rubbish inclined to be found within unattended ruins:

As Mr Wyndham found a curiously engraved tile on this hill, I thought it behoved me to peep about for something to carry off with me and write about, so I was lucky in stumbling upon the fragments of a Roman brick on which some letters are very legible. During the last night fell so much rain that when I woke this morning it was a perfect deluge, so I did not regret a late rising.

---

[9] Here, Wyndham is assuming the building rose from the present ground level, whereas the 'lost' walls were buried beneath his feet.

We hope that August will prove fairer than July, lest we must buy Lunardi jackets and go on swimming through our tour.[10]

On cycling into Caerleon, Elliot-Stock and friend observed that scarcely a soul noticed their arrival beyond an old drover with his bunch of heifers for Newport market, and he only because they rather upset the uniformity of his little bovine army plodding sleepily 'like the old river flowing to the sea'. Like others of his time, he was convinced of Caerleon's historic claim to have been King Arthur's Camelot, and wrote:

> Certain it is that Pendragon's son lived, and that at Caerleon he held his court. There would seem also little doubt cast upon his (Arthur's) twelve great battles with the Saxons in his successful endeavours to stop their encroachment upon Gwent.

After travelling here on the Monmouth bus, Stuart Mais compared Arthur's legendary destiny to rise again with the Saxon thegn, Wild Eadric, awaiting a call to arms from his Shropshire cave:

> Here, under grassy mounds, King Arthur still sits sleeping over the ashes of his last banquet, his knights around him and his sword by his side, waiting to be summoned to England's aid.

Amphitheatres were the traditional stadia of entertainment for Romans, where mass slaughter was played out for the enjoyment of the audiences. This usually involved theatrical executions of criminals and Christians. The amphitheatre at Caerleon was no exception, and here in AD 304 it is alleged that three victims in particular – Aaron, Julius, and another Christian, Amphibalus – met whatever gruesome death was planned for the day. Aaron was a local Briton, but it is thought Julius was a Roman soldier who had converted to Christianity. Amphibalus was a native of Caerleon and said to have preached in Verulamium (St Albans),

---

[10] In the mid-18th century, the Italian pioneer balloonist, Vincenzo Lunardi, invented a coat that claimed protection for the wearer in the case of sudden immersion or contact with the ground when falling from a balloon.

where he is thought to have converted St Alban himself, another Roman soldier, before escaping back to Wales. There were, of course, no indications for our early travellers of the extraordinary excavations that were to follow years later. How much excavating the likes of Elliot-Stock, Arthur Bradley, or Charles Harper had seen is unclear, because digging didn't start in earnest until 1909, and it wasn't until 1926 that funds were provided to allow a young archaeologist, Mortimer Wheeler, to complete the work.

The Romans built a timber bridge across the River Usk as an extension of the Via Praetoria, their central roadway, connecting the quarters they called Ultra Pontem with their headquarters in the centre of Isca. The bridge had to be replaced several times during the Middle Ages, the last was destroyed in a storm in 1779. The present stone version was erected a few yards further west in the early 19th century. At the end of its time, around AD 300, Isca itself was being demolished and re-used for defences elsewhere in Britain as the Roman Empire began to break up and usurpers took positions to challenge for the top jobs. The legionnaires had lost their significance as invaders and expansionists and became field armies for the leading players in the battles for power, whether in Europe or in Rome. The ruins began to disappear stone by stone, tile by tile, as relics, or souvenirs to build a growing Caerleon new town. The church of St Cadoc was erected over the basilica, probably with its debris. The Norman castle was built entirely of Roman stones, as the only remaining bit of it, a surviving tower next to the Hanbury Arms, clearly shows. H.J. Massingham suggested that there were doubts that the Romans had created Isca in the first place, and quotes an ancient manuscript suggesting that the Silurian leader, Beli Mawr, Beli the Great, built a fortress at this point by the Usk. The evidence against is that Beli's camp was likely to have been the fort on Lodge Hill overlooking the river plain, and in any case, he had already moved on in the wake of the Roman advances. Massingham wrote later:

> I unconsciously took the image of Caerleon away with me and many times in the heavy labour of writing my chronicle my thoughts have wandered back there and I see it in the beams of the

sun sinking behind Twm Barlwm as though it were engraved upon my retina. I came to realise that, historically speaking, no place in the marches can compare with it. I think of it now for its thousand years of cultural wealth and learning as the Rome of the Cymric West.

Substantial excavated Roman remains can still be seen in and around Caerleon, including all that is left of the military barracks that were occupied by the Legionnaires. Much of their bath house has been rediscovered and preserved in a purpose-built museum in the centre of town, and with the aid of modern technology the visitor is given a vivid image of its former grandeur. The recent discovery of a quay where Roman ships might have docked has raised the likelihood that more buildings have yet to be unearthed from the empty fields around Caerleon.

Lower Usk and Far Off Things

The Roman road from Ultra Pontem runs for a short distance alongside the Usk before becoming an unclassified lane known as the Bulmore Road, which for the first 2.0km has been hemmed in by a section of the Celtic Manor golf course. There is little, if any, traffic along this narrow stretch of road, and care and patience is necessary if two vehicles should converge. After eight more miles the lane meets the B4598 Abergavenny road in the centre of Usk town. A closer look at the map indicates that this pleasant country route extends at either end to connect the A40 at Raglan to the M4 motorway at junction 25 beyond the suburb of St Julians. The Bulmore Road was a favourite route taken by Welsh mystic author, Arthur Machen, when walking in the valley near his home. In his personal account, *Far Off Things*, he described it as:

> That most wonderful, enchanted, and delicious road that winds under hillside, under deep Wentwood, above the solemn curves and esses of the river. We went on our way by the river and passed

under Kemeys, a noble, grey old house with mullioned windows and Elizabethan chimneys. There is such a peace about this place, such a sweetness from the wood, such a refreshness from the water, so grave a response upon it.

He would frequently recall his growing-up years here with his friend Bill Rowlands, when they would 'swing along' the winding lane beside the winding river:

> And as we went, the sound of pouring water sang to us. For now, the over-runnings of the wells of Wentwood came from the hill as rivulets, and about each stream the twisted thicket grew, accompanying it all down the steep to the river below. We passed little Kemeys Church, watching above the pools of the Usk, and there on the hillside, almost in the shadow of the forest, was Bertholey, that solitary house that has awed me for years, so that in another time I made my awe into a tale.

Unlike his contemporary, W.H. Davies, who was born in a pub, Machen started life opposite one, the Old Black Bull in Caerleon, in 1863. A writer of supernatural fantasy and horror fiction, his first book, a novella called *The Great God Pan,* was hailed by Stephen King as a classic horror story. Machen's writing career is a far cry from his early childhood years spent in innocent isolation in this lovely part of Monmouthshire. From Caerleon, the central vale road to Usk town runs through a lush green, hilly landscape, crossed initially by the Afon Lwyd – a thirteen-mile long river which flows down a heavily industrialised valley from its source near Blaenavon. The waters of this river were so severely affected by industrial pollution, mine discharge and fly-tipping that it was once named the dirtiest river in Wales. Hidden in the folds of the lower Usk valley, the church of St David's at Llanddewi Fach where Machen's father was parson, is perched on a small hill overlooking the tiny Sor Brook. The old Rectory is by the roadside a little way off, the two separated by fields of quietly grazing sheep. The bedrooms of Arthur's childhood home face west, from where the young boy would look out towards the valley wall made up of the distinctive tump of an Iron Age fort called Twm Barlwm and the Mynydd Maen ridge beyond Pontypool:

> I shall always esteem as the greatest piece of fortune that has fallen to me that I was born in that noble, fallen Caerleon-on-Usk in the heart of Gwent. The older I grow, the more firmly I am convinced that anything I may have accomplished in literature is due to the fact that when my eyes were first opened in early childhood they had before them the vision of an enchanted land.

Long before the upper Sôr valley was dammed and flooded for the Llandegfedd Reservoir, Machen recalled there were still hills within sight of Llanddewi yet untrodden, lanes and footpaths of which he knew the beginnings but not the ends:

> We have tramped about hill and dale, by mountains and river through this delicious land to our heart's content. We have tasted of the native beverages, beer and cider: we have drunk from holy wells and the mountain torrents, we have laughed, sung, and joked in a thoroughly Silurian manner.

Years later, on his return from London to his beloved county, he found happiness again strolling in what he called 'that delicious air', where he would watch the morning mists vanishing from the mountainside, see again the old white farms beneath Twm Barlwm and Mynydd Maen gleaming in the sunlight. And after his walks, he would lie in deep green shade and feel that he was home again. Massingham wrote of the area almost with the same deep emotion:

> North-eastwards from Caerleon along the right bank of the Usk, an utterly different country succeeds the southern levels and above them the little hills stick like currants into the domestic landscape. Up through Bulmore, Abernant, Kemeys Inferior to Newbridge skirting the long tongue of Wentwood to the east, the traveller loses himself in as wild, hill-tossing, passionately beautiful, retired and bewildering a countryside as any in all the Southern Marches.

On another day, author and traveller, Percy Thoresby Jones, was approaching from the opposite direction, and he too wrote in dreamy tones about the scenery:

> The river goes gently strolling along below you with alternation of loop and short reach. Fine old groups of trees grace the water meadows. Continuing our gentle road along the Usk bank, soon after parting with a skyward lane we skirt a long flank of Wentwood, showing bits of cliffs known as Kemeys Craig.

All these testimonies are now lost memories. The dreamy world of quiet lanes and rolling hillsides, of birdsong and gentle Usk lapping against riverbank, no longer exists. In 1970, the A449 dual carriageway was opened to run between the Coldra interchange of the M4 motorway and Raglan, following almost exactly the line of the Bulmore single track road. Sir Terry Matthew's Celtic Manor golf course has cut that off from the river, and now the busy highway to the English Midlands isolates it from the Great Went Wood, too. In the process, the little family church of Kemeys House has been demolished, wiped off the map. And now the noise, that dreadful noise of traffic thundering along the new way, has destroyed the idyll forever. Fred Hando did not live to experience the dramatic changes; he died in February 1970, just weeks before the new road's opening. After the little church's demolition, he was not surprised at what he saw on his final visit:

> Although I knew what to expect, I shall not forget the shock of that sudden emptiness. Always on other days the little church had appeared, sweet and appealing between me and the screen of trees and the river. Now there were a pile of stones, a couple of stone columns the screen of trees and the river, and one bird in the tallest tree twittered a requiem.

At the head of the valley above Pontypool, Llandegfedd Reservoir appeared in 1964, formed by damming the little Sôr stream that flooded the very fields walked by Arthur Machen and his pal Bill in his Llanddewi days. Its water is mainly for the needs of the

Welsh capital, Cardiff, but there was enough to satisfy the thirst of the gigantic steel works at Llanwern in its heyday. On the hillside above the Llandegfedd visitors' centre, a 'Hando' seat was erected encircling a young oak tree in memory of our wandering man of Gwent. In May 2016, I saw the seat in a sad state and on the point of collapse. Although I made many attempts to bring it to the attention of the local authorities, I failed to find anyone, or any department that either knew what, or to whom the landmark referred, or could do anything to activate a rescue. There were several other 'seats', all funded by public subscription, erected at various locations known to be favourites of Hando's during his life, and as far as I know may no longer be in good order, have long since collapsed or been taken away. I have searched in vain at the top of the Wyndcliff at St. Arvans, and near Keeper's Pond on the Blorenge Mountain. Such is the inevitable fate of today's short-term support for local heroes.

The valley's river gives its name to its main town, Usk. It's Welsh name is Brynbuga and in Roman times it was Burrium. The town stands by the river, and access on its western side is by an attractive five-arched stone bridge. Roman occupation seems to have started around AD 55 when a fortress was built to aid Ostorius Scapula in his campaign against the Silures. His army was the best that Rome could provide, the all Roman nationals 20th Legion, not long from the Rhineland but more recently from their Kingsholm camp at Gloucester. After they left Burrium, it continued as a civilian settlement until taken by the Normans. They recognised the town's geographical and military importance, and around 1120 the powerful de Clares built a castle to control the people and the area's resources. Nearly 70 years later, Gerald of Wales and Archbishop Baldwin met at the castle with the Archbishop of Llandaff and after sermons by both Archbishops, claimed to have convinced many men to take the cross and join their crusade. The large, grassy expanse of the inner ward of the castle still lends itself these days to open-air gatherings and surrounded by high walls it has naturally resonant acoustics, good for musical events. For added authenticity and picturesqueness, the ruins have been left with their natural vegetation cover. Simon Jenkins wrote in his *Wales: Churches, Houses, Castles*:

> Usk Castle is everything a CADW castle is not. It is wild, unmanicured and idiosyncratic. Where a government castle is scrubbed and tidy, Usk respects the dishevelment of age. If ruins must be ruins, let them be like this.

In 1402, Usk was virtually destroyed during a raid by Owain Glyndŵr. There are no houses before that date still surviving, except for one, now the town's Rural Life Museum. Two houses nearby date from soon afterwards and will have been part of the 15th century re-building work. When William Coxe arrived in 1798, he reported seeing Roman remains still exposed or recently excavated, as well as ruins of houses still visible from Glyndŵr's raid:

> Usk is undoubtedly a place of great antiquity and was of considerable extent. In digging wells, and making foundations for buildings, three ranges of pavement have been discovered, and in the adjacent fields pitched roads traced which are supposed to have been streets of the Roman town. Many ancient houses are in ruins, and a considerable district is much dilapidated, exhibiting the appearance of having been sacked, and recently quitted by an enemy; the natives consider these ruins as the effect of Owen Glendower's devastation.

In 1949 Massingham saw long rebuilt cottages and newer developments on the outskirts, with some lively colour wash among the houses by the prison and the marketplace:

> But the best of Usk is the river, not the town, glittering under the arches of its stone bridge and singing over its pebbly shallows. Those were the days when salmon, lamperns and lampreys were speared by the coracle men.

45

Usk has been for many centuries a popular place to fish for salmon. There are everlasting tales among local fishermen of a salmon of 68lbs caught there in 1782, and 4,391 were taken in 1891. In the town centre is the four hundred-year-old Three Salmons Hotel, a favourite with Arthur Machen and his pal Bill Rowlands. Percy Thoresby Jones stayed at the Inn in 1938 while on his cycling tours in Wales:

> It has old interior modernised in the way of bathrooms and lighting, and the beds are soporific. Expensive? Far from it. This is not a resort of nouveaux riches or the suburban genteel. Most of the guests are engrossed in piscatorial achievements and technicalities.

It was Richard de Clare who founded a Benedictine nunnery at Usk in 1170 – the only one in Wales – which became St Mary's Priory Church after the dissolution. Adam of Usk wrote that 'in this monastery only virgins born of noble ancestry were want to be received'. This may well be true, as it has been suggested that de Clare sought a solution for redundant women in his castle who may well have been the daughters of nobles attending to the marcher lord's needs. Set into the east face of the wooden screen in the chancel of the church is a rectangular brass plaque written In ancient Welsh text commemorating Adam, priest and chronicler, and his death in 1430. His chronicle, written around 1421, paid attention to events in his native Wales and his account of the progress of Owain Glyndŵr's rebellion, with whom he spent some time in refuge while in self-inflicted disgrace with King Richard II. Perhaps in view of Glyndŵr's eventual destruction of Usk, it is as well Adam never lived among his fellow townsfolk. However, as with Gerald's *Itinerary* then also with Adam's *Chronicle*, there is a fascinating insight into the workings of another highly intelligent mediaeval mind. Outside the west door of the priory church is the burial place of the martyred Jesuit priest, David Lewis, of whom I have told the dreadful story in my previous book, *In My Own Time*. The grave slab here is new; the worn original now forms a replica grave in the churchyard of St Francis Xavier and St David

Lewis on Porthycarne Street. Inside that church, a reliquary is on display containing a piece of cloth said to be stained with the blood of the martyred priest. Such material memorials were accepted by the Catholic Church as true relics, as if they were a piece of bone from the martyr's body.

Meanwhile, team Elliot-Stock had already learned that cyclists of the early 20th century were not spared the ravages of road surface variations and occasional demand for some bicycle maintenance:

> Our travels were not bettered by the odd patch of repair the road had recently undergone, and tyres suffered in consequence. Granite seems plentiful in these parts, an unalloyed mercy in comparison with the flint dressing on some of our Home County (London) roads, and considering our isolated state during the major part of this tour and the remoteness from that great essential, a bucket of water for the discovery of minute punctures, we were almost disposed to bless each patch of repair as we rode across or round it.

Before leaving Usk to take the high road to Clytha, Elliot-Stock was keen to do some photography in the town square but was surprised when he attracted an audience:

> Usk possesses a work-a-day air and is probably considered quite a metropolis in the countryside. The flattering little crowd to witness the setting up of a camera below the castle shows the town can even sit up and take notice of the alien and his doings.

About 5.6km (3½ mi) north of Usk and a few miles south of Clytha, is the village of Bettws Newydd. Its church was founded in 1188 and is uniquely dedicated to St Aedan, after Aedan of Ferns in the Irish county of Cavan. It may be no coincidence that the foundation year of the church was also that of Archbishop Baldwin's crusade, as it is known that Aedan and Gerald had preached before in the area around Abergavenny. As so often happens in the marches, the church at Bettws is isolated from its hamlet on the crown of a steep hill. It was reconstructed in the

15th century, at which time its fabulous rood screen and loft carved in black oak was installed. It is a blessing that although the rood has gone, the screen and loft have remained untouched for six hundred years, reason alone for Its Grade I listing. In the churchyard are two ancient yews – one ruinous and riddled with holes like a cheese; the other upright, evenly corrugated, and of classical proportions.

Rood screens were ornate partitions between the chancel and nave – a common feature in late medieval church architecture. The screen would originally have been surmounted by a loft carrying the Rood, normally a large wooden cross, a sculptural representation of the Crucifixion complete with the attendant figures of Mary and St John. Towards the end of the 15th century, nearly every church had a screen and loft. Each varied in character, material, and detail, and even in the most remote places they were often elaborately carved and painted. Though many screens remain, the destruction of their Roods took place during the reign of Henry VIII and Edward VI, and there are no known instances of complete roods surviving. The screen at Bettws still has its loft, and both are in a magnificent state of preservation. Together with its tympanum, they are the most complete set of rood furniture to survive anywhere in England and Wales. Massingham, an advocate of country church furnishings, was overwhelmed by what he saw here:

> Suddenly inside the little belfried church I was confronted with a rood-loft and screen not only of the most opulent and delicate ornamentation but containing as a very rare feature a boarded and panelled tympanum pierced by a pair of three-light openings with traceried heads like windows. I never get over my wonder at seeing these rood screens; they continue to electrify me, though I have now seen many. Bettws Newydd of the decidedly Welsh type is one of the most perfect.

High on a wooded promontory overlooking Bettws Newydd, is Coed-y-Bwnydd, the largest and best-preserved Iron Age hill fort in Monmouthshire with a history of human involvement stretching back more than 2,000 years. Its steep and densely wooded slopes provide a challenging scramble in places, and the well-preserved ramparts have earned it the status of a Scheduled Ancient Monument (SAM). It is a very old fort and may have been abandoned by the Silures even before that at Sudbrook. In his book, *Gwent*, Fred Hando described the view from the summit:

> I know few viewpoints more thrilling than the north-west edge of Coed-y-Bwnydd. On a clear day, Blorenge, the Black Mountains, Sugar Loaf, Skirrid an Craig are dramatic points on the skyline, the middle distance is green and pastoral, the fruit blossom forming white pools among the green, the brown churches and white farms peep out from among the trees, while our exquisite river steels out of Breconshire and slips sweetly passed and away.

Raglan, the village, is located midway between Monmouth and Abergavenny on the A40 road, and very near to the junction with the A449. It was an important mail coaching stop in the 18th and 19th centuries and still retains its three coaching inns – the Beaufort Arms, the Ship, and the Crown. The 14th century church of St Cadoc has been associated with the lords of Raglan Castle since the earliest days of the de Clares. Since then, the Herberts and their successors, the Somersets, have continued to expand and repair the building. The Beaufort Chapel contains the remains of three reclining stone figures, representing the 3rd and 4th Earls of Worcester and Lady Elizabeth Hastings, all mutilated by Parliamentarian troops during the English Civil War. On the chapel wall above them is a tablet placed there in 1868 by Henry Somerset, 8th Duke of Beaufort, which details all of the Somerset internments in the vaults beneath.

As soon as the motorist leaves the A449 and joins the A40 road westbound, the magnificent remains of the ancient home of the Herberts, Raglan Castle, fills the view. This most castle-like of medieval fortifications, and the last one to be built, stands guard over the point where the old Gloucester to Caerleon and Chepstow to Abergavenny roads cross. The buildings we see today were started in 1432 by William ap Thomas, a Welsh nobleman and servant of Lancastrian kings from Henry IV to Henry VI. After William's death, his son, also William, allied himself to Richard, Duke of York, and supported the Yorkist cause in the Wars of the Roses. After Edward of York succeeded to the throne as Edward IV, he rewarded William with the title of Baron and 1st Earl of Pembroke, but insisted the Earl take the defunct family name Herbert, his Welsh patronymic. In his versified guidebook of 1587, *The Worthies of Wales,* Thomas Churchyard was one of few to see and record Raglan Castle in all its glory:

> *Not far from thence, a famous castle fine,*
> *That Ragland height, stands moated almost round:*
> *Made of freestone, upright as straight as line,*
> *Whole workmanship, in beauty doth abound.*
> *The curious knots, wrought all with edged tool,*
> *The stately tower that looks o'er pond and pool:*
> *The fountain trim, that runs both day and night*
> *Doth yield in show, a rare and noble sight.*

During the civil war, the Somerset family supported Charles I, and after the disaster at Naseby in 1645 the king sought refuge at Raglan and sent Henry Somerset to Ireland to canvass support while other envoys tried to raise an army in Wales. Neither effort succeeded. After moving on to Chester, the king's misfortunes continued when he saw his army lose the final battle at Rowton Heath. In the aftermath, Raglan was taken by Parliamentary forces, and the castle was deliberately damaged enough to put it beyond further military use. In spite of the restoration of Charles II, the Somersets decided not to restore their castle home but left the ruins to become a source for local building materials and eventually a dramatic shell. Writing of Raglan's demise, Massingham tells of an awful truth:

The castle's library, one of the choicest in Britain, was totally pillaged, all the pictures were destroyed or sold, the woodwork was burned, the painted glass destroyed, the roofs pulled down, the lead sold for £6,000, the park timber all felled and Cromwell himself swelled his private fortune out of the loot.

The Rt. Hon. John Byng also wrote of the material loss at Raglan, though on a more simplistic level:

Many of the bastions are converted into cow stalls and pigsties and every part is in rampant disorder. If the Duke of Beaufort has the merit of abstaining from dilapidation, he should incur the shame of neither fencing, cleaning or adorning this much remembered ruin.

Halfway between Raglan and Abergavenny is Llansantffraed House – a modern mansion, built in the late 17th century style and converted into a luxury hotel around 1952. During William Coxe's attention to his tour of Monmouthshire, it became his local base and where he conceived the plan to write a book about his adventure. The house was then occupied by James Greene, MP for Arundel, but long before Raglan was the seat of Thomas ap Gwyllym, from whom the Herbert earls of Pembroke are descended by the male line, and the dukes of Beaufort by that of the female. Coxe wrote in his diary:

Unacquainted with a single gentleman when I first entered the county, I was introduced to Mr. Greene, by my friend Sir Richard Colt Hoare; his hospitable mansion was open to me at all times and on all occasions without form or ceremony; I was left at full liberty to make excursions as my fancy or inclination suggested, and on my return, after the fatigues of the day, I enjoyed the comforts of an agreeable society. In this delightful residence, I first conceived the plan of writing a tour in Monmouthshire.

Coxe's host died in 1814 and is buried in the churchyard on the estate. The house as it stands now was rebuilt impressively in 1912 and has been extended and modernised again since.

Four miles north west of Usk on the B4598 road is the village of Llanfair Kilgeddin. Its medieval parish church is some distance

Figure 4 Archdeacon William Coxe

away, isolated in its ancient churchyard and no longer offering services to the community; a redundant church. However, St Mary the Virgin is a Grade I listed building. It was reconstructed in 1876 by the Gothic-style architect, John Dando Sedding, who reused some of the original fabric and medieval features. The rebuild was instigated by the rector, Rev William Lindsay, and following the death of his wife, Rosamund, in 1885, he invited painter, George Heywood Sumner – an advocate of the arts and crafts movement and a contemporary of William Morris – to decorate the interior walls in her memory. Sumner introduced a graffito-style of painted panels direct onto the plaster, unique in Wales. The scenes are of well-known local mountain landscapes, Blorenge, Sugar Loaf, and Skirrid Fawr, and in recent times it had become a favourite hideaway for Labour MP, Roy Jenkins of Hillhead and Pontypool, who often used it for quiet reflection away from his Parliamentary commitments.

In 1982, St Mary's was overdue for refurbishment and close to collapse, and Jenkins voiced his concerns and support for urgent repair. In fact, the church's condition was so bad that demolition was considered, with the inevitable loss of Sumner's artwork. That extreme decision, however, was prevented, thanks to the attentions of the Friends of Friendless Churches. They canvassed successfully for grants from CADW and the Pilgrim Trust, and the repair was done. The refurbished church is now held in the MP's memory, and the incredible art forms are once again available for public viewing. Although the building is kept locked, a key is readily available at Pant-y- Goitre farm.

Directly across the river from St Mary's Church is another building dedicated to a deceased wife. The very visible Clytha Castle, a crenellated stone folly with gothic windows, is set on a rounded hill amid chestnut groves. It was built in 1790 by William Jones of Clytha Park to realise his ardent wish for a memorial to his late wife, Elizabeth, last surviving child of Sir William Morgan of Tredegar House, 'for the purpose of relieving a mind sincerely afflicted by the loss of a most excellent wife'.

Riding passed both these monuments to well-loved wives, Elliot-Stock and his companion were nearing their night stop:

> The humble push bike, like the day light, has its limits and we were still eight miles from night quarters yet to be found in Abergavenny. All thought of the camera had to be abandoned and we dropped down to join the main road running east and west a bare mile from Llanvihangel Gobion and by the banks of the Usk where they make their first sharp bid for a southerly course to the Severn.

At this point, the OS map tells me that I am looking at the site on agricultural land close to the river Usk of Castle Arnold, but the translation of the original Welsh is questionable. Castell Arnallt was once the fortified house of Seisyll ap Dyfnwal, the Welsh Lord of Over Gwent, before it was destroyed in a ruthless purge by William de Braose in the late 12th century. The Seisyllts of Monmouthshire eventually became the Cecils of Hatfield House in Hertfordshire and regulars of the Elizabethan court. There are no remains visible at Arnallt, but no excavations have ever been carried out either, so it is entirely possible that the stone foundations remain below ground waiting to be exposed.

Directly across the river is the wooded Llanover Estate. Lady Augusta Hall, Baroness Llanover, was born Augusta Waddington here in 1802, the youngest daughter of Benjamin Waddington and his wife, Georgina. They lived at Ty Uchaf, a 15th century manor house on the estate midway between Pontypool and Abergavenny, which Augusta would eventually inherit. In 1823, she married a Welsh civil engineer, Benjamin Hall, and a new house, Llanover Hall, was built as their marital home. Benjamin was an elected Member of Parliament for Monmouth, but his engineering prowess was required in London where he eventually became First Chief Commissioner of Works, collecting a knighthood on the way. It was he who was made responsible for the final stages of the rebuilding of the Houses of Parliament and the erection of the clock tower. Sir Benjamin was six feet four inches tall, so the name 'Big Ben' was given to the tower's great hour bell in his honour. A few years later, Prime Minister Palmerston rewarded his achievements with a place in the House of Lords as Baron Llanover.

Augusta wasn't idle while her husband developed an illustrious career in London. She already had an interest in Welsh lifestyles from childhood, and with the help of Thomas Price – the bard with the unpronounceable name, Carnhuanawc, whom she met at the Brecon Eisteddfod in 1826 – set about learning to speak the Welsh language and re-inventing herself. She became an enthusiastic proponent of all things Welsh, structuring her household at the Hall and insisting her staff wore Welsh costumes. She maintained an interest in Welsh culture and traditions, including the national instrument, the harp, one of which she kept at Llanover.

Baron Llanover died in April 1867, aged 64, and was interred in a mausoleum in St Bartholomew's churchyard close to the banks of the Usk. Having survived him by almost thirty years, Lady Llanover joined him there in 1896, borne, so Fred Hando tells us, by twenty maidens dressed, not unexpectedly, in Welsh costume. A wreath of white roses was sent by the Princess May of Teck, later to become Queen Mary to George V. In his *Monmouthshire*

Sketchbook written in 1954 and reminiscing on a later scene at Llanover, Fred Hando wrote in his most nostalgic mood of a world we all longed to keep but he knew it could never be again:

> The cool sunlight of a March morning silvers Old Llanover. Set against the backcloth of clouds and great hills, church and cottages dream. The church glows between a vast yew tree on the one side and a weeping willow and lone pine on the other. A sparkling mountain stream joins the Usk under the arch of Ty'r Afon, the fishing cottage.[11]

It was a bitterly cold and very wet January day when I stood alone beside the impressive catafalque in the churchyard by the river. It was not quite like the misty graveyard scene from Dickens' *Great Expectations,* but the similarity was not lost on me. The contrast couldn't be less akin to the banks of the River Thames far from here, where Big Ben lives on amongst the doubts and ignorances of those walking by the Parliament buildings in pursuit of busy lives.

Gateway to the Beacons

Abergavenny, one of many towns labelled as a gateway to Wales, sits at the eastern end of the Black Mountains by the confluence of the river Usk and the tributary stream Gavenny, after which the town is named. It is not a pretty town, but being surrounded by two mountains, Blorenge and Sugar Loaf (Y Fal) – both not far short of 560m (1,640ft) in height – and five other hills, the Skirrid (Ysgyryd Fawr), Little Skirrid (Ysgyryd Fach), Deri, Rholben, and Llanwenarth Hill (Mynydd Llanwenarth), the overall impression comes close to picturesque. Ernest Elliot-Stock perceived Abergavenny's position an enviable one to the smoke-dried Londoner:

---

[11] There is a footbridge over the river by Ty'r Afon, but there is no public right of way now.

Especially as seen bathed in the last ray of a July sun that floods the upper Usk Vale road to the 'Gate', and paints the western slopes of the Sugar Loaf with a warmer colour than it had appeared capable of taking to itself when seen a dozen miles away. Utopian in every detail was our verdict; and thrice blessed he whom fate has willed shall ply his trade in and about so perfect a paradise.

The town is described in the *Rough Guide to Wales* as being just a couple of miles and a few hills away from the iron and coal towns of the Welsh valleys. Indeed, Abergavenny's prosperity was once due to the proximity to the South Wales mining districts, but the town's industries took a different path. Whichever way it is written, Abergavenny translates as 'mouth of the Afon Gafenni' or River Gavenny, barely a brook and an unglamorous one at that, with a very short life from its birth four miles away in the Blaengavenny Wood. Looking at the OS map, it is tempting to be pedantic and put the stream's entrance a little further north near Penyclawdd Court, or even from a spring on the north face of the Skirrid, but it would still be a short water course. Though the town has had the right to hold two weekly markets and three yearly fairs since the 13th century, Abergavenny was once renowned for the production of Welsh flannel and for the manufacture, whilst the fashion prevailed, of goats' hair periwigs. Coxe was familiar with this local habit:

> During the prosperous fashion formerly prevalent among the beaux of decorating their heads with flaxen periwigs of an enormous size, and not infrequently sold at the price of forty or fifty guineas, a method was discovered and supposed to be invented in this neighbourhood, of bleaching hair, an employment which supported many persons and was productive of considerable profit, until the fashion changed.

Not all early visitors were pleased by everything they saw here. Arriving twenty-five years before Coxe, Henry Wyndham decided that:

the environs of Abergavenny though rich and beautiful, and like the rest of the vale of Brecknock, abound with the most charming variety of landscape, the streets in general are narrow, ill paved and ill built.

Abergavenny began to develop alongside the military fortress the Romans called Gobannium. The word *Gobannia* has Brythonic origins meaning 'river of the blacksmiths', and the relative use of it by the Romans relates to the importance given to the town as a centre for their iron smelting activities. Gobannium/Abergavenny later became a medieval walled town complete with a Norman castle – the site of a particular nasty event. In 1175, the resident marcher lord, William de Braose, attempted to wipe out the established leadership of the local Welsh community at a Christmas gathering. Having persuaded his guests to leave their swords by the castle gate, de Braose treacherously called in his soldiers, who slaughtered them while at table. Among the dead was Seisyllt ap Dyfnwal of Castell Arnallt by the Usk. Not content with his death, de Braose attacked Seisyllt's base and killed his seven-year-old son and heir. The marcher lord's murderous plan ultimately failed and Abergavenny Castle was sacked in retaliation by surviving Welsh chiefs. Gerald of Wales described the effective use by the Welsh on that occasion of the longbow – the favourite weapon even then of the men of Gwent. Later, during the Hundred Years War, Welsh longbow men would be instrumental in victory for the English House of Plantagenet armies at Crecy, Poitiers, and Agincourt. William de Braose did not receive any accolades for his cruel streak but was henceforward in conversation given the title 'the Ogre of Abergavenny'.

On an elevated position within sight of the town's bridge over the Gavenny Brook, is the priory church of St Mary, formerly a chapel for the Benedictine Priory which once stood beyond the town walls, and now one of the largest parish churches in Wales. It is significant for two other reasons. As Abergavenny was on the road to London from Pembroke Castle where the first Tudor King Henry VII was born, his children Arthur and Henry came to know St Mary's Church well. So much so that when the young Henry, as King, decided on dissolving Catholic ownership of religious houses, he did not include St Mary's Church which by then was already being used for parish use. Secondly, there are a number of high status monument tombs and rare medieval effigies in the Herbert chapel, which contains the tomb of Sir William ap Thomas, the ancestor of all the Herbert families, and lords of Somerset and of Raglan, and Dukes of Beaufort, whose home now is Badminton House near Bristol. These and others lying here represent one of the largest collection of effigies in Britain outside of Westminster Abbey. The real treasure of St Mary's is the large fifteenth century reclining wooden figure in the form of Jesse, in the north transept. Carved from one solid piece of oak, it is ten feet long and was originally highly coloured and part of a larger tree depicting the life of Jesse and the lineage of Jesus Christ based on the Bible. It is unique in Britain and is described by Tate Britain as one of the finest medieval sculptures in the world. Art historian, Andrew Graham Dixon, described it as "the only great wooden figure to survive the wreckage of the British Cultural Revolution".[12] Returning to Abergavenny in June 1802, Sir Richard Colt Hoare described St Mary's as:

> A handsome Gothic edifice, very rich in monumental stone. Indeed, few parish churches can surpass it, either for the number or richness of its sepulchral effigies. Those of the Herbert family are very costly in their decorations and good execution in alabaster. The church has lately gone considerable repairs and unfortunately, in the general whitewash, some of the old effigies have not escaped the brush.

Rising early to make their plans for the remaining leg of their cycle tour of Monmouthshire, Elliot-Stock and companion were encouraged by a turn in the weather. Their introduction to the day was helped considerably by the addition of a brilliant sun, and so they rode forth to discuss their future route beneath the castle

---

[12] A project to integrate the wooden Jesse with a stained-glass window in the Lewis Chapel of St Mary's, depicting the remainder of the tree, was completed in 2016 and unveiled on July 7th by HRH The Prince of Wales.

walls with the aid of a map and a post-breakfast pipe. Abergavenny has been known for centuries as a gateway to or from Wales, and roads from here lead in all directions of the compass.

> We had but two possible roads to choose from; that northward round the flanks of the Black Mountains to Pontrilas and the Golden Valley and Westward by the 'gate'. The latter looked decidedly the more interesting. The upper Usk, a rampart of hills on either hand, a hill pass at Bwlch, Llangorse lake, all crooked a beckoning finger. We could do no less than obey.

Meanwhile, in the river plain below the broken castle walls, the River Usk passes by, unruffled by all that has gone on over 1,000 years of history. Beyond this scene, the skyline to the southwest is dominated by the Blorenge Mountain – an eastern corner hill of the Brecon Beacons National Park. At the foot of the Blorenge's steep eastern wall is the Monmouthshire and Brecon Canal, affectionately called the Mon and Brec by those who use it, while the northern headland of Llanfoist Fawr looks down now on one of South Wales' major highways, the A435, at this point the Abergavenny bypass but further west becoming the Heads of the Valleys Road carrying traffic westwards towards the coastal region around Swansea Bay.

On the east side of Abergavenny, partly hidden in tree cover, is the quietly spoken-of red brick collection of buildings known as Maindiff Court. It was previously home to Mr Crawshay Bailey junior and his family. Bailey was the son and namesake of the great iron-master Crawshay Bailey and inherited all his father's lands and properties – some 12,000 acres in Wales alone. His father had sold his interest in the iron manufacturing business in 1851, leaving his son to his inherited estates and to develop his own future. When Bailey junior died in 1924, the estate was bought by the Monmouthshire Asylum Committee and turned into a hospital for the mentally ill. During and after World War 2, the hospital was used to care for wounded soldiers, but in 1942 Adolf Hitler's deputy, Rudolf Hess, was held here until his trial at Nuremberg, and had half the building to himself. He was allowed out once each week to walk in the nearby hills, no doubt enjoying this generous touch of freedom for such a high-ranking detainee. His guard was a man named Joe Clifford who said later that Hess had a comfortable life at Maindiff, treated like an officer, well fed and well looked after. After the Nuremburg trials in 1945, Hess was incarcerated in Spandau Prison in Germany until his death in August 1987 at the age of 93. Joe Clifford was 94 when he died in June 2011. Today, Maindiff Hospital remains as a mental health care centre, operated by the Aneurin Bevan Local Health Board.

It is not known whether Hess climbed the Skirrid, the Holy Mountain, on one of his freedom days, but it would certainly have not escaped his notice, being practically just outside the gates of his temporary accommodation. Skirrid Fawr is an outlier of the Black Mountains and forms the easternmost part of the Brecon Beacons National Park. The mountain's distinctive shape comprises a long ridge oriented north-south, with a jagged western side, the result of an Ice Age landslip. There are other landslips of a similar nature on the nearby hills, although the Skirrid has perhaps the most well-known owing to its weird formation – like a broken tooth which can be seen from afar in several directions. On the summit is what is left of a Roman Catholic chapel which was used during the time of brutal persecution by Titus Oates. Services on the Skirrid were ended in 1680 by John Arnold, lord of the nearby manor of Llanfihangel Crucorney Court and the county's infamous Jesuit hunter. The lower slopes of the mountain are clothed in scattered woodland of oak and sweet chestnut. The long spinal column of the mountain, these days bearing the Beacon Way footpath, rises steeply and smoothly for a mile or so, hardly ever wider than thirty or forty feet and narrowing to ten or twelve and ending abruptly by the ruins of St Michael's Chapel in a hook on the skyline. Here is the awesome site of the landslip that took place allegedly at the moment of Christ's crucifixion, and is the reason for the mountain's reference to being 'Holy'. The split in the hillside opened a precipice nearly 100m (300ft) down, and at its foot lies a great mound of red earth now overgrown with a tangle of thicket and bramble. The final stretch takes walkers close to the dramatic edge. Coxe made two attempts on Skirrid, the first being unsuccessful:

> I felt mixed sensations of animation and lassitude, horror and delight, such as I fearfully ever before experienced, even in the Alps of Switzerland; my spirits almost failed, even curiosity was suspended, and I threw myself exhausted to the ground. These sensations increased during my continuance on the summit. I several times attempted to walk the ridge, but my head became so giddy as I looked down the precipitous sides, and particularly towards the great fissure, that I could not remain standing.

Massingham never climbed the Skirrid, nor any kind of height in the Black Mountains, due to his unfortunate disability[13]. Never was the frustration more bitter to him than when standing disconsolate on the lower slopes of the Skirrid. Later, in the shadow of Waun Fach mountain a few miles to the west, he brooded a second time:

> In my disappointment of being stopped at the open door of these heights, I felt I'd rather climb them than write this book,[14] breathing their rarefied air and holding in my mind every detail of their configuration, rather than, as I'm doing, dully scribbling their mere names and craning my neck to get a glimpse of them.

A short distance beyond the Skirrid, in the river meadow emerging from the Ewyas Vale, the Honddu stream ends its journey through the southern valley of the Black Mountains and meets up with its brother stream, the Monnow, from the northern valleys. At their very confluence is the ancient manor house of Alt-yr-ynys, an early home of the Cecils – their familiar name by now anglicised from the Welsh Seisyllt,[15] the clan almost extinguished by the murderous

---

[13] See introduction.

[14] *The Southern Marches*, written in 1949.

[15] The founder of the clan is said to be Robert Sitsyllt, a follower of the Norman lord, Robert Fitz Hamon, during his takeover of what is now Glamorgan in the eleventh century. Seisyllt may have acquired Allt-yr-ynys around that time as reward for his services with Fitz Hamon.

Ogre of Abergavenny. This ancient, rather ill-shaped Tudor mansion had for a time degenerated into a farm, but even in its heyday Alt-yr-ynis has never have been one of the attractive border manors, being too plain and lacking the graces of Monnington, or Kentchurch Court and other Tudor manors of the southern marches. However, William Camden, being closer in time to the original owner, was not slow in his praise:

> Alt-yr- ynys lieth in manner of a river-island, insulated within waters: the seat in old time of that ancient family of the Seisyllts or Cecils, knights, whence my right honourable Patron, accomplished with all the ornaments of virtue, wisdom, and nobility, Sir William Cecil, Baron of Burghley, and Lord High Treasurer of England, derived his descent.

Alt-yr-ynys is Grade II listed but in 2006 when I last looked on from the gate, the house was a tired, run-down hotel. Later, it became empty and deserted and was eventually sold at Christie's auction house in September 2014 to a family from Surrey.

Empty Landscape to Heritage Protection

The stars were like little moons in the darkness, for the night was black and freezing, but flashing red and hot over the top towards Merthyr, Nantyglo was smouldering crimson on the clouds.

Alexander Cordell's *Rape of the Fair Country*

On August 24th, 1798 Sir Richard Colt Hoare accompanied a party of friends on an excursion into the mountains and the hidden industrial valleys beyond the Blorenge. They forded the Usk at a place where a tram road had been built to transport iron ore from the mines to waiting barges on the Mon and Brec Canal and thence to the docks at Newport. That place was probably Llanfoist, from where the tram road snaked across the hillsides below Blorenge and Gilwern Hill and into the deep gorge of

Clydach. The experience for Colt Hoare and his party would have been startling in its stark industrial reality, as he wrote later:

> A deep cart with iron wheels is made to fit exactly the iron track. The friction is by this means so small that they run with the greatest facility. It is curious to see a number of these carts laden with ironstone running with great velocity down the sides of the mountain without any horses. One or two men stand behind the cart and by means of a lever stop the motion of the wheels instantaneously. These carts carry the weight of three tons. We followed this road for near four miles. There were Ironworks at the bottom of the hill.

The Clydach Gorge (Cwm Clydach) is a steep-sided valley down which the River Clydach flows eastwards from its source on the southern slopes of Llangattock Mountain, Mynydd Llangattwg, before joining the Usk. The gorge was one of the first locations in South Wales to be industrialised and was a crucial transport corridor between the lowlands of Monmouthshire and the coalfields of the Welsh valleys. In spite of those dark days, the gorge has retained its rugged beauty, is now included within the Brecon Beacons National Park, and has become a tourist attraction in its own right. The 18th century ironworks mentioned by Colt Hoare is today a Scheduled Ancient Monument, and the tram road which he and his companions followed has become part of the National Cycle Network. William Coxe was with the group and wrote in his diary:

> We turned down to the left by a steep path to see a cascade. Our party consisting of twenty dined under the canopy of the skies, our cloth spread on a large flat rock. A rapid rill at its foot cooled our wines and afforded us a delicious beverage. The scene was alpine and gay, such as I could have fancied oft occurred in Switzerland, but in its past happy days. In the evening we returned to Abergavenny.

Previously within the boundary of Monmouthshire, the town of Blaenavon has become an electoral ward of Torfaen County

Borough Council. It started from nothing and grew around the great ironworks built in 1788 by an enterprising business partnership led by a Midlands banker, Thomas Hill, and industrialists, Thomas Hopkins and Benjamin Pratt. Steel-making and coal mining industries followed, boosting the town's population to over 20,000 at its height. On August 27th, 1798 Colt Hoare and Coxe made another excursion together towards Blaenavon, this time over the western flanks of the Blorenge. As the B4246 road climbs out of Llanfoist on the outskirts of Abergavenny, the landscape is of industrial dereliction where a few centuries of iron ore and limestone quarrying has left its mark. Near the summit are the remains of the Garnddyrys forge, built by Thomas Hill II in 1817. Hill had earlier built a road for horse-drawn trams to transport pig-iron from the ironworks in Blaenavon to connect with the canal at Llanfoist, passing through his works at Garnddyrys. At one time 450 people lived around the forge, but by 1854 the railways had reached Blaenavon turning the tram roads and canal obsolete. It was the end, too, for Garnddyrys and the site was abandoned. All this happened long after Coxe and Colt Hoare had passed this way. Today, though little of Garnddyrys is visible, it is archaeologically well-preserved. Beyond Garnddyrys, our travelling duo arrived in the valley of the Afon Lwyd, the Grey River, where Thomas Hopkins had been tempted by the promise of great richness just ten years earlier, established a considerable ironworks and mined the ore and coal to feed the furnaces. Colt Hoare recorded the scene, first in his diary but later famously in a sketch:

> The whole is a busy sight, the noise of the forges, the fire and thick volumes of smoke occasionally bursting forth from the furnaces, the numerous mules, asses and horses employed in carrying the lime, coal etc., the many cottages and habitations disposed all around; together with the picturesque forms of the buildings, being very irregular, massive in their forms, produced a new and pleasing effect and a perfect contrast to the deserted castles and solitary abbeys we had lately been visiting.

At some distance, the ironworks would have had the appearance of a small town, surrounded with heaps of ore, coal, and limestone, and enlivened with all the bustle and activity of an abundant and developing establishment. Coxe claimed the view of the buildings, partly constructed into the rocky outcrop of an adjoining hill, was strangely picturesque, and heightened by the volumes of black smoke emitted by the furnaces. While Colt Hoare was sketching this singular scene,[16] Coxe set about examining the mines and works where, although only completed in 1789, three hundred and fifty men were now employed. After nearly 110 years, the ironworks closed in 1900 and the coal mine that fed it in 1980. In 2000, the Blaenavon landscape became a UNESCO World Heritage Site, and the town's population, having lost its original means of livelihood, is now only a quarter that of the 19th century Victorian boom years.

A Promise of Paradise

One hundred and forty years after the visit to Blaenavon by Sir Richard Colt Hoare, William Coxe and friends, author, broadcaster and ardent omnibus rider, Stuart Mais arrived on the edge of the Brecon Beacons in August 1937 but chose to avoid the smoky darkness of the foundries and took a westward high road. He followed the road that runs above and alongside the gorge of Cwm Clydach below the imposing slopes of Gilwern Hill, then down below high limestone rocks and whitewashed cottages of Mynydd Llangatwg, Llangattock Mountain, that reminded him strongly of the dales in Derbyshire. The cliffs had by now been eaten away by quarries and lime works, exactly as they were in the Peak District:

> Then, rounding a corner, I found myself looking out on that fairytale like Table Mountain above Crickhowell that I had

---

[16] Sir Richard Colt Hoare was the first to depict the ironworks when he painted his now famous watercolour.

already seen from so many different angles. At Gilwern I walked along the canal bank for a mile or two, long enough to prove it one of the jolliest walks in this part of the border.

The origin of the name Crickhowell is the Iron Age hill fort of Crug Hywel, hanging 451m (1480ft) above the town. These days, Crickhowell is a popular tourist destination that during the summer is notably busier. Without doubt, the main attraction is the river and the grand 17th century bridge that carries the A4077 road across thirteen arches. Here, the Usk is wide and shallow and a favourite spot for salmon fishermen. Many early visitors of the 20th century conceded that the view from the old bridge was at a time of huge unwanted industrial influences and, here particularly, it showed the waters of the Usk poisoned by chemical and industrial effluents, and the salmon fry destroyed in myriads by unslaked lime.

Behind today's seasonal hustle and bustle, Crickhowell is a quiet and pleasant place. On my last visit there, I strolled down Bridge Street to the river, along cobbled pavings and passed old cottages, some still with the bow shop windows of a previous age. If you take heed of the traffic trying to push you over the parapet, it is worth a short linger on Crickhowell's bridge to take in the scenery all about. The views are still of limestone rocks of Llangattwg, but now worn and cut into a thousand fantastic forms reflecting back the light in many hues, the Blorenge range lying against the sky like a huge whale, and the cone of Y Fal, known to all hill ramblers as Sugar Loaf. Beyond the flat topped tump of Crug Hywel they call Table Hill and forming the southern flank of the Black Mountains are the Pen Allt-Marr range – a lofty mountain mass of irregular formation, including Pen Cerrig-calch, Pen Allt-Mawr, and Waun Fach. Just outside the town is the Manor Hotel where, in 1798 as Gwernvale Manor, George Everest was born. In later life he became Surveyor-Governor of India and gave his name to the highest mountain in the world. It may be a surprise to some high enthusiasts that Sir George's surname was not pronounced as in 'ever-rest' but 'eve-rest'. There's no available explanation as to who first adopted the mountain's name as it is known, but the time has long gone for

Figure 5 Sir Richard Colt Hoare

any challenges. Relief, too, one might think, for the double-glazing windows company that took the same appellation.

In 1802, Sir Richard Colt Hoare had taken a new companion for his travels around Wales – Richard Fenton, a Welsh lawyer and topographer. As on previous tours, the Angel Hotel at Abergavenny served as his base for a night or two:

> On our way back to Abergavenny, we stopped at Crickhowell to see its church and dine with a fine old veteran tar, Admiral Gell, who has lately built a pretty villa on the banks of the Usk.[17] The Vale through which we passed stands unrivalled for its beautiful and happy mixture of wild and cultivated nature, which it presents to the admiring and astonished eyes for the distance of about thirty miles. Few villages are more delightfully situated that Crickhowell. I reviewed with pleasure the spot where in the year

[17] Glanusk Villa (not to be confused with Glanusk Park) was designed by the architect John Nash for Admiral Gell. He died in 1806 and the house later became the home of another Royal Navy man, Commander John Hotchkiss. The name of the house was changed to Glanwysg, a Welsh version of the same name, sometime during the 20th century when it became part of the Glanusk Estate.

1793 I had spent so many pleasant days. My ardour for monumental antiquities had not then begun, nor had I ever seen the inside of the parish church which contains food for the artist and antiquarian.

A few miles west of Crickhowell is the Glanusk Park Estate. Another of the great Bailey iron masters, Sir Joseph Bailey, built a huge Gothic mansion here in 1826 from the proceeds of the Cyfarthfa ironworks at Merthyr Tydfil. The mansion was severely damaged by fire in 1952 and had to be demolished, but the Bailey descendants still live nearby across the river in Penmyarth Park. The iconic view of what remains of Glanusk now is the highly photographed Tower Bridge over a section of the river which runs through the estate, still one of the largest privately owned in Wales. Ten years after Glanusk was built, author Thomas Roscoe passed through Crickhowell, following the river on his way to Brecon. There are few prospects, he determined, that could equal the valley of the Usk:

> The gigantic barriers in the distance consist of the Brecknockshire Beacons on one side and the dark range of the Black Mountains on the other. From the champaign lying within these spring mountain after mountain of inferior elevation, with tiny vales running from their bases, and filling the intervening space with fallowed fields and green meadows through which run the whimpering rivulets that feed the noble stream, shadowed by foliage and dressed in all the coloured pigments of the season.

Seen from the long hill descending from Pengenfford, or the summit road above Talgarth to Crickhowell, these mountains display typical moorland colouring – green of varied shades, and russet browns diversified by dark patches of heather and blazing clumps of gorse. The whole mountain block is composed of old red sandstone, all but one single peak top that flaunts a white crest of limestone above Crickhowell and bears the appropriate name of Pen Cerrig-calch, Chalkstone Head. As he continued his ramble alongside the river, Stuart Mais observed:

That the Usk Valley road is one of the most charming in all Wales. It is less frequented than the Wye Valley roads, and for this reason the Usk has retained the greater glory. The Way is thickly lined with tall trees which add greatly to the river's beauty by only half revealing it. These tests add, too, to the mystery of the great hills above, for it is only occasionally that you get a peep at their changing shapes.

Twenty years beforehand, Elliot-Stock astride his bicycle, rode the Brecon road thinking of Owain Glyndŵr, and the coincidence of who and what was to follow his violent rebellion 500 years before:

What a magnificent country for military strategy! And what a training ground for the North West frontier! One cannot help being lost in admiration at the pluck, ambition and endurance of those knightly free-lances, who with little or no map-knowledge of what lay before, forced their way through these narrow passes held by a natural fighting race of foot soldiers that only one hundred years later became the flower of England's foreign armies.

His words almost present great foresight of the presence today of Special Forces activity on the Brecon Beacons filling his view from the saddle as he rode away from Crickhowell.

The church at Llansanffraed, a village name repeated regularly in the Welsh countryside, is dedicated to St Bridget. It has mediaeval origins and, though largely restored in 1690, was completely rebuilt in 1885. It may surprise many then, that It has a Grade-II listing. This is partly due to the unique design of Stephen Williams, a local Victorian civil engineer and architect. The building stands beside the A40, mainly hidden behind trees and ignored by almost everyone who drives by. It is a fine-looking church, and if there are any visitors at all other than those who to take part in the services, they have come to see the grave of the poet, Henry Vaughan, who died in 1695 and is buried at the very back of the churchyard beneath an ancient yew. Vaughan titled himself 'the Silurist', not only to distinguish himself from other Henry Vaughans, but to mark his deep affection for this area of south-east Wales and the British tribe which inhabited it before Roman times. He spent almost his entire life in his family home at Scethrog, a hamlet less than two miles further along the Brecon road. The first-time visitor could be forgiven for assuming at a glance that an enormous catafalque near the church door is Vaughan's, but that is occupied by Gwynne-Holfords, previous residents of Bucklands Hall across the river. Helpful signs point the way to Vaughan's burial place, and a seat awaits the weary by the grave. Massingham would not have and did not resist the opportunity to pay homage:

> On the crest of the sloping yard above the church is a spreading yew tree and under it, protected by a rusty iron railing, is the long grave slab of the Silurist. The inscription upon it is only partially decipherable, giving the date of his death, 1695, and his age, seventy-three, and ending with the words

> SERVUS INUTILIS, PECCATOR MAXIMUS, HIC JACEO, GLORIA MISERERE[18]

> The grave of the greatest of the Vaughans, the supreme spirit of mysterious Siluria, is within sight, almost within sound, of his own Isca.

Henry Vaughan (1621-1695) was a Welsh metaphysical poet, author, translator and physician. He is chiefly known for his religious poetry contained in his work, *Silex Scintillans*, published in 1650 and wrote in English. The term 'metaphysical' was coined by the supreme critic Dr Samuel Johnson to describe a loose group of 17th-century English poets whose works were characterised by the inventive use of excessive opinions, especially of a far-fetched nature – a sort of early social media channel. Vaughan was descended from the Somersets of Raglan through his maternal grandmother who bore him no fortunes, so it seems he chose an unorthodox lifestyle that his forebears would have had no incentive to follow. His father, Thomas Vaughan, had lived as a

---

[18] A meaningful translation might be "Here lies a useless slave, the greatest sinner. Glory, Mercy."

child at Tretower Court but it was his elder brother Charles who inherited that. Henry, however, could not fail to have an interest in Tretower which was barely six miles from his home at Scethrog House. In the late 16th century, the manor of Scethrog was owned by Blanche Parry, lady-in-waiting to Queen Elizabeth I and is buried in St Faith's Church in Herefordshire's Golden Valley.

Henry eventually inherited Scethrog by virtue of being born before his own twin brother, Thomas, and lived there practically the whole of his life. But there was no wealth to go with it. His father, though a country gentleman, had little or no assets other than the house and a small landholding for his family's livelihood. Living so close to the Usk, Henry grew to love the river and, in his poetry, called it his 'Isca':

> *So, where swift Isca from our lofty hills*
> *With loud farewells descends, and foaming fills*
> *A wider channel, like some great port-vein,*
> *With large rich streams to feed the humble plain.*

Stuart Mais had once attended the Brecon Hunt Ball at Scethrog House in his undergraduate days, and it was from that house of the poet that Mais first set eyes on the Usk valley. During that brief visit, Mais read some of Vaughan's poems but was clearly unimpressed:

> Vaughan wrote a little that was very lovely, and he wrote lovingly, if sadly, of his own sweet land but he did not write great poetry. There is little of the quality of memorableness that all great poetry possesses but Vaughan has his niche.

High up on a hilltop ridge above Llanhamlach, the next parish to Llansantffraed, is an ancient chamber tomb which is named on the OS map as Ty Illtyd, the house of Illtyd. It is made up of several hefty stone slabs, some of which bear incised crude crosses and other hieroglyphics, some enclosed in lozenge shapes. In his book, *A Life and Interpretation*, F.E Hutchinson suggested that Henry

Vaughan referred to this ancient monument in *Vanity of Spirit*, his poem of childhood reminisces:

> *Weak beams and fires flash'd to my sight,*
> *Like a young east, or moonshine night,*
> *Which show'd me in a nook cast by*
> *A piece of much antiquity,*
> *With hieroglyphics quite dismember'd,*
> *And broken letters scarce remember'd.*

Passing near the site in 1803, Colt Hoare referred to a passage by Gerald of Wales, who said that Illtyd lived here a hermit's life, but Colt Hoare offered a cynical, though perhaps realistic, view on the stones' artwork.

> I think there was probably a small cell or chapel on the summit, but the crosses and other figures cut into the stones of the cromlech are certainly only the playful handiwork of those who have visited the hermit's cell.

Graffiti, in other words.

No Better Place for a National Park

Sited at Llangorse between the River Wye to the north and the River Usk to the south, and within the Brecon Beacons National Park, is the largest natural lake in Wales. It has been known by several different names during its history, including by original Welsh names Llyn Syfaddan and Brycheiniog Mere. The lake is glacial and occupies an ice-scoured rock basin. It is renowned for its unusually high numbers of fish and birds, and as a result is a site of international conservation importance. The largest pike ever caught by rod in the UK was said to have been at Llangorse in 1846, and supposedly weighed 31 kg (68 pounds). That was never substantiated but if it was true, that might still be a world record. There is mention in Welsh folklore of a Llangorse lake monster known as *afanc,* thought by many to be a giant pike. The word translates from Welsh as *beaver,* but with a lake full of pike it would not be difficult for an imaginative fisherman to slip *afanc* into his description for the one that got away! In the 15th century, the poet Lewis Glyn Cothi slipped the creature into a poem:

> *The afanc am I, who, sought for, bides*
> *In hiding on the edge of the lake;*
> *Out of the waters of Syfaddon Mere*
> *Was he not drawn, once he got there.*

The diarist, Francis Kilvert, noted several visits to Llangorse lake, including a July 1878 outing in the company of his father when the pair caught a brace of perch. Perch, pike or beaver, there would surely be no mistaken identity by a visiting honest curate. The lake lies only five miles south of Talgarth, and with two hours of daylight still to their credit, Elliot-Stock and friend felt justified in lingering to obtain a distant photograph, though the sun had commenced to dip behind the distant dark mass of the Epynt Mountain:

> This is not, perhaps, the time to choose for a camera, but there is no better to bring out all there is of the best in a lake's romantic atmosphere, especially when it lies below one, polished as a mirror, with the faint outline of the brown fells lying deep down in its placid depths.

It was on an autumn day in 1897 that another cyclist travel writer, Arthur Bradley, temporarily abandoned his bike and strolled along the banks of the lake before tackling the 600m (1,970ft) ascent of Mynydd Troed:

> As I stood in the autumn sunshine on the peak of Troed, no fitter place could well be found. For here I could trace the windings of the Wye northward as well as the Usk beneath, my sight ranged over the sunny wastes of Radnor Forest, or travelling westward along the Epynt hills, caught the dim summits of the Carmarthen moors. And as I looked down once more upon the Vale of Usk,

73

with Llyn Syfaddan shining like a jewel in its bosom, and the noble Beacons of old Brycheiniog growing in stature and mystery before a drooping sun, one cannot wonder that Henry Vaughan found inspiration here.

Forty years later, Percy Thorseby Jones stood on that same summit and was likewise moved to powerful descriptive prose, but with an added glance at the Black Mountains behind him:

> On the west side of Pengenfford, though not more than 600m, Troed is a conspicuous landmark and offers extensive views. From the top the western prospect centres on the Brecon Beacons but also includes immediately below the gleaming level of Llangorse lake. Best of all is the eastward view, the two western ridges of the Black Mountains, with Waun Fach (811m) and Pen-y-Gadair Fawr (800m) in lofty serenity.

Following Bradley's route from Llangorse village, I left the hill road after a mile or two for the open bracken-covered slopes of Mynydd Troed's companion hill, Mynydd Llangors, which rose to 550m (1,800ft). There is no obvious access now to the summits, so I joined the only right of way available on these twins and marked on my OS map as Three Rivers Ride, part of the National Bridleroute Network. The route travels along the western flanks of the Black Mountains, and after half a mile or so turns quite suddenly down a secret valley, the presence of which I had not expected. It was marked on the map as Cwm Sorgwm, and in a patch of green in the hollow sandwiched between steep inclines stood a solitary farm. It looked the kind of place for a holiday for an out-of-this-world experience. The Cwm road leads to another valley, where the Rhiangoll stream greets you on the way south to its meeting with the Usk by Tower Lodge in Glanusk park. Not far from this point, Stuart Mais came across his first view of the Brecon Beacons from a bend in the road:

> There, outstretched before me over the hedge, was the great wild panorama over the intervening gracious green valley of the Usk.

The vivid lush green stopped suddenly at the foot of the hills, and the deep bracken that followed was in its turn succeeded by slopes of greyer hue where the rocks peeped through the worn green and the shadows formed by the great peaks in the distance were black.

The historic county of Brecknockshire was created in 1535 by the Laws In Wales Act with Brecknock as it's county town. The name Brecon derives from Brychan, the founder of the old kingdom of Brycheiniog, and seems to have been adopted over time by the town's folk as an easy-off-the tongue replacement. The official name, Brecknock, was itself eclipsed with the formation in 1974, of the county of Powys. However, Brecon remains the county's third largest town. Its Welsh name, Aberhonddu, means 'mouth of the Honddu', referring to the river which flows, often roars, down from nearby hills, passed the old castle, and into the Usk. In the Dark Ages, the territory in which Brecon stands was part of the small independent petty kingdom of Brycheiniog which acted as a buffer state between England to the east and the powerful south Welsh kingdom of Deheubarth to the west. That is, until the arrival of Bernard de Neufmarché, a minor Norman lord, but one of the second batch of Knights after the Conquest who rose to power in the Welsh marches. He successfully invaded Brycheiniog in 1088 and then created the Anglo-Norman lordship of Brecknock.

Neufmarché's castle was a motte and bailey affair, which he built in 1093. The great earth mound, now in the Bishop's Palace garden opposite the Castle Hotel, was the motte on top of which he erected a timber keep. The bailey or courtyard below the motte extended to cover what is the present Hotel and gardens. After the Conquest, the Normans embarked on a massive programme of castle building throughout the Welsh borders, and in almost all cases they started as motte and baileys with timber buildings. Eventually, the more important ones were enlarged and strengthened, and this occurred at Brecon where the castle became the administrative and military headquarters of the lordship. Its important strategic position also warranted making the castle more powerful, so timber was replaced with stone.

During the English Civil War of the 17th century, unconfirmed reports referred to Brecon Castle and town walls as having been demolished by the non-aligned Welsh inhabitants to prevent suffering a damaging siege by either Parliamentary or Royalists factions. It is known that by then the castle was already an impressive ruin, so perhaps nature had pre-empted the townsfolk's needs. The Rt. Hon. John Byng saw what was left of the castle in 1774 while stood for a time on the keep:

> Nothing else now remains of the castle but a small bastion where stood the Ely Tower. The inner space is converted into a bowling green and the old hall which fronts the Honddu bridge.

By the end of the Georgian era, Brecon Castle had practically gone, but in 1809 the Morgans of Tredegar Park stepped in when the remaining section of the curtain walls and a few outbuildings were renovated by Sir Charles Morgan into one of the first tourist Hotels in Wales. The result is the Castle Hotel – an interesting, if not bizarre mixture of medieval and Victorian. Bradley could have thought so, too, when he chose to stay there at the end of the 19th century:

> The old hostelry has the advantage of a delightful situation entirely removed from the clatter of the town. The tourist in south Wales has often cause of complaint that has nowhere to lay his head, or at any rate no refuge of a tempting kind, but in Brecon he may make himself happy in a good many different quarters.

We stayed in the hotel, too, for a few days in September 2016, and as we sat on our veranda were blessed with a wonderful red sunset over the Beacons stretching across to the distant Carmarthen Fan mountain ridge.

Within sight of the castle, in the plain beyond the south bank of the Usk, is an impressive, mainly late sixteenth century farmhouse, dated around 1582 but still with 13th and 14th window headings. Newtown farmhouse was once the home of the Games family from which they dominated Brecon for a time. The family name was originally Llywelyn, but in the 15th century their famous ancestor, Sir Dafydd Llywelyn, was given, perhaps cruelly, the surname Gam because of an eye deformity, a squint. His home then was near Abergavenny and his fame was being killed at Agincourt when throwing himself in front of King Henry V as he was being attacked. For that supreme sacrifice, he was knighted on the battlefield. Newtown farm went into decline from the early 18th century and is now surrounded by a golf course.

Brecon's Cathedral Church of St John the Evangelist is a beautiful building, not lacking in anything due to its minority standing in the league of cathedrals. It certainly isn't in the same class as, say, Canterbury or Lincoln, but is without doubt in one of its own. In Wales, it is regarded as second only to St David's, about on a par with Llandaff, but distinctly superior to those of St Asaph and Bangor. Its elevated position amid a spacious and well-kept graveyard, its venerable trees and the ancient buildings of the adjoining priory, make up a picture of which Breconians should be proud and absent ones might recall with fond memory. Until 1923, the cathedral was merely Brecon's parish church, but following the disestablishment of the Church in Wales it became the seat of the Bishop of Swansea and Brecon. Regardless of the extensive reconstruction and restoration by Gilbert Scott in the 1860s, it is still described as one of the finest examples of Gothic architecture to be seen, and I liked what I saw. Among the mass of stone and marble commemorating the dead in the nave is a wooden figure of a lady – the sole relic of the mausoleum of the Games family of Newtown farm, erected in 1555, but despoiled by Cromwellian soldiers in the civil war. The figure is elaborately dressed in the costume of Elizabethan times. The Games' monuments were intact in Thomas Churchyard's time, and inspired that worthy poet to the extent of a stanza:

> *These are indeed the ancient race of Games*
> *A house and blood that long rich armies must give,*
> *And now in Wales are many of their names,*
> *That keep great train and doth full bravely live.*

At the eastern end in the sanctuary, part of the 1201 build, the five stepped lancet windows fill the eastern wall above an elegant stone reredos, with carved panels and rows of saints and worthies connected with the cathedral and the diocese. Among those is a statue in one of the niches of the Silurist, Henry Vaughan.

The Rt. Hon. John Byng had little complimentary to say about the priory church as he saw it in 1774: "the inside is a filthy display of Welsh dirt!" Neither had Sir Richard Colt Hoare any better words for it in 1802:

> The venerable church is in a dilapidated state and the paved floor sadly disfigured by the horrid custom of digging graves within it and burying corpses.

The Brecon of today is a busy market town and a thriving community, and being on the northern edge of the Brecon Beacons National Park it has grown into a popular holiday destination. One of the town's top attractions is the annual Jazz Festival, conceived in 1984 by a group of enthusiasts, one of whom, the well-known jazz personality, George Melly, became the first musician to be contracted for the opening festival, and remained a supporter until his death in 2007. There was little of such pomp and entertainment in Stuart Mais's day, but there were interests, of sorts:

> On leaving the museum I visited the picturesque inn once called *The Shoulder of Mutton*, now *The Siddons Arms*, where Sarah Siddons and her brother Charles Kemble were born. I learnt to my sorrow that the whole place was to be sold a couple of days after my visit, and I asked the landlord to bid for me for the decorated taps and old oak settles. As I heard no more, I took for granted that the dealers had descended on it.

As the River Usk nears Brecon and gathering force from tributary streams, it flows passed the grassy remains of Roman Cicucium on a flat meadow overlooking the river from the north bank. This was their military camp which guarded the western approach to South Wales. Some of the massive walls, in places 3m (10ft) high, can still be seen while within are traces of their buildings. When the Legions left, the Britons of Brycheiniog moved in and renamed it Y Gaer. By the time Bernard de Neufmarché arrived with his Norman troops, Y Gaer had already become overused and suitable only as a temporary base while the marcher lord built his own new town a short distance further east. Y Gaer fort site is on private land, and although CADW say visitors are permitted along a narrow farm road, parking is limited to sharing spaces with farm vehicles.

At the time of my visit, the fields around had been drenched by days of heavy rain, making it difficult to walk to the site, and my camper van was just too much for the very limited parking. The fort was initially made of timber and built around AD 80 as a base for a five hundred-strong cavalry unit. Romans were not known for their equestrian skills, which is why they brought in Spanish Vettones tribesmen who had a reputation for being experts at handling horses. They were under the command of Sextus Julius Frontinus and the Second Augustan Legion of Caerleon.

In the second century, the timber structure was replaced by a larger stone one, and it is the remains of this that can be seen today. In its time, Cicucium was one of the largest Roman auxiliary forts in the Welsh border region – an important centre for controlling military progress into South Wales and eventually protecting their network of roads linking exploited territories, mines, and harbours with their border fortresses. The activities and deployment of the military units here were dependent on what was happening elsewhere in the Roman world, and the garrison was often on the move. On at least two occasions, large forces were despatched to the border with Scotland where, in AD 120, Hadrian was building his wall, followed twenty years later with another by Antonius. Then there was rebellion back home requiring the need for the battle-hardened Legio Secunda Augusta, and once again Cicucium was left light on defence.

There is evidence to suggest that in the remaining years of Roman occupation, the Welsh continued their resistance and there were several phases of refortification at Cicucium until the final trauma of withdrawal in 410. The young exposer of Caerleon's amphitheatre, Mortimer Wheeler, practiced his excavation skills here first in 1925, and the fort is now an SSSI – a Site of Special Scientific Interest. Colt Hoare was much struck with the situation here, but thought it was a legion's summer station, a holiday retreat perhaps for hard-working soldiers from Caerleon. Probably for that reason, he didn't stay long:

> We descended from the Gaer to the banks of the Usk and pursued a meandering path by the water's edge through the noble wood, and more beautiful and natural scenery of wood and water can be seen nowhere. The fine bend of the river adds great variety to the landscape. It reminded me of the scenery of Mr Knight's at Downton Castle.

In the village of Llanddew on the outskirts of Brecon, the church of St David – the oldest in Breconshire – is thought to have been the parish church when Gerald was Archdeacon of Brecon from 1175 to 1203. It is the third church on the site, the first being a timber one around AD 500 and though much restored, the present building contains some original work. Gerald's home was the Bishop's Palace, the castellated ruins of which survive in the garden of the Rectory across the road from the church and about which he wrote, 'in these temperate regions I have obtained a place of dignity'. Here, Gerald is said to have compiled his *Itinerary* and in it wrote affectionately of his home county:

> Brecknock, is a country having sufficient store of corn; and if there be any defect thereof, it is plentifully supplied out of the fruitfulness of England bordering so near upon it; a country likewise well stored with pastures and woods, with wild deer and herds of cattle, having abundance beside of fresh water fish, wherewith Usk on the one side and Wye on the other serveth it. For, both these rivers are full of salmon and trout, but of the two the Wye is the better, affording the best kind of them.

Even as he wrote and prayed in his Llanddew Palace, Gerald was burdened by not yet being Bishop of St David's. He had set his heart on replacing his uncle as bishop, restoring its metropolitan status, and making the Church of Wales free from subservience to Canterbury. When his uncle died in 1176, he thought his chance had come, but King Henry II chose the prior of Much Wenlock, Peter de Leia, an Anglo-Norman by birth. Gerald was again a candidate for the see of St David's in 1198 but was excluded a second time. Bitterly disappointed, and considering his chance had gone, he returned to his old teaching college in Paris where he continued his academic studies until his death in 1223.

There is no doubt that the Beacons and the National Park named after them, is a special place. It is an area that contains a diverse range of beautiful environments, from the steep escarpments of Pen-y-Fan and Cribyn – the highest points in southern Britain – to picturesque reservoirs, mountain lakes, dense forests and woodlands, wide open moors and the unforgettable waterfalls of the Afon Mellte. If you are fortunate, you may see a Red Kite or two in the skies over the deciduous woodlands of the National Park, one of the great ornithological conservation successes of recent years in Mid Wales. Even from the tea shop terraces of the Beacons Centre on the moors above the village of Libanus, the mountains put on a powerful show. The A470 mountain road climbs steeply from Brecon to its high point at Storey Arms, where Beacon busters assemble for the easier climbs to the summits. The panorama is awesome but the lay-bys and off-road parking areas in summer and at holiday weekends can be packed to overflowing. Traffic is heavy and descending back to Brecon is fast and often furious. The road surface is good and in parts straight and long but it's the automotive equivalent of a ski jump. Accidents are common, and attending services expect things to be bad when they get to an accident. Local newspaper reports of a recent horrendous tragic pile-up not far from Storey Arms doesn't seemed to have influenced any slowdown in motion.

The climb from the Storey Arms Outdoor Centre is the shortest walking route to the tops, taking in Y Gyrn and Corn Du before reaching Pen y Fan, the highest point at 900m (2,953ft). As the way approaches the ridge above Llyn Cwm Llwch, a conspicuous obelisk appears close to the edge. This marks the spot where the body of five-year old Tommy Jones was found in early

September 1900 after a search of twenty-nine days. Tommy was the son of a miner from Maerdy in the Rhondda valley and on 4th August the family went to visit the boy's grandparents who farmed at the small hamlet of Cwm-llwch below the Pan-y-Fan peak. After taking the train to Brecon and walking some distance, they met up with the grandfather and Tommy's 13-year-old cousin William. The party was by now just a quarter of a mile from the farm, and the older boy ran on to warn the grandmother of their approach. Tommy went, too, though he couldn't keep up with William and eventually became lost in the growing darkness. The poor wretch had no sense of direction or distance and must have kept going in the hope of eventually reaching the farm.

It cannot be imagined what terrors the little lad went through as he stumbled around and the darkness closed in on him, nor the fears and panic of his father and grandparents as they searched frantically through the night and all the following day. They did not guess that Tommy might have climbed further up the mountain, but tragically that is what happened. His cold, dead body was eventually discovered accidentally by two hill climbers enjoying their sport, less than 200m (650ft) from the top of Pen-y-Fan. Tommy's father had never given up hope, returning time and again to the mountain, still believing he would find his son alive. He must have got so close to discovering him. Like many before him and since, Stuart Mais stood by the stone pillar and pondered on the obvious questions:

Two things seem very surprising: the fact that his cries were not heard, as sound carries here through the still, hot, August nights much more clearly than it does in the valley; and then the fact that his little legs carried him so far.

Figure 6 Stuart Petrie Brodie Mais

Southwards beyond Storey Arms, the B4059 high moor's road leads to the spectacular waterfall country which has impressed travellers for centuries. This can be a lonely forbidding road at the best of times, but in winter can be a test for nerve and steady driving. Wandering sheep can be a hazard and the occasional victim of a collision by the roadside is not surprising. At one point, a moorland lane leads over the youthful Hepste River from where streams building on the soaked moors begin their tumble through narrow rock-strewn, wooded ravines, cascading spectacularly over broken riverbeds and ridges down towards the Neath Vale. During his stay in Brecon, Mais was invited by Colonel Jock Lloyd, then the curator of the Brecon Museum, to accompany him on a sightseeing tour of the Hepste and Mellte valleys. The Brecon Beacons National Park didn't exist then, but the colonel was a keen proponent for introducing free access to the area known as Forest Fawr to the public to encourage tourism. After many postponements, the two men finally agreed the time and place and set off to explore the unknown heights of Breconshire. They drove along the high ground above the Mellte valley, passed stone farms as remote as crofters' cottages in Scotland's Outer Hebrides. And so, came to Ystradfellte, a tiny hamlet of white-washed cottages lying completely hidden below the high wastes. In the excellent Inn, with its low ceilings, oak settle, great beams hung with smoking hams, and vast kitchen range, three cyclists and a couple of carters were taking their ease. It looked none too easy a place to reach on a bicycle and a considerable achievement, too, for two warring 13th century lord marchers to find the place at all![19]

And so Mais recalled:

> We came to a superb waters meet at the junction of the Hepste and
> Mellte, and watched the great waters tumbling down a fifty-foot

---

[19] Following a land dispute between Earls Hereford and Gloucester in 1291, King Edward the First decided to resolve the matter himself and demanded the Earls assemble on 12th March at Ystadfellte. The King brought with him the Bishop of Ely, the Earl of Pembroke, and two regular judges, to hear the case. Gloucester didn't appear, so they adjourned to Llanddew near Brecon.

fall. Then as we climbed again on to the wild waste moorland, the Colonel spread his arms and said: "Can you think of a better place for a National Park? Here is the ideal happy hunting ground for all South Wales." And indeed, it seemed to be admirably placed within cycling and good walking distance of the great coal centres. I have never seen a lovelier land than the whole range of Forest Fawr.

One hundred years before Mais, Thomas Roscoe was pursuing a similar trek. Starting from the Angel Inn deep In the Neath Valley, he took the southern path that leads over the Craig y Dinas and first caught sight of the Afon Hepste – one of the targets of his search – peacefully gliding through a richly wooded dingle to the point where it joins her sister stream, the Afon Mellte. The whole of this extraordinary valley is a mass of waterfalls and geological wonders. One of the most remarkable is a cave system called Porth-yr-Ogof:

> Here, I traced a zig-zag path on the high ground above the stream of the Hepste, and then threading my way down the Cwm amidst a forest of trees and underwood, with the noise of the cascades constantly breaking upon the ear, reached the higher fall of the river, which descended forty feet into a large and deep basin below. I climbed down and came to a vast cave where the cool, crystal Mellte river suddenly disappeared. This cavern gate has an arch forty-three feet wide and twenty feet high, and as I wandered along over the boulders, I found many side passages where the stream was flowing on its underground course. Having remained a considerable time amongst these remarkable scenes, I once more turned away to the high ground, almost relieved that the deafening sound of the roaring cataracts had subsided into a solemn and ceaseless murmur.

In September 2016, I set out on a walk along the Nedd Fechan River. This was my first visit to the waterfall country of South Wales, and one which I had looked forward to with heightened enthusiasm. There's an easier path from the Angel Inn than

Roscoe's tramp over Craig y Dinas; even so, there was no doubting the increase in degree of difficulty to come. The compensation would be the waterfalls. My walk started well, following the path upstream and the detour along the Afon Pyrddin to Sgwd Gwladus, the Lady Falls. To get to my next waterfall, Sgwd-y-Bedol, the Horseshoe Falls, I had to return to follow the banks of the Nedd Fechan, but after half a mile I arrived at a point where, to my forever unending disappointment, the path had disappeared beneath a substantial and impassable landslip, and suddenly my walk was over. The non-fulfilment of expectations was hard to take at that point, but the thought that I might have been on the wrong side of the slip with no way back was sobering.

Paragon of Miniature Valleys

It is twenty-five years since I climbed Y Fal, the Sugar Loaf Mountain overlooking Crickhowell. Twenty-five years younger, leaner, and fitter. I remember my rambling friends and I started early from Glangrwyney near to where the Grwyne Fawr crosses under the A40, climbed the steep south face to the summit, then down the eastern side by the Deri to the Crown Inn at Pantygelli for a few well-earned beers and lunch. The weather that day had been unfriendly, and our disappointment was not having much of a view through the mist on reaching the top of the mountain. On a fine October day in 2016, I drove my camper van from Pandy to Crickhowell, along very narrow lanes behind the northern flanks of Y Fal, with hardly a passing place to make a difference for a tricky meeting with another vehicle of any size travelling in the opposite direction. Below and occasionally besides, enclosed by a continuous line of alders, I was accompanied by the running waters of the Grwyne Fawr. This delicious mountain stream rises on the southern slopes of Rhos Dirion in the Black Mountains and follows a southeastward course for several miles before being interrupted by the huge white elephant of Grwyne Fawr Reservoir.

Built in 1928 to hold up to 1,800 megalitres (400 million gallons) of drinking water for the rising population in the South

Wales valleys, the reservoir was decommissioned in 1994 by Dwr Cymru, Welsh Water, because the lake had become permanently discoloured with peat sediment, and therefore undrinkable. It was decided that any attempt at a remedy would be uneconomical. In 1938 Percy Thorseby Jones reached the reservoir on his walk over from Talgarth, having climbed over Y Das via Rhiw Cwnstab and into the Grwyne Fawr gorge – an achievement any time, except he was carrying a bicycle! Y Das can be reached directly from Pengenffordd cart track, skirting the base of Y Grib. The terrain is rough and undulating, but en route offers delightful views of bracken-clad spurs of the escarpment and the cone-shaped Y Das from this angle:

> The track at first winds through high bracken, then mounts the flank of Y Das by steep pitches; higher up comes a series of zigzags. On the left is a deep gully Cwm Cwmstabl, formed by a stream that has cut its way back into the escarpment. It's almost precipitous sides, scored and riven by countless storms, show bare red rock and patches of scree. Two more miles of rough walking and at last the level expanse of the reservoir comes into sight ahead. In its deep hollow it seldom sparkles and with its rim of confining concrete it is undisguisedly utilitarian.

Thoresby Jones was enthralled, and recorded the twin Gwryne Fechan valley as, "the very phoenix and paragon of miniature valleys, unaccountably ignored, unsung by poets, unpainted by artists, unsnapped by Zeiss-Ikons and dismissed by admirable guidebooks". But it's the quality of the Border countryside that pleases to excess here. The miles of deep green valleys, the narrowness of the roads and the loneliness of the whole area, give the traveller solitude and peace of mind rarely found anywhere in the whole of Britain.

Massingham, too, was in awe of this landscape and described it in impassioned tones:

> This is the narrowest and wildest of all the five valleys of the Black Mountains. A lane ascends from Crickhowell and passes between

Llanbedr and the foot of Crug Hywel, whose upshooting flanks and flat rocky cap give it a geometrical prominence. The river, with anger not insignificantly fierce, foamed below the lane. From Table Hill, lane and stream were deep in the wilds and from the southern slopes of the Gadair Ridge east of the intense river a series of bold promontories projected over the valley in tawny, purple and bright green between gleams of whitened sunlight and the darkening of rain clouds.

The Grwyne Fawr gorge ends about three-quarters of a mile below the turning for Partrishow. Where four lanes meet, the stream is crossed by Pontysprig bridge, Bishop's Bridge – the prelate referred to is Archbishop Baldwin who passed this way during his preaching tour of 1188, accompanied by Gerald of Wales. They had climbed Rhiw Cwmstab from Talgarth and followed the rugged track amongst the heather, bilberries, and bog-cotton alongside the Grwyne Fawr, until it descended into the treeless glen under the Fwddog Ridge. Here, Massingham hit the dreamy prose button again:

> There are no views among these niches, recesses and serpentine ways, but a succession of woods, hill and water so intimate and embroidered with luxuriant vegetation that there could be no sharper contrast with the mountain austerity of the stream higher up. Nowhere in the marches do the trees grow more lustily, especially the alders by the stream. The little river is overhung with magnificent timber all along its route to the Usk, but the trees are just as upstanding and vigorous on the banks, down the slopes and along the hedgerows.

The man in his camper van following the same course that October day should not say more, lest he spoils the moment but notwithstanding the descriptive excellence, this idyl was once tarnished by murder. Fifty years before Gerald and Baldwin moved on to Abergavenny following the Grwyne stream and the rugged Coed Grwyne pass, this very route was taken by the unfortunate marcher lord, Richard de Clare. Somewhere along the woodland track leading to Partrishow, de Clare was ambushed and killed by a small Welsh force. The incident lead to a period of conflict and unrest between the English and Welsh. Today, on the bare mountain ridge overlooking the Grwyne Fawr forest, is the Crug Dial, the Cairn of Revenge – a stone erected to commemorate de Clare's demise.

Somewhere, too, along this same track in the 6th century, an early Christian hermit by the name of Issui (Ishow) founded a cell on a sloping hillside beside the Nant Mair stream. In the 14th century, a church was erected on the site, and church and cell now sit side by side, undisturbed and protected by their isolation. The church retains a stunning 16th century rood loft and screen that spans the entire width of the nave where there is an even earlier pre-Norman font. Neither the religious reformers nor the Puritan iconoclasts who took strong exception to these lofts, knew where to find them, so Partrishow was fortunate that their treasures survive. The present building is mainly Tudor, but an extension at the west end, the anchorite's cell, is two hundred years older – not old enough to be Issui's cell, but there is a presence here that makes it as genuine as one could hope. For below an altar in the cell is a grave, discovered in 1908 complete with the unidentified bones of its occupant.

A few yards down the road from the church is Ffynnon Issui (Well of Ishow), a place of pilgrimage long before Christianity came to these parts. The position of this ancient well, much frequented by walkers and cyclists, is by an extremely tight bend on a very narrow lane in thick Grwyne woodland. No room here, thankfully, for motor vehicles. A flagstone staircase leads down to the well where the spring's water runs into a drystone, open-ended, slab-roofed chamber. One cannot ignore the silence and isolation of this place, unless of course you are with a group of walkers or cyclists and wonder how even a Celtic hermit could have first discovered and then survived in what would have been hidden in a deep, inaccessible forest.

The Vale of Ewyas is a steep-sided and secluded valley in the Black Mountains. Often called the Honddu (pronounced Hondy) Valley, after the river that separates the great wall of mountains on each side, and occasionally Llanthony Valley but only by those who visit the vale with the famous priory ruins in mind. The vale was named after the small Welsh kingdom of Ewias, formed after the Roman withdrawal from Britain and which, following the Norman invasion of Wales, became an autonomous lordship within the southern march. In 1536, King Henry VIII's Act of Union with Wales made the vale part of the new county of Monmouthshire, while the remaining part of Ewias to the north east of Hatterall Hill was incorporated into the county of Herefordshire. Just a few miles into the vale, along its narrow entrance lane from Llanvihangel Crucorney, the tiny village of Cwmyoy clings to the broken flanks of Hatterall – probably the result of the same subterranean upheaval that caused the collapse on the Skirrid. The debris is still plain to the eye beneath the cliff it must have left with such disturbance.

Consequentially, Cwmyoy has become best known for St Martin's Church – the most crooked church in Great Britain. Standing on the steep hillside, it survived the land slippage but was left with bit of a wobble. Inside, the evidence of sideways chancel movement has created a 'weeping chancel', where the straight nave represents Christ's body and the deflected chancel his head fallen sideways in death. A remarkable instance of natural artwork.

Arthur Bradley had begun a tour of South Wales here in the spring of 1897 and believed there could have been no finer place to start. He thought the vale one of the gems of Wales, even in full consciousness of more striking claims of many other valleys throughout the Principality. In defence, he concluded:

> There is no outstanding ruggedness here, no great wealth of waterfalls, nor yet any broad surging river and no wilderness of woodland. But then one does not approach the Vale of Ewyas by way of Snowdonia, or the Cadair range, or the Berwyns, or the Cardigan Mountains.

During early spring, and for as long before the start of the tourist season as you can get to be here, it is a pleasure to find a five-barred gate to lean over and absorb the near silence of the day. I see Bradley now, deep in thought, eyes glazed, and holding a smoking pipe:

> How gratefully the Honddu's crystal waters wash the thirsty rushes and grasses by the road edge on one side or flick the pendent fern leaves and the trailing greenery of the fence bank on the other. How the ducks rejoice in it, and what a pace they come sailing down, and even the water flies seem conscious of their immunity from their quick eyed foe, as they skim the surface of their short and merry day. If I were a trout, I should retire for the summer solstice to these cool and bubbling depths, and indeed an odd one or two will generally be found possessed of such measure of sagacity.

In another time, I was walking on Hatterall Hill, following the section of the Offa's Dyke Path which runs the length of the range to Hay Bluff. The high back of the ridge is broad and soft, and bog grasses grab your knees. On that hot day, there was not air enough to stir the wild cotton bloom of the bogs. A few carrion crows floated lazily about and a restless curlew or two broke the silence with their melancholy cry. Once, I almost stumbled on a clutch of young grouse that fluttered gallantly up from the deep heather in search of parents and safety. The prospect from here is sublime, even in the simmering heat of the July day. Down in the vale, a thousand feet below, the great grey pile of Llanthony Priory, with its two west towers and its long line of Gothic arches lying conspicuous and solitary, struck a wonderful note. Looking south, I could see every detail of the vale, with the Skirrid rising progressively from its lower base, and on the right the Sugar Loaf looming hazily in the near distance.

When Archbishop Baldwin's cavalcade of priests and princes crossed the Black Mountains from Talgarth and descended by the sources of the upper Grwyne, it was the recognised way to travel along hillsides, or to climb over their crests. For one thing, they liked to see who was about; for another, the valleys were often tangled swamps. The main routes to Llanthony lay over the Hatterall ridge on the east and over the Fwddog on the west. Access to the Ewyas Vale at the end of the 18th century was not yet easy, as William Coxe pointed out:

The access to the vale though unsafe for carriages is not difficult on horseback, and the latter part of the way is extremely interesting to pedestrian travellers; pleasant walks lead through the fields above the precipitous banks of the Honddu and present a constant succession of romantic scenery which is concealed from those who traverse the hollow roads in carriages or on horseback.

Coxe visited Llanthony Priory several times and described the going through the vale when probably at its worst:

I would not recommend timid persons to pass this way in a carriage, for in the whole course of my travels, I seldom met with one more inconvenient and unsafe. Excepting in very few places, there is not room for a single horse to pass by a chaise; and should two carriages meet, neither could proceed until one was drawn backwards to a considerable distance.

At that time, the priory ruins were in a delicate state and seemed to Coxe to have lost more of its structure with each visit. He had been informed that in the previous year a part of one of the fine Gothic windows in the western front had given way, and now he had the sad mortification to find that all these three elegant windows had fallen to the ground in the preceding winter:

The Saxon tower, I fear, from the present unconnected state of the stones which compose its masonry will soon follow the same fate. It is a melancholy sight to the traveller who frequently revisits the same ground and object of antiquity to witness the progressive ruin of these fine specimens of ancient architecture.

At the turn of the 19th century, Manchester born, alderman, philanthropist and adventure cyclist, Fletcher Moss, arrived in the vale, unhindered by any early signs of tourists' traffic:

To cycle up the pass in the dark lone hills to Llanthony was a veritable pilgrimage, for there no motor car or vulgar tripper shocks the senses; the curlew or the peewit calls, the patient angler, or the still more patient hopeless shepherd, calmly waits for death.

Behind the Skirrid Inn, the road climbs through a cleft carved out by white water for mile after mile. Mounting steadily, the track runs between hedges of hazel and holly. For all Coxe's concerns, the going is easy enough to walk a steady four miles an hour. In 1968 travel writer and long-distance rambler, John Hillaby, on foot in the Ewyas Vale, was untroubled:

> I chose the track that follows the Honddu River. It gets progressively steeper towards what is indelicately called Lord Hereford's Knob, but for most of the way you could drive up there in a bus. I walked fast because I wanted to get over the ridge by nightfall and sleep near Hay on Wye.

The ruins of Llanthony priory church of St John the Baptist stand in a wild and beautiful setting in the valley of the Afon Honddu, about seven miles along the narrow valley road from Llanvihangel Crocorney towards Hay on Wye. The priory is Grade 1 listed, as is the Hotel which is part of the priory buildings, and the church of St David next to them. It was built on the site of the 6th century monastic cell of Dewi hiself and considered one of the most sacred sites in Wales. Long before Walter de Lacy built his priory here in 1108, this place had already seen out five hundred summers. The Norman nobleman discovered Dewi's tiny ruined chapel while out hunting and decided he would spend the rest of his life in that very spot in prayer and penance. What made a battle-hardened knight have such a catastrophic change of heart is difficult for a modern man to fathom, but so he did, and with the help of his chaplain companion, Ernisius, who had joined him in his personal sacrifice, they established one of the most isolated communities of dedicated men of prayer anywhere in Britain. Eventually persuading forty more monks to join them in this wild setting, Llan nant Honddu priory became one of the earliest Augustinian houses of canons. Gerald of Wales knew of the priory's existence, which he described in the opening of the third chapter of his *Itinerary* and it is likely he spent time here in the latter part of the 12th century, even as the buildings were still new, and experienced the healthy feel of the surroundings:

> In the deep vale of Ewyas which is about an arrow-shot broad, encircled on all sides by lofty mountains, stands the church of Saint John the Baptist, covered with lead, and built of wrought stone; and considering the nature of the place, not unhandsomely constructed, on the very spot where the humble chapel of St David, the archbishop, had formerly stood decorated only with moss and ivy. A situation truly calculated for religion and more adapted to canonical discipline than all the monasteries of the British Isle. As the monks sit in their cloisters in this monastery, breathing the fresh air, they gaze up at distant prospects which rise above their own loft roof-tops, and there they see, as far as any eye can reach, mountain peaks which rise to meet the sky, and often enough at herds of wild deer grazing on the summits.

Massingham was not so impressed. He thought the wildness and the loneliness enclosed a kind of pastoral amphitheatre of Arcadian grace and hospitality, but the wide floor of the vale didn't feel wild at all:

> I have been to the priory several times in many weathers and seasons. Yet despite its magical environment it seems to me to be almost entirely lacking in atmosphere. Sensibility is unmoved and admiration keeps its distance.

Stuart Mais was equally unmoved. He expected to see a Tibetan-like fortress with black-cowled monks, or at any rate some striking reminders of the eccentric, Walter Savage Landor:

> This really is the heart of the Black Mountain country, which to me has always spelt mystery and romance, but I must confess that Llanthony was a disappointment. All I saw was a ruin, once a superb building, turned into a tea shop. There was a lot of barbed wire about, which seemed unnecessary. It is quite time that the Office of Works took over and restored it.

Fred Hando had seen the ruins many times, and on the last occasion he turned his attention to Llanthony village along the river's bank:

> Always we have found enough in the priory to hold our interest but below the ruins at the foot of the hill the cluster of cottages caught my fancy. Set against the swelling green of Bal Mawr they were a study in old-time grace and harmony. The old mill, long since silent, was a favourite subject for painters in water colour.[20]

As many had done before me, on a hot day in early summer I wandered from the pastures of the priory, through a large field of upland grasses alive with butterflies, and there at the foot of the climb to Hatterall Hill ridge and at the head of a densely-wooded dingle was the roofless ruin of a house choked with ivy, nettles, and cow parsley. For strangers to the territory and its history, the sight would be puzzling, for no fire had apparently ever scorched it, nor was its decay that of a long age, nor were there any signs of garden, grounds or outhouse enclosures. The scene is very picturesque but strangely unpractical and may suggest to those seeking mystery the possible odd desire of some modern Walter de Lacy without the hair shirt, the rusty armour and the rope girdle, but with no less an enduring passion for solitude. What was before me were the remains of the abandoned unfinished home of Walter Savage Landor, poet and writer, and a friend of Robert Southey.

Although Southey rated Landor's poetry as 'exquisite', Landor himself seems to have been poor at holding on to friends. He had few, and those he made didn't hang around for long. Landor's life reads like a Charles Dickens novel that didn't have a happy ending. The hero's story starts badly and continues downhill for the rest of the way. His schooling had been a disaster, being expelled first from Rugby and later from Oxford, and for the rest of his life he found it easier to make enemies than friends. Not surprisingly, he fell out with his father and left home, penniless, to

---

[20] J.W. Turner rendered his superb watercolour vision of 'Llanthony Priory, Monmouthshire' in 1794, now held for the nation in the Tate Gallery in London.

live in South Wales. Despite the family bust-up, after the death of his father in 1809 Landor ended up with a healthy inheritance. He had already decided to buy Llanthony Priory where the previous owner had constructed a house into the ruins, but Landor wanted to pull that down and build his own place nearby. He planned to plant trees, rear sheep, and improve roads in the vale, but his intention to become a model country gentleman was to be another of his short-lived ideas. His arrogance and volatile attitude towards subordinates prevented much work being done on his plan. After three years of constant disagreements and petty squabbles with neighbours, tenants, magistrates, lawyers, and even the Bishop of St David's, he decided he had had enough, left his house half finished and emigrated to Italy. However, he never forgot Llanthony, nor his perceived unfriendliness of his fellow Llanthonians, and wrote a poem in memoriam.

Llanthony! an ungenial clime
And the broad wing of restless time,
Have rudely swept the massy walls
And rocked thy abbots in their palls.
I loved thee by streams of yore
By distant streams I love thee more;
For never is the heart so true
As bidding what we love adieu.

Walter Savage Landor, from *Fiesolan Musings*

From Llanthony, the vale road narrows further and becomes challenging for vehicles wider than a horse, as far as Capel y ffin. In one of those strange tales where history repeats itself, a wandering Anglican cleric, Joseph Leycester Lynne, arrived here in November 1869 and decided to build his own religious community. He adopted the name Father Ignatius, and with the help of local masons and a few followers, constructed a building in which to lead an eccentric monastic life. Alleged visions of the Virgin Mary helped his convictions of a fulfilled existence in this wild place. The appropriately named Vision Farm, nestling below a spur of the Black Mountains, reflects this questionable event was adopted, though placed higher up nearer the national border with England, by Bruce Chatwin in his classic story *On the Black Hill,* published in 1982. Ignatius's commune was enough to attract the diarist, Francis Kilvert, because he walked from his home at Clyro to the monastery on at least two occasions. An entry for September 2nd, 1870, described a meeting with Ignatius:

> The face is a very saintly one and the eyes extremely beautiful, earnest and expressive, a dark soft brown. When excited they seem absolutely to flame. He wears the Greek or early English tonsure all around the temples, leaving the hair of the crown untouched. His manner gives you the impression of great earnestness and single mindedness.

The experiment was never successful for when Father Ignatius died in 1908, it all came to an end and the Benedictine monks of Caldey Island were forced to take control of the estate. While expressing himself neither to be a believer of established religions nor disapprover of dissenters, or non-conformists, Arthur Bradley had strong feelings about the New Llanthony at Capel-y-Ffin, which he was not slow to share – the reason being that Father Ignatius's 'abbey' was then recent news, and the real 'priory' not yet a popular attraction:

> One bone I feel free to pick with the zealous founder of the new Welsh Augustinians. For beyond all doubt he has created the most hopeless confusion in the minds of the British public in the matter of Llanthony by appropriating its name for his modern establishment some miles away. One of the most beautiful of monastic ruins, having due regard to its unique situation, has been quite obscured in the public mind by a modern society whose eccentricities, as plain people mostly think them, have been more widely bruited about than their more solid characteristics. Be that as it may, should you mention Llanthony in any company outside the district, nine people out of ten will vaguely attribute its foundation to Father Ignatius, which is hard on William de Lacy and something of a shock to anyone familiar with the facts of the Vale of Ewyas.

In 1924, another experiment of a very different sort was reaching a crisis point at a Catholic artists' community on Ditchling Common in Surrey, amidst rumours of unorthodox goings-on. Sculptor Eric Gill was about to be thrown out for persisting in excessive sexual activity of a forbidden kind. He had been raising eyebrows for some time and his fellow artists considered it was not in keeping with his faith, nor compatible with normal behaviour. Jumping before he was pushed, Gill sought alternative surroundings away from the modern industrialisation of London that he hated and the tittle-tattle at Ditchling which he had created and found instead for his small band of followers an available hideaway here at Capel-y-ffin. He obtained a rental agreement from Caldey for the unused monastery buildings, and moved in with his family and David Jones, a fellow artist. In time, others would join them. The monastic buildings were still used occasionally by the Caldey monks as a place for retreat or convalescence, and they provided continuing connection with the Catholic services that Gill still wanted. And so, life of sorts had returned to the Anglican clergyman's hideaway.

Gill and his company carried on with their life's work, carving, chipping, drawing, and writing in isolation. There was no let-up either to Gill's liking for incest or bed-sharing, regardless of his deep religious beliefs. Nevertheless, personal hang-ups apart, Gill's work was highly sought-after and that meant regular returns to the London scene to retain contact with his markets and acquire orders for his artwork. He kept in close contact with old friends there, particularly the Irish artist and author Robert Gibbings. He visited Gill at Capel several times during 1926 but couldn't get used to the austerity on offer:

> It is certainly as cold a spot as any anchorite could wish for. I can still remember the dinners by candlelight at the long refectory table, everyone wearing overcoats or shawls, while members of Gill's family took it in turns to read the Epistle and Gospel of the day. But if the stone floors were cold, Eric was as lovable a man as you could meet.

For Gill, however, the constant travelling to and fro took its toll. After four years in the wilderness, he decided to leave Wales and continue his complex life nearer London again.

Beyond Capel-y-ffin, Massingham avoided the need again to hide his physical disability and described a view which a climber might have otherwise seen from the mountain top but which he probably saw from the roadside:

> Here, on the hammock of high land slung between Darren Llwyd and Hay Bluff, among the scattered hornbeams and nodding foxgloves, the whin bushes and the bilberries, the wheatears and the meadow-pipits, I could look down on a cluster of white cottages and farm buildings, chapels and monastery which is Capel-y-ffin. I could see its cornfields in gold, red fallows, blue-dark woodland, green meadows and green-brown mountainsides, with the shadows playing overall.

At the head of the vale, the Gospel Pass (Bwlch yr Efengel) single track road, so called as justification for an impossible suggestion that SS Peter and Paul came this way to convert the Silurians, is often blocked by snow during the winter owing to its height at 549m (1,801ft) and subsequent exposure. It has become a very popular route for walkers aiming for the vale's high peaks, and motorists and cyclists aiming for the glue pot of Llanthony Priory. At holiday times and weekends, particularly from the Hay end, the Pass and the priory have become places to be avoided. The road's narrowness makes travelling along it a hazard for all at times, although one can still easily find solitude on the mountains, and there's no arguing about the splendid views. The erstwhile stony mule-track – for that is what it was – up from Capel-y-ffin, crosses the flank of Darren Lwyd, a flawless grass dome that closes in the valley. For a time, the infant Honddu River, gleaming and bounding over its stones, can be heard still piping musically down the valley. As the road ascends more steeply, Darren's dome is squeezed into a thin hog's back, dominated now by the massive shoulder of the Twmpa, the less personal alternative title for Lord Hereford's Knob.

As you look northwards from the top of the pass deep into Siluria, towards the wild moor of Pumlumon, ponder on the activities a century or so ago of the utility giant known then as the Electricity Board, who had proposed to acquire 30,000 acres of land to the west of Pumlumon for a hydro-electric scheme by which the headwaters of Wye, Severn, Rheidol and lesser streams, were to be diverted from their natural courses into artificial channels culminating in a series of huge reservoirs. As you would expect, there was a huge outcry by a nation concerned about the destruction of the Cambrian landscape and the possible irreversible damage to the surrounding environments of several Cardigan Bay seaside towns. Objections were denied and Rheidol power station was eventually built near the Devil's Bridge, east of Aberystwyth, between 1957 and 1962 and was officially opened on July 3rd, 1964. As it turned out, there has been little or no disruption to the landscape on Pumlumon and holiday visitors still flock to the seaside towns. A century and a half ago, George Borrow cast about for and found the sources of the Wye and the Severn but the concern remained for a long while that if the power companies finally conquered Pumlumon Fawr, his spirit would hunt in vain for them through a labyrinth of pathways, earthworks, canals, and storage chambers.

By Epynt and Aberedw

The small town of Talgarth lies below the western edge of the Black Mountains. According to traditional accounts, it was once the capital of the Welsh Kingdom of Brycheiniog (Breconshire) before Bernard de Neufmarché arrived from Normandy and changed things his way. After posting a dozen exposed plates back to London at enormous cost, Ernest Elliot-Stock planned a night stop at:

> From here one is treated to a fascinating picture of the old town of Talgarth, crowned by its Norman church with the Gadair ridge as a noble background; and comfortable night-quarters found, we

wandered down to the Llynfi brook with our map and a pipe apiece to enjoy the afterglow upon the Gadair's russet slopes, and thrash out our route for the morrow.

St Gwendoline's Church, a Grade II listed building, was named after St Wenna, one of the 24 daughters of King Brychan who governed Brycheiniog from his palace here. He also had 22 sons and an unknown number of grandchildren, so the Lord only knows where he found the time to organise and rule. The historical importance of Talgarth should have meant there was a castle of some kind within its boundary but the nearest obvious one is Castell Dinas, an Iron Age fort above Pengenffordd four miles away. A couple of miles outside Talgarth, in a field close to the edge of the rising mountain block, is the redundant 13th century church of St Ellyw. It is designated by CADW as a Grade I listed building and is one of three remarkable medieval churches in the area. It has a 15th century rood screen complete with its loft, described as being an exceptional example of medieval work and is the reason for its high grading. Massingham saw it, too, as a cell of delicate and complex workmanship:

> The real mastery in this mountain sanctuary is its 15th century roughly hewn oak double-rood screen and rood-loft with the skeleton floor between them and the tympanum faintly tinted (or painted red and decorated with white roses?) with a cross on it to replace the ancient rood between the rood-beam and the tie-beam of the roof. The rood-loft gallery has gone, but the socket for the rood is still there.

And travel writer Jan Morris wrote in her book, *The Matter of Wales:*

> The screen has a nobler symbolism than more famous and sophisticated examples, for it seems to to stand there between nave and altar, a little tilted with age and perhaps woodworm.

Not far away at Llanfilo, St Bilo's Church, also 13th century, has been said to rival St Ellyw and St Ishow at Partrishow 'in its beauty, peace and holiness'. St Bilo was another of the many daughters of Brychan, and like the church at St Ellyw there is here also a 15th century screen and rood loft of the highest quality, and these and the plaster tympanum escaped the Gothicizing zeal of the Victorian improvers. The exquisite trail carvings of vine leaves and grapes with acorns are matched by the six carved timber pillars of the screen. To crown it all, the cross appears still in place with St John and Mary on either side and would have indicated a uniqueness of combinations if it wasn't for the note on the church guide that the latter was added in 1925.

Further north by a pleasant lane bisecting park-like country, is the 15th century church of St Matthew at Llandefalle built on the site of a Celtic foundation. It, too, has a contemporary screen, this one of sandy brown oak, but there is no loft and no rood. This church is renowned locally for the misfortune of location – it is extremely difficult to get to unless on foot or horseback. It is so hopelessly situated as to make access practically impossible for any mode of modern transport, the lane up to the entrance being so narrow and so steep no modern vehicle wider than a scooter could complete the journey and park conveniently, and even then, there is room only for one! At the inn, I was told that guests to a wedding taking place there recently had not been warned of this and had experienced the most horrendous of times. A challenge too far maybe for any satellite guidance aid.

From Talgarth, the A470 turns west to run alongside the Wye as the river heads east before kinking northwards around Hay then realigning east again to Hereford. Hence forward, the combination of river and the accompanying roads will be the northern border of my 'Southern March', the separation of Breconshire from Radnorshire and Herefordshire from Powys. In 2008, the village of Llyswen – a sleepy little hamlet on the fringes of the Brecon Beacons – was named as one of the ten most desirable villages in which to live in the UK. Nearby on the banks of the river, the elegant Llangoed Hall was created in 1912 by Bertram Clough Williams-Ellis, the architect known chiefly as the designer of the Italianate village of Portmeirion in North Wales. He redesigned the existing 17th century mansion on the site into a large country house fit for a millionaire. Sir Bernard Ashley, Laura's husband, bought Llangoed Hall in 1987, opened it as an Edwardian-style hotel three years later but died of cancer in 2009 before it really got going. Llangoed is now run under new ownership as a country hotel. Massingham stayed there in 1949 as a guest:

> What amazed me most was the spotlessness of this vast rambling inchoate mansion, monument of a period just before closed for ever were the spacious days of country life, and demanding, one would have thought, especially in the riverine damps of winter, the mops and brushes of a whole corps of housemaids. It owed its spruceness and order to our hostess, whose mother had been Kilvert's friend in the seventies of the last century and her companion of much the same years [21]. What tenacity still lies in the old stock of the country gentry of Britain!

The village of Erwood sits beside the Wye on the Breconshire bank some 6 miles south-east of Builth Wells. It is overlooked from across the river by the ancient hill-fort of Twyn y Garth. Bradley thought it an unmissable treat to climb to its summit for a rare view of the valley and surrounding hills:

> It is well worth while, if time allow, to cross Erwood bridge and climb to the top of the rock-crowned hill of Garth above the little station, for the Cambrian railway is all this time working its way through the woodlands on the Radnor shore. A pleasant walk of turf up the long heather and bracken slope almost invites you to the summit, and when this is reached you have your reward. There are higher hills by far than Garth all around from which the prospect might be better, for this is but some five hundred feet above the valley, yet so easy of ascent and of such ready access to a railway station, it is perhaps more noteworthy on this account.

---

[21] Massingham's hostess's maiden name was Elinor Crichton. Kilvert's friend was Emma Charlotte Crichton.

To go down to the river again and re-cross by ferry to the main road would, in mere point of time, have been Bradley's shortest route to Builth. But there is no reason, even now, why anyone should not take the lane along the Radnor side of the river passed the old railway station and on to Aberedw. In his day, Bradley would have had to bear a full three miles of rough and tortuous by-way before the easier track was reached, but there was sufficient consolation in the glorious glimpse one gets above the tree-tops or framed within their trunks and foliage of the river below and the mountains towering above. The cliff that is made up of the Aberedw Rocks thrusts its huge back to all across the way, and the cyclist must dive out of sight of the woodlands reaching up towards the heights of the Epynt range on the opposite shore into a dingle, where the Edw brook hurrying down through damp grassy hollows, bright with marsh marigolds, drowns the murmur of the Wye with its merry gurgling. In earlier years, Thomas Roscoe's journey from Builth and Hay was along the Breconshire side of the river:

> The now wide and full-rolling stream of the Wye is here plentifully strewn with fragments of rock of all shapes and sizes, from the huge mass, like an overthrown tower rising high above the swelling water, to groups of weed-grown stones that only serve to chafe the impetuous torrent into momentary foam and fury. Huge mountains on either side confine the valley as we advance. Aberedw Hill rises

Figure 7 Harold John Massingham

on the Radnor bank and Allt Mawr erects its stern precipitous front high and frowningly over the shadowed path.

The town of Builth Wells (Llanfair ym Muallt)[22] began its existence when the Normans built their timber motte and bailey castle above the ford in the river where the Wye bridge is now. It occupied a strategic position but had a somewhat turbulent history until, in 1277 King Edward I had the castle rebuilt in stone. That stone structure has long gone, presumably recycled into town houses, and its remaining overgrown grassy mounds still peer over the rooftops but attract little interest. The old Cambrian line closed in 1962 under the Beeching axe but the town is still served by a railway station at Builth Road on the Heart of Wales line a mile to the north. Just above the town bridge that supports the A483 Llandrindod Wells road, a winding tributary, the Irfon, falls into the Wye from its birth in the Cambrian Mountains. Beyond the outskirts, the Wye receives another tributary – this time of the Ithon, whose course through the Radnorshire countryside is marked by the same features of grandeur that distinguishes its more graceful senior.

Builth was at one time described as the spa town of the Welsh working classes. The first recorded mention of mineral waters there was around 1740 but it wasn't until the 1830s that the Park Wells and the Glanne Wells became well known. As at Llandrindod Wells, the discovery of mineral springs meant large numbers of visitors came to Builth during the 19th century following the fashion to 'take the waters'. Not surprisingly, a huge collection of hotels, guest houses and shops were built to accommodate them. This was a time of great expectations for pleasure-seeking Victorians. It didn't seem to bother most that the waters might not be as pleasant in the taking as it was just being there. Many visitors to the Park Wells in 1747 agreed that the waters tasted strongly of sulphur and smelled like gunpowder. In the holiday season heydays of the coal mining era, the town was given over to

---

[22] The Welsh name refers to the foundation of the church dedicated to St Mary

the workers of the Glamorgan collieries who gathered in large numbers to drink the most saline waters they considered their bodies required, and then to wash it down when the day's regime was over with generous volumes of Cwrw-dda (Welsh beer). However, the moment came and went. Today, the Glanne Wells has disappeared beneath the town's golf course and Park has returned to pasture. The Rough Guide describes Builth now as an 'earthy agricultural town that has little to detain anyone'.

The Royal Welsh Agricultural Society has played a leading role in the development of agriculture and the rural economy in Wales for over a century since its formation in 1904 and has come a long way since those early days. The successor to Builth's town fairs, the Royal Welsh Show, has become an important event in the Welsh calendar, attracting some 250,000 people over the course of four days. This achievement has allowed for the extensive development of a permanent showground across the river at Llanelwedd, first used in 1963. Each year sees the cream of Welsh livestock on parade, the finest produce from across Wales on sale in a purpose-built food hall and plenty of entertainment for all the family. My first ever visit, in 2016, was quite an experience. I have no tolerance generally for being in a large crowd at any time, and one of up to 100,000 and a temperature in the high twenties looked like being too much. My partner, Linda, has a strange fascination for large muscular beasts, her favourite being the Hereford breed, so she was content to watch and admire. In my analasys of the event, the overall impression I was forced to admit was a favourable one. The huge attendance was always under control and seemed far too enthralled with what was on show for there to be any bother.

But all this used to take place in the town's narrow streets. In his visit to Builth in 1774, Henry Wyndham found the experience a little overwhelming:

> We passed through Builth on market day, and our ride through the crowds in the street was attended with difficulty. It at first amazed

us to see the fullness of these weekly meetings in such little towns, for they appeared like large fairs than common markets; the houses were not sufficient to contain the people who thronged to them, nor were the stables capacious enough for their horses.

Bradley, too, in 1897, considered the whole thing challenging. He thought that if Builth had its serious moments, there could be none more so than when it held its fairs, for it had one of the best stock markets in South Wales:

> It has not succeeded, however, in shaking off the time-honoured but inconvenient custom of holding these functions in its main street, which for the most part is some twenty feet wide and presents in these momentous occasions a scene of indescribable and congested animation. Every vendor of stock is strained to the uttermost to keep his terrified four-footed wares separate from those of his neighbours. Such capering and bellowing of Herefords. Such tossing of long horns, such whacking of sticks, such shouting of men and barking of collies never was heard in so cramped a space.

Bradley later suggested that, in the course of time, there should arise here one of those establishments of which South Wales stood so woefully in need during the industrial revolution, and thought Builth could become the ideal resort, being perfectly equipped with attractions for the active and enterprising to have plenty of convenient outlets. Furthermore, half an hour by train from Builth Road station would, in one direction, provide transport to the foot of the Black Mountains; in another, to the slopes of the Radnor Forest; in a third, to Rhayader with its recently built lakes in the Elan Valley; and in a fourth, amid the splendid solitudes that look down on the Vale of the Tywi in Carmarthenshire. By the close of the 19th century, not only were there lines here run by Cambrian and North Western Rail but good highways leading to each of those four points of the compass. In September 1874, the diarist Francis Kilvert caught the train from Hay to Newbridge on

Wye, where his friend and mentor, Richard Lister Venables, lived at Llysdinam House:

> I never had a lovelier journey up the valley of the Wye. A tender beautiful haze veiled the distant hills and woods with a gauze of blue and silver and pearl. It was a dream of intoxicating beauty. I saw all the old familiar sights, the broad river reach at Boughrood flashing round the great curve in the sunlight over its hundred steps and rock ledges, the luxuriant woods which fringe the gleaming river lit up here and there by the golden flame of a solitary ash, the sudden bend of the river below Builth, the Irfon mouth above the ancient town, and last but not least the grey-towered house of Llysdinam sitting on its green sunny hill backed by dark woods, and looking towards the river and the mountains of the south.

At Cilmeri, two miles west of Builth, is a huge granite monolith beside the Llandovery road. It marks the spot where Llywelyn ap Gruffydd, the last Welsh Prince of Wales, met his end. It happened on a bleak December day in 1282 after being ambushed by soldiers of Edmund Mortimer. The monument was erected here on a grassy mound in 1966, together with two plaques – one in English, the other in Welsh – that explain its commemoration. On a bleak day a long time after, flowers and flags still adorn the monument put there by proud Y Cymry hands.

Back on English Soil

According to Arthur Bradley, the railway junction at the Three Cocks was not like that at Bletchley or Rugby, a type with which he was obviously familiar. Here, on calm summer days you can hear birds singing, brooks gurgling, and even cows munching grass in nearby fields:

> But when the trains pour out their loads and Welsh and English meet on common ground, rosy-face farmers, black bearded tall

hatted preachers, buxom matrons, light-hearted maidens bound for Llandrindod or Llanwrtyd Wells - will have more to say to each other by a great deal than the people at Bletchley or Rugby.

Three Cocks, yes, that *is* the name of the village and it gets it from the celebrated old coaching inn which gave its name also to the railway station at the time when the trains still ran. Its Welsh name is Aberllynfi and refers to the mouth of the Afon Llynfi which enters the River Wye a mile or so downstream at Glasbury. The inn is now known more commercially as the Three Cocks Coaching Inn and Restaurant, but this fine old rambling building by the A438 Hereford to Brecon road has been serving travellers for over 500 years. Massingham seems to have thoroughly taken to it:

> The Three Cocks is an inn in which I feel at home, and that is by no means only because of its good looks and ample though variable food. It really is an inn, not a stuffy purse-proud cold-hearted modern hotel. It allows my bullterrier to wander at will from the kitchen to the big log-fire in the sitting-room, nor does it enslave its fishermen and others to punctuality.

The structure has changed little from the front view, which sits at a different angle to others around it, due presumably to long-forgotten highway re-alignments, but its original cobbled area forecourt survives. Within the ancient walls, customers are presented with modern, small hotel surroundings, while the residents' lounge surprisingly maintains an air of Edwardian comfort, if the ubiquitous widescreen TV can be ignored. I particularly liked the limed oak wall panelling, but I couldn't really picture Massingham's dog wandering freely about in the clean modern hotel environment. Interestingly, on the opposite side of the road. the inn's old stable block is still in situ and has itself been converted into a public house. Three Cocks was an important junction of the Hereford, Hay & Brecon Railway with the Mid Wales Railway until 1962. Now nothing remains of the Bradley's busy platforms whose ghostly foundations now lie beneath a vast garden centre complex.

The village of Glasbury lies at the crossing point on the River Wye connecting the old counties of Brecknockshire and Radnorshire. Following severe flooding sometime in the 17th century, the river changed course and cut the parish church of St Peters off from its community that was now on the north side of the river. Today, Glasbury has *two* churches after a second one, All Saints, was built a short distance from the village centre along the B4350, while a rebuilt St Peters is south of the river on the A438. Since 1974, *all* Glasbury has been in the county of Powys and has become a place to pass through en route to Hay or Brecon.

Despite its title, the delightful town of Hay on Wye evolved on a hill, and entry from any direction is by a fairly steep ascent. On the north side of town there is an abrupt drop to the river, where the broad and shallow stream is crossed by the bridge that carries the road to Clyro. Immediately to the south rise the foothills of the Black Mountains. In *Welsh Border Country*, author Percy Thoresby Jones described:

> Its buildings a not an unpleasing medley of the picturesque, the stolidly respectable and the purely utilitarian. On market days the town is full of life and colour and during these weekly feasts the inquiring stranger can get plenty of local colour by visiting the bar of the Crown.

Hay is unique in being wholly in Wales within the county of Powys but having an HR3 Hereford post code. The English/Welsh boundary is the Dulas Brook which flows down from Cefn Hill passing the edge of town and into the Wye, placing the adjacent village of Cusop on the English side. Hay also has *two* Norman castles within a short distance of each other. The mound behind the Swan Hotel was a motte likely to have been built by William FitzOsbern as part of his Welsh border barrier. The stone castle in the centre of town was probably constructed later by the marcher lord of Brecon, Bernard Neufmarché. It has had a very chequered history, even into modern times, having been captured in battle or disputed on a regular basis since it was first built.

The town is known by most people as a mecca for second-hand bookshops, the first of which was opened by the eccentric Richard Booth in 1961 and the first of several 'Book Towns' to be so labelled in the UK. When Booth declared Hay an independent kingdom in 1977 for a publicity stunt, he decided to compound the move by purchasing the castle for himself and moved in. Thence, on celebratory occasions, he would dress in a monarch's clothing and tour the town, waving regally to the amused and bemused crowds. This bibliophile's paradise is also the venue for the Hay Festival which attracts over 100,000 visitors every year. Not that the residents of Hay benefit directly from the proceeds. The first one was held on the town's streets amongst the books and the antiques, until the celebrations turned annual and were hijacked by large corporations and moved to an out-of-town venue where entrance is by ticket only. It has subsequently become disconnected from Hay town life. In recent years, however, the community has tried hard to get its own back by staging a not-for-profit Winter Festival in November, this time within the town's perimeter. And no large corporation has yet, as far as I know, made an unwanted attempt to influence the proceedings. Be all that as it may, for most of the year Hay has a feel of unhurried charm. The people, though mostly not indigenous, blend happily together. It is a very nice place to visit and, so I am told, in which to live.

Rambling author, John Hillaby, continuing his walk around the border area, preferred to keep to his own tracks. Along the disused rail bed from Hay, he made use of an old line-side hut for his overnight accommodation, where he was joined by a friendly ginger cat, apparently happy with his company:

> At dusk, near Clifford, I came across a disused plate-layer's cabin, clean and serviceable, with a fire grate, and decided to spend the night there. On impulse, I lit the fire. The wooden chocks that clench the rails are bituminous and burn wonderfully well. Immediately the spell began to work as surely as I had touched the sorcerer's wand. In the amber-coloured light the hut became the log cabin of everyone's dream.

In 1904, a Mr C.J. Lilwall of Cusop-by-Hay undertook some private excavations on the site of Craswall Priory at Abbey Farm. 60 members of the Woolhope Club, including their guest Arthur Bradley, visited the site on Mr Lilwall's invitation:

> We trained to Hay and walked thence up the sequestered dingle of the Dulas brook and over its watershed, dropping down through the yard of the solitary homestead of all this picturesque wild to the woody dingle which holds the ruins of the priory church. Little more than the moss-grown foundations of the church remain, sunk in a thicket and shaded by a large oak or two. But the enterprise of a neighbouring landowner had done some excavations preparatory to our visit, unearthing a bit of the chancel floor and increasing the obligation by entertaining us in sumptuous fashion on a remote hillside where one might well have been thankful for a packet of sandwiches and a flask.

Craswall Priory was a monastery of the austere Grandmontine order. At over 375m (1,230ft), it is the highest monastic site in England. Nestling in an isolated valley below the Cefn Hill, surrounded by the Black Mountains and the heights of the Golden Valley wall, a confused collection of ruins is all that remains of this wealthy alien foundation. It was started in 1220 by Roger de Lacy, whose family gave largely to the monastic establishments in Herefordshire and adjoining counties. The priory was subordinate to the Abbey of Grandmont in Normandy, and flourished for more than two hundred years, supported and enriched by great lords of Herefordshire. Other donations came from English Kings, Henry III and Edward III, who still had strong French allegiances. When the Mortimer Edward IV came to the throne, such generous backing for foreign religious establishments that had cared neither for the priests of the parishes, nor for the bishops of the Diocese, was ended.

The valleys of the Escley brook and the young Monnow river could be conveniently explored on a single circular trip from Hay. The lanes are narrow for the most part, so the use of a small car might yet be preferable. In Bradley's day, the tramp-cum-cycle method was more satisfactory. In any case, it is pleasant to follow the river up the deep vale of Longtown, with its 'long town' street of equally pleasant houses, hamlet, and old castle mound. Nor could a summer's day be more delightfully spent than in climbing up to these same springs of the Monnow, which rise in that half wild tract of upland once the chase of Craswall monks. After leaving Welsh Hay, cyclist Ernest Elliot-Stock added a note of pleasure, almost signifying relief to be over the border and back in his own country:

> The sheltered position of the Golden Valley lends itself to a more profuse growth than do those of the Llynfi and Wye but in any case, the atmosphere was entirely delightfully English.

Despite its remoteness, strewn at its southern end with farmsteads and cottages, the Golden Valley is one of the most countryfied of countrysides, and I have spent many happy days just wandering about among its green-tunnelled lanes. Signposts are at times confusing and at others a luxury, and the way is guessed and groped to St Margaret's, a hamlet on the western fringe of the valley. The parish church of St Margaret gives its name to nothing more than the odd collection of farmsteads and cottages, but everything other than the church will be forgotten when you reach it. The distinctive building stands in a field with a few gravestones. Its interior is of the customary Welsh type in the continuity of nave and chancel, but I had no eyes except for the silver-grey oak rood screen and loft that literally stopped me in my tracks. I was so surprised at the apparition that, before going closer to examine it, I retreated to the porch and back to try to take it all in. In the sheer exuberance and complexity of its decorative scheme, it seemed to me to outclass any of the screens which I had seen before. Any art that can turn oak planks into a portrait of a paradisal garden must rightly claim our wonder and honour as a creative masterpiece, both of richness and delicacy. Only by its remoteness and the trouble of finding the way here could it have escaped the Tudor reformers, the Cromwellian fanaticism, and a Victorian restoration, not to mention the contrary present extreme of guidebooks and maps. It is fitting that the view from St Margaret's west and south-west towards the Black Mountains and south to the great hills of Gwent, should be on so epic a scale. For the jewel within the humble setting of this little church, forms the perfect foil and contrast to both.

As the traveller crosses the wild and hilly common above Ewyas Harold, which parts the waters of the Dulas and the Dore, in due course he sees the Golden Valley stretched out below him and the fine old monastery church of Dore Abbey immediately beneath, rising grey and massive from the level land beside the river from which it is named. This is the great Cistercian monastery founded in 1147 by monks from Morimond Abbey in North Eastern France. Construction of the present stone buildings started in 1175 and was finally consecrated more than one hundred years later, in 1280. Cistercian monks were skilled at managing their agricultural lands; in the case at Dore, it was breeding sheep with wool of exceptional quality.

A large part of the original medieval building has been used since the 16th century as the parish church, with remaining parts including the north and south transepts, the interior columns, together with some tiles, wooden fittings, and fragments of stained glass incorporated into the present church. Inside, the building is a scaled-down model of the monastery as it was in the 13th century. It was indeed a huge outward sign of the monks' wealth and must have been an imposing sight to the natives whose homes were lacking in any kind of quality, and barely adequate to sustain a comfortable life. In spite of Gerald of Wales's known anti-Cistercian bias, there is good reason to believe that these monks were not only wise, provident, and far-seeing farmers, they were great flock-masters, the best horse-breeders, gardeners, carpenters, millers, cloth-workers, iron-masters, beer-brewers, wine-makers, fishermen, and estate owners from the twelfth to the fourteenth centuries. They quarried their own stone and built their monasteries and churches with their own hands. Moreover, they possessed a widespread reputation for their austerity, frugality, and simplicity of living. Their houses were renowned as being inns and hospitals, as well as sanctuaries for prayer and contemplation.

They had an expert eye for the beautiful site and deliberately chose the lonely places for their settlements. When they left, as Massingham points out, it was down to others to repair the ruin that the dissolution created:

> I have been in the abbey when the rain was dripping on the floor from the roof, and yet far worse must have been the condition in which John Scudamore left it. It was his descendant, Viscount Scudamore of Holme Lacy, who in reparation for his grandfather's rapacity, in 1634 repaired the church, built the tower, added the timber fittings and furniture, and replaced the fallen stone vault with John Abel's roof.

An eighteen-mile long railway used to run through the Golden Valley from Hay on Wye to Pontrilas, where the single track joined the main line, passing by Dore Abbey on the way. The route served some of the loneliest parts of Herefordshire, though Its existence was always precarious, and didn't run at all from 1889 until 1901 after running into financial difficulties. The service closed finally to passengers in 1941, but trains continued to be used by the military base near Pontrilas junction for a further sixteen years. Bradley had used the railway on at least one other previous occasion:

> Some years ago, I remember, when as a stranger in the land, I had taken it on a certain occasion into my scheme of travel for the ensuing day, and at the same time taken too much for granted. For it was not till I had bundled out my effects on the Hay platform that I discovered it to have been in a state of suspended animation for some twelve months. So much for putting foolish reliance on a two-year-old Bradshaw Guide in a country inn.

Charles Harper's opinions of the Golden Valley Railway would linger in his memory, not for any train ride but for a day of unexpected inclement weather:

The line is poor in the extreme, the station weed grown and platforms mouldy. But we shall ever remember Abbeydore, chiefly for the rainy afternoon that rendered our walk thence to Peterchurch in the Golden Valley as penitential a pilgrimage as ever a holy friar made or mediaeval evildoer vowed as a salve for grievous sins. We would have taken the train but that three hours was a long while to wait, so we walked along the railway track instead; and all those weary five miles it rained with a deadly and most dreadful persistence.

The wooded slopes above the B4348 road entering the valley from Hereford shelters a mystery. At Monnington Court, many believe lie the remains of Owain Glyndŵr. The Welsh rebel is thought to have died around 1415 after 'retiring' undefeated from a murderous campaign in the marches, which he himself had started in September 1400. There had been no sight or sound of him since, and speculation abounds as to where he eventually settled. He had very cleverly allowed his five daughters to marry English lords, perhaps in the likelihood that his safety might eventually be assured, and here at Monnington Straddle, one of them, Margaret, had married Sir Richard Monnington. It is more likely that this Monnington Court and not the Court of Monnington-on-Wye is where Owain Glyndŵr remained in safe obscurity under the protection of his daughter and son-in-law, and possibly even where he died. The error of locating Monnington-on-Wye as his place of refuge has been repeated throughout history by one writer after another. The evidence for that is a tomb slab said to have covered his burial site in the churchyard there. This has never been proven, and further evidence that the Wye-side Monnington at the time was part of the manor of the Audleys who were strongly anti-Glyndŵr, weighs heavily against that theory. In spite of this, the diarist Francis Kilvert seemed content to accept the popular vote:

Under the shadow of the old grey church the strong wild heart has rested by the ancient home of his kindred since he fell asleep there more than four hundred years ago.

But Massingham knew better and took full advantage of two mistaken observers:

> It is entertaining to recollect that here Mr Bradley, that eloquent champion of Glyndŵr, indulged in an almost lachrymose lament over the reputed gravestone of his hero. Kilvert makes the same error. It would be difficult to judge who wins the prize for sentimentality.

The name Golden Valley probably derives from an incorrect recognition by the Normans of the name for the River Dore. The French word '*d'or*' means 'of gold'. The Welsh word for water being *dŵr* is similar sounding and may have added to their confusion. Percy Thoresby Jones offered his own thoughts on the origins of name 'Golden':

> The honey-sweet efflorescence of gorse and broom, or the ripening cheeks of russet apples, and the tawny sheen of cornfields:

In early spring, the hillsides of the valley are covered yellow from daffodils and fields of rape, providing the modern traveller with a more plausible and happier explanation. The large village of Peterchurch, locally proclaimed the valley's capital, is recognised from any point by its very tall church spire – a fibre glass replacement of 1940. St Peter's Church itself, however, is anything but a modern rebuild. Mainly Norman in origin, there are Saxon remains in the stonework, and the four chambers, which include a double chancel, are unique in the marches. The theory behind this anomaly seems to suggest the presence once of a central tower that may have collapsed, and the replacement spire built at the west end. In 2009, a plan to redevelop the nave as a community centre was proposed and accepted and has received national acclaim for its inventiveness and effective use of redundant church space. This idea is being taken up elsewhere, particularly in Herefordshire, and must be applauded at a time when old fashioned neighbourliness has dwindled in recent years. Charles Harper wrote of two notable objects in St Peter's churchyard:

An ancient monolith of great age and unknown origin or purpose, and a fine yew tree, of all yew trees, the largest and most patriarchal of aspect.

The monolith of which he speaks confusingly, and the great yew tree, appear to be one and the same structure, as there is no other and the tree has long been known for its great age. Historically, it was originally thought to be 750 years old but a re-dating has put it at over 3,000 years old! There are many yew trees in the marches ware known to be over 2,000 years old, but one of this great age is extremely rare. Even as Harper was looking at the great Norman church, so 41-year-old Private Robert Jones was trying to deal with his recurring nightmares of hand-to-hand fighting with Zulu warriors at Rorke's Drift in 1879 – action that earned him the Victoria Cross. It would be another four years before, worn out and seemingly defeated by the horrific memories, he took his own life. In those dark days, suicides were forbidden entry to churchyards, so his tragic end was made more poignant when his coffin was carried over the wall rather than through the gate. His gravestone stands out in its position beside the path leading to the church door, not only for its whiteness but, as was the custom, because it faces away from those memorials around him. It is, however, good to see that his heroics are still remembered every Armistice Day when an unknown hand leaves a poppy crucifix on his grave.

While in the Golden Valley, Bradley left us such a dramatic and descriptive episode, we would be less wise for not absorbing it. It was a few days after his visit to Abbeydore, and on this occasion taking his bicycle, he set off along the winding lanes with a view to crossing the valley's eastern wall at Stockley Hill and returning down the east bank of the Wye into Hereford. The ridge to be surmounted is just under 250m (800ft), but the stony lanes which wriggle over it squeeze through a notch in the summit at somewhat less than this:

This narrow crown of Stockley cannot easily be forgotten, first on account of the uncompromising directness with which it plunges down at an angle of forty-five degrees to the vale below, and secondly for the fine scenic effects with which this heroic method of descent provides the hardy traveller. For the banks here rise thirty or forty feet above the sunken lane, and when I went down between them were a perfect blaze of foxgloves and ragwort, of briar-rose, honeysuckle, and flowering elder, springing from deep carpets of ferns. And far beneath lay outspread the many-tinted lowlands of Herefordshire with the Wye curving through their centre.

Three Castles of Gwent

Three castles fair are in a goodly ground,
Grosmont is one, on hill it builded was:
Skenfrith the next, in valley is it found,
The soil about, for pleasure there doth pass.
White Castle is the third of worthy fame,
The country there doth bear White Castles name.
A stately seat, a lofty princely place,
Whose beauty gives the simple soil some grace.'

Thomas Churchyard, 1520-1604

The term Trilateral Castles is used by historians to collectively describe White Castle, Skenfrith Castle, and Grosmont Castle – all located in an area east of Abergavenny close to the Monnow valley. They were built within eight miles of each other in the 11th century by the castle-building Earl of Hereford, William FitzOsbern, to protect Norman access to the fertile plains of South Wales. From his base at Chepstow, FitzOsbern was the first Norman lord to conquer central and eastern Monmouthshire, including the future sites for the Three Castles. The defences raised at that time would have been of earth and timber in the classic Norman motte and bailey style. The castles eventually became part of territory under the control of a single lord, Hubert de Burgh, justiciar to King John in 1201.

The Three Castles briefly saw action during the rebellion of Owain Glyndŵr in 1404-05, but never played a major role in any military affairs after, and by 1538 all were in ruins and abandoned. The remains for a time later belonged to the Duke of Beaufort until, in the years around 1922 they were given to the State and the National Trust. All three castles are now conserved and maintained by CADW.

Situated in silent countryside off the B4521 Abergavenny to Ross road, White Castle is the largest of the Trilaterals and the least damaged. Leland described it as 'standeth on a hill and is dry moated. It is made almost of great slate stone and is the greatest of the Three Castles'. At the time of the first Queen Elizabeth, White Castle was seen as still a magnificent place. Thomas Churchyard called it 'a statelie seate, a loftie pricely place'. The name White was so-called simply from the whitewash put on the stone walls, traces of which can still clearly be seen in the outer ward. The moat encircling the inner ward is still wet. To get to the site requires a steep climb up nearly five hundred feet to the castle crowning the summit. That is, assuming my reader is tackling the very enjoyable but challenging Three Castles Walk. Access roads are extremely narrow in places and parking is limited for two or three small cars. It is hard not to believe that both will be problematic during holiday periods. Percy Thoresby Jones had no such concerns when he came here in 1936, and his description is as good as any guidebook:

> The special excellence of White Castle is its marvellous state of preservation. The walls and the towers, though roofless, are otherwise almost intact; so that from outside it looks pretty well the same as it looked more than six centuries ago. Unlike the other two castle of the Trilateral, Grosmont and Skenfrith, White Castle was never used as a residence: it was purely military, it's garrisons being accommodated probably in penthouses ranged along the inner faces of the walls.

Five miles to the east is Skenfrith Castle. William Coxe didn't like Skenfrith village much. He saw it as 'a miserable place containing a church, a few cottages, and two public houses. Charles Harper's description at the end of the 19th century was a harsher extension of the same theme. He wrote:

> The place has dragged on a decrepit existence in this unhealthy sink between the hills, saturated with the showers and melting snows, scarcely dried by the heats of summer, inundated with the rains of autumn, and by the spates of the river; so that rheumatism and bronchitis, diphtheria, whooping cough and agues are the common ailments of its unfortunate inhabitants.

Even Elliot-Stock, from within his bicycle clips, was unimpressed when he described it as:

> Prettily situated as it is, the Skenfrith of today cannot be exactly Utopia to live in. The circling hills make a deep cup of this section of the Monnow valley, and this, together with a river often well above its banks, must make the darker months dark and damp indeed for Skenfrithians.

But Stuart Mais gave us a change of view for the better when he called Skenfrith one of the most attractive villages on the whole length of the border:

> First, there is the Bell Hotel by the grey stone bridge, a favourite haunt of anglers. Then there is a working watermill and houses built into the tall walls of the ancient castle. Behind the castle rises the square, stout, wooden belfry of one of the most attractive churches in the country.

And Bradley provided an old-world English view of the bridge linking England and Wales – an old stone structure of three arches, beneath which the Monnow river glides to spread out below into wide sunny ripples washing the edge of overhanging woods:

> It is a bridge for the angler to smoke his evening pipe upon, warmed with a good dinner and the memories of a good day. And the thought is doubtless prompted by a snug-looking old inn

which stands at the end of it, and was in former days, the landlord informed me, a favourite haunt of the disciples of the renowned angler and writer, Izaak Walton.

I have been to Skenfrith many times in recent years, and on my last visit in the summer of 2015 I found it glinting in the sun as bright as any jewel. The castle, of course, dominates, but it isn't much of one – four walls and a central round keep, unlike her sister castles at White and Grosmont. St Bridget's Church was built around the same time as the castle in the 13th century and is as solidly built, with a massive tower complete with dovecote – all part of a defensive plan in case of attack. The Bell Inn is now its only house of refreshment.

On the way to Grosmont, beech hedges line the lane, oaks and sweet chestnuts shade the weary traveller, and road and river pass between the high meadows of Craig Syfrddin and the equally protuberant dome of Garway Hill. Travel-hardened Fred Hando was used to seeing beautiful places, especially in his home county of Gwent, but even he was taken aback by his first visit to Grosmont:

> Approaching Grosmont from over Cupid's Hill, you pass a school and a few flower-filled cottage gardens and now, travelled hardened though you be, gasp with delight. You pause: do you hear the sound of trumpets 'on the other side'? For surely this is heaven and you are about to enter.

The road into the village is somewhat of a by-road, but quite a reasonably good one for either motor vehicle or bicycle. But in any case, it is a pleasant road, and as Elliot-Stock discovered, not too arduous:

> Grosmont village is so high and so close to the border that its views extend into both England and Wales. Very few vestiges now remain of its departed glory as an important Marcher town with a charter, but it retains something far more fascinating that would seem to reproduce so faithfully the dead and gone days of Marcher rule. The only possible inn about the village (the Angel) offered us

an excellent brew, and with apologies to temperance advocates,
I should like to place on record that the ale of Gwent is excellent.

As preserved villages often are, Grosmont can indeed be likened
to a cut and polished precious stone and has remained a hidden
one for most of its existence. I've seen older and prettier places,
but none as well preserved as this one. Jan Morris described it as
'the most beautiful village in Britain'. Its impressive St Nicholas's
Church, cruciform with transepts, aisles and chancel, indicate
its pretensions as an important mediaeval town. At its centre, the
sandstone market house built in 1832 stands guard beside the
Angel Inn in a street of many old and structurally undisturbed
buildings. The long single street stretches downhill passed church
and castle. Considering how long it has been in its ruinous state,
Grosmont Castle is still recognisable as a strong fortress, and is
the most elaborate and the best preserved of Hubert de Burgh's
Trilaterals. Here was the site of at least two major battles – the
last in 1405 when Glyndŵr's ally and trusted captain, Rhys
Gethin, marched in with a force of 8,000 men, burning town and
castle, such was its importance as a medieval border township.
Grosmont never recovered. According to Camden, in his time
there were fragments of causeways and buildings, no longer
visible today, that were evidence of a once larger, prosperous
community.

I was there on a glorious roses-round-the-door warm late June
day, but apart from me with camera in hand, mooching about the
castle ruins and later in the dark, empty, unfinished thirteenth
century nave of church, there was no-one else around. Standing by
the eastern side of the ruined castle which hangs over the precipitous
banks of the Monnow, shaded by a rich grove of wide spreading
oaks, I watched the river below, singularly beautiful as it gleamed
through the foliage, suddenly bends into a horse-shoe form to
almost encircle a field of maturing wheat. At this point, the traveller
along the B4347 might look down on the Monnow and across it
into Archenfield, the target for Welsh pike and arrow from the days
of the Saxon invader, but a sun-bathed peace rested upon it today
from its river boundary below to the bracken-crowned summit of

Garway opposite. Here, if Hando had been in *his* heaven, then I, too, was most definitely now in mine.

Being just over the Monnow and so in Herefordshire, Kentchurch Court is a 14th century Scudamore mansion, and said to be another refuge where Owain Glyndŵr escaped detection during his later years. The house, built of castellated stone, was rebuilt and restored by Nash in the 19th century. The front face has an oriel window of five lights, a porch with a Cotswold-like roof, Gothic windows, and a corner tower where Glyndŵr is said to have died, and in which the lady of the house – herself a Scudamore – mischievously accommodated me for the night, thinking I might welcome an atmospheric and, as it turned out, a guaranteed sleepless night! Additions elsewhere on the estate reveal the high days of the Scudamores, one of whom, Glyndwr's son-in-law, planted the magnificent sycamores and oaks that climb the slope of Garway Hill above the alder-lined water meadows of the Monnow.

In writing this book, I have the opportunity here to correct a previous mistake I made about the village of Ewyas Harold and hope that it cures a lingering embarrassment. The motte and bailey castle seen today is Norman and built around 1086. It replaced a Saxon castle that *wasn't* built by Harold, Earl Godwinson, as I had once written, but which may have been *destroyed* by him in a dispute with the then Earl of Hereford, a nephew of King Edward, the Confessor. However, the village *is* named after *a* Harold – ironically, the son of a previous Earl of Hereford, and grandson of King Æthelred the Unready and builder of the Saxon fortification.

Meanwhile, Charles Harper's mood hadn't improved after his short walk from Pontrilas:

> In the dull church with its squat, plain, powerful buttressed tower, the heart of a de Lacy enclosed in a casket once reposed for half a millennium.[23] Its western background is the mountains and it is girdled by upland common, woodlands and lowland meadows.

---

[23] Harper was mistaken. The heart belonged to Lady Clarissa Tregoz who died in 1290. In 1865, a small casket was discovered beneath her effigy, and it was assumed this was a medieval heart burial, popular at the time.

History and nature both have conferred distinction upon it, and it possesses the further notability of a caustic epitaph in the churchyard:

Reader pass on, not waste your time
On bad biography, and much worse rhyme
For what I am this cumbrous clay immures
And what I was is no concern of yours

Yet, in fact it is a forlorn and miserable little place, semi-modernised and gone to seed the more and not the less for that.

Archenfield: Herefordshire in Wales

The ancient district of Archenfield, or Ircingafeld, is the historic English name for the area of southern and western Herefordshire located between the Rivers Monnow and Wye. Its origin was the once larger Welsh kingdom of Ergyng which spread into modern Monmouthshire to where the old Roman iron town of Ariconium was thought to be. It is possible that Ergyng extended across what is now the Forest of Dean to the River Severn, but when Offa built his Dyke he used the Wye as it edged passed Hereford, Ross and Monmouth, as a natural boundary, keeping Wales west of the river. Ariconium survived in the Anglo-Saxon Chronicle of 918 AD as Arcenefelde, and two hundred years later the name reappeared in a local charter as Erchenefeld. William Camden's 16th century understanding did little to explain away the confusion:

How far that little region Archenfeld reached I know not, but the affinity between these names, Ereinuc, Archenfeld, the town Ariconium, of which Antonine in the description of this tract maketh mention, and Hareford or Hereford, which now is the chief City of the Shire, have by little and little induced me to this opinion, that I think every one of these was derived from Ariconium. Yet do I not think that Ariconium and Hereford were both one and the same?

The Welsh inhabitants of Archenfield continued to live mostly in peace and privilege thereafter in a shadowy border land that was neither part of England nor Wales. The rebellious Owain Glyndŵr considered it entirely in Wales when his men raided the area in 1405. Speculation still lingers that the battle-weary Welshman may have eventually died after all at Kentchurch Court, the home of his daughter Alys, which was inside the assumed Archenfield boundary. In the 6th century, the British monk Dyfrig (Dubricius) was an evangelist of Ergyng and much of southeast Wales. Legend has it that he was born near Madley, and Ergyng/Archenfield became the centre of his work. He is said to have collected many disciples around him and built a monastery at Llanfrother near Hentland, and another later at Moccas. The remoteness of Archenfield must have appealed to those Celtic holy men during the troubles of the Dark Ages, both as a secure shelter from pagan invasion and as a setting for their hermitages in countryside where relative seclusion can still be found even today.

Uncertainty over the English/Welsh border persisted until Henry VIII's Acts of Union in 1536 sorted out many of the administrative anomalies within Wales and the marcher borderlands. Archenfield was bundled into Herefordshire as the Hundred of Wormelow, but it remained a predominantly Welsh-speaking region until at least the 17th century. Bradley refers to ancient gravestones engraved in Welsh in the isolated churchyard of St Dubricius near Kilpeck. There was once a railway station near that church on the Hereford to Abergavenny line, presumably serving the communities of Wormbridge, Kilpeck, and Didley – a neighbourhood of few people that hardly justifies stopping a main line train, although it is no coincidence that one of the many Clive family homes at Whitfield was in the same vicinity.

When I wrote of the little church at Kilpeck in 2005, I used the words of a first-time visitor overwhelmed with what I was looking at. No other church in the marches approaches it in picturesqueness or reputation, and it is probably better known more for it's appealing diminutiveness than Hereford Cathedral is for all its vast architectural grandeur. Our wandering cyclist, Alderman Fletcher

Moss, tells us of his reaction to seeing the incredible carvings at Kilpeck attributed to the Hereford school of stonemasons:

> It is beyond my powers to describe the wonderful doorway to the church. Slippery serpents climb up and down trees of knowledge and life. Dragons and monsters are in such an endless tangle that enthusiastic decipherers of symbolism might become confused and driven crazy. Round the eaves of the church are seventy grotesque heads of fiends, some with long curling tongues. It is a failing of modern imaginations to conceive the monstrosities of the good old times, when men heard more of and took more interest in the legions of the devil.

This miniature cell of worship is dedicated to St Mary and St David and is in remarkably good preservation, having been restored with astonishing discretion and good taste in 1848. Though the screen and rood loft have long disappeared, (and who knows what magnificent glories we have missed as a result), it remains exceptionally beautiful, far more so than Dubricius' Norman church at Moccas with which it has often been compared. Since that first introduction, I've made many re-visits, unable to avoid its magnetism. On the last occasion in 2015, I was met by the warden – a man of the village, who first volunteered years before to sweep up after the daily influx of tourists and generally keep his eye on the place. He told me that he had reluctantly decided to hand in his broom and spend more time in his Kilpeck cottage garden. It is to be hoped another volunteer could be found. There will be who knows how many thousands yet to gaze inside and out at this miniature wonder, bringing with them Herefordshire dust which must be swept up afterwards. Massingham reminds us of what sometimes happens in these lonely places:

> As we sat on the castle mound, half asleep in a little world that was itself rounded with a sleep, people from far and wide arrived at the church for the Harvest Festival. There were only a few walkers, for Kilpeck itself is but a Queen Anne house, a farm and a cottage or two. The people drove up not only in cars but in gigs,

pony-carts and farmer's traps, while from the church the singing
of the hymns from a full congregation - where did it all come from
in this lonely neighbourhood?- swelled out upon the golden air to
join the cawing of rooks and the twittering of the house-martins.

Further along the river valley, clinging to the hillsides, is Moccas
Park, a National Nature Reserve, which by necessity is closed to
the public. It is one of the most important sites in the country for
its ancient trees, glacial kettle-hole pool, and extraordinary
variable species of wildlife. The oldest oak, the Moccas Old Man,
is estimated to be pushing 900 years, yet still said to be churning
out acorns 'as big as quails' eggs. The origins of the park are
uncertain. The Old Man excepted, many of the veteran trees pre-
date 1660 but it is thought that large scale planting began around
1793 and continued for 40 years. Chestnuts were planted here
when people elsewhere in the country were planting chestnuts.
Towards the end of the 18th century, landscaping work was
carried out by 'Capability' Brown, during which time there were
extensive plantations of beech, oak and yew. Humphrey Repton
also gave a hand to Sir George Cornewall's plans for more
planting, and later had further help from Richard Payne Knight
and Uvedale Price when more exotic planting was carried out in
the 19th century. Perhaps the most treasured description of the
ancient residents of the park was written by Francis Kilvert in his
diary of 1870:

> I fear those grey old men of Moccas Park, those grey, gnarled,
> low-browed, knock-kneed, bowed, bent, huge, strange, long-
> armed, deformed, hunched-backed, misshapen oak men that stand
> waiting and watching century after century.

A little further down the road at Bredwardine, the Norman church
where Kilvert held his final services is carved with Kilpeckian beasts
on the lintel of the doorway and possesses inside an elaborate effigy
of Sir Roger Vaughan of Agincourt. The church stands on a knoll
above the Wye, girdled by a ring of hanging woods and trees casting
cool shade around the rim of the churchyard into which an avenue

of cherry trees lead. Kilvert's Rectory of white roughcast plaster with scalloping in the eaves stands above the river – a house that poet as well as vicar would have been pleased to live in, and he was both. Let Massingham bring down the curtain on the arboreal scene and a tragically cut-short life:

> The church is close beside the bridge over the Wye, the same of which Kilvert was Vicar at the end of his life, and between a lordly beech and a sycamore in the churchyard he lies, himself under a Victorian white cross he would have loathed for its pretentious discord among the decent sandstone gravestones of the marches. But if he has an ignoble monument it has the setting that in his lifetime he knew and loved.

Hereford: City of Treasures and Cider

Hereford is a cathedral city and the county town of Herefordshire. It lies on the River Wye, 26km (16 mi) east of the border with Wales. As cities go, Hereford is not particularly large. It has 60,000 or so inhabitants and is easily the biggest settlement but being the county hub as well as sitting on the marches' central artery, the A49, traffic chaos akin to the much larger conurbations of Bristol or Southampton is rarely avoided. Like Brecon, Hereford curiously enough shares a similar tradition as regards its origin. For as the Welsh town is said to have been built out of materials brought from the Roman military station of Cicucium, so with as much probability can the creation of Hereford be attributed to the abandonment of the Roman settlement at Magnis. Little remains of the city walls, though passing traffic may glimpse what is left here and there. The city gates have vanished, and so too has the castle. More's the pity, for its origins date back to 1046 and it became Earl Harold Godwinson's base for his invasion of Wales. From the slopes of the Black Mountains in the distance, the wild and needy Welshmen would cast a hungry eye at the prosperous and promising city on the Wye, so the castle was seldom idle, often besieged, and not infrequently captured. Its days ended brutally in the English Civil War, and it seems hardly fair that the most conspicuous object left in view on the site should be a column which commemorates a sailor, even if that sailor be Lord Nelson.

Hereford's pink sandstone cathedral dates from the late 11th century and has a double dedication, to St Mary the Virgin and to St Ethelbert the King – the second dedication being an attempt at appeasement by King Offa, who had been the young Ethelbert's jealous executioner in 792. By that murderous act, the new cathedral's first treasure was created with Ethelbert's quick progression to sainthood and subsequent claims of miraculous cures. The Hereford chained library is the largest surviving with its chains and books intact. Assembled over 900 years ago, the oldest chained book found in the library is the Hereford Gospels, written in the 8th century, and it is one of 229 chained books in this unique collection. The cathedral possesses one of only four remaining Magna Cartas of 1217, but Its most famous treasure eventually became the Mappa Mundi – a mediaeval map of the world dating from the 13th century. However, in 1988, the cathedral was presented with a financial crisis and was forced into putting the Mappa Mundi up for sale. The general feeling at the time was that it would be sold out of the country, so desperate measures had to be taken if the map was to stay in Hereford. This situation was not new to the cathedral's congregation. Twenty years earlier they lost a magnificent Gothic-style iron choir screen – a creation of Sir George Gilbert-Scott built by the Coventry metalworking company of Francis Skidmore. The screen was judged to be no longer appropriate for a medieval building, so was dismantled in 1967 and confined initially to a Victoria & AMuseum storage cellar in Battersea. It is a relief to know that Gilbert-Scott's masterpiece was eventually put back together and has been on display in the V & A ironwork gallery since 2001, thanks to the mammoth effort of their metal conservation team and a financial contribution from the National Lottery Fund.

There was no similar financial help available to save the Mappa, but a charity – the Mappa Mundi Trust – was created with Sir John Cotterell, 6th Baronet of Garnons as chair, and he used his skills to attract interest from leading financial institutions to support his fundraising campaign. At the same time, Sir John put forward plans for a new building to house the map and the cathedral's other asset, its chained library. During excavations of the site alongside the cathedral's west door, more than a thousand skeletons were unearthed which had to be sympathetically dealt with, so some were reburied on Sir John's own estate at Garnons. The resulting award-winning building in Hereford was acclaimed 'Building of the Year' by the Royal Fine Art Commission Trust and opened in 1996 by Her Majesty Queen Elizabeth II.

In 1720, Daniel Defoe came to Hereford and was impressed by the great cathedral:

> It is a magnificent building, however ancient, the spire is not high but handsome, and there is a fine tower at the west end over the great door or entrance.

But this 'fine tower' was poorly built and it collapsed in 1786. It was never replaced and consequently the west end of the cathedral is shorter than it was. The Rt. Hon. John Byng, 5th Viscount Torrington, was in Hereford around the time of the disaster and witnessed the aftermath.

> A fellow who stood near to us related the circumstances of this accident, and what a glorious clash it made. He said the inside roof began to give way in the morning and continued to fall so rapidly that people were placed around the close to hinder any from entering. As the crumbling and dissolution increased, this noble tower began in some hours to totter and after many shakings at last sunk upon itself a heap of ruins, with half the body of the church in sight of the whole town assembled.

When Sir Richard Colt Hoare arrived in 1798, he didn't mention the cathedral's west front, so perhaps the debris had been removed by then. Instead, he resorted to criticism of the internal whitewashed walls:

We stayed the night at the New Inn where we enjoyed our dinner, a sober glass of wine, a good fire, and pleasant conversation. After breakfast we went to see the cathedral. Some very fine specimens of Saxon architecture in rich ornamented style but the effect and solemnity of the cathedral much injured by its being painted a dead white.

While attending a service at the cathedral in 1903, Fletcher Moss had to swallow a little pride after realising he wasn't dressed in his Sunday best:

As the congregation slowly gathered, I asked the verger for a seat, although I lacked that emblem of respectability, a top hat, and he showed me to a place in the front under the central tower, where in faded clothes, with cap in pocket, and boots on which patches of hotel blacking overlapped flakes of dried dust, I was set before the congregation as an awful example of what a man might be reduced to by much cycling.

Arriving through the suburbs of Hereford in 1842, William Makepeace Thackeray seems to have been suffering from a surfeit of Wye Valley black and white which he had witnessed earlier in the day.

Of Hereford, it behoves me to speak in terms of the most bitter reprehension. The houses are, for the most part, square with small regular windows of the hideous sort of style prevalent, say, in the year 1780, and they are formed of a sort of dirty crimson coloured brick, the most disagreeable to the eye of all brick I ever saw.

Then later, he is further unimpressed with the shabby air of quality of the hotel in which he was to spend the night. As he contemplated the cheerless prospect to hand, a coach pulled up at the hotel door driven by an old man dressed in black. A younger man also in black, apparently in profound mourning, descended from the coach and took the arm of another old gentleman also in mourning and evidently on the verge of death. The scene was too much for our celebrated traveller:

> By Heaven, it is all too bad! Thinking there was some fatality hanging over me, I made a rush for my hat and went abroad into the streets. They were not much more cheerful, but at least the sun was shining his best and giving as gay an aspect as he could to this Herefordshire Palmyra. I passed a gaudy new Roman Catholic chapel painted yellow and so distinguished from the scarlet abominations about it.

Hereford is indeed a noble city, but its transport facilities leave something more to be desired. The railway station at Barr's Court is outside the centre and beyond the ring road, requiring a lengthy walk to reach the top tourist attractions near to the cathedral's precinct. Matters might be improved considerably if there was a direct bus service connecting both. Neither are parking facilities adequate. The main car park is on the opposite side of the city centre beyond the Wye bridge, again with no public transport connection and requiring another uncomfortable hike. Nor has time improved the travellers' lot. Transport in and out of the city has perennially struggled to satisfy, as Stuart Mais found in 1937:

> Hereford is ill-served in the matter of trains. The quickest train in the day from London takes over three hours. Unless you are careful, the journey is more likely to take five. Hereford is also ill-served in the matter of buses. A glance at the elaborate Midland Red and complicated Yeomans' timetables betrays the fact that the only chance of reaching most neighbouring places by bus is once a week, on market days.

Arthur Bradley thought Hereford a humdrum cathedral town deeply concerned with the wholesale production of apples and the ubiquitous red and white bullocks. The most famous name on Hereford lips is H.P. Bulmer, the English cider-making company founded in 1887 by Henry Percival Bulmer, the twenty-year-old son of the local rector at Credenhill. It is said that he had followed his mother's advice to make a career in food or drink, 'because neither ever go out of fashion'. Draught cider has been produced in Herefordshire since the 14th century. The making of it had been essentially very much a farmhouse and cottage industry. By the mid-17th century, most Herefordshire farms had – and some still have – their own cider presses, and until the appearance of Bulmer's, privately-owned apple orchards were common in every part of the county. The Bulmer cider business was incorporated as a private company on June 27th, 1918 and remained in the family's hands until 1970 by which time it had become the largest producer of cider in the world and shares were offered on the stock exchange. The owners are now (2017) Heineken International, and the Bulmer name has become merely a brand.

Cider consumption became widespread in England after the Norman Conquest in 1066, when cider apple orchards were first established. Production developed into a major industry in medieval times, and monasteries sold vast quantities of their strong, spiced cider to the public. Farm labourers received a cider allowance as part of their wages that was increased during haymaking time. The cider made and matured in the ancient ways was usually potent, and not surprisingly overconsumption in rural communities in the late 18th and early 19th century was commonplace, often leading to violent breakdowns in law and order, particularly in the town centres. When commercial cider-making eventually reached industrial proportions and attempts were made – mainly by the Herefordshire clergy – to take their fight to the Licensing Commission, the secret cider drinkers retaliated.

In spite of church or chapel,
Ungodly folk there be
Who pluck the cider apple
from the cider apple tree
And squeeze it in their presses
Until the juice runs out
At various addresses
That no-one knows about

And, maddened by the orgies
Of that unholy brew,
They slit each other's gorges
From one a.m till two,
Till Ledbury is a shambles
And in the dirt and mud
Where Leominster sits and gambles
The dice are stained with blood.

But still, if strength suffices
Before my day is done
I'll go and share the vices
Of Clungerford and Clun,
And watch the red sun sinking
Across the March again
And join the secret drinking
of outlaws at Presteign

E V Knox

The City of Hereford is surrounded by natural scenery of exceptional beauty, more so than its more northern neighbour, Shrewsbury. For Shropshire only rises above the ordinary level of pleasant midland landscape on its Welsh side and in its southern districts, while Hereford looks eastward over a region which is a good deal more and is still further fortunate with the most imposing background to the east being the Malvern Hills. I have said little yet about the Wye, the Roman's wandering Vaga, which is part and parcel of the Hereford scene. I give that last word to Bradley:

It may be noted that the Wye on its journey towards Hereford is but a short distance off hidden in a narrow trough between the wooded steeps of Breinton and the waving parklands of Belmont. It is running briskly over gravelly shallows or gliding with deep current between lofty and leafy banks. It is a river adapted perhaps to the strenuous rather than to the loafing oarsmen and furnishes periodical rapids to lend excitement without serious danger to the many boating excursions that pass up it on summer days.

Part Two

The Middle March

Roman Road to the Welsh Border

I have yet to leave the shire of Hereford, and though there is no defined line on any map, I have chosen the Roman road north of the city of Hereford as the beginning of my Middle March chapter. Arthur Bradley chose this route in leaving Hereford to head west towards the Welsh border lands:

> A few hundred yards below the village, at a small railway station bearing its name, the highway is lifted over the Hereford and Hay railroad by an arch, and standing upon this you look immediately over two or three large fields covering the Roman site, in all perhaps fifty acres, and sloping gently upwards from the line. It is one of those spots, like the field of Waterloo, concerning which the man in the street will tell you there is nothing now to be seen.

On low-lying ground 7km (4½mi) west of Hereford is the outline of the Roman town of Magnis, or Magna Castra which, as Leland remarked, 'is far more ancient then Hereford itself and was celebrated in the Romans' time'. The site lies in the parish of Kenchester, on the Roman road which passed through it from Glevum (Gloucester) heading into the middle reaches of the Wye valley and thence the Roman military frontier-system of Wales. It is interesting to note that the road from Gloucester did not pass through the centre of Hereford, indicating that the Romans may have thought it an unsuitable spot to set up camp.

Magnis is a hexagonal flattened mound of about 22 acre, and excavations from time to time have discovered evidence of many Roman buildings. Here, the Romans weren't far from the Wye, and as they needed access to the river, their crossing point was achieved at the place called Old Weir. Half a mile north of the Roman town are the ramparts of the substantial Iron Age hill fort of Credenhill, the second largest in Britain (Maiden Hill in Dorset being the first). The fort had been constructed around 80 BC as a tribal capital of the Dobunni tribe and was said to have housed up to 4,000 people. They were still there when the Romans arrived, and therefore a situation ripe for conquest. Today, another army is stationed at Credenhill, for it is the home of the British Army's Special Air Services Battalion, the SAS.

Continuing west along the Roman road, the wooded heights of Foxley rise on the right. They and the mansion within them belonged to the Price family through the 18th century. It was a later son of that family, Sir Uvedale Price, who became a renowned landscape gardener of his day and a promoter of the Picturesque movement. His son after him, was unfortunately less successful, especially at maintaining the estate, and sold it in 1856 when he fell heavily into debt. Nothing of Sir Uvedale's house remains, nor do the gardens any longer reflect the beginnings of his revolutionary ideas. It is a curious coincidence that the other great planters and gardeners of that period should have been neighbouring squires. For the Knight brothers, Richard and Thomas, of Wormsley and afterwards of Downton Castle near Ludlow, were no less famous throughout England than Sir Uvedale. In 1802, Sir Richard Colt Hoare owas on his way to North Wales in his customary post-chaise carriage and paid a visit to Foxley to see 'Mr' Uvedale Price:

> I was accompanied round a large part of his grounds, which are highly gratifying to the lover of picturesque scenery. The house is of brick, old and indifferent in every respect. The chief beauty of Foxley consists in the irregularity of its hills and woods, the variety in which the different sorts of trees are grouped and the extensive views it commands from the high grounds.

At the foot of the wooded Garnons Hill, rising 230m (760ft) through which passes a section of Offa's ubiquitous Dyke, sits a large country house built on a raised terrace. When the Garnons estate was inherited in 1790 by John Geers Cotterell, he invited James Wyatt to make alterations to the house and Humphrey Repton to redesign the grounds. While Wyatt planned to reduce the great house to a more manageable size, Repton recommended that the turnpike road laid out on the line of the Roman road and passing in front of the house, be moved further south – in the process, creating the modern line of the A438.

One of the delights of Herefordshire is the popular Black and White Trail – a collection of picturesque villages featuring timber-framed buildings, many dating from the medieval period. To the north of Garnons Hill is the historic and, arguably, the best Village of all, Weobley, with its prodigious assembly of houses ranging from the 14th century to the 17th. There, you find a diversity in gables, overhangs, dormers, porches, squares, and diagonals, the like of which is hard to find anywhere else in the marches. In addition, the village's 13th century church of St Peter and Paul has a 14th century tower with a spire that is the second tallest in the county. When alderman Fletcher Moss arrived there with his cycling companion, he declared:

> This is the most picturesque little town we have yet seen, and I have not heard of one in this or any other land that would surpass it as a beautiful specimen of a little country town of our forefathers. It is an ideal place for a lazy photographer who would like nice easy subjects all around him. He could set up his tripod in the wide grass-grown street where, if any traffic comes, it will idly pass him by; and turning north and south, east and west there are black-and-white houses of all sorts and ages that have not moved for centuries, and will long outlast his little life.

A few miles further towards the Welsh border is another of Herefordshire's Black and White Trail villages which demonstrates its own individuality. Eardisley once belonged to the Baskerville family for almost 600 years while they held the castle. However, when Glyndŵr passed this way in 1403, the Baskervilles' home had already long been in ruins. Some of Eardisley's cottages are plain white and this eases the monotony of the magpie image. Stone roofs are a common feature, and like Weobley, gables and overhangs are everywhere. Recent dendrochronology dating work on some timber-framed buildings along its high street have revealed that parts date back to the 14th century. The church is dedicated to St Mary Magdalene and is 13th century – one of many of that age in Herefordshire. However, this one stands out, not least because its Norman font was carved by the renowned

Herefordshire School of Sculptors. The bowl and base are decorated all over with the sceptical religious theme of the Harrowing of Hell into which Christ is supposed to have descended for the three days before his resurrection. It is one of the finest Romanesque fonts anywhere in England, and a must for font baggers like me. The present south aisle occupies the whole of the site of the first church built here in the 12th century, and a carved stone windowsill in the aisle is said to be a fragment of the doorway of that earlier building.

A turning at the crossroads by the Tram Inn leads to something quite special. Nestled between a few houses in a narrow lane is the Eardisley Oak, also known locally as the Great Oak. This ancient tree is truly a magnificent sight in any season of the year and is rumoured to be between 600-800 years old. Bradley expressed surprise at its apparent liveliness in spite of its great age:

> The grandeur of this oak lies not in being a megalithic-looking ruin of antiquity, but in its extraordinary combination of hoariness with health and vigour, the more remarkable since some years ago it was struck by lightning. Its girth is said to be 45 feet, but I found it impossible to measure because sections of the roots project above the paving that surrounds the tree into huge rounded bosses that form a ramp round the trunk. This trunk is hollow, though the slit into its interior is so narrow that you would never guess it to be so.

Along its course, the River Lugg excels in natural beauty, but it is the River Arrow that is adorned more by beautiful villages. One such is Eardisland, which has the right to a place on any short list of England's loveliest. Though Herefordshire is rich in black and white villages, I know no rival to the quintessential beauty of Eardisland on a summer's morning. To some, it is a Kate Greenaway[24] village, a magical place, a thing of perfect joy, but its superior charm need not be too closely analysed. One factor may

---

[24] Catherine 'Kate' Greenaway was a 19th century English children's book illustrator and writer.

be the way the buildings are spaced out, straggling in careless irregularity along the road's broad green borders. Another is the presence of the meandering Arrow that passes silently under a bridge near one end of the village. The approach from the bridge has on one side a rambling black and white house that. Bradley identified as the Old Vicarage; on the other, a Tudor dovecote of red brick and greying timbers, whose four gables are mirrored in the silvery river:

> Scattered about on either hand on the edge of a pool and velvet banks of the stream are timbered cottages that lose nothing in some cases by having occupants that are conscious of the part their dwellings play in a quite idyllic scene. It is this scattered outskirt which gathers about the pool and bridge and stream that gives Eardisland its modest fame. I have been here several times of late, and standing on the banks of the Arrow here it pleases me to think its limpid waters have made but a few hours joyous pilgrimage from the remote hill villages of Radnor and the upland farms that lie under Brilley mountain and the heath-clad wastes of Squilver[25], where in former years I have spent pleasant hours in its merry company.

To many of its visitors, Pembridge is the jewel in the crown of north Herefordshire's magpie villages, that is if the A44 road passing through it could be ignored. There's no doubting its inconvenience, but so far, no plan to bypass the village has ever succeeded. It would not take great powers of imagination to picture a traffic-free Pembridge as an even bigger, bustling tourist attraction throughout the whole year. It has the backdrop to beat all and the potential to compete well at Christmas with Hereford or Ludlow. A leisurely stroll through its few streets will display its historic timber-framed houses and cottages in great variety. Percy Thoresby-Jones, might have become more warmly attached to Eardisland had he not moved on, perhaps too soon:

---

[25] Squilver lies at the southern end of the Stiperstones.

Pembridge and Eardisland are so delightful that no mere 'once over' will so much as skim the cream of their beauties. Pembridge should be approached from the south so as to enter the main street at a point where you are close to the three principal sights: the church, the primitive looking Market Hall, and the venerable New Inn. The pleasing irregularity of the inn's exterior reflects the rambling waywardness of the rooms and passages within. The open Market Hall formed by eight stout pairs of timber supporting a broad roof, is now but a shelter from rain and a place for smoking and salivatory rumination.

From Pembridge's marketplace, a flight of steps leads up to the churchyard, and immediately the magnificent detached 14th century belfry claims attention. Inside is a roomy octagon of stone with a high-pitched pyramidal roof and two further roofed stages supported on ancient rough-hewn tree trunks, the whole building resembling a pagoda. Pembridge is one of several Herefordshire parishes whose bell tower stands separate from the church, but none are as remarkable as the one here. Not to be outclassed by its detached neighbour, St Mary's Church is itself Grade I listed, the oldest part of the church is 13th century and most of the rest is 14th century. In spite of its obvious attractions to the modern eye, Charles Harper thought Pembridge a depressing place:

> Quaint, though untidy, and given over to memories of the good times that were, but shall never come again.

Neither was C V Hancock, journalist and zealous gourmand, all that impressed when he visited in 1956:

> Pembridge was a market town and remains a decayed one. I first new it as a slattern, a slovenly place. It has spruced itself up, yet still fails to make the most of its charms and to bother enough about its blemishes. It is hard to avoid comparison with the more charming near-by Eardisland, yet they are too different to be close rivals. Eardisland never forgets it's good looks; it has a proper

regard for its appearance, and jealous neighbours might say it uses make-up.

Massingham seems to have agreed with Hancock, as he compared Pembridge with Eardisland but then declared a strong preference for the latter:

> For myself I decidedly prefer Eardisland. Pembridge to my taste is too bunched up against the knoll that carries the church with its engaging oddity of the three-storeyed detached belfry. The huddle of Pembridge brings confusion to the eye. Much to its advantage, Eardisland has given itself more room and the luminous Arrow flows right through it without for a moment forfeiting its rural graces. Eardisland is like those snatches of poetry we knew by heart in youth - "Oh, to be in England now that April's here", for instance - that have long become cliches, hackneyed prettinesses shut up in a dusty drawer of memory.

Kington is the smallest of Herefordshire's market towns, and along with Hay on Wye, the most westerly on the Black and White Trail. It is 31km (19 mi) north-west of Hereford and just 3.2km (2 mi) from the border with Wales. Despite being constantly in the Welsh firing line throughout much of Its early history, this quiet border town has been English for over a thousand years. It sits on the River Arrow in the shadow of Hergest Ridge, where it is crossed by the main English Midlands to Mid-Wales A44 road. Kington has been a market town from its earliest days and there is still a thriving prime sheep market held every Thursday. The town's location and historic character is the reason why so many old tracks and long-distance footpaths pass through it, including the Mortimer Trail, the Herefordshire Trail, and the Offa's Dyke Path. There is a small tourist industry, though concentrated in the summer months. However, it is still an unspoilt town, loved by many, and an important marketplace for local farmers, as John Hillaby pointed out:

> Kington is a little squashed-up, narrow streeted market town on the Welsh frontier where they sell sheep dip fertilizer and men's

flannel underwear. A town for farmers. Everything feminine or fripperish comes from Hereford fifteen miles away. Even in the best pub in town there were snuff-coloured fragments of what the customers had recently been walking on!

The turfed mound high above the bypass section of the A44 is all that is left of Kington Castle, after King John ended William Braose's border rebellion in 1210. On an adjoining rise stands St Mary's Church, dominating the town as the castle once did. The impressive spire reaches up from a heavily constructed 12th century tower, believed in some circles to be the rebuilt castle keep. To the west of Kington, a few miles along the Huntingdon road, is the very, very old house of the Vaughan family. Hergest Court sits on a high spur overlooking the Arrow and has done so since the 13th century. It was once one of the great family houses of Wales but is now a mere shadow of its former self. At first, a fortified stone building stood on the site, and is thought to have replaced the motte and bailey which can be seen in the field on the opposite side of the road, as the functioning military presence. By the late 15th century, the Court had become the home of Thomas Vaughan and had grown considerably. The poet, Lewis Glyn Cothi, likened it to 'a house on the plan of the towers of Alhambra'.

It remained in the hands of the Vaughans for three hundred years, although age and history had taken its toll and some remodelling had to be carried out in the 17th century. Eventually, the Vaughans moved away and the old house became neglected and ruinous once again. By the 19th century, the walls were gone and much of the timber-framed building had been taken down and re-used to construct outbuildings for storage and farm livestock. Such was the state of Hergest Court when

Figure 8 Robert Francis Kilvert

I visited it in 2005 in the company of Mr Lawrence Banks, himself a distant relative of the Vaughans and owner of a large chunk of Hergest Ridge hillside, which includes the renowned Hergest Croft Gardens and the old Court itself. While we wandered around dark corners and dusty rooms, Lawrence told the story of the Black Dog of Vaughan, said to be the mean and intolerant Thomas Vaughan himself in reincarnated form and haunted the lanes and fields hereabouts for centuries. Arthur Conan Doyle, who stayed occasionally with the Baskervilles at Clyro, will have heard these stories, too, and is likely to have used the idea for his famous tale of *The Hound of the Baskervilles*.

A minor road from the centre of Pembridge passes over the River Arrow via an ancient bridge and skirts Shobdon Airfield, formerly a wartime glider training base but these days home of the Herefordshire Aero Club. In Shobdon village, the old court was home to the local Bateman family for over two hundred years until the last Lord Bateman died in 1931. The great house was demolished two years later, and a replacement Shobdon Court was created from the service and kitchen ranges of the old one. It Is grand enough to have been awarded a Grade II listing. Close by the house is the extraordinary church of St John the Evangelist, the third on this site but a hugely important work of architecture which has a direct connection to Horace Walpole's Gothic-style house at Strawberry Hill in south west London. It is Grade 1, and these two buildings must be the only listed pairings where the church is graded higher than the parent house. The church was created in 1756 by Richard Bateman for his elder brother who had other properties to care for in London. Richard was a close friend of Walpole, and the church's extraordinary white interior and matching furniture is the sole example of Walpole's influence. Simon Jenkins, in his book *England's Thousand Best Churches*, considers St John's 'a complete masterpiece of English Rococo', while Sir Nikolaus Pevsner described it as 'the finest 18th century church in Herefordshire.'

During Bateman's 18th century remodelling, the Romanesque chancel arch was carefully removed from the existing 12th century church and reassembled on the nearby hillside, linked to two arched doorways to create an unusual folly. The carvings of the arch were the first commission of the so-called Herefordshire School of Sculptors, the same team of craftsmen responsible for the church at Kilpeck, and a forerunner of their work which later appeared in many other sites in the county. Though now somewhat eroded, the arches' exquisitely detailed Norman features remain. Ironically, the Rococo decor in the replacement church did not escape the destructive action of a leaking roof which needed urgent repairs, completed in 2013 at a cost of £1.25 million. When Massingham arrived at Shobdon, he described the arches on the hillside in his usual eloquent but never too simple fashion:

> On the skyline of the crest among the trees stands what I have called Shobdon's Folly, and I had no idea how queer and exotic a picture-book of ancient symbolism, mythology and Christian ico-nography I should find when I walked up to it. It consists of three arches with their orders, shafts, doorways and tympana covered with an extraordinary profusion of Celtic and Romanesque imagery, much of it so rubbed and worn by the siege of vandal weathers as to be hardly decipherable. What an astonishing trou-vaille upon an eighteenth-century terminary in a park! The era of common sense, my thoughts ran on, lacked even the average pru-dence of realising that ornament so exposed to wind and rain, frost and sun, would be a short-lived spectacle.

On the day I first saw Bateman's folly, I mused thoughtfully as I walked towards the more recent church which had displaced one that must have been viewed by many as a second Kilpeck. Once inside, what I saw took my breath away. I was confronted with a fairy chamber of Walpole Gothic in white, gold, blue, and rose; an Aladdin's Cave of 18th century fantasy. Except for the addition of a west gallery in the Regency style, and the font of the original church, this masterpiece is what it was in 1756 – a perfect example of escape from the as-you-were mid-18th century into the land of dreams. Charles Harper's visit to Shobdon pre-dated the demolition of the old Court, and he neither saw inside the church nor noticed the arches in the park:

> Field-paths led from Pembridge to Shobdon, a scattered village situated on a gentle hill. It is notable only for the neighbourhood of Shobdon Court, a red-brick and stone mansion of great size built during the last century by Viscount Bateman. The entrance to the lovely wooded park is untidy, and the great range of stables melancholy with broken windows. Everything around is unkempt and dishevelled and the court wears the appearance of a superannuated workhouse.

The 19th century Irish sculptor friend of Eric Gill and a fond advocator of the Herefordshire School's work, Robert Gibbings, detested Bateman's decision to destroy the Romanesque church:

> Kilpeck church, though one of the smaller in England, is one of our richest examples of Anglo-Norman Romanesque architecture. It is unfortunate that Victorian prudes defaced many of the quaint corbels that encircle the outside of the building. But that is nothing to what happened at Shobdon, when the second Lord Bateman pulled down a church which was at least the equal of Kilpeck, and probably grander. He did this not only in order that he might indulge his taste in Strawberry Hill Gothic, but also that he might have some ruins as features in his park, a form of absurdity then in fashion.

Curious Old Leominster

How many miles. How many
From Leominster to Llanllieni

The historic market town of Leominster (pronounced 'Lemster') is the second largest in Herefordshire, and dates to the 7th century. Contrary to popular folklore, the town name has nothing to do with Leofric, the 11th century Earl of Mercia and husband of the more famous Lady Godiva. Its name derives from the first minster church, built around that time for an Anglo-Saxon community of clergy in the ancient district between the Rivers Lugg and Arrow, then known as Leon. The Welsh name for Leominster, Llanllieni, is still used today by a few on the Welsh side of the nearby border. According to the *Anglo-Saxon Chronicle,* a raid by the Welsh in 1052 ended with the Battle of Llanllieni against a combined force of Saxons and Norman guerrillas.

The Priory Church of St. Peter and St. Paul, which now serves as the parish church, is the remaining section of a Benedictine monastery founded in 1121 by Henry I. The site as a monastic foundation is a lot older than that, possibly as a house of 7th century nuns, but that building – and we must assume the inhabitants – was destroyed in an attack by an army of wandering Danes. The Norman rebuild included a remarkable pointed, arched west doorway and window, containing unique Herefordshire School carvings. Today, it stands, in Pevsner's words, 'pale red on a juicy green, in a curious isolation surrounded on three sides by lawn'. But the *pièce de résistance* of Leominster's collection of black and white buildings is Grange Court[26], John Abel's Market House of 1633 that once stood in the centre of town on Broad Street. It was an ornate and beautiful structure, composed entirely of carved oak and designed by that famous of Herefordshire men whose work is almost exclusively of wood. The Grange was sold in 1853 to John Arkwright of Hampton Court for £95, then pulled down and re-erected by the recreation ground. In 1949, Massingham saw an analogy of the structure in a nursery rhyme:

The first thing that struck me about it now is that it looks bogus and indeed it is partly bogus. No building can be taken down,

---

[26] Grange Court was used as offices for the Borough Council, then the District Council, and later the County Council until 2008, when redevelopment began again to turn the Court into a Community, Enterprise and Heritage Hub, and the inevitable wedding celebrations.

removed, and put back together again in a different place, in spite of the warning of Humpty Dumpty, without looking so.

John Abel was largely employed by the corporations and the landed gentry of the county, and his work may yet be seen in many mansions and churches. But to the shame of those towns, his town halls of Brecon, Hereford, Kington, and Weobley were swept away to make room for modern improvements. Leominster was no better in a sense than those graceless towns. Sir Richard Colt Hoare saw Leominster's Market House still in situ at the top of Broad Street and described it as 'a curious piece of old woodwork!', while his travelling companion of the day, Richard Fenton, called the town 'a dirty, dingy, scrambling place, the church the only thing worthy of note. Arthur Bradley took less notice of Leominster than making an issue of the local price of apples and the care and attention of the orchards in which they are grown:

> The whole of the district is the most noted in Herefordshire for its apples. Yet the growers of this premier county of England generally appear to leave their trees to their own wild will, untrimmed and unpruned, and to make grass paddocks of the land they stand on. The orchards are more often than not conspicuous for their picturesque disarray and the freshness of the perennial turf which mats about the roots and catches stray sunbeams that can only pierce the wilderness of boughs above. Yet cooking apples are sometimes three pence a pound even in Hereford!

Though Leominster's broad main street gives a spacious and genial air, it is only by nosing about the back lanes and alleyways that its historic fabric is exposed, dominated by medieval buildings and conjuring up images of centuries ago. Names such as the Buttercross, Drapers Lane, Cordwainers Lane, and Corn Square, are not just reminders of Leominster's commercial past but remain a crucial part of the town centre today, a bustling hub that includes a range of antique shops featured frequently on a television programme associated with bargain hunting.

Lonely Radnorshire Roads

Travelling in early May through Herefordshire and South Shropshire, the light green shoots of spring show an encouraging hue on the landscape, and occasionally, where winter sown rape has begun to blossom, the familiar patches of cheering bright yellow split bare ploughed fields of red earth, the whole resembling a giant patchwork quilt on the surrounding hillsides. The A438 road and River Wye now run side by side and set back on a bend in road and river is the Rhydspence Inn, known in earlier times as the Cattle Inn. In a field opposite in bygone days, the Welsh cattle droves were re-shod after being driven from the barren moors of Epynt, across the Wye ford near the Erwood bridge, climbing Llandeilo Graban Hill and along the high ridge tracks, before descending like 'a slow black river' from Painscastle. Massingham had made the inn his headquarters for an exploration of the Radnorshire bank of the Wye between Whitney and Hereford:

> It is an inn, too, that, like a many a good inn in the past, has a little farm attached to it, and being just in Hereford, a little orchard as well. It is full of draughts and crooked and creaking timbers like all black and white houses, and voices in one room keep no privacy from those in another.

Figure 9 Mr Fletcher Moss at ease.

Having arrived hot and thirsty, which is how all travellers ought to arrive here, Fletcher Moss and friend entered the bar in garters and cycle clips and asked for cider. "The hostess told us it was threepence a quart but if we could spend fivepence she had some super-excellent brew. We said, 'blow the expense!" At another time, also on his cycling tour, Arthur Bradley did not call at the inn but continued along the A438 towards Hay on Wye, absorbing the scenery around him and the joys to come:

> We are in Wales but not yet of it. Yet one could never guess what a comparatively wild and Welsh country it is whose southern slopes we are now unconsciously brushing, and what chaos of hill and valley, dimpled here and there with red patches of tillage, but pasture for the most part. Tortuous and narrow lanes, sometimes stony, sometimes grass-grown, sometimes torn by unruly streams, clamber about from homestead to homestead and from hamlet to hamlet.

In 1865 the Reverend Francis Kilvert was appointed curate at St Michael's Church at Clyro and began his curateship in a new building completed a dozen years before. Originally a 12th century building, only the base of the tower remained medieval. Kilvert's duties were mainly to take Sunday services at St Michael's, and an isolated chapel at Upper Bettws, a two-mile walk away. He was also expected to perform visits to the sick and the poor of the parish, which inevitably required him to walk to whoever and wherever they might be – an exercise he grew to enjoy doing. I, too, have walked many of the lanes above Clyro following in the diarist's lonely footsteps, as many have done after him. Wandering these hillsides is a wonderful and a memorable experience. The ways are steep in parts and as you climb slowly – for there is no other way to do it – thoughts of the tall gangly Kilvert striding forth, and in all weathers, to visit his scattered parishioners make you tire more:

> Shall I ever forget that journey up the hill to Cefn-y-Blaen in this burning Easter Eve, under the cloudless blue sky, the scorching sun and over the country covered with a hot dim haze? I climbed up the Bron panting in the sultry afternoon heat. Went up the fields from Court Evan Gwynne to Little Wern y Pentre and envied the sheep that were being washed in the brook below. The peewits were sweeping, rolling and tumbling in the hot blue air about the

tall trees with a strange deep mysterious hustling and quavering sound from their great wings.

I am not sure why Bradley doesn't mention Kilvert when he was in Clyro in 1897. After all, it had been less than 20 years since the curate's untimely death, and the memories of his time there would have lingered among his parishioners almost as the fateful day itself, despite his unexpected transfer to Bredwardine. On the contrary, he dismisses it almost with nonchalance:

> In the meantime, the road has struggled for a moment out of the Wye valley in fetching Clyro, which is a village of some note for its general charm of appearance and general situation. It is of the Herefordshire type and includes an ancient and stately church. There is not much, however, to detain us here, or if there is, we must resist temptation.

The Radnorshire foothills run parallel with the Middle Wye from Llyswen, where it takes that double bend from the south-east to north-east to Rhydspence, and thence its wide sweep southward towards Hereford. On the hillside above the Radnorshire half of Glasbury is the very visible Maesllwch Castle – a vast pseudo-Gothic pile, complete with towers, battlement walls with arrow-slits and mullioned casements. This, however, is no previous marcher lord's statement of power. It was constructed in the mid-19th century for a Walter of the de Winton family, one of many sons bearing the name Walter to inherit the estate. This Walter's father had been a Wilkins, the old family name, but in 1839 he decided to adopt a simplified version of their Norman ancestral name de Wintona. Maesllwch is the third house on the site – the first being a 16th century hall house belonging to the Vaughans. That house was replaced in 1729, but when Walter Wilkins moved in barely seventy years later as Member of Parliament for Radnorshire, he drew up plans to construct the fantasy castle. Part of it was later demolished to reduce the costs of upkeep, but what was left remains an imposing private residence and now a Grade II listed building.

Of all his walking excursions, Kilvert's favourite was to Aberedw, a village on the Radnorshire bank where the small river Edw converges with the Wye, and where the remains of two castles share the landscape – an early motte and bailey and a later stone fortification which Llywelyn ap Gruffydd, the last of the medieval princes of Wales, used as his hunting lodge. Near to the remnants of the stone castle is a cave in which Llywelyn is said to have hidden from his enemies and is now adorned with flags and memorabilia put there over many years, presumably by Welsh nationalist supporters, in memory of the prince who was killed in December 1282. When the railway was built to connect Hay with Builth, much of Llywelyn's castle overlooking the Wye was destroyed to make way for the line. There is no railway now, but a footpath crosses the old rail bed from the main road and leads along the edge of the hill above the rocky riverbed towards St Cewydd's 13th century church. On the one hand is the flat green water meadow of the Wye, and on the other is the deep narrow valley of the Edw rushing by the older castle mound to meet its more powerful watery neighbour. It is a truly beautiful place.

Bradley described the dingle where the Edw spends its last half-mile as 'deep and striking'. The church's squat tower, with a pyramidal roof, appears high above the tree-shadowed glen on what is thought to be another ancient site. A few 18th century gravestones have been placed in the outside walls of the chancel, although the churchyard doesn't appear to lack burial space. Inside the church by the north door, a glass case displays the flute and pitch-pipe of William Williams, the church musician in Victorian times before they had an organ. As well as accompanying the choir, he would also play seated in the timber-framed porch while the local swains and damsels danced on the church green. Dominating the nave is a huge 14th century screen which survived restorations in Tudor times and again in the Victorian period. The rood loft appears to have been replaced at some stage by a further two tiers of wavy balusters on the screen, leaving the structure looking like a large gate which, if it wasn't for the aisle-wide entrance, has the appearance of a barrier preventing access to the chancel.

Close to the village and overlooking the Wye are the extraordinary exposed cliffs of the Aberedw Rocks, which Kilvert loved almost to the point of obsession. As you travel north west between the Wye and the gorsey hills of the Radnorshire bank, the river narrows and then widens, occasionally cluttered with banks of shingle and sometimes revealing its bed of ledges of limestone where cattle used to browse on the grasses growing between the narrow spaces. Here, suddenly, the Aberedw cliffs appear towering in terraces 215m (700 ft) above the shelf of land between them and the river, their summit crowned with scrub and trees curving their talons over the rock masses. The huge slabs of limestone are piled one above another in such regular horizontal courses, and with such precision in their vertical alignment, that they look exactly like dry-walled masonry. It is no wonder Kilvert was inspired to poetry in his most impassioned mood:

> *Oh, Aberedw, Aberedw,*
> *Would God I might dwell and die by thee.*
> *Memory enters in and brings back the old time*
> *In a clear vision and walking dream,*
> *And again, I descend from the high moor's half encircling sweep*
> *And listen to the distant murmur of the river*
> *As it foams down the ravine from its home*
> *In the Green Cwm and its cradle in the hills.*
> *Once more I look up at the cliff castle towers*
> *And mark the wild roses swinging from the crag*
> *And watch the green wood wavering and shimmering*
> *With a twinkling dazzle as they rustle in the breeze*
> *And shining of the summer afternoon, while here and there*
> *A grey crag peeps from among the tufted trees.*
> *Oh, Aberedw, Aberedw.*

From Aberedw, Bradley thought at first to go down to the river again and re-cross by ferry to the main road, which would have been the shortest way to Builth. But he decided there was no reason why he should not take the lane along the Radnor side of the river, along which the farmers of Aberedw get to the main highway that runs into Builth:

> There is a full three miles of rough and tortuous byway before the excellent artery is reached, but there is sufficient consolation for the rudeness of the path in the glorious glimpse one gets above the tree-tops, or framed within their trunks and foliage, of the river below and the mountains towering above. Aberedw hill thrusts its huge back to all across the path which has to struggle around between its gorse and heather-clad base and the river. Sometimes we dive out of sight of the woodlands reaching up towards the heights of Epynt range from the opposite shore into some dingle where a tributary brook hurrying down through damp grassy hollows, bright with marsh marigolds, drowns with its piping voice the murmur of the Wye.

Beyond the eastern bank of the Wye between Glasbury and Builth Wells lies an almost empty landscape of moorlands and valleys stretching far to the north to where the Radnor Forest meets the Shropshire border and the land of Clun beyond. A single lonely road, the B4594, winds its undulating way from Erwood, through Painscastle, Newchurch and Gladestry, passing west of the Hergest Ridge to meet the A44 Kington road near Burlingjobb. For much of the journey along this road there are spectacular views of the Black Mountains. In 1938 Percy Thoresby Jones described the lanes as:

> Too steep and narrow for motor cars, winding between vigorous, intricate hedges planted on high banks that are richly adorned with unstinted profusion of wildflowers characteristic of Radnorshire.

Massingham's view of the 'lonely road' had not improved by much in the ten years since he first passed this way:

> Idling along this road, the traveller is as remote in situation if not in mileage from the arteries of traffic as though he were footing it among the Dartmoor Tors. Both wayside scene and long-distance

change at every corner, and for sheer rural retirement in a period
when it is becoming an Arcadian dream, I know nothing outside
mountain country to touch theses foothills.

The pleasant hilltop village of Painscastle takes its name from its
large castle mound, the Castle of Payn, but there is some doubt
who the man was. It is probable that it was Payn FitzJohn, an
Anglo-Norman nobleman and an administrator for Henry I and
owed his position and wealth to the king. Payn's family originated
in Normandy, but he appears to have spent most of his life in
England and the Welsh marches. He built his castle here on top of
the remains of a Roman fort, but he didn't hold it long. During
one of many land ownership disputes between Welsh chieftains,
he was ambushed and killed in 1137. The castle was never held
for any length of time by anyone because the site was so important,
yet so vulnerable. If any power-seeking prince was on the road,
Painscastle would be in his way and a target for attack. It was the
scene of major Anglo-Welsh battles in 1196 and again in 1198.
Henry III rebuilt the castle in stone in 1231, but within 30 years it
had been destroyed again. By the time Glyndŵr was on the
rampage, there was little left to protect and the remains were
abandoned. The castle earthworks are substantial but are presently
in private hands on farmland and there is no public access.
Historically, the site remains an important one, and if the land
ever comes up for sale, I expect an authority like CADW to step in
and obtain it for a grateful nation.

Another destination for one of Kilvert's walks from Clyro –
a route now appearing on the OS map as the Offa's Dyke
trail – was the village of Newchurch. He had become friends
with the vicar, David Vaughan, and his family. One of Vaughan's
daughters, Emmaline, who Kilvert had known, died suddenly
at the age of fourteen. He was deeply affected by this sad event
and visited her grave in the churchyard on each of his following
visits:

As I stooped over the green grave by the churchyard gate, placing
primrose branches in a cross upon the turf, the large flakes of

snow fell thickly upon us but melted as they fell, and the great yew
tree overhead bent weeping upon the grave.

The great tree is no longer there. It came down in a storm in 1990,
and the old graves are gradually being engulfed in tall summer
grasses, the exception being that of Vaughan himself, where
mowing had taken place around the grave to allow clear viewing
by pilgrims. Vaughan had rebuilt St Mary's in 1856 at his own
expense on a tight budget, and corners were cut to stretch the
costs. The church is now at risk of falling apart and requires some
urgent attention.

The lonely road eventually descends to Gladestry (Llanfair
Llwyth Yfnwg), a village close to the border with England at the
end of the Hergest Ridge. Approaching Gladestry, the Ridge fills
the view and lingering behind it is the great hump of Hanter
Hill. The village is part of a thriving farming and agricultural
community and not far away at Burkingjob is a huge quarry.

For the final stretch of the road, the traveller will be in an
industrial landscape of grey dust where the Tarmac Company have
been digging up Old Radnor Hill for nigh on one hundred years.

In the 14th century, the inn at Gladestry was a favourite haunt
of the bard Lewis Glyn Cothi:

> *There is in Llanfair, by Saint Llywenfel*
> *Money for me, and sweet honey*
> *Ale from Ludlow there would make me healthy*
> *And drink of Weobley ale completely restore me to health.*
> *I shall have wine with no refusal or frown*
> *From eight harbours in Llwyth Yfnwg*

The Royal Oak has a lasting memory for me. In 1987, while
walking the Offa's Dyke Trail with a band of friends, we stopped
at the inn for a lunchtime drink. At the time, licence restrictions
on Sundays did not allow drinking beyond 2pm and knowing we
had taken longer than planned to arrive in Gladestry, we had
practically run the last three miles to get there before closing time.
Being first to the bar by a few hundred yards, I ordered as many

beers for our group as we might be allowed to consume, but after filling sixteen glasses with the very welcoming liquor, the puzzled landlord asked why I was in such a desperate hurry when, in his twenty-three years as the licence holder, he had never closed on a Sunday before 4pm! Ah, the memories of agreeable publicans and a misspent adolescence!

Lying below the eastern flanks of the Hergest Ridge is the village of Huntington, founded as a medieval borough to replace the nearby town of Kington which had been destroyed in 1216. Huntington's Castle still retains fragments of two of its towers and indicates that it may have been larger than that of Kington. Thanks to the efforts made to clear excessive overgrowth on the site, it is now possible to capture the landscape beyond the castle grounds, though even in Massingham's day the prospect was still clear:

> The magnificent view of the Hergest Ridge and Colva Hill from castle mound of Huntington with its fragment of masonry is coloured predominantly russet. An immense solitude enfolds the traveller, and the more comforting are the endless companies of primroses that deck the steep roadside banks in April, like the swarm of Titians putti.[27]

On the south eastern edge of the village is another castle mound, an earlier motte probably built by William FitzOsbern as part of his campaign to secure the Welsh border. Nearby is the curious little church of St Thomas à Becket, which it is believed was built as a penance by one of Becket's killers and is one of only four churches so dedicated – fitting, maybe, to remind us of the four knights who were responsible for the crime. With the introduction of the Protestant Reformation, a proclamation was made that Becket's death was 'Untruely called martyrdom'. He was therefore de-canonised and thence referred to only as Bishop Becket. The churches dedicated to Becket were changed to other saints, but for some reason that did not happen here.

---

[27] Titian called his questionable paintings of hordes of naked children as 'the putti'.

Mortimers Rising

Moving northwards out of Kingsland, one is soon among the level fields where, in 1461, the followers of the Red Rose fell in the ferocious fight which made young Edward, Earl of March, the King of England. It is a particularly evocative battlefield, for there, at the end of the level tract of pasture, are the outer ramparts of gentle wooded slopes. Between them and the River Lugg, the Yorkist forces from the last centre of Mortimer influence at Wigmore, longbow men itching to test their arrows and their skills, and battle-worn Lancastrians, weary from the slog across Wales from Pembroke, assembled as three distinct suns, a parhelion, rose on that second morning of February.

> *Three glorious suns, each one a perfect sun,*
> *Not separated with the racking clouds*
> *But sever'd in a pale clear shining sky.*
> *See, see! they join, embrace and seem to kiss,*
> *As if they vow'd some league inviolable.*
> *Now are they but one lamp, one light, one sun.*
> *In this the heaven figures some event.*
>
> Shakespeare: Henry VI, Part 3

They had no idea what the parhelion was, so there was an added fear on both sides, though Edward Mortimer seems to have seen it as a good omen. It would not have been a good time for a battle; early February was out of season for fighters in the 15th century, and the vision in the sky indicated it was probably very cold. Edward's men lined up at the crossroads where the Mortimer's Cross Inn is now, and Owen Tudor's chose the site of Luctonians Rugby ground. The numbers have long been speculated upon, but it looks like the death toll was a horrendously large percentage of combatants. At the end of the fray, it is claimed that 4,000 lay dead in the mud or drowned in the river out of an unsubstantiated total of 6,000. The killings weren't restricted to the battlefield. Scattering Lancastrian soldiers were pursued and slaughtered where they were caught, and captured commanders, including Owen Tudor, were ceremoniously executed in Hereford. A field somewhere south of Mortimer's Cross Inn was used as a burial ground, and eventually a monument was erected at the Kingsland end to record the whole messy story.

And so, to Croft Castle, a lavish country mansion – now in the hands of the National Trust – started life in 1055 as a timber motte and bailey stronghold for 'Bearded' Bernard de Croft. There has been a Croft home on this site, overlooking the North Herefordshire plain, since then. In the 15th century, John Croft married one of Owain Glyndŵr's daughters, Jane, and it was about this time that a wounded black dragon was adopted as the family crest, in support of their Glyndŵr heritage. In spite of this history, financial pressure during the 18th century forced the Crofts to sell the castle, and it was nearly two hundred years before they could buy the estate back. Interestingly, it was during the time they were away that the castle received its internal Gothic makeover, the work carried out by the designer of the world's first iron bridge, Thomas Farnolls Pritchard. The idea for this came from Richard Bateman's Rococo decor in his church at Shobdon; his friend, Thomas Johnes, was then the resident of Croft.

The Gothic stairway is the only surviving example of Pritchard's work. Eventually, it was Sir James Croft, 11th Baronet, who retrieved the estate from the then owners, the Kevill-Davies family, in 1923. Sir James was killed tragically in 1941 while training with the Commandos in Scotland and is buried in the castle's churchyard. He had no heir, so the estate went to his cousin, the 1st Lord Croft, who was the Under Secretary of State for War in Churchill's government at the time. Although ownership of Croft is no longer with the family, one of them still retains an apartment within it. In the 1940s, Massingham's acquaintance and friend, and then owner of Croft Castle, was Major Owen Croft[28]. Brigadier General Henry Page Croft, whom Massingham

---

[28] Major Croft was the last of the family to own the castle. His wife, Stella Bouwer, wanted to demolish it and clear the estate of its trees, but the Major's sister, Diana Croft, agreed to look after the estate until it could be saved for the nation.

also knew, helped him in Parliament with attempts to get the Plumage Bill[29] passed into law in 1921.

> Many are the days I have had picnic lunches and teas in the castle, for my friend of Pomona Farm now owns it. He bought it not in order to live there, an impossible expense, but partly out of ancestral piety and partly because he is determined that his highland estate shall be properly farmed. Hence, I have many memories of the castle and not least of them the good company I have enjoyed there.

Above the castle, on a long narrow hilltop ridge, is Croft Ambrey Iron Age fort, the 5th century citadel of Ambrosius Aurelianus. Here, in 2007, where the raven's nest and sandstone meet limestone once more, I had the south of the Northern as well as the north of the Southern Marches in my view. The south-westward prospective is even further, etching the Black Mountains and the Radnor Forest in a half-arc, and on a clear day the Brecon Beacons, which to the Silurist, Henry Vaughan, where Solomon's mountains of myrrh and hills of frankincense are.

Beneath Ludlow Bells

The landlocked county of Shropshire forms a large part of the middle march, is rich and fertile and the scenery varied from plains to mountains. The rivers are plenty, too, from the mighty Severn, wandering Teme, and gentle Onny, born from a myriad of spring-fed streams and picturesque brooks. The western boundary of Shropshire is also the national border of England with Wales and its principal area of Powys, which now covers the historic counties of Montgomeryshire, Radnorshire and most of Breconshire. Ludlow is the largest town in south Shropshire.

---

[29] Known as the Importation of Plumage (Prohibition) Bill, the object of which was "to prohibit the importation of the plumage of birds and the sale, or possession of plumage illegally imported".

It is a market town and has been so since the 13th century. The old walled settlement occupied the summit of a rocky limestone hill, separated from neighbouring heights on the south and west by a deep gorge through which the River Teme winds its confusing way.

On the northern side, beyond the encircling wall and extended suburbs, the River Corve joins the Teme in sight of the great castle ruins rising sheer from precipitous western cliffs. Ludlow's magnificent castle was founded by Walter de Lacy and was one of the first stone castles to be built in England, initially as a military defence against the Welsh. But when the last male de Lacy died in 1240 the castle passed to Piers de Geneville, who began to turn the military outpost into a luxurious fortified palace. In 1301 de Geneville's daughter, Jeanne, married Roger Mortimer, 1st Earl of March. Having moved in from his ageing quarters at Wigmore, Mortimer extended the internal complex of castle buildings, and the Mortimer family went on to hold Ludlow Castle for over a hundred years. After 1470 Ludlow became a royal castle, when the victor of the War of the Roses, Edward Mortimer, was crowned Edward IV and chose it as a haven for his two young sons, Richard and Edward. There they remained, protected by a team of courtiers led by their uncle, Earl Rivers, who may have been oblivious to the power struggles back in London. In 1483 their father the King, died at the age of forty, and the two young princes were recalled to London to be murdered in the Tower by Edward's ambitious brother, Richard of Gloucester.

During his brief reign, Edward IV set up the Council of Wales and the Marches in 1472 – a regional administrative body based in Ludlow Castle and initially responsible for governing the lands held under the Principality of Wales, lands directly administered by the English crown. The Council was made up of a President, his deputy, and just twenty members – mostly from the Woodville and Stanley families but all friends and allies of the monarch. The king's eldest son, while still under protection at the castle, was installed with the Council as Prince of Wales and the figurehead of the monarchy. It met only intermittently but remained a significant place of appeal for many Welsh landowners. Under the presidency of Bishop Roland Lee of Lichfield in 1534 the Council developed a reputation for its ruthless suppression of lawbreakers and for Lee's prejudices against the Welsh. He even protested Henry VIII's Act of Union in 1536, believing his own iron fist approach would be enough to hold the Welsh in check. His law officers had taken full advantage and gained a bad name themselves for corruption. In the early part of the 17th century Parliament took notice of the intolerable state of affairs in the marches and the Council was disestablished. Charles II briefly revived it In 1661 but following the Glorious Revolution that overthrew the Stuart monarchy, William of Orange had little enthusiasm for maintaining the Council and it was abolished finally on July 25th, 1689.

At that point the castle was abandoned altogether and the people of Ludlow helped themselves to whatever materials they found useful. In 1720 Daniel Defoe saw Mortimer's great house sliding into oblivion:

> The castle itself is in the very perfection of decay, all the fine courts, the royal apartments, halls, and rooms of state, lie open, abandoned, and some of them falling down; for since the Courts of the President of the Marches were taken away, here is nothing to do that requires the attendance of any public people; so that time, the great devourer of works of men, begins to eat into the very stone walls and to spread the face of royal ruins upon the whole fabric.

After the castle, the parish church is regarded by many as the real glory of Ludlow. Author Simon Jenkins described St Laurence in *England's Thousand Greatest Churches* as 'the cathedral of the marches'. In 1540 Leland called the church 'very fayre and large and richly adorned and taken for the fayrest in all these parts'. Camden declared in his great work *Britannia* in 1577 that 'then the Inhabitants in process of time, built in the very bosom of the town, and on the highest ground a very faire church, and the only church they have'. Built of red sandstone and cruciform in shape, St Laurence's graceful and lofty tower is a landmark over miles of country and beautiful in the near approach. The north side of its graveyard rests against a northern section of the old town wall overlooking the Corve river and beyond to the Clee Hills that fill the eastern sky.

Inside the great church, beneath the floor of the Choir, is the heart of the fifteen-year-old Prince Arthur, the younger brother of Henry VIII. He had lived at the castle with his young wife, Catherine of Aragon, and held his Tudor princely court where once Mortimers had ruled; he died there of the mysterious sweating sickness. It is interesting to consider the consequences of Arthur's premature death, not least that Catherine became his brother's first wife, Henry believing that her marriage to his brother was unconsummated. More significantly perhaps is the likelihood that had Arthur survived to become king instead of Henry, there would have been no break with Rome and no dissolution of monasteries, and England and Wales would be blessed even now with those magnificent abbey buildings which Henry had so belligerently destroyed.

Old houses abound in this town, among them the Reader's House – a 17th century building of timber and plaster standing next to St Laurence's, and as fine an example of a black and white timbered building as may be found anywhere. Queer old shops, cavernous and gloomy, are to be seen throughout; many of them with richly decorated ceilings, and others contrived in the most unlikely places. A walk around Ludlow's main streets and quiet lanes is to walk through nine hundred years of architectural history. There are over four hundred listed buildings in these streets. One of the oldest is the Norman chapel of St Thomas of Canterbury, built just outside the castle walls not long after the Archbishop's martyrdom in 1170. The old grammar school in Mill Street, now forming part of Ludlow College, was founded circa 1200, making it one of the oldest schools in the country. Heading north from the Bull Ring at Ludlow's central crossroad, Corve Street is littered with eye-catching Georgian facades, many with a medieval core. There is just one flaw now in this otherwise unblemished collection, and that is the abomination of a modern Tesco store built over the site of the old market where local farming stock used to be bought and sold every week.

Ludlow was poet A.E. Housman's favourite town and he referred to it often in his writings.

> *Oh, come you home of Sunday*
> *When Ludlow streets are still*
> *And Ludlow bells are calling*
> *To farm and lane and mill*
>
> *Or come you home on Monday*
> *When Ludlow market hums*
> *And Ludlow chimes are playing*
> *The conquering hero comes'*

(from The Recruit)

Contrary to the perception, Housman was not a Shropshire lad but a Worcestershire one who grew up outside Bromsgrove. Those 'blue remembered hills' were his western horizon from a nearby hill near his home. To some, it is hardly surprising that his ashes are buried in the grounds behind St Laurence's Church. The stump of a cherry tree planted in his memory marks their location and his memorial tablet is fixed on the outside north wall. Ludlow was also a favourite of John Betjeman's, who wrote in 1943:

> Ludlow is probably the loveliest town in England with its hill of Georgian houses ascending from the river Teme to the great tower of the cross-shaped church, rising behind a classic market building.

Arthur Bradley, too, thought highly of Ludlow:

> There are towns of Ludlow's size perhaps as quaint and boasting as many ancient buildings, but they do not in all probability crown an eminence amid really striking scenery, nor yet again share such distinction of site with one of the finest medieval castles in England, and one possessed of a military and political history unique in the annals of British castles.

165

The many fine large townhouses in the centre of the town within sight of the castle itself, are a direct effect of the times of the Councils of Wales and its serving members. Councillors and visiting dignitaries would stay in the inns just off the Square as well as the quaint and architecturally superior Feathers Hotel, where the Victorian artist, Henry Thornhill Timmins, stayed while on a tour of Shropshire in 1896:

> We observed how this venerable house seems to stand at ease, as it were, in these days of its ripe old age, it's tall beetling gables and quaintly carved beams leaning this way or that, quite regardless of perspective. With what picturesque effect its diamond-paned oriel windows jut forth from beneath the deep-browed eaves, and the queer carven monsters ogle the passer-by from bulging bracket and beam end, and how charmingly the flowering creepers on the balcony relieve its grim old timbers.

When the pioneering travel writer, H.V. Morton, stopped for the night at Ludlow in 1927 he also chose the Feather's, and after checking in decided on a late afternoon stroll:

Figure 10 Henry Vollam Morton

> I put on my dusty hat as if it had been a helm with a plume towering above it, and strode out into the hilly streets of Ludlow to admire those raiding, fighting border men, those sturdy Salop knaves, still driving before them, between rows of half-timbered houses on market day, big brown cows and fatted sheep.

Victorians never shied away from ideas of pretentiousness in their buildings. The early 18th century Market House in Castle Square had become so dowdy and drab that on the eve of the Queen's Golden Jubilee in 1897, the council replaced it with a larger elaborate structure that was architecturally fashionable. At the time, it was received with great local pride, but the liking for its style did not last. Pevsner described it as "Ludlow's bad luck. There is nothing that could be said in favour of its fiery brick or useless Elizabethan detail." It was demolished in 1986 and the space today is used for regular weekday markets.

Built against the south side of the curtain wall of the castle, Dinham House is yet another fine residence. This nine-bay, red brick, 18th century two storeyed mansion became the detention centre for Lucien Bonaparte, younger brother of Napoleon. He was held here from 1810 after capture at sea while attempting to make his way to the US with his family, seven children, and twenty-three servants. The Bonapartes' arrival prompted great excitement and curiosity in Ludlow, but the in-town location of Dinham House made it difficult for them to escape attention, particularly from the upper classes who sought them out. After a few months, the Bonapartes escaped for less intrusive living near Worcester but with his brother Napoleon defeated and exiled on Elba, Lucien's prisoner-of-war status was lifted. Within a few weeks, he had left finally for Italy.

Ludlow's famous festivals take place throughout each year around the town. An open area within the castle grounds serves as the stage for Shakespearean plays, and elsewhere several venues give space and time to musicians and varied entertainers. During the second weekend in September, the Food and Drink Festival, for which Ludlow is justifiably proud, comes to town. Over the last weekend of November, the Medieval Christmas Fayre fills the castle grounds and the market square, including a candlelit evening on the Saturday. On quieter days, the market square fills with what it was intended for – market stalls displaying goods from the crafter or farm. There seems to be something going on almost every day of every week.

In 1634 John Milton's *Masque of Comus* was presented in the halls of the castle in celebration of the appointment of John Egerton, Earl of Bridgewater, as President of the Council of Wales. Masques were a 17th century form of entertainment of poetry, pantomime, dialogue and song, played out in front of royals or lords and ladies of the courts. Milton's play was cleverly based on an incident involving the Earl's daughter, Lady Alice Egerton and her younger brothers, when returning home from visiting relatives over the county border in Herefordshire. The innocent facts appear to indicate that Alice and the boys became separated at some point a few miles south of the Ludford Bridge. Alice got herself lost in Haye Park Woods, a Saxon deer park which became part of the Mortimer Forest and is rather dense in places even now. Lost became benighted, a pretty scary matter for any young child, and so you have a ready-made plot for Milton's imagination.[30]

According to Percy Thoresby Jones, after a climb of three hundred feet or so from either Dinham or Ludford Bridge, up the grassy slope of Whitcliffe Hill towards the fringe of the Mortimer forest, there is a view of the town and castle like no other and includes the distant Clee Hills as its background:

> Thence look down over Ludlow, camera at the ready, and you will not grudge the trifling climb. Before you is a clean old town of red and grey complexion, with roofs and gables above black and white facades, and a glimpse or two of its steep streets, while on the town ridge crest rises the finest parish church in Shropshire, if not in England. On the western and highest portion of the ridge stands the noble fortress, with its long array of ancient towers and curtain walls scored with the outlines of battlements. It's the perfect subject point for the painter, too.

Nowadays, Whitcliffe Common is a reserve under the management of Shropshire Wildlife Trust who have made a point of making sure the trees don't grow so dense or so high as to spoil that view.

---

[30] The story of Comus is well known to some, but those readers to whom it is unfamiliar will, I hope, forgive the author's presumption and seek it out online.

168

Though a considerable river, the Teme is not navigable at Ludlow. It is too shallow most of the year, for one thing, and for another, there are no less than five substantial weirs within a space of half a mile. The tumbling of these weirs on still summer nights fills the air with a continuous murmur that in time of flood rises to angry roaring that fills the streets and alleyways of the old town with menacing reverberations. When Charles Harper published his book, *The Marches of Wales,* in 1894, the Teme flowing beneath Ludford Bridge was the county boundary. Since then, Herefordshire has lost ground and the border – crossed by the A49 – has slipped five miles south to the crossroad by the Salwey Arms at Brimfield. Little has changed since Harper's visit, and his words described cobbled corners of old-world charm which exist even now:

> On Ludford Bridge the view hence is delightful, look which way we will. Trees, rocks, bustling rapids and deep, calm pools that reflect the sky, combining to form a scene of rural harmony. A picturesque old flour mill and some dilapidated tanneries still cling to the bank hard by, having been swept away in an unprecedented flood a dozen years ago.

Dust Under Wigmore Grass

Continuing his second tour of the Welsh border in 1903, Arthur Bradley left Ludlow by the Ludford Bridge and set his attentions towards the western sun:

> We now thread the devious and hilly ways that wind south west by Wigmore and Brampton Bryan. I have made note of the unforgettable prospect which Ludlow offers to the climbing the steep heights of Whitcliffe, a feat the Wigmore road easily accomplishes by much judicious grading. But when these giddy heights are surmounted you have only in fact begun the ascent of one of the biggest banks that any important border highway is called upon to face, and that is saying much. The ascent, however,

is lengthy rather than steep and for more than half the distance the way lies through the edge of a thick forest, which opens almost at the moment the ridge is gained and you seem of a sudden to be looking out over all the kingdoms of the earth.

The village of Wigmore is located on the A4110 road, about 13km (8 mi) from Ludlow, in the far north west corner of Herefordshire. For a long time this was the old home of the Mortimer clan, and after they took ownership in 1071, Wigmore Castle became the centre of their power. That would last for 400 hundred years, until Roger Mortimer moved to his new home in Ludlow in 1330. During their time, Wigmore became one of the main English border castles in the marches. When Edward the Confessor reigned, the barony of Wigmore belonged to Eadric Sylvaticus, the Saxon Earl of Shrewsbury, sometimes referred to as Wild Eadric on account of his refusal to submit to Norman invaders, and the skirmishes he organised while trying to slow down their takeover. His reluctance to submit to the Norman rule led to the loss of his estates to William FitzOsbern, Earl of Hereford. He it was who built the first castle at Wigmore, an earth and timber affair replaced with one of stone in the 13th century. Before the Wars of the Roses, Wigmore was a flourishing little town sheltering under the former Mortimers' fortress. From this stronghold the lords of Wigmore conquered and for long periods overawed a large part of the Welsh marches. The steep, stony track leading passed St James' church to the grassy mound that is the last vestige of the castle gate, was once climbed by companies of knights and men-at-arms, and sometimes kings and queens, but the glory of this place ended centuries ago. A short distance across the vale from the castle lie the remains of an Augustinian abbey, another Mortimer foundation, now in private hands. Buried within the ruins of the abbey church, eleven lords of Wigmore – among them five holders of the title Earl of March – lie in forgotten tombs, and there the Mortimers and their turbulences are now mere dust under Wigmore grass.

Clearly visible from the southern approach, long before you reach Leintwardine, is the tall, gaunt tower of its church. Entry to the town is by a delightful five-arch bridge over the Teme which has just been joined by the River Clun, and the accumulated water broadens suddenly into a pool where Mallard and an occasional coracle enthusiast paddle around in dappled shade. Percy Thoresby Jones, again on bicycle, recalled an unexpected embarrassment:

> The first building beyond the bridge is the principal hotel, (the Lion), a pleasant place of low-ceilinged rooms. Once, its trim parlourmaid, pardonably doubtful of my solvency - I must have resembled a tramp cyclist - warned me that a plain tea was one shilling and sixpence!

Although the A4113 High Street in Leintwardine follows a similar line as Roman Watling Street, it is not the original route. That title goes to an insignificant lane running parallel to it down the centre of the old village where picturesque cottages line the narrow way on either side. The sign of the old Swan Inn still hangs over the door of one of them but there are no customers in the bar, nor have there been for forty years or more since it became a private house. Butchers, bakers, and candlestick makers have all come and gone, too. Between the two 'streets' is the previously espied tower belonging to yet another church of St Mary Magdalene, which was built on a section of the defensive ditch of Roman Branogenium, resulting in the chancel being raised above the level of the nave. The legionaries built the civilian settlement here around AD 160, but the cause for the duplication of the Roman road may rest on the final position of the settlement and whether the original line of Watling Street may have been diverted for some convenience of its eastern edge. The area around Leintwardine had been an important strategic centre between Deva (Chester) and Isca (Caerleon) for the Roman military for many years, and nearby military forts at Jay Lane, Buckton, and Brandon Hill serve as a reminder of the changes that needed to be made over time to maintain their hold on power locally and resist the constant attacks from Welsh tribesmen.

Having been joined by the Clun, the Teme now bends and winds its way in short shrift fashion towards one of its outstanding stretches. Downton Castle, a Grade I listed 18th century castellated country house, stands in a hilly and wooded picturesque landscape park laid out above a deep gorge. Richard Payne Knight, who along with Uvedale Price introduced the aesthetic ideals of the Picturesque movement, inherited Downton in 1772 and set about creating a new house on the site in a Gothic revival style. The building was completed six years later resembling a medieval castle with embattled parapets. Nikolaus Pevsner considered the finished article a semi-fortified house rather than a castle. Downton is now a private shooting estate, its steep valleys and high hills attracting parties from across the globe who enjoy exceptional facilities in spectacular surroundings. Sir Richard Colt Hoare arrived at Downton on June 2nd, 1798, as a guest of Payne Knight, and recognised the place had been justly celebrated by travellers for its picturesque situation and the taste shown by its owner in having laid out the grounds according to the true principles of nature:

> The house has great variety in its architecture. Built of a yellowish stone of good colour it has a round, square and octagon tower, a Gothic porch, Gothic and modern sash windows, all embattled. Of the interior apartments the most conspicuous is an elegant rotunda, used as a dining room, fitted up with niches supported by columns representing porphyry. In each niche is a bronze figure holding a light. The ceiling is ornamented with compartments. The whole room is very similar to the Pantheon in my garden at Stourhead and I have heard that the idea was taken from thence.

A section of the Herefordshire Trail long distance footpath passes near the castle as it follows the river between Castle Bridge and Bringewood House. I have walked this track myself, as Colt Hoare did during his stay. Much of what he saw is either no longer there or, more likely, hidden by over 200 years of tree growth:

> From the house I descended to a stone bridge over the Teme and entering a a narrow walk followed its left bank for a mile and a half till I came to a rude and picturesque wooden bridge thrown

across the river. On this spot the scenery is grand, pleasing and romantic. The rocks on the opposite bank are of a considerable height and perpendicular. The scene is animated by some picturesque cottages and a mill and a waterfall occasioned by a weir, where the water is penned up for the mill.

Town on the Dyke

From Leintwardine it is a matter of some three miles to Brampton Bryan and its pleasant village green, large groups of lime trees and pretty cottages, lying midway between Leintwardine and Knighton. Much of the village and surrounding parkland is still owned by the Harley family who have controlled the area since the Mortimers left in the early 14th century. The manorial home, Brampton Hall, was built to replace the old castle destroyed in the English Civil War in spite of Brilliana's stubborn defence. The new Hall stands alongside its ruined predecessor behind a great yew hedge. Daniel Defoe, almost contemporary with this episode, recorded that the castle may have remained necessarily inhabitable:

> Brampton is a stately pile, but not kept in full repair, the fate of that ancient family not permitting the rebuilding it as we were told was intended. Yet it is not far decay'd as Ludlow, nor is it abandoned, or like to be so, and the parks are still very fine and full of large timber.

Rising above the village, the hill called Coxall Knoll has been identified as a multiple enclosure Iron Age fort, that is, comprising an inner and one or more outer enclosed areas, and as such is rare in the marches. Beneath the substantial tree cover, its well preserved defences were designed to take full advantage of the natural steep slopes of the hilltop, and the enclosures are protected by a substantial ditch and bank system. The Knoll dominates the area in which there was plenty of early Roman activity. It faces the hill fort of Brandon Camp, some 3km (2 mi) across the river plain containing the sites of three further Roman camps from different times, at Jay Lane, Buckton, and Leintwardine. The battle to defeat the British chieftain, Caractacus, took place in AD 51, and according to Sir Richard Colt Hoare and Richard Fenton, here was proof enough where the scene of his tussle with Scapula was located:

> We ascended the steep hill called Coxwell (Coxall) Hill and there found a camp occupying the whole summit of the hill, fortified with a prodigious rampart and covered now with fine oaks. On the eastern side, the rampart much stronger and more filled with stones being the most accessible side and the one opposed to the enemy. At the foot of the hill, exactly corresponding with Tacitus's account, the Teme flowing by, and in several places very deep. In short, nothing can be more satisfactory than the site of both the camp and the course of the river to prove them the very places referred to by the Roman Historian in connection to the battle with Caractacus.

The area hereabouts is very hilly, and in the dips and valleys lie small hamlets, some of great age. Between Clun and Knighton is one with an inexplicable name, New Invention. It is made up of just four dwellings. one of which used to be the Stag's Head public house and all sit by a central crossroads. There have been many attempts at guessing the origins of the name, and that is all they have been – guesses. No historical explanation has ever been recorded. Stuart Mais found more strange village names hereabouts of a singular loveliness, some of which he pointed out had once been commemorated by E.V. Knox in *Punch* magazine, in these lines:

> *And oh! I'm filled with yearnings*
> *To tramp it down the slope*
> *That takes you passed Five Turnings*
> *And leads to Lurkenhope;*
> *Or, best of all, go roaming*
> *Beside the tiny beck*
> *To where it falls a-foaming.*
> *At Water-breaks-its-neck.*

But I cannot honestly claim to like Knighton, even though it was my childhood home when my father was curate there. Yet the approach to it from the north could scarcely be fuller of promise. Knighton stands grandly among the wooded hills of the Teme valley, and the temptation to explore this water by going further up the Teme was very nearly irresistible.

Like many border towns, Knighton is built on a hill. The main street climbs steeply, narrowing towards the top where the 12th century castle once stood. The castle's history was short, having had the unenviable distinction of being systematically knocked about, first by Llywelyn the Great in 1213, then by his grandson Llywelyn the Last in 1262, and finally by the serial town-wrecker, Owain Glyndŵr, in 1402. The town is the sixth largest in Powys and straddles a regular feature of this part of the English-Welsh border, the River Teme. While most of Knighton is in Wales, the railway station is over the border in the English county of Shropshire. It probably started life as an Anglo-Saxon settlement and later became a Norman fortified town. Its Welsh name, Tref-y-Clawdd, means 'town on the dyke', i.e Offa's Dyke that passes through the town.

The 11th century church is only one of two in Wales dedicated to St Edward, the patron saint of England before he was replaced by St George. There is a second castle here on the edge of town but there is confusion which one was built first. The town centre castle is probably the favourite, if only for where it is and the fact that the streets radiate from it, whereas Bryn, or Brian's Castle, sits above the river on a lower level. Its title seems to suggest a history of disputed ownership, perhaps after the town castle was left in ruins.

The 1840s and 1850s saw considerable railway building right across Great Britain, but the old county of Radnorshire had a small population and little industry. Knighton, then in Radnorshire, was deemed too remote from the centres of commerce and it seemed likely the railway revolution would pass it by, or at least fail to reach the town. It was down to local landowners and businessmen that progress was eventually made, and so the Knighton Railway Company was formed to build a line from the junction at Craven Arms in Shropshire. The connection was completed in March 1861 and trains continue to call here as part of the Heart of Wales service.

Market days in Knighton have been a major feature for centuries for farmers, butchers and stockmen of every kind. Instead of being tourist-conscious, the local people were farmer-conscious, concerned that rain might keep the visiting folk away. Each Tuesday, buses from outlying villages to'd and fro'd, unloading and uploading their passengers, the menfolk to look at sheep, and the women to eye up the merchandise on the stalls that perched on the edges of the streets around the clock tower. At the sheep market, black-faced Clun were packed in with the speckle-faced Kerrys. Shepherds and farmers greeted each other cheerfully, cracking jokes in Shropshire or Welsh tones. To most accustomed ears, the border accent sounded like rural English when men were speaking but Welsh when high-voiced women and children joined in. These people were themselves a special breed, more friendly than pure Welsh and English farmers. When the auctions began, they bid with palms raised. Sometimes a sheep escaped into the town, to be brought down with a flying tackle and either dragged back to the pen by the scruff of its wool or walked back pinned between a cowboy-like pair of legs. On Friday, it would all happen again with cattle.

Marchland writer, Cledwyn Hughes, began his border tour near Oswestry for his 1953 Regional Books contribution, *The Northern Marches*. We will meet him later as he moves about, sometimes with his home farm at Llansantffraid-Ym-Mechain as his starting point. He included parts of North Radnorshire on his agenda, which even then would be an imaginary line on his map somewhere south of Ludlow:

This is the southernmost point of my journey. I am on the borders of Herefordshire and Shropshire, land of orchards and gentle farms, of cider and daffodils and old men. After a stiff climb over the flank of Cwm Whitton Hill comes a long smooth descent to Knighton. Prosperous villas fringe the outskirts of the town, then after passing between rival inns, you must climb again towards one of those dreadful municipal clock towers, all made to one compulsive pattern of which so many Welsh towns possess a specimen - Hay, Rhayader, Machynlleth, Ruthin, to name a few. But a pause now, and then I must away again. Away to the Northern Marches of Wales. I think I shall travel next in summer. Cold winter is a time for crackling logs of the fallen apple tree, a time to read, to write and remember. Winter is no time to travel. It shall be sun for Montgomery and Ludlow, Church Stretton and Shrewsbury.

Two national trails meet and cross here at the top of the town. Glyndŵr's Way was granted National Trail status in 2000 to coincide with the beginning of the third millennium and the 600th anniversary of the long-running rebellion started in 1400 by the Welsh folk hero Owain Glyndŵr. The Offa's Dyke Path was officially opened In 1971 by Lord John Hunt, for a time resident at nearby Llanfair Waterdine – the same John Hunt who'd led the British Everest expedition of 1953 that culminated in Sir Edmund Hillary's successful ascent to the summit. In 1999, the Offa's Dyke Centre opened on West Street in Knighton to manage the whole route.

Between Wye and Severn

Alas, alas poor Radnorshire,
Never a park nor even a deer,
Never a squire of five hundred a year
Save Richard Fowler of Abbey Cwmhir.

Presteign (Llanandras) is the most charming of border towns, and having ready access to the Radnor Forest, the Deerfold Forest region, the middle valley of the Wye and the Shropshire highlands, is a useful strategic centre for the lover of varied scenery. Here, too, is a comfortable inn to go with all the charms – the Radnorshire Arms, a half-timbered genuine antique. The town sits on the south bank of the River Lugg, which forms the border as it passes the town, and at the corner of the three counties of Shropshire, Herefordshire and old Radnorshire, now Powys. After the Acts of Union in 1536, Presteigne was the county town of Radnorshire until the end of the 19th century, when its larger neighbour, Llandrindod Wells, usurped the role of administrative centre. However, Presteigne remained the venue for the assize courts until they were abolished in 1971. It is indeed a time-warp of a place but with a relaxed feel. Musty second-hand bookshops sit side by side with antique shops, old-fashioned greengroceries, and laid-back cafes. But, as if to pay a little homage to modernism, it has its own electrical white goods shop.

From the centre, Broad Street, running down to the Lugg is lined with numerous architecturally pleasing buildings, some whose previous residents warrant a blue plaque. At number 25, the Red House, Naval Officer Admiral Peter Puget lived from 1806 to 1812. In 1791, under the command of Captain George Vancouver, 2nd Lieutenant Puget was given the task of surveying the US Washington state coastline for the Northwest Passage. In recognition of his work, Vancouver named the southern stretch Puget Sound. By the oddest of coincidences, also resident in Presteigne was retired Royal Naval Officer Captain Joseph Baker. He, too, was stationed on Vancouver's 1791 Expedition, as Third Lieutenant. During this expedition, Baker became the first Englishman to recognise and map the second highest prominent volcano on the Washington skyline. Although the Spanish claimed to have first recorded it in 1790 and had named it Great Mount Carmel, Vancouver had recorded the sighting on April 30, 1792 and renamed the mountain Mount Baker.

Another high-profile building on Broad Street is the Judges Lodgings, an award-winning museum housed in Radnorshire's disused Shire Hall. The interior is a Victorian fossil, a judicial environment complete with living quarters, court room, and even the cells, re-created with original furnishings discovered in antiques warehouses and the occasional attic. It is clever theatre and has made it onto our TV screens at least twice in recent times, to the delight of presenting historians, Lucy Worsley and Simon Schama. On a visit in 2014, HRH Prince of Wales, appeared in the judge's dock in front of accompanying dignitaries. Presteigne's Town Council are rightly proud that this most appealing of small museums has been called 'the most remarkable survivor of all UK court buildings' and 'Britain's Best Hidden Gem'. However, there is a sad and desperate side to this story.

The most infamous case ever heard at the legal seat of Radnorshire in Presteigne was that of an uneducated seventeen-year-old, Mary Morgan, in 1805. Mary was charged with the murder of her newborn baby while serving as a servant girl at Maesllwch Castle near Glasbury, at the time the home of Walter Wilkins, MP and former High Sheriff of the county. The judge of the day was Justice George Hardinge, the senior justice of the Welsh counties of Breconshire, Glamorgan and Radnorshire since 1797. It would be no help for Mary's fate that Hardinge was known to be revolted by child murder. He called infanticides 'the vice of the poor' and would have felt genuine compassion for the baby she had allegedly killed. Illegitimate births were commonplace, but even so, and notwithstanding the rarity of the harsh sentence, Hardinge condemned Mary to hang.

Two gravestones erected in her memory stand in the shadow of St Andrew's Church expressing separate and contrasting sentiment. On one, Thomas Bruce, the Earl of Aylesbury and a friend of Hardinge's, praises a *'benevolent judge'* while denouncing Mary as *'a victim of sin and shame'*. On the other, a simple sermon, *'He that is without sin among you, let him first cast a stone at her.'* Hardinge remained at his post in Presteigne until his death in 1816, before when he may have had the time and certainly the opportunity to visit Mary's grave to reflect. There can be no doubt that he had been vehemently criticised for his harsh punishment, so could it be he may have been troubled eventually and found a need for some soul-searching?

St Andrew's medieval church at the bottom of Broad Street is a fine building, mainly of 14th and 15th century, but still containing Saxon and Norman remnants in its structure. Hanging on the north wall of the nave is its treasured Flemish tapestry, woven in 1510 and depicting Christ's entry into Jerusalem. It was donated to the church in 1737 and was used for over one hundred years as the altar piece. In *Exploring Radnorshire*, a 1964 entry for the Radnorshire Society Transactions,[31] local historian Ffransis Payne paid particular attention to the churchyard:

> It has an unchurchyard atmosphere. I don't know why, unless it is the effect of the weather because I have been here only on fine days. I find it hard to believe that people lie beneath the sunny surface. Indeed, there is something light-hearted about some of the grave inscriptions I noticed. I remember one referring to '*My death so suddenly and quick, Occasion'd by a horses kick.*'

But there is an altogether different epitaph on the stone relating to Mary Morgan:

> *To the Memory of Mary Morgan, who young and beautiful, endowed with a good understanding and disposition, but unenlightened by the sacred truths of Christianity became the victim of sin and shame and was condemned to an ignominious death on the 11th April 1805, for the Murder of her bastard Child. Rous'd to a first sense of guilt and remorse by the eloquent and humane exertions of her benevolent Judge, Mr Justice Hardinge, she underwent the Sentence of the Law on the following Thursday with unfeigned repentance and a furvent hope of forgiveness through the merits of a redeeming intercessor. This stone is erected not merely to perpetuate the remembrance of a departed penitent, but to remind the living of the frailty of human nature when unsupported by Religion.*

The spire of Kington Church has scarcely faded from sight when a sign by the wayside proclaims the boundary of Wales. There are many gates to Wales, and this one – through which so few strangers enter – is by no means the least beautiful. On one side of the narrow valley, the hulk of Hergest ridge terminating in Hanter

---

[31] Written originally in Welsh and translated for the Transactions of the Radnorshire Society by Dai Hawkins.

Hill is worthy of Wales in altitude, form and colouring. On the other, through the gap around Herrock Hill to the westward, bright strips of green meadows, musical with the babbling Riddings Brook and twinkling with the stir of alder leaves in the soft June wind, make a bewitching foreground to the blue masses of Great Creigiau and Whimble, of Fron Hill and Black Mixen that fill the distance. Bradley wrote that after climbing by an easy gradient over a moderate pass:

> Their path drops down out of the hills, and we find ourselves at the hamlet of Walton, looking out over the Vale of Radnor, beyond who's green and level floor the rolling solitudes of Radnor Forest for the whole length of the horizon from north to south fills the sky.

After staying the night at the Kings Head Hotel in Kington on May 24th, 1802, that he described as being 'remarkably clean', Sir Richard Colt Hoare rode to New Radnor to begin following in the footsteps of the campaigning monk, Gerald, his highly curious *Itinerary* through Wales, and to make a collection of drawings to illustrate it:

> The first place he mentions is Radnor, most probably Old Radnor. This morning I rode first to Old Radnor from Kington on the road to Rhayader and passed through a pretty valley; where the country begins to assume a mountainous appearance; hills rocky in parts and well wooded. New Radnor is situated at the foot of a hill. It was formerly surrounded on three sides by walls and guarded on the fourth, viz the north, by a castle built in a strong situation on an eminence.

Radnorshire ceased to be a county in 1974 having been swallowed up in a newly formed larger Welsh county of Powys. However, in 1989 the name Radnorshire was re-born as one of three new districts of Powys. The area covered by the old county is still one of the most sparsely populated regions south of the Scottish border. According to the 2011 census, the population was just 25,821. Little surprise then that the main employment in this vast semi-empty space is tourism and sheep farming. It has remained mostly English speaking because the fertile areas are situated along the border and always had the largest part of the sparse population. Visitors to the county will notice the prevalence of English place names, and the people have a pleasant detached outlook on life, as witnessed on a Radnorshire tombstone:

Him as was has gone from we
Us as is must go to he

Rich in remains from ancient times, the landscape abounds in Bronze Age circles, burial mounds and standing stones. There are ruins of castles practically everywhere you look, most of Norman origin. From the 11th century, this was the battle ground for marcher lords, often fighting among themselves for a piece of border land and power. Previously it was home territory of Welsh princes of Maelienydd and Elfael, but their efforts to regain lost ground had nothing more than nuisance value. All that would change by the end of the 12th century with the rise of the Llywelyn princes of Gwynedd. A little below the western lip of the much-quarried Old Radnor Hill, yet still at 260m (840ft), is its rocky hilltop community of Old Radnor, dominated by one of the most interesting churches in Wales. St Stephen's was built in the 15th century on a spur of volcanic rock, from which one looks across a green diamond of level pastures to the swelling bulk of the Radnor Forest. It has a fine perpendicular tower – a rarity in Wales - but its most impressive feature is the extraordinarily long rood screen separating the chancel and north and south aisle chapels from the nave. This is one of the finest screens in either Wales, or England, and it is claimed to be the work of the Gloucestershire Carvers, renowned for the excellence of their workmanship. In its original form, its grace and beauty were enhanced by being richly painted and gilded. Sadly, a 19th century restoration removed both paint and gilt. Maybe the result is better to our modern influenced eyes. In the chancel stands a linenfold crafted 16th century organ, thought to be the oldest in Britain. No-one knows exactly when it was made, but it is not stretching imagination too much to think that it was made *before* the dissolution of the monasteries. It is also interesting to note that one of the great early organists, John Bull, was born in Old Radnor in 1563, and must have practised, or been taught to play on this very organ. The font is claimed to be 8th century and seems to have been crudely fashioned from a massive block of stone – possibly the fifth monolith of a group near Knapp Farm in these parts and known now as the 'Four Stones'. All these extraordinary features have rightly contributed to the church's Grade I listing.

Before the Normans arrived in the vicinity, there was an older church here dedicated to a Welsh Celtic St Ystyffan. They mistakenly thought it to be Stephen, who they knew as a Christian martyr, and so the name stuck. When he arrived, H.J. Massingham was relieved to find that this church-on-the-hill was little changed:

> It was a heart-warming gratification to find the interior of the church one of the grandest in all the Marches, and I cannot in fact think of any to compare with it for bounty of beauty, variety of interest and harmony of proportion. It is not only extremely well kept, which is more than can be said of many. The tub-font alone is not only the biggest in Britain and pre-Norman but it looks like a sacrificial monolith hauled up out of the deeps of history. The screen stretching across the full length of the church is a glory to behold, but is part of a beauteous whole and not, as so often happens among the restored churches of the Marches, a bright jewel in a commonplace mounting.

The town of New Radnor (Maesyfed) was created in the 13th century to replace Old Radnor, though that may be more likely due to a geological than a military reason. It was a planned medieval walled town, with streets laid out in a grid pattern and was initially made the county town of Radnorshire. The first thing that greets you as you turn into the town from the A44 is a memorial of astronomical size commemorating the deeds of Victorian MP, Sir George Cornewall Lewis. Erected in 1864, it was designed by John Gibbs who was also responsible for Banbury Cross. Lucky old George must have been well thought of because he has another monument in the form of a statue outside the Shire Hall in Hereford. The 21m (77ft) high Gothic carved stone monument at New Radnor is Grade II listed and appeared as a promise of great things to come as you entered the town. However, the vision never quite materialised. The A44 highway eventually became a by-pass and when they arrived, trains stopped short of the town at an end-of-line minor halt, now a caravan site. In the 2001 census, the community had a population of 410, split evenly between male and female. Until March 2015, it also had a pub – the Radnor Arms – but after twenty-five years of neglect, the owners were served with a closure order. Since then, there has been an ongoing community effort to persuade the absentee landlord either to restore the ailing building or sell it to someone who might. At the time of writing (2018), there has been no new developments, so presumably the battle of New Radnor goes on.

In an area where many castles were built by Norman lords as part of a multi-defensive system against Welsh attacks, New Radnor's always seemed to be particularly vulnerable and was sacked many times before Glyndŵr, in his usual fashion, destroyed it completely in 1402. It was rebuilt again later in the 15th century and was described as square with massive towers, a fitting bastion for a county town. During the civil war, Parliamentary forces finally sealed its fate when they dismantled it to prevent it falling into Royalist hands. Today, only the earthworks remain. As befits the fate of many castle ruins, the stonework became a ready supply to the local people for their homes and farms. Henry Wyndham wrote that New Radnor was a wretched and miserable place, with as ill-conditioned an inn as any traveller would have wished to avoid:

> Its poverty is so remarkable that it cannot maintain a barber! From Radnor we rode through stony and miry lanes, sometimes crossing the hills, and sometimes traversing the little valleys which indeed rarely surprise the impatient traveller in this disagreeable part of the tour, till we arrived at the extreme brow of this bleak and uncomfortable county. From hence we began to view and

enjoy the beautiful prospect which arose before us in an assemblage of woods, meadows, and cornfields on each side of the Wye.

Thomas Roscoe agreed when he wrote in 1836:

It may perhaps appear to be correct that proper respect be paid to the county town of New Radnor, which is however but a mean, squalid looking place, though in the far distance times of much greater importance, having been enclosed by a wall with four Roman gates, bearing some resemblance with those at Caerleon and Caerwent.

The view from the castle tump of the vale of Radnor, the rich farming country towards Presteigne, the flat-topped summit of Great Rhos and the great cleft of Harley Dingle, was all quite beautiful and worthy of any rambler's attention. However, a word of warning. Although there are rights of way in the Radnor Forest, some are on a Ministry of Defence firing range, and the signs 'RIFLE RANGE KEEP OUT' and 'DANGER LIVE FIRING WHEN RED FLAGS ARE HOISTED' ought to deter foolhardy walkers when it matters.

On the other hand, the 10km (6mi) drive along the A44 from New Radnor to Penybont is even more spectacular. Surrounded initially by the highest of the Radnor Forest hills on one side and the slightly isolated Fron Goch on the other, the view opens out dramatically across to the jagged tops of the Llandegley Rocks and the fort-like humps of Bwlch-y-Cefn bank. Located on a hilltop beside the highway fronting this dramatic scene, the grassy remains of Crugerydd Castle emphasises its position was likely intended to block the mountain pass into the ancient Welsh kingdom of Maelienydd. Here, on 4th March 1188, Gerald of Wales and Archbishop Baldwin met with Lord Rhys ap Gruffydd and stayed for two nights, recording but few additions to the conversion rates. Their destination was St David's in Pembrokeshire, so on Monday the 7th, Gerald and Baldwin travelled south east to Hay on Wye, where their accommodation was Hay Castle. Crugerydd Castle was destroyed in 1403, another victim of Owain Glyndŵr, adding more material damage in Rhwng Gwy a Hafren, between Wye and Severn, than all the plunderers of the ages put together.

The whole western side of Radnorshire, and a great deal more besides, lies spread beneath a beautiful confusion of outstanding hills, with their slopes of cloud-flecked greenness and summits wrought into fantastic shapes by the Silurian rocks that give such character to this Mid-Wales landscape. Ffransis Payne described its dramatic effect in *Exploring Radnorshire:*

> Here is the loneliest and highest land in the county. This is a district of prominent hill slopes covered with bracken and gorse and of long, bare slopes of peat and heather rising more than 600 m (2,000ft) above sea level. This mountain country appears like a windy island in the middle of the green of the surrounding valleys.

In these mostly uninhabited uplands of the upper Edw valley is the remote village of Glascwm. It is an area of scattered farms and dwellings, but even so, Leland found his way here in the mid-16th century and wrote "Glascumbe, where is a chirche but few houses". But he also told us that Glascwm lay on an important drovers' road through central Wales which functioned during the post-medieval era. St David's Church consists of a 13th century nave and a 15th century chancel and was built on an earlier monastic foundation said to be connected to St David himself. Francis Kilvert called here to see the Vicar one day in 1871:

> First, I went to the vicarage. A pair of shears lay on the doorstep and a beautiful, luxuriant, sweet briar climbed a trellis by the door and filled the whole porch with fragrance. I met the old Vicar in the hall with his stout frame, ruddy face, white hair, seen long sweeping eyebrows and a merry odd twinkle in his eye. One of the last of the old-fashioned parsons. He gave me some splendid Herefordshire cider and some bread and butter. 'I am Bishop here,' said the Vicar. Then fetching the church key, he added, 'Come and see my Cathedral.'

Formerly Llandegla, the inconspicuous village of Llandegley derives its name from the church of St Tecla. The saint was known for her kindness to sufferers from a form of epilepsy, although it is not known whether that was in her lifetime or as a result of praying to her memory. The reader may remember her name has connections with Chapel Rock, just off Beachley in the Severn estuary. But Llandegley is on the map for a very different reason. In 2002 Nicholas Whitehead conjured up the idea for the mother of all pranks when visiting friends in the village and noticed that the roadside advertising sign was vacant. He paid for the sign to read 'LLANDEGLEY INTERNATIONAL AIRPORT' and the rest, as they might say, has been fun. The sign attracted interest from around the world, including its own Facebook and Twitter fan clubs. There has even been extra emphasis on a story of two planes landing and taking off from a local field during the war, giving the whole thing a strange credibility and everlasting puzzlement. Not many aircraft now over Llandegley skies but there have been many buses running through the village, and Stuart Mais arrived on one of them during his tour of the borders in the spring of 1937:

> At Llandegley I got off the bus. It is a tiny grey hamlet with a little stone church which was, after the manner of all churches in Wales, locked. There was no shop and no chance of getting any refreshment. There was once sulphur springs here, but I didn't want a sulphur spring. The bus driver had said there was a good eight-mile walk over the moors to Llandrindod.

The Happiest Town in Wales

The first signs of life in the area around Llandrindod Wells were Roman ones. The advancing army of the Second Augustan Legion arrived around AD 70 and set up a military base, Castell Collen, on a spur of land above the River Ithon within a mile of the eventual site of the modern town of Llandrindod, known affectionately to the locals as Llandod. The Romans built a vicus

– a village – around their fort, from which a civilian population serviced the garrison's needs, an early indication that a large town might develop. That it didn't happen in that place is probably due to the restrictions of the land within the curve of the river where the fort was built. By AD 330 the Romans had moved on and no others moved in to take their place, so the area remained relatively uninhabited for another 12 centuries.

Llandrindod's saline and sulphur springs were first uncovered in the 16th century but it was the prestigious Vaughan family of Herefordshire who came here in 1696 to 'take the waters' and were followed by more of their contemporaries thereafter. The wells were discovered on a bleak common in what was the village of Old Llandrindod, but in the early days and into the 18th century, there were few comforts for visitors. In 1732 a certain Mrs Jenkins, a local farm tenant, began to sell water to travellers who sought their healing properties from wells on her farm. That farm was later to become the Pump House Hotel, the nucleus of Llandrindod Wells as a major spa town. Meanwhile, at Old Llandrindod, accommodation was provided at farmhouses and farm cottages dotted around the common and at the wayside Llanerch Inn on the main road from Newtown (now the A483), though facilities were primitive. One of the more frequented farmhouses was eventually turned into the resort's first ever hotel by the owner, a Mr Grosvenor, which by all accounts became fashionable with its excellent accommodation and entertainments. Grosvenor's hotel was enlarged in 1749 and renamed Llandrindod Hall. But it was Dr Wessel Linden who, in 1756, wrote a scientific paper on the medicinal effects of the waters that brought the benefits to the attention of the wider world. Consequently, Llandrindod Hall's attraction increased. It became the centre of revelry and extravagant living for more than thirty years and was very much part of the 18th century spa and cultural scene. At its height, it had one hundred beds and the great hall could accommodate a thousand dancers, apparently not near enough for the vast numbers who visited.

Towards the end of the 17th century, the new town was sporting two groups of mineral springs – the original saline and sulphur springs investigated by Dr Linden based at the Pump House; and the chalybeate rock springs on the Rock Park estate. Both were attracting more and more visitors, and by 1790 had effectively replaced the old facilities at Llandrindod Hall. The introduction of more hotels and the rise in the number of private residences ready to accommodate vast numbers of tourists, was too much. Llandrindod Hall's bubble had burst and, no longer answering the expectations of the owner, it was converted back into a farmhouse.

During the prosperous years of the 19th century, many of the new buildings in Llandrindod (by now with the added Wells in the title) were of quality and distinctive brickwork. There was a major programme of hotel construction carried out to cope with demand for rooms. The Metropole was built in 1870, the Gwalia (now a training skills centre of Powys Council) in 1900, and the Ye Wells Hotel in 1906 (now part of the campus of the NPTC Group of Colleges). Consequently, the town had taken on a unique Victorian Spa aura. It was being described as the queen of the Well towns of Wales and one which competed with the fashionable English Spa Centres of Bath and Buxton.

However, after 1970 the concept of the Spa lost credibility and a spiral of decline ensued. The National Health Service became the main financier of hospitals and medical establishment and withdrawal of long-term local authority investment was a major factor. Llandrindod's spa infrastructures became decayed and less relevant. In 1972 a new physiotherapy unit was opened in the town's hospital and the Rock Park centre closed. The Pump House Hotel was purchased for Powys County Council Headquarters and by 1978 Llandrindod's spa treatments had ceased. After 200 years, the party was over.

The National Cycle Collection of Wales is here in Llandrindod – a fine collection of bicycles through the ages — established in 1997. It contains around 250 bicycles from the years 1818 to 2005, including a large collection of penny farthings, solid-tyred safety bicycles and the earliest velocipedes to interest the likes of Fletcher Moss, Percy Thoresby Jones, Arthur Bradley and others of the age. Among those was Tom Norton. Born in Newtown in 1870, he was a keen cyclist from an early age and regularly rode the 43km (27mi) to Llandrindod. He became influenced by the impressive buildings going up in the increasingly fashionable town. In 1898 he opened up a cycle centre in the High Street and became one of the first agents for the Raleigh company. When he outgrew his business there, he bought a new site on Spa Road and replaced the existing facility with the present art deco-style building that became known as The Automobile Palace. It was given Grade II listing in 1985 as an exceptionally early grid-pattern, steel-framed building, surviving largely unaltered.

Unlike many heavy industrial towns where dead hearts were ripped out in order to rebuild new life, Llandrindod had something good to show for its dabble with chalybeate springs. In *Exploring Radnorshire,* Ffransis Payne wrote:

> This must be the cleanest town in Wales. I don't know of any other town where the yellow bricks stay so yellow. There is neither dust nor smoke, and the air is like wine. Here you have houses between gardens and trees, and the green of the town is more obvious than the red of the bricks that there is so much talk about.

Bradley saw something new happening and gave his approval, albeit a mild one:

> Even before it boomed some ten years ago[32], Llandrindod was no dream of brick or stone. There was no nucleus of any old village or town to spoil. I am not going to criticize the architecture of the red brick villas that have sprung up by the score on these heathlands within recent memory, nor wax sentimental because I can remember the gorse blooming where many rows of them now stand.

However, the town doesn't appeal visually to everybody. Mike Parker described it in *Real Powys* as pure hallucination:

---

[32] A G Bradley's *Highways and Byways of South Wales* was published in 1903 but was likely to have been prepared well before then, in the late years of the 19th century

Coming off the A4801 from the A470, it suddenly looms across the fields like a mirage, a fake film set of redbrick suburbia and Victorian turrets.

Llandrindod is a nice town but I can see where Mr Parker is coming from. It is not a Welsh-looking town. Parts of it remind me of childhood holidays at Lytham St Annes on the Lancashire coast, where the streets were lined with elegant red-brick houses and I expected to find the sea around every corner. A recent survey in the somewhat obscure 'Happy at Home Index' identified Llandrindod Wells as the happiest place to live in Wales and 12th in the whole of Britain. No matter the source, the people of Llandrinod won't argue with that discovery.

Perched along a high, narrow ridge in a loop of the Ithon river east of Llandrindod, the imposing site of Cefnllys Castle is really two castles in one. At its northern end, Ralph Mortimer – aided by his young son, Roger – built the first castle around 1240. It was badly damaged in 1262 by the forces of Llywelyn ap Gruffydd (Llywelyn the Last), so Mortimer thought a new castle would be better defended at the opposite end of the ridge to the south east. This second castle, built in 1267, lasted over a hundred years, during which time a small community grew in the river plain alongside St Michael's Church. It did not, however, escape the ravages of Owain Glyndwr's revolt, and the formidable castle was attacked and burned in 1406. By the late 16th century Cefnllys was a ruin, and today there is little left of Mortimer's fortress. St Michael's stands alone now in its remote setting close to the river. In 1893 the rector of Llandrindod had the roof removed to persuade the parishioners to attend a new church in the town, but his move was unsuccessful; they refused to abandon their old church, so he had to put the roof back. The building was restored in 1895, though is still basically a medieval structure, and the 15th century screen, without doubt its most interesting feature, has survived abandonment and having no roof above it for two years.

A few miles west of the Crossgates junction, in a secluded valley of the Clywedog Brook, are the Grade II ruins of Abbey Cwmhir. This former religious house is another alleged burial place of Llywelyn ap Gruffydd (Llywelyn the Last), but with the presence of a burial slab at what is presumably the altar end, is certainly the most believed. The abbey was built here in 1143 amid a secluded amphitheatre of Cambrian hills – a typical isolation calculated to inspire devotional thoughts — on the instructions of the Prince of Maelienydd, Cadwallon ap Madog. It was enlarged in 1176 to accommodate sixty Cistercian monks and, encouraged by Llywelyn ap Iowerth (Llywelyn the Great) in the early part of the 13th century, there was a plan to extend again to become the largest Cistercian abbey church in Britain. When Llywelyn died in 1240, work did not continue and a visit from Owain Glyndŵr and his demolition gang in 1403 ended any future for the project.

One of Llywelyn ap Gruffydd's lifetime achievements, though short-lived, was Dolforwyn Castle and townlet which he built high above the Severn bank in 1273. It is a fine example of Welsh castle design, fairly primitive in its concept as opposed to those built by the English during their conquests of Wales. Llywelyn's aim to become the supreme Welsh leader were in the ascendency but his mistake was to test the English King, Edward I, by building his castle here, practically within sight of the castle at Montgomery. Despite his efforts, the last castle ever to be built by a Welsh prince lasted barely five years before it was sacked and handed to Roger Mortimer. A steep, stony track winds its way up to the battlements high above the River Severn where, in the imagination, Edward's Royal Standard can be just seen peeking over the eastern horizon atop the bastion of Montgomery. What was left of Dolforwyn remained in limited use for the next 100 years, although it was not kept in good shape, and by 1398 was in ruins. You can still see several grass-covered platforms before the old castle entrance, where half-timbered and thatched houses once stood, but abandoned in 1277. As if in some way in tribute to Llywelyn, Mortimer rebuilt the settlement outside Dolforwyn's walls a little further down the valley and is now known as Newtown.

Newtown: Made with Flannels

In 1774, Henry Penruddocke Wyndham appears to have taken the road now the A489 over Brimmon Hill to Newtown. From this high point, about 300m (985ft), the vista is spread out across the Severn Valley:

> Our road led us over a hill from Montgomery to a beautiful valley, which was enriched with the Severn meadows and pastures, and bounded on each side of the river with moderate hills generally mantled with woods. The houses in this country are generally framed with timber, and the intermediate parts are secured against the inclemencies of the weather with laths and plaister. Newtown is built in this manner, which, in other respects is a neat and agreeable town situated on the banks of the Severn at the extremity of the valley before described.

Roger Mortimer's 13th century New Town grew steadily as a medieval border market town but more rapidly from the 18th century when a cloth industry developed with wool from the sheep walks of the Kerry Hills. Newtown became a principal cloth manufacturing centre with eighteen flannel mills, six shawl mills, and five tweed mills. It is believed that cloth making had been in existence in the march lands since Saxon times and in the 14th century, Flemish weavers, renowned for their expertise with wool were introduced by Edward III. They settled initially in the far south-west of Wales and gradually moved inland towards the borders where there was a regular source of materials. By the 15th century Montgomeryshire wool was recognised as the best in Europe. However, before long the drapers of the marches' region were having problems with French merchants buying up the local cloth stocks and shipping them back to France.

According to the Welsh Assembly Government's Agricultural and Rural Affairs Department, the higher altitude, heavier rainfall and poor soil quality mean that 80% of agricultural land in Wales is considered low grade. While this makes the land unsuitable for arable crops, the conditions provide perfect grazing land for sheep. As much of Powys falls into this category, it is not surprising that the county was the most important centre of the Welsh woven textile industry, and Newtown took full advantage. In 1859 a local man, Pryce Pryce-Jones, started a drapery mail order business – the first mail order business of any kind. The success of the business called for larger premises, so in 1879 he built the iconic red-brick building, the Royal Welsh Warehouse, that still dominates the town. Pryce-Jones is credited with the invention of the sleeping bag, patented under the name of the Euklisia Bag. At the time it looked less like a bag – more a folded rug – but the Russian Army, who bought sixty thousand of them, would have been extremely grateful for the invention. By 1887 Pryce-Jones had in excess of one hundred thousand customers and his success was acknowledged by Queen Victoria with a knighthood. At the end of the 19th century, the cost of transporting finished goods out and of bringing coal supplies in, led eventually to the loss of trade to the mills of Lancashire and Yorkshire. It is befitting of the man that the warehouse where he made his mark has been preserved and remains part of the Newtown landscape.

Newtown old hall which used to be in the park near the centre of town, was once home to Pryces – no relation to the bag maker, but a race of controlling squires who's humbler neighbours had learnt to understand the moments of submission and acceptance. This family, which had supplied seven sheriffs of Montgomeryshire and was for long prominent in the affairs of the county, claimed lineal descent from one of the five royal tribes of Wales, as compiled by 15th century bards. Some of them were also inclined to be eccentrics and squanderers. While at Newtown, Thomas Pennant wrote of the 5th Baronet, Sir John Pryce, being a gentleman of worth, but of strange peculiarities. He had married three wives and kept the first two who died in his room, embalmed and laid out – one on each side of his bed. The third wife declined the honour of his hand until her defunct rivals were committed to their proper place. When she died, Pryce decided to call on a local miracle worker, one Bridget Bostock, who healed all diseases by prayer, faith, and embrocation of spittle. Multitudes resorted to her from all parts and kept her salivary glands in full employ. Sir John, with a high spirit of enthusiasm, wrote to the woman in 1748 to ask her to visit the hall to restore his third and favourite wife. His letter will best explain the foundation on which he built his strange hope and very uncommon request.

Madam

Having received information by repeated advices, both public and private, that you have of late performed many wonderful cures, even where the best physicians have failed, and that the means used appear to be very inadequate to the effects produced,

I cannot but look upon you as an extraordinary and highly favoured person. And why may not the same most merciful God, who enables you to restore sight to the blind, learning to the deaf, and strength to the lame, also enable you to raise the dead to life! Now, having lately lost a wife, whom I most tenderly loved, my children an excellent step-mother, and our acquaintances a very dear and valuable friend, you will lay us all under the highest obligations, and earnestly entreat you, for God Almighty's sake, that you will put up your petitions to the

Throne of Grace on our behalf, that the deceased may be restored to us, and the late Dame Eleanor Pryce be raised from the dead.

If your personal attendance appears to you to be necessary, I will send my coach and six, with proper servants, to wait on you hither, whenever you please to appoint. Recompense of any kind that you could propose would be made with the utmost gratitude, but I wish the bare mention of it is not offensive to both God and you.

   I am, Madam
      Your most obedient, and very
         much afflicted humble servant
            JOHN PRICE

The 6th Baronet continued the process of squandering the estates and died in 1776 in a debtors' prison. The title and the family became extinct when *his* son, the heirless 7th baronet was found dead on 28th June 1791 in a field near Pangbourne in Berkshire. It was assumed that death was due to the effects of destitution.

Newtown's most famous son is without doubt Robert Owen. He was born in a draper's shop in 1771 and is best known for his efforts to improve the working conditions of factory workers, particularly in the mills of Manchester, and his later attempts to create communities where unemployment and poverty would be abolished. He famously established a factory village in Scotland which he called New Lanark and tried a similar experiment in America calling that New Harmony. It was his socialist theories which led to the setting up of the Co-operative Movement and its first shop in Rochdale in 1844. Towards the end of his life, Owen returned to Newtown a sick man and died while in residence at The Bear Inn in 1858. His altar tomb surrounded by magnificently decorated iron railings lies in the churchyard beside the ruins of St Mary's on the banks of the Severn. However, this wasn't his original resting place. Long after his internment in a simple grave close to that of his parents, Owen's friend and fellow reformer George Holyoake discovered it, neglected and in a state of decay, and used his influence with the Co-operative Movement to construct a memorial more suitable for a personage of his singular success.

St Mary's was built in the 13th century with a fine carved wooden rood screen erected between chancel and nave, more work of the Newtown School. But the church was badly sited and subject to constant flooding which eventually led to its decline and eventual abandonment in 1856. The carved screen was removed and installed in a new church dedicated to St David, erected on higher ground in the town. In the meantime, steps had also to be taken to preserve and protect the burial site of the Pryce family of Newtown Hall, whose mausoleum stands in the open nave of St Mary's in the form of a small house. It was erected by one of their descendants one year before Holyoake's tribute to Robert Owen. The building of St David's church wasn't a great success and was itself subject to constant repairs and alterations. By 2006 the problems with its infrastructure proved

Figure 11 The remarkable Gregynog Hall, Powys

insurmountable, so the parish of Newtown merged with the neighbouring parish of Llanllwchaiarn. The much-travelled rood screen, or what was left of it, is now in its third home in their church, north of the river.

Strategically, the small town of Caersws in mid-Wales was the furthest west any invading Roman force could get before meeting the natural barriers of the Cambrian Mountains. Beyond here, the upland roads become hedgeless and the landscape turns to scrub of gorse and bracken. And there on the high Pumlumon plateau, Wye and Severn – the two greatest rivers of the marches – are born. The Severn is the longest river in Britain, a trickle and noisy brook, eager and fast in the beginning, but at the end the great slumbering waterway to the Bristol Channel. During Glyndŵr's rebellion, Henry IV with an English force followed him beyond Newtown through the Severn valley towards Glyndŵr's capital at Machynlleth. At the time, the mountainous terrain hindered the king's men. Constant rain sweeping across Pumlumon was not the best preparation for war, especially against a master tactician ready to make the most of the local conditions. Bad weather was what Henry had come to expect of Wales. Author Jan Morris agrees with him and paints an appropriate picture in *The Matter of Wales:*

> The drizzle seems never likely to stop, the mountains look permanently concealed in mist, the sea is grey and queasy, the towns damp and dingy - you can bet your life it's early closing day. The sheep in the field out there are huddled miserably against the wind. The river roars sullenly beyond the wood. Nothing, one feels, is ever going to change, or even perhaps to happen.

In a hidden valley, seven miles north of Newtown, Gregynog Hall is a house of ancient origin, set within a National Nature Reserve, and has a surprise Victorian face. At first glance, the house appears as a magnificent Tudor mansion of black and white timber. The 'surprise' is that what you see is a concrete-cladded facade over a very old brick structure. It was to this place that Thomas Pennant came in 1776:

> We reached Gregynog, the seat of Arthur Blayney esq, whose hospitality I experienced for two or three days. Under his conduct I saw everything in the neighbourhood which merited attention. This very worthy owner is descended from Brochwel Yscythrog, Prince of the House of Powys.

Arthur Blayney's garden was designed by William Emes, who had already worked on the estate gardens of Powis, Chirk, and Erddig – the home of Blayney's friend Philip Yorke. The gardens at Gregynog have been given Grade I status, however, Emes' masterpiece here is the Great Wood, a Site of Special Scentific Interest, where some of the oak trees are three hundred years old. Arthur had no children and was the last Blayney to live at Gregynog, so after his death the estate passed to Viscount Lacy, husband of Arthur's cousin, and in turn to their daughter Henrietta who had married into the Hanbury family – renowned iron masters of Pontypool. It was Charles Hanbury-Tracy who decided in 1840 to rebuild Gregynog and encase the whole exterior of the house, along with many others on the estate, in painted concrete to replicate the black and white timber-framed architecture.

In 1920 the estate was bought by Gwendoline and Margaret Davies who, over the next twenty years, put their own romantic stamp on the gardens. These two remarkable sisters had inherited substantial wealth from their grandfather, the Victorian industrial entrepreneur, David Davies. Being aware of the debt they owed to Welsh labourers who had helped the Davies family build their businesses and make their fortune, the sisters contributed generously to good causes in return. They established Gregynog as a centre of excellence for the arts and crafts with which they hoped to enrich the lives of the people of Wales. It became famous for music festivals, the printing of high-quality books and the sisters' art collections, which they bequeathed to the nation that can now be seen in the National Museum of Wales in Cardiff. In 1960 the surviving sister, Margaret, gifted Gregynog to the University of Wales, and from that time the hall has hosted seminars, conferences and summer schools with a wide range of academic disciplines. At its height, Gregynog could call on the services of up to twenty-six gardeners for year-round care. Nowadays, under the ownership of the University of Wales, these magnificent grounds are maintained by a team of just three.

A dozen miles or so north west is Llanfyllin, in the valley of the River Cain. It is a pleasant market town with an 18th century Grade II listed bridge, and not far from it – as if in a curious biblical reunion – the Cain is joined by the Abel. Formed at the confluence of the Nant Alan and Nant Fyllon, itself a collecting pot for several other streams falling from the surrounding hills, the Cain will become the River Vyrnwy at Llansantffraid-ym-Mechain which then merges with the mighty Severn at Crewgreen on the Shropshire Border. A few miles westwards of Llanfylin is Llyn Efyrnwy, Lake Vyrnwy – a man-made water basin built in 1860 to supply the people of Liverpool and surrounding areas with their drinking water 109km (68mi) away. It is fed from over 300 streams and brooks and is Severn Trent's largest reservoir. At the head of the lake is the impressive Rhiwargor waterfall but the River Vyrnwy now starts from the base of the reservoir's dam and flows east into England. To create the lake, the whole valley was flooded, including the village of Llanwddyn. In real terms that added up to 37 houses, 10 farmhouses, 3 pubs, 2 chapels, a church and Eunant Hall owned by Sir Edmund Buckley, MP for Newcastle under Lyme. All were either demolished, or abandoned and submerged. To their undeserved credit, Liverpool Corporation built a new village of Llanwddyn further down the valley beyond the dam for the living and reburied their dead in a new churchyard. A twelve-mile drive around the lake in early May was a big disappointment. Apart from the occasional break in the lakeside tree cover, I saw nothing much of a view worthy of a photograph. No doubt the best views will be from the surface of the lake itself. At least Bradley thought so:

> It is in the intervals of a day's fishing, when out on the broad bosom of the lake, that you best take in both the beauty and romance of the place. Then is the time, after straining your eyes for an hour or so at where you know your flies to be among the dancing ripples, to lie back and rest them on the silent crags towering to the sky, on the emerald turf fresh with mountain mists and warmed by the suns of May that sweep upwards to their feet. The middle heights, too, are all ablaze with golden gorse and sprinkled thick with feathery birch trees. From the straggling woods of primitive oaks, hoary with trailing moss and waist-deep in bracken that dip here and there to the water, comes at such times the note of the cuckoo, full and clear.... But perhaps after all it is at sunset, when the day's work is over and the breeze is dead, and we are stealing slowly homeward down the lake, that the spell of its strange association is strongest.

Red Castle by a Welsh Pool

William Emes' great oak wood at Gregynog grew to fill the land between the draining waters of the Bechan Brook, which adds itself to the Severn as it flows north below the two great Welsh strongholds of Dolforwyn and Castell Coch, Powis Castle. Here is a bustling market town located by the Severn just 6km (4m) beyond the border and surrounded by the rolling hills of Montgomeryshire and the glorious unspoiled hilly countryside of Mid Wales. Welshpool has been called the most English town in Wales, but when Sir Richard Colt Hoare first arrived in 1799, it was still in the early stages of development:

> The town consists of one long broad street with houses of brick. A new town hall of handsome proportions is now being built. It is advantageously situated for trade being a short distance from the Severn and close to a canal.

Later, in 1836 Thomas Roscoe considered the town had become the most spacious and important of the towns of Montgomeryshire. He judged that the spoken language and the manners of the people were almost certainly English. The origin of the town's English name is said to come from the murky waters of the Black Pool, a small lake in Powis Castle park. The town's Welsh language name, Y Trallwng, literally means 'the marshy or sinking land'. Initially known as Pool, the name was changed to Welshpool in 1835 to distinguish it from the Dorset town of Poole. However, the old name still exists a short instance north along the A483 in the riverside village of Pool Quay, after the wharf where small boats from Bristol carrying merchandise could moor at a time when the Severn was navigable to this point. Sandwiched between the town's access roads and the railway line, and surrounded by trees, is a motte and bailey, Welshpool's first castle. For all the approach of modern developments on all sides, the old castle mound has remained largely intact and undisturbed for almost 900 years. The bailey is occupied today by a bowling green – a place of more sedate confrontations.

Welshpool's 16th century Grade 1 listed church of St Mary occupies an imposing site above the centre of the old town. An earlier church was built in about 1250 part of which survives in the lower courses of the tower. Roscoe reported that the church possessed a golden chalice which had been gifted to the parish in 1662 by Thomas Davies, a local man and previously an agent of the East India Company. He had worked briefly on the West African coast and was apparently so relieved to have survived the experience, he considered the amount of gratitude he felt warranted the expense of the chalice which had been made from the purest Guinea gold plate. So grateful, that he decided to pay whatever undisclosed price for one of only five gold chalices ever to have been made before the 19th century. Gratitude indeed! Davies was at his African station for only one year and though it is not known from what mishap he had felt deliverance, it is likely to have been disease which he may have seen as being rife among the natives and caught himself, yet somehow lived. The chalice survives in the security of the National Museum of Wales in Cardiff on permanent loan.

Beside the church steps is Grace Evan's Cottage, named after a maid of Lady Winifred Herbert, a daughter of the 1st Marquess of Powis who took part in a remarkable and daring rescue of Lady Herbert's husband, Lord Nithsdale – a Jacobite supporter – from imprisonment in the tower of London in 1716. On the eve of his execution, Lady Winifred persuaded the guards to let her and Grace visit him in his cell where they dressed him in a woman's clothing and smuggled him out. The 'dress' became known as the Nithsdale Cloak, still kept at Traquair House in Scotland. While the Nithsdales escaped to join the Stuarts biding their time in Rome, Grace made it back to Welshpool where she was given the cottage to live in as a reward for her bravery and dedication to duty.

The local economy of Welshpool today is primarily based upon agriculture. Livestock sales have been held in the town since 1263. In 2009 a new Livestock Centre was opened on the outskirts of Welshpool, capable of holding 1200 cattle and 15,000 sheep. This huge complex is now home not only to the main auction outlet for livestock in Mid Wales and the borders but is recognised as the largest prime lamb market in Western Europe. Still with its platform beside the bypass road, the architecturally pleasing old railway station was built in 1860 by the Oswestry and Newtown

Railway Company and later became the headquarters of Cambrian Railways. The old station closed in 1992 and is used now as a clothing retail store and restaurant. The railway line is now on the opposite side of the by-pass, leaving the occasional commuter left confused on the wrong side of the tracks, unaware of the change of use for the previous station building.

The Montgomery Canal, the 'Monty' – these days a leisure feature of the local area – passes through the town centre. Built over 300 years ago by local landowners as a means of transporting lime around the county to help improve their soil for better productivity, its presence became very convenient for moving wool to the town's flannel factories. Towards the end of the 18th century, Thomas Pennant recorded that:

> Flannels, both coarse and fine, are brought every other Monday (except when fairs intervene) to Welsh Pool; and are chiefly consumed in England, to the amount of about 7 or 800,000 yards. The Shrewsbury drapers go every market to Welsh Pool, for the sake of this commerce.

When this activity became less profitable, its popularity and use declined. Essential repairs were no longer carried out and the canal was left too long for any recovery and so was abandoned. In 1969 the forgotten canal bed was threatened by moves to construct a new bypass for the A483. In some places the canal had already been filled in or built over and bridges lowered to road level. In a desperate bid to preserve it, partial restoration has been carried out where possible, and there are now ongoing plans to restore the whole canal as far as Ellesmere in north Shropshire.

Without doubt, the star attraction of Welshpool is Powis Castle, also known as Castell Coch, the Red Castle, formerly the seat of the Earls of Powis. The medieval fortress, built with stone of bright red hue, hence its reference to that distinctive colouring, has dominated the landscape from a high, steep-sided, narrow ridge above the town for seven hundred years. It was never captured by any marcher lord. In the mid-13th century Gruffudd ap Gwenwynwyn, the prince of Powis and builder of the earliest first with the English crown, then with Llywelyn of Gwynedd, in an attempt to retain his lordship. In 1274 Llywelyn turned against him, drove him into exile and destroyed his castle. But in 1277 Gruffudd returned with the support of Edward 1 and was restored as ruler of Powys. He and his successors re-built Powis Castle and held it for over three hundred years.

In 1587 Powis Castle became the property of Sir Edward Herbert, whose great grandfather from various illegitimate liaisons was William ap Thomas of Raglan, the founder of all Herberts after being persuaded to change his family name by Henry V. Powis remained in the hands of the Herbert family for the best part of another 350 years before it was bequeathed to the Trust in 1952. Housed within one of the castle rooms are the treasures that were brought home from India by Robert Clive and his son, Edward. They had collected their spoils – some say illegally – during service with the British East India Company. In 1801 George Herbert, the 2nd Earl of Powis, died without heir. The title died with him but the castle and its estates were inherited by his sister, Henrietta, then married to Edward Clive. Their marriage had led to the union of the Clive and Powis estates, and the earldom was then recreated for the third time for Edward Clive who had taken the Herbert surname.

These days, the castle is known for its attractive formal gardens, balustraded terraces, deer park, and heavily wooded estate. The crowning glory of the castle gardens is the great three-hundred-year-old yew hedges, known as twmps, first introduced in 1680 by the 1st Marquess. Further plantings were carried out by Mary Preston, the wife of the 2nd Marquess until her death in 1724 interrupted progress. Irish yews were added to the mix during the 18th century by the 1st Earl, Henry Herbert, and a single golden yew was planted on the top terrace 200 years later by Violet Lane-Fox, wife of the 4th Earl. Clipping of the hedges was introduced during the mid-Victorian period after the twmps had begun to obscure the view from the castle windows, however from 1970 the yews were allowed to maintain their own shapes

Figure 12 18th century yew hedges known as twmps at Powis Castle

and 'drift' over the edges of the terraces. All this seems a long way from the condition of the estate towards the end of the 18th century when Sir Richard Colt Hoare considered It was suffering from neglect:

> The gardens were laid out in the foreign style with terrace above terrace, vases, statues, parterres, etc. This type of garden will not suit all situations, but it is the only one fit for Powis Castle, from whence you could descend by no other means into the gardens but by a long flight of steps. The walls overhung with fine ivy have a very good effect, but at this time the gardens and terraces are in a very neglected state.

Later, Thomas Roscoe observed that the magnitude of this elevated pile is best seen with the greatest effect from the road leading towards Montgomery, whence its embattled turrets rise above the surrounding trees. But, like the paying visitors of today who arrive in their thousands to gaze in awe at the old Powis home, the Clive treasures and glorious gardens, many still have time to wander the grounds:

> I was delighted with my ramble over different parts of the park, which is formed of gently rising hills clothed with many magnificent specimens of trees and pleasant lawns where the deer added to the charm of the scene. For the artist who delights in wild forest scenery, or pastoral quiet, Powis park will supply a continued treat. The verdant spreading lawns, the swelling hills and the rich variety of wooded views, together with the distant hills mingling with the sky at the moment I witnessed them in the soft glow of an autumnal evening had a everlasting effect on my mind.

At Pool Quay is the site of the abbey of Strata Marcella, a Welsh Cistercian monastery built on the banks of the Severn. It was founded in the 12th century by Owain Cyfeiliog, a powerful Welsh prince of his day and it seems the abbey was quite a size. The nave alone has been estimated as being 60m (200ft) long. If the building conformed to the usual design for abbeys and had a choir, two transepts and a presbytery, it would have been one of the largest in Wales. The library is said to have been very rich and its reputation widespread. The abbey's eventual destruction is attributed, not to Glyndwr, but to the later Dissolution and not one stone of the immense edifice survives. What few remains there were have more than likely been washed away by the numerous Severn floods of the last 600 years.

As was often the case with idle men of power in those far-off days, Owain Cyfeiliog's high position allowed him time to have a hobby when not warring with neighbouring princes, or Norman lords, and his was poetry. His Drinking Horn poem did achieve some acclaim. Whether he was satisfied with that one success is not recorded, but no other notable compositions have survived, so he may have chosen instead an early retirement to his riverside abbey.

The Long Mountain above Severn's eastern bank is well named, partly to differentiate from the identical mass of the Long Mynd, its sprawling cousin by Church Stretton. It starts to rise near the village of Westbury and quickly reaches 300m (1,000ft). Along its summit a narrow road – part of the Roman route from Uriconium (Wroxeter) to Lavobrinta (Forden Gaer) – extends for ten miles, crossing the national boundary and the county boundary between Powys and Shropshire. Its western flanks carry a section of Offa's Dyke. The highest point on the Mountain is Beacon Ring, Cefn Digoll, an Iron Age fort and the site of conflict in 630 at which a Welsh alliance of Gwynedd and Mercia defeated a Northumbrian force led by the ambitious Edwin. On an eastern spur, Robert FitzCorbet built Caus Castle in the late 11th century to guard the route from Shrewsbury to Montgomery and the border. FitzCorbet owed fealty to Roger of Montgomery, the 1st Earl of Shrewsbury, and vowed to help him control the Welsh marches in that part of the Severn valley. The name Caus, derived from the town of Pays de Caux in Normandy, became sufficiently important for it to be granted borough status, and a small town grew up from the mid-13th century inside the castle's outer bailey. The town's layout contained at least two streets and in one a church was built dedicated to St Margaret. A hundred years later there were 58 burgesses living in Caus, but further residential progress ended abruptly in 1349 with the arrival of the Black Death. When the last resident Corbet died in 1347, the castle passed to the Earl of Stafford, then through marriage to the Thynnes of Longleat in Wiltshire. From that time, Caus was rarely used and was abandoned by the end of the civil war. The site is in private hands now with a large modern house, itself called Caus Castle, on the old ramparts looking out towards Shrewsbury. In the early part of the 19th century there were no access restrictions existing here when Fletcher Moss and his companion rode up the approach lane:

> We leave our bikes by a lonely cottage and climb over fastened gates and up a steep path in a wood until we stand on a precipitous conical mound where remnants of masonry are overgrown with wild peas or vetches in great profusion of pods. From the topmost peak there is a fine view over the Salop plain to where

the Wrekin dimly rears its lonely height, brooding in aristocratic aloofness, and round to the west are the mountain strongholds of Powysland.

The broken mass of Breidden Hill is a feature of the scenery hereabouts and is well known to every traveller along the A483 bound for Chester and the coastal resorts of North Wales. The Breiddens are a group of five peaks forming an extinct volcano, the summit of Breidden Hill itself reaching to 367m (1,204ft) while its undisturbed neighbour Moel-y-Golfa is the highest at 403m (1,322ft). On Breidden, there are remains of an Iron Age hillfort, one of the many candidates for the disputed site of Caractacus' last stand against the Romans, but with the close presence of the River Severn which Tacitus gave credence to as possible watery barrier for the attacking soldiers, it must be a strong one. On the highest point of its northern ridge there is an obelisk commemorating Admiral Rodney placed there in 1781 by the gentlemen of Montgomeryshire, suppliers of the oak timbers that they transported down the Severn to Bristol where the Admiral's naval fleet was being built. At the time, Rodney was already a national hero, though had no other local connections with this area. The original Welsh inscription on the pillar reads, 'The highest pillars will fall, the strongest towers will decay, but the fame of Sir George Brydges Rodney shall increase continuously, and his good name shall never be obliterated.' The obelisk was struck by lightning in 1835 and a golden ball that originally topped the pillar was destroyed. The golden ball became a copper one when it was re-installed in 1847. In the early part of the 19th century, Rodney's followers formed a club, the Breiddenites, whose custom was to meet and dine annually at the base of the pillar. Toasts were proposed and patriotic speeches made, followed by the singing of the Breidden Glee, a song especially composed in honour of the pillar. The summit is no longer all celebration and glory. The huge Criggion quarry on Breidden has been blasting the western side of the mountain away for road stone since 1866, too early maybe for Henry Thornhill Timmins to have noticed much damage:

Yonder a few miles rise the Breidden Hills, 'brewing the weather, like a Lapland witch', and looking wonderfully mountainous for their inches; with lights and shadows chasing each other athwart their wooded flanks, and their summits wreathed in a cope of lowering storm cloud. Rising abruptly from Severn-side, this isolated range is a conspicuous landmark for many a mile around, keeping watch and ward over the broad Vale of Shrewsbury, much as Gibraltar Rock guards the entrance to the Mediterranean.

After crossing the Severn, Thomas Pennant's route lay at the foot of the mass of these rocky hills, their bases skirted with woods above which they suddenly present a most tremendous and precipitous front. There was no reason then for him to complain of any industrial activity. More obvious difficulties would have been in the way of Cledwyn Hughes, but they either did not bother him or his mood helped him to ignore any disruption to his walk:

> It is Maytime and as I go down from Breidden Hill on which I have been standing I pass a stone cottage. There are damson trees all around it and the blossom is breaking in the wind and the petals steam out like wild confetti at a village wedding. An old woman is carrying water and a petal has stuck with a flutter in her grey hair. She scoops out the water from the well with a chained hand bowl; it sparkles in the sunshine, breaking the light and ugly only when it stains the ground.

Nestling below Middletown Hill, within a stray quarry-blasted boulder distance of Breidden and the Welsh border, there is a small out-of-the-way village in which an unpretentious church has a brass plate set into the wall. Engraved upon its surface is a portrait of an old man and the following inscription:

> *The old, old, very old man Thomas Parr was born at the Glyn in the township of Winnington within this chapelry of Great Wollaston and parish of Alberbury, in the county of Salop, in the year of our Lord 1483. He lived in the reigns of ten Kings and Queens of*

England (viz.), K.Edwd 4th, K.Edwd 5th, K.Richd 3rd, K.Hen 7th,
K.Hen 8th, K.Edwd 6th, Q.Mary, Q Eliz., K.James 1st, and
K.Chars 1st. Died 13th and was buried in Westminster Abbey on
the 15th November 1635; Aged 152 Years and 9 months.

Thomas Parr lived in an isolated cottage at Winnington, near Middletown. He had no neighbours, and the likelihood is he would have had few friends. Little is known about his alleged extraordinarily long life, if we are to believe what we read in the history books. There are few records, and what there are differ to the extent that it has been difficult to prove his claimed age, his marriages, or the births of his children and there are no descendants to support his story. What we do know is that in 1635, the Earl of Arundel, Thomas Howard – on whose land Parr lived – persuaded him to leave his isolation in the Shropshire countryside and go with him to London to meet the king, Charles I, live thence a life of luxury, and become a spectacle. We know, too, that the celebrated painters, Rubens and van Dyck, went to the trouble of putting him on canvas. Whatever else the good Earl had in mind for his protege would not last long, because Thomas was dead before the end of the year – from the stress of the move, the change of diet, or the unhealthy environment.

Many legend-breakers have attempted to explain old Tom's secret of longevity but have shied away from conclusions. No-one today believes the story, and it is difficult to understand how or why such dignitaries as the Earl of Arundel and the monarch could be so convinced. Even then, there was plenty of reason to doubt: no record of a birthdate; vain and vague memories of an old man living alone; Arundel, a prominent influential courtier to the king and seeing an opportunity to please and increase his popularity. Thomas himself would surely not have turned down the chance to get away from his basic existence and boredom. Then there was the evidence of William Harvey, the court physician, who declared after the postmortem that there was nothing unusual with the condition of the old man's organs, that they were good to go for a while longer. Hardly proof of extraordinary ageing.

In 1933 Herbert Forrest, then owner of Thomas's cottage at Winnington, discovered that the wattle and daub construction of the building was no earlier than 1550, very close to the findings by the Society for the Protection of Ancient Buildings, whose dating range was 1570-1620. So, Thomas could not have moved in before 1550, 85 years before his death at the earliest estimation. Unfortunately, without proof of birth we can only guess his age at the earliest date. The cottage is still on its original isolated pitch, a long way from modern day traffic. The current owner has been there since she put it back into habitable repair in 1986 and tells me she has every intention of remaining there until she reaches 153, at least.

While narrowboat pioneer Lionel Thomas Rolt's *Cressy* was at her overnight Cheshire moorings at Church Minshull, he discovered a record in the parish church register which challenges Tom Parr's claim as Britain's oldest man. Thomas Damme of Leighton near Crewe is said to have died on the 20th February 1648, having seen off seven score years and fourteen!

Three Castles of Montgomery

Montgomery (Trefaldwyn) is the traditional county town of the historic county of Montgomeryshire. Named after Roger de Montgomeri, who was created Earl of Shrewsbury by King William I and given this part of the Welsh marches in recognition of his support in the Conquest. When Earl Roger first arrived in the region in 1070, he constructed a timber motte and bailey fortification at Hen Domen, a raised field one mile away, to control a narrow, vulnerable ford over the nearby River Severn at Rhydwhyman. Roger didn't stay much time at his new fortress, for his home had to be in Shrewsbury where he had built another castle for his function of government and, as becomes any Norman chief's wish, an abbey church for his salvation.

Following Roger's death, Hen Domen ended up in the hands of the de Boulers family of whom one, Baldwin, would have the ensuing new township named after him (the Welsh for Montgomery, TreFaldwyn, means 'Baldwin's Town'). In 1223

Henry III decided on a stone castle for the new town and left it to his justiciary, Hubert de Burgh, to build it on a high crag above the settlement. Centred between these two Norman defences, and built long before either, is the tree-covered Neolithic hill fort of Ffridd Faldwyn, one of the largest hillforts in Wales. Due to it being visible for miles around, this substantial multivallate site was probably a regional centre for the Ordovices tribe and is likely to have served as a gathering point for other travellers and traders. When Thomas Pennant visited Montgomery in 1776, he noted:

> On a hill, not far from Montgomery Castle, is a stupendous British fort. The approach is guarded by four great ditches, with two or three entrances towards the main work, with two or three fosses running across the hill, the end of which is sufficiently guarded by its steepness.

That this area has been strategically important for a very long time is further borne out by the presence of Roman occupation at Forden Gaer – their second largest auxiliary fort in Wales – just 2.5km (1.5m) away, and Offa's great earthwork just 0.8km (0.5m) from Montgomery town centre. The national border is a short distance beyond that. Thomas Roscoe recognised that here was an important and significant place:

> No spot in the Principality is more memorable in Cambrian history for the singular events, the wild and daring feats of arms, the fierce contests, and succession of masters, which the castle of Montgomery witnessed from the very foundation of the fortress to the period of the Civil Wars.

Beneath what is left of the old castle walls, Montgomery lies still partly forgotten, a quaint and quite alluring little place on a gentle slope at the foot of castle hill. The market square is dominated by the large town hall, built in 1748 as a courthouse, around which 18th century houses still stand, all red brick. Roscoe wrote that the town had an air of peculiar neatness and gentility, not very usual, he thought, in the Principality:

> It is chiefly inhabited by persons of middle rank, or small fortune, some of whom have selected it by way of economy, and some for learned leisure. They have everything which reason and nature can supply, and a succession of lovely and luxuriant scenes around them to charm the site, with the rich prospect of Salopian woods and mountains gradually fading into the clouds.

When Hubert de Burgh fell from power in 1232, Montgomery Castle reverted to the Crown which at that time would grant land and property guardianships to the Mortimer Earls of March. Until, that is, in 1490 a new name appeared as the key-holder, Sir Charles Somerset. He already had his own castle at Raglan having married into the Herbert family and succeeded as Lord Herbert of Raglan, so it was a kinsman, Sir Richard Herbert, who became the first of the family to reside at Montgomery where they are landowners still. After Sir Richard's death in 1539, he became first Herbert to be buried in St Nicholas's Church. The early 13th century church is the oldest surviving building in the town and houses a wonderfully carved rood screen, choir stalls, and misericords which had been brought from Chirbury Priory after the dissolution of the monasteries. Another of the interior highlights is the ornate tomb of the 2nd Richard Herbert, Lord of Chirbury, father of the remarkable 1st Baron Chirbury, Edward Herbert and his brother, the poet and cleric, George Herbert. During the civil war, Lord Edward, the last Herbert to live in the castle, surrendered the family seat to Parliamentary forces led by Sir Thomas Myddleton. Edward was allowed to travel to London to submit to Parliament and receive a pension of £20 a week. Montgomery castle was rendered ruinous and unusable, and Lord Edward's magnificent house which he had built in the middle ward just twenty years before, went too, every brick. In 1903 Alderman Fletcher Moss stood on the end wall of the ruins and gazed across the northern Montgomery landscape:

From this lofty fortress how sweet and pure seems the air. Far below us, farther than the eye can see, there stretches Powysland, the paradise of the Cymru. There seemed no limits to its wealth and beauty. Straight as a dart for miles the road gleams white through thousands of acres of fertile fields, where white-faced Herefords and black Welsh cattle chew the cud in peace together, and Shropshire sheep climb up into the ruins of the castle to seek its shade and breath the fresh breeze as we do.

During his lifetime, Lord Edward Herbert cut a unique figure. As an Anglo-Welsh soldier, diplomat, historian, and religious philosopher, Edward achieved high distinction. He even found time to compose poetry to match that of his illustrious brother. After the failures of the civil war, Edward returned to Montgomery to live for a while at Lymore Lodge, a beautiful timbered house on

Figure 13 The abandoned Lymore Lodge near Montgomery shortly before it collapsed in 1921.

the outskirts of the town. It was said to be one of the most superbly beautiful half-timbered mansions in the whole border area, but it was rarely used as the family seat and remained unoccupied for much of its existence. Tragically, in 1921, while empty and abandoned, the house collapsed and what was left was pulled down. Sir Richard Colt Hoare saw the house long before its demise:

> It presents a curious specimen of the style of architecture in use in this county at the era of its being built. Its construction is of timbers and plaster with several gable end roofs and bears the date 1675.

Fletcher Moss somehow managed to gain entry to the Lodge and left us with a marvelous description of how it was before the end:

> The oak in this house is wonderful. All the floors are waxed and polished, but the panelling, doors, and other oaken work is simply dusted, neither oiled nor waxed, and consequently is a light grey colour, very different from the ordinary conventional idea of oak. It is four storeys high, and even the attics are crowded with enormous oaken beams roughly adzed to shape. It must have taken a thousand oaks to make it. The house has not been inhabited for nearly two hundred years, and yet there is the old furniture, the bandy-legged chairs, the faded tapestry, the dim pictures, even the pewter on the pantry dresser, with the willow patterned plates. The whole house seems full of secret chambers, or dark passages which lead to nowhere in particular.

Set on rolling ground to the east of Montgomery, Lymore is now a well-preserved deer park which the Earls of Powis still own and maintain. The parkland is characterised by informal tree planting, ponds, and woodland, and includes a section of Offa's Dyke forming the eastern boundary. There are sweet chestnuts here and ancient oaks. One monster survives on the boundary of the Montgomery cricket ground – the oldest in the county, and a delightful backdrop in which to play or watch. On another day in 1898, Arthur Bradley witnessed a different sport:

> Winding my way leisurely through the park, I was startled by the sound of a horn and the loud cheering cry of a pack of fox hounds taking their first autumnal field day, with all the pomp and circumstance peculiar to the first breaking ground on these stirring occasions. The whole pack with riders and pedestrians of all kinds passing quickly before me had such an enlivening and animating effect upon my mind that I was induced to extend my walk to the neighbouring plantations. The fox, however, although seen in one of them that same morning, was nowhere to be found, to the chagrin and disappointment of all present. Sly renard, probably, was in one plantation while the hounds were in another, and being aware of the danger, quietly stole away to the Shropshire hills.

From the mid-18th century, the local roads of the border country had become turnpike roads with tollgates, but by 1840 the roads of Montgomeryshire were in a most wretched state. Mail was still carried on horseback until the following year when a mail coach service began running across the county. At about that time, a report produced on the condition of the roads suggested that the practice of making wagon wheel shoes with three-inch projecting plates resulted in road surfaces becoming harrowed.

Montgomeryshire is a gentle country of river valleys and mountains. On its eastern border is Shropshire and England and the western side rises to mountain ranges of Mid Wales. The Severn flows out of Wales at Llandrinio, where the banks are bare and dark, deep pools swirl and twist in the currents. Cattle drink at graveled watering places, keeping an anxious eye for fast darting pike. Not far from the road bridge, by a place called the Mount, the great river's early route north came to a halt by the great ice barrier of an ancient age and was forced to change course eastwards, eventually pushing its way through the narrow valley at the head of Wenlock Edge and gouging its way south towards an unpredictable meeting with the Wye at Chepstow.

Boundaries of the Marches

The village of Bromfield on the A49 road is 3km (2m) northwest of Ludlow, and close to the confluence of the Rivers Teme and Onny. These days, travellers along the A49 cannot help noticing the Ludlow Food Centre opposite the turn into the village, described as 'a farm shop like no other'. Just visible from the same spot is the broad tower of the parish church of St Mary the Virgin, once the chapel of Bromfield Priory, a pre-Norman college of secular canons founded by Edward the Confessor sometime before 1061.

After almost 100 years, royal support by Henry II persuaded the prior to attach the college to the Benedictine monastery of St Peter's in Gloucester, and being hence dependent on the wealthier Gloucester abbey, Bromfield survived until the surrender of St Peter's in 1538. It was then leased, together with its lands which included Oakly Park, to Charles Foxe, the son of the Ludlow Member of Parliament. After he purchased the property outright twenty years later, he converted parts of the priory and the chancel of the church into a private house, unfortunately mostly destroyed by fire in the 17th century. The remains can be seen still attached to the chancel which was restored for the use of the parish. The timber-framed 14th century monastic gatehouse that was the entrance to the priory has also survived, complete with its wide archway containing iron-studded oak doors. Beyond the gatehouse and across the river is a picturesque water-mill – the perfect scene for the painter's brush. Here, too, is the entrance to the 400-acre Oakly Park, the estate of the Earl of Plymouth. Their family name is Windsor-Clive, the result of a union in 1855 with the designation of Lady Henrietta W, wife of Edward Clive, the 2nd Earl of Powis, as Baroness Windsor. The Earldom of Plymouth is a Windsor inheritance. Oakly became another of Robert Clive of India's house collections in 1771, and when his wife died in 1817 the estate then passed to her grandson, Lady Henrietta Windsor's youngest boy.

In 1896 Henry Thornhill Timmins arrived at Bromfield by train:

> Alighting at Bromfield station we make our way to the village, as
> picturesque a spot as one could wish to see, situated in a pleasant
> fertile vale close to the place where the Onny and Teme unite. At
> the end of the village street we traverse an old grey many-arched
> bridge spanning the lively Onny near which rises a row of lofty
> storm-rent poplars, still known as the Twelve Apostles, though
> several veterans have succumbed to the gales in recent years.

The hamlet of Stokesay, fleetingly visible from the A49 across the
winding Onny, gets its name from the ancient family of de Says,
descendants of Picot de Say who fought for the Conqueror at
Hastings. The de Says did not own the estate but rented it from
the powerful de Lacys, holders of the manor of Stoke and
Ludlow from their base at Stanton Lacy. Peeping over the trees,
is Stokesay Castle, built in the 13th century by the fabulously
wealthy Laurence of Ludlow, a successful wool merchant who
had become one of the richest men in England. Laurence intended
his new home by the highway between Ludlow and Shrewsbury
to show to all who passed that way that he was now one of the
country's landowning classes. His castellated house was not
constructed with defence in mind, for it would not have
withstood a serious attack, but the walls and moat were not
entirely decorative either. Laurence's status symbol still needed
to be protected from wandering rogues, opportunistic robbers,
and Welsh marauders. The visitor today would see first the
golden charm of the now famous and much photographed
gatehouse. It looks, and is, a later addition built in 1641 by the
1st Earl Craven. The elaborate carvings and panel work indicate
yet more wealth and high standing, this time of a cultivated
supporter of Royalist restoration. By the early part of the 18th
century, Stokesay Castle was looking its age. The buildings had
been let to a series of tenant farmers and parts of the complex
were used as stores and workshops. The hall became a granary,
the basement of the south tower converted into a smithy, and
almost inevitably, a fire there in 1830 burnt out the floors above.

So much of Stokesay had influenced Stuart Mais that he based a whole novel on it years before he ever came to know it:

It was a drawing by Cecil Aldin that first set my imagination on fire about Stokesay. I have always been lucky with my visits there. On my first visit it was festooned with snowdrops and yellow crocuses. On my last visit a riot of hollyhocks, lupins, sweet-peas and carnations.

While sketching the castle in 1920, Aldin had stayed at the Stokesay Inn in Craven Arms for ten consecutive days, getting to the castle early in the morning and returning to the inn late in the afternoon. It was January, and he had the place to himself:

Not a soul disturbed me, or interfered with my wanderings from gatehouse to keep, keep to solar chamber, great hall to priests' rooms or buttery and kitchens. Rushing over a house of this description on a warm summer's day while your chauffeur turns the car round is all very well, but that way you can never know your house or their inhabitants.

Fletcher Moss arrived at Stokesay in an earlier time and a different season, but still found the castle as deserted as Aldin had discovered:

The country road is white with hawthorn, refreshed with the rain and redolent with perfume. Onward we

Figure 14 Jaggery's Sheep Tracks sculpture at Craven Arms

219

glide until there rise before us the embattled walls and towers of Stokesay. They seem to be solid, yet they are deserted; substantial and in good repair, yet all is silent. There is no sound but the jackdaw's querulous caw and the plaintive bleat of cade lambs. The winds toss about the trees and the clouds are chased over the surrounding hills, while the charming buildings seem to be a mansion of the dead.

In early spring 2017, I took time out from my writing for a country hike. I took the path through Stoke Wood to the Rowton road that climbs steeply passed a deserted quarry to the top of View Edge Wood. From that height there is a magnificent view of the Clun country I was about to explore. A billowy sea of hills, some showing clear evidence of cultivation, others deeply wooded, and beyond these the soft purple contours of loftier heights which roll away to lose themselves in the mist.

Craven Arms is Shropshire's newest town that started to grow the day the Shrewsbury & Hereford Railway Company moved in during 1852. The local lord, Earl Craven, had already built a coaching inn bearing his name to serve horse-drawn travellers between Shrewsbury and Hereford, and as the settlement developed and began to fill the gap between Newton and another village just up the road at Newington, so the name 'Craven Arms' was adopted for the budding new community. Throughout the early years of its existence, Craven Arms sprang up for all the world like a prairie town of the American Wild West, to many just as ugly and forlorn in appearance. The more aristocratic suburb of Newton containing some beautiful black and white houses, stood aloof from it nearer the river, as if it despised its upstart neighbour. As the railway appeared, all it had to serve at the time was a set of crossroads where the Craven Arms Hotel is now, but then the customers to start with would have had four legs – sheep and cattle. From that time, immense auctions of livestock were periodically held at this by now important railroad centre, when the loud clamour of Hereford cattle and black bullocks of Radnor and Cardigan, or Shropshire sheep and collie dogs from the

Cambrian Hills and march land meadows filled the air. Erected on the opposite corner to the hotel is a modern sculpture that tells the story of Craven Arms; rail and sheep have paid for it all. On another corner of this central junction is one of the most unusual of graded buildings, in this case a milestone obelisk. Its plinth bears the names and distances of 36 UK major cities and industrial towns, should anyone need to know. From here, it is 283 miles to Berwick on Tweed!

Today, the town and its surrounding suburbs are reasonably pleasant. Traffic tos and fros busily from the Clun valley, but in 1955, C.V Hancock saw it otherwise:

> Nowadays most people who travel along the main A49 road from Ludlow to Shrewsbury rush through the township of Craven Ams with a pardonable shudder, for it is a wart on the landscape, a nineteenth century agricultural centre that sprang up around the railway junction that takes its name from the coaching inn. However, unless the travellers break their journey here, or take to the Clun Valley road they may never discover the delectable country leading to the towns and villages of the Clun Forest.

A back road running parallel to Roman Watling Street leads towards Leintwardine and a house of murder and mystery. In September 1987, Simon Dale, a retired architect, was found bludgeoned to death in his countryside mansion at Hopton Heath. A long time before that event, Henry Thornhill Timmins had been invited to include in his touring schedules of Shropshire a visit to Heath House, the scene of the later tragedy:

> We alight at Hopton Heath station, shoulder sketching gear, etc., and trudge away to Heath House, which lies a short mile to the southward. Charles Seaton Esq's. residence is a large, substantial edifice dating mainly from the latter part of the seventeenth century and seated in a broad park-like demesne. The interior of the mansion contains several handsome panelled apartments adorned with pictures and curios that reflect the artistic taste of the proprietor. But the most notable feature of the house is the

elaborate old staircase hung with ancient tapestry and is a marvel of massive construction. Its huge oaken handrails and newels, and even the twisted balusters, look as strong and simple as possible, and much of the work has the appearance of being fashioned with an axe!

The modern-day mystery of the Heath House affair was choked with jealousy, hate, adultery, and the fraudulent actions of a Baroness; one Agatha Christie might have written for her favourite detective, Hercule Poirot. As it turned out, the murder was never solved, though the Baroness who was Dale's ex-wife was never far from an accuser's lips. After dinner at Heath House, it is feasible that Timmins took a short stroll around Hopton for a later addition to his diary:

> In the nook of the hills to the westward stands Hopton Castle, a grey old Norman keep-tower seated in a curiously low exposed position near the banks of a stream. Traces of ruined outworks indicate that the place was much more extensive in former days, when it figured in some stirring episodes of Marchland history.

Not a true castle, Hopton is more a high-status stone tower house, built in the early 14th century on the site of a Norman motte. It had served purely as a fortified home with few features built in as security against attack. In 1644, Sir Michael Woodhouse, a Royalist with a force of about 500 soldiers, laid siege to the castle which was being defended by thirty Roundheads under the command of Samuel More. After three weeks of desperate fort-holding, More agreed terms and surrendered. Woodhouse decided to allow More his freedom but not so his men, who were cut down mercilessly as they emerged from the castle. In spite of the relatively small number of casualties, Hopton became one of the most infamous incidents of the English Civil War.

Still habitable at the start of the 18th century, the castle fell into disrepair soon afterwards and was left a crumbling ruin. In 2006, the remains were purchased by the Hopton Preservation Trust with the help of a £1million donation from the Heritage

Lottery Fund and cleared and repaired the building for public access use. Grateful though we must be for such spirited action, the result is less than complimentary. Externally, the ruined keep looks stable and even spooky in the right autumnal light, but inside, the refurbishing is modernistically too clean and tidy. Only the diving, darting swallows create much excitement.

In 1932, a schoolteacher from London, Magdalene Weale, was spending her summer break on horseback in the Shropshire hills. Her hired steed was a racing pony called Sandy. After gazing briefly in awe at the castle ruins, horse and rider continued their lonely cross-country journey:

> I went on my way up the hill and turned into a lane which led me through the woods of Hopton Park up the steep side of Hopton Titterhill. A thousand feet up I stopped to look back at the wonderful view of the Clun valley hemmed with trees and ringed all round with hills. I chose this lovely woodland spot to eat my sandwiches, while Sandy found much to interest her on the borders of the wood. For liquid refreshment I relied, as usual, on meeting with a stream and later on, if I were lucky, an inn. The pony, the pheasants, the grouse, and the rabbits were my only companions, and these plied their various trades, quite regardless of me.

I imagine her ride was one of great satisfaction. Beautiful in a quiet way, not with the rugged grandeur of the heights but with a soft charm of a land of quiet hills and dales. The section through the emerald Darky Dale, tucked away between the wooded slopes of Hopton Titterhill and Bedstone Hill, must have been a surprise but a pleasing discovery. At Aston-on-Clun, Magdalene and Sandy put up for the night at the Kangaroo Inn. The name has no connection with the Australian marsupial, rather a 19th century cable runner ship, about which nothing much else is known. Across the road from the inn is a tree, continuously decorated haphazardly with flags. Ancient pagan worship, perhaps? It is known that in many parts of the English countryside villagers celebrate regularly by ritual, for instance Oak Apple Day, on May 29th. Its origins go back to the restoration of the monarchy and Charles II in 1660. At that time, the story of the Boscobel Oak, inside which, the fleeing monarch allegedly hid from his parliamentary pursuers, was well known. And in recognition of the King regaining his throne, a 'day for the oak tree' became a national holiday. But that was more than two hundred and sixty years ago, and if that is what was going on here, what is being celebrated in autumn? The Aston tree is not oak but black poplar, and according to Dorothy Nicolle in her *Shropshire's Oddities*, not even original because that fell in 1995.

One of the attractive features of the Clun country is its variety. From the level of the tableland the hills rise with folded valleys in between. River, wood, and high open spaces complete the picture. From the tiny hamlet of Chapel Lawn, Magdalene Weale made her way on pony back to Obley and thence along the road to Cwm, passing east of the Black Hill – the very eminence Bruce Chatwin used as the background for his 1982 classic story, *On the Black Hill*. Presently they took a lane which climbs steeply to an ancient track of flint men leading to Pen-y-wern circle, the often-suggested Clun Hill stone axe factory and Rock Hill settlement. It is haunted ground; how could it be otherwise?

> What, think you, are those ghostly hammer sounds the shepherds hear at night, those lights that twinkle amid the hills? Those dark shapes that flit noiselessly along the ancient trails after sunset, are they only the sheep at pasture or the shadows of clouds across the moon? I know better.

Down in the meadows, the meandering Clun is at one point overhung by Clunbury Hill. In the village below it, Ida Hony made her home briefly in 1930. She was born in Bishops Canning, Wiltshire in 1885, but after marrying Dr Thomas Gandy persuaded her husband to move to Shropshire. They settled in Clunbury where they found a practice for sale. In her book, *An Idler on the Shropshire Borders*, she described her love for the local countryside around her new home, the many walks she took before breakfast on Clunbury Hill and along the banks of the Clun, where trout swam, and red squirrels foraged in the woods. She had developed an infatuation with nature, like Mary Webb. On the hill there were no houses, but Ida discovered rock dwellings – in one lived two elderly sisters who she befriended. She came to know every hill in view from the summit of Clunbury by name. Many of Ida's walks ended with an invitation to tea and cake from farmers and cottagers she met on her ways. If freely given, this was hospitality rarely shown these days.

The uplands of southern Shropshire bear the densest concentration of hill forts, and Caer Caradoc a few miles south of Clun, is one of the finest. This massive earthwork lies in a high position overlooking the Redlake stream, and the views from it in all directions are exceptional. As with the hill of the same name at Church Stretton, it relates to Caractacus and the British tribal leader's last stand against the Roman forces of Ostorius Scapula. Tacitus described the site of battle as having steep gradients and 'a river of uncertain depth flowing passed, and here bands of fighters were stationed to provided defences'. It is unlikely that this Caer was the one to which the Roman historian was referring; the Redlake is far too tiny at this point even to be called a river. Regardless of this evidence, William Camden was convinced that this was the site of the British chief's final conflict:

> But where the Clun meeteth with Teme, among divers doubtful fords, there mounteth up an hill of a very ancient memory, which they call Caer Caradoc, because about the year of our Salvation 53, Caratacus a most noble and renowned British King, raised in the front of it a mighty wall of stone, and with his people resolutely made it good against Ostorius Lieutenant for the Romans and the Legionary Roman Soldiers. Until the Romans having forcibly broken through that fence of stones so rudely laid, (the remains whereof are to be seen at this day) forced the unarmed Britons, to quit the place, and hie up to the mountains.

On nearby Stow Hill, a track runs for more than a mile along the summit ridge 400m (1,300 ft) above the sea. According to our adventurous pony lady, Miss Weale told us if you want to experience one of those rare moments of exhilaration which life occasionally offers, she recommends you gallop across it – or next best thing, run across it. Here you are on top of the world, the air is like wine, the hills would flash by as you speed along. At times, the track is higher than Caer Caradoc itself:

> I felt as if I could have gone on forever. Even Sandy, who did all the work, did not seem inclined to stop!

Land of Lords and Romance

> *Clunton and Clunbury,*
> *Clungunford and Clun,*
> *Are the quietest under the sun.*
>
> *In valleys of springs and rivers,*
> *By Ony and Teme and Clun,*
> *The country for easy livers,*
> *The quietest under the sun.*

A.E. Housman: from A Shropshire Lad

The little town of Clun is at the centre of what author and broadcaster, John Seymour, called 'the Welsh Bulge' where the national border from Bishop's Castle encroaches westwards for a while in a semi-circular blip before re-joining the boundary line at Knighton:

> And I will say here and now that this part of the country is the most attractive and satisfying countryside that I have found anywhere in the world, and I have travelled somewhat in four continents.

The town's name is taken from the River Clun (Welsh: Colunwy), which rises in the high western forest that also takes the name.

According to the Campaign of the Protection of Rural England (CPRE), Clun is one of the most tranquil locations in England. Towards the end of the 7th century, it began to grow around a late Saxon church that was replaced in the 12th century with the present church of St George. In the surrounding area, there was a scattered population as early as the Neolithic period, about 5000 years ago. Presumably by design, Clun ended up on the historic drove road, the Clun-Clee Ridgeway, along which sheep and cattle were driven from Wales In the west to the markets in the Midlands and London. At the time of the Norman Conquest, Clun formed part of the extensive lands of Wild Eadric, the wealthy Saxon thegn whose unsuccessful revolt against William the Conqueror led to his lands being confiscated and given to Roger de Montgomery. In turn, Roger granted twenty-seven manors, Clun being the largest, to fellow Norman, Robert 'Picot' de Say. It was he who built Clun Castle, owned for many years later by the FitzAlan family and today forming a picturesque ruin. In their hands, the castle played a key part in protecting the region from Welsh attack until it was gradually abandoned in favour of a more luxurious one which they owned at Arundel in West Sussex. The 14th century pack horse bridge that even now crosses the river connecting Saxon Clun to Norman Clun, has given rise to a local saying, 'Whoever crosses Clun Bridge comes back sharper than when he went.'

St George's Church stands on a hill slope at the top of the Saxon town. The tower is low, with the appearance of great strength, and doubtless was of useful service in times of conflict. In the large graveyard, the border names are constant: Cadwalladers and Merediths, besides the Hughes, Pughes, Prices, and Watkinses, which with Brunts, Gilleys, and Gittoes, make a curious variety. Robert Luther lies here, a famous local sportsman and Master of the United Pack – a farmers' hunt that still flourishes in these parts. Also, among the deceased are a number whose epitaphs declare an artistic life, including playwright John Osborne, famous for his *Look Back in Anger*. He lived at Clun from 1985 until his death in 1994. Buried next to him is Osborne's fifth wife, Helen, a journalist in life who was known for being as self-opinionated as her husband. Their home, The Hurst, is now used as a retreat for budding artists who can spend quiet time contemplating their future careers.

According to the brief notes available inside the church, the lych-gate – a charming bit of ancient carpentry built in 1723 – appears to have been well travelled. In fact, when Henry Timmins arrived in Clun in 1896, it had not long been restored to its original position, having stood elsewhere since 1841 on at least two other sites. The oldest feature in the churchyard is a somewhat untidy expansive yew tree. It is claimed to have begun life here beside the first place of worship in Saxon times.

Henry Timmins entered Clun along the Bishop's Castle road:

> By and by, as we march passed the castle and enter the town, the westward-looking houses are painted in crimson and gold by the glow from the setting sun, while we dusty wayfarers bear away for the Buffalo Inn whose hospitable roof is to be our shelter to-night. So taking up our quarters in the Blue Room, we will give the benefit of the doubt to the local legend and hold that this is the chamber in which Sir Walter Scott once slept, and yonder table the very one upon which the 'Wizard of the North' wrote the first three chapters of *The Betrothed* - there is nothing like being precise in matters such as these.

The Buffalo is the most famous of Clun's inns, and is where many visitors of note have stayed, including Scott. This imposing building in a corner of the square has a sinister air about it, as if Scott's ghostly hero has taken up residence in the Blue Room, ready to terrify the next person to enter. With Sandy happily accommodated in a field next to the bridge, Magdalene Weal booked a room for the night at the Buffalo.

> While strolling around Clun, on old man directed me so I offered him a cigarette. At that time, I was partial to Russians, which I had found impossible to buy in Clun. I opened my case and saw my last

Russian lying there, brown amid the white Gold Flakes. I hoped it would escape the old man's choice, who, thought I in my presumption, would have no particular regard for it. He selected it. 'That's a Russian, that brown one,' I ventured. 'Perhaps you won't care for it.'

'Ah, but I likes em brown,' said he.

And so good-bye to my last Russian. But he was welcome to it.

Business at the Buffalo ceased in 2004, and since then the owners have resisted any sale regardless of the many offers to take it on, including one from a consortium of parties representing the villagers. It has since been given a Grade II listing, which means it can't be demolished or altered in any way without planning consent. So, what are the owners planning to do with it?

The lofty keep of Clun Castle, set high on the sharp slope of immense grass-grown earthworks with the prattling river washing two sides of them and the western sky for a background, fills a distinct place in the memory. Its grandeur persuaded Scott to use it as the Castle of Garde Doloreuse in his classic story. I was fortunate in having the peaceful hour of a glorious sunset for my first introduction to it, with nothing more inharmonious to disturb it than some heavy-uddered milking cows crunching greedily at the grassy moat on their way to the parlour. The towering square keep, long since bereft of its inner wall, blackened gradually against the fiery sky, and its ragged windows blazed like furnaces. Far away over the folding hills of the still wild upland of Clun Forest to the distant heights of Kerry, the shadows deepened into the grey of twilight. Charles Harper liked the old-fashioned shops of little country towns, wayside villages, and rural hamlets, although he once admitted that the cosmopolitan blast of their comprehensive stock is, on first acquaintance, somewhat trying:

> But one soon becomes used to the warring scents of tea and coffee, of strong home-cured hams and yet stronger cheeses, and then this rural mart is not without its own peculiar interest. The space within is, as a rule, restricted indeed, what with biscuit-boxes, piles of pails, barricades of brooms, and shining arrays of bright

tin goods. However, the cavernous little place makes an unconventional picture filled with lots of colour and great rich shadows which send you at once harking back to Rembrandt to point to the force of your impression.

Though old houses are plentiful enough here, there is little of architectural interest, with one striking exception. That is the small hospital built in 1618 for old men by Henry Howard, 1st Earl of Northampton, an ancestor of the FitzAlans. The old low-pitched picturesque building, profusely covered with varied creepers, its chapel, dining hall, and quadrangle gay with well-trimmed lawns and flower beds, is an even more seductive spot than the Conningsby Hospital in Hereford. *33

The Clun Forest, an undulating area of moorland and upland pastures sprinkled with copses and belts of mixed deciduous and coniferous trees, is crossed from east to west by the B4368

Figure 15 Clun Castle

---

33 Described in my earlier book *In My Own Time*

connecting Clun with the A489 Newtown road at Glanmule, followed closely for most of the way by the river. The area was once royal hunting ground, largely forested to the east as far as Ludlow. These hills and the adjacent Kerry Hills, once noted for prehistoric camps and stone circles, are famous now for their sheep breeds. Nearing the small village of Newcastle, Offa's Dyke descends either hillside north or south. Beyond the village, a steep lane starts up for Bettws-y-Crwyn, and hence continues southwards to Beguildy in the valley beyond where flows the River Teme. The road from Clun climbs more steeply now to the lonely Anchor Inn – the highest, possibly oldest continuous licensed, but certainly the most fascinating public house in Shropshire, if not the whole United Kingdom. Incorrect impressions on arrival are that it is derelict, with the front garden overgrown and signs that no-one is at home. But seek the rear entrance, ignore the leaf-strewn floor and peeling walls, and you will find yourself in the most basic of bar rooms. Pick your time, or more importantly the owner's, for they open only when it is convenient for them. If entry is gained, take it all in, for you may never see the likes again.

Magdalene Weal and Sandy left Clun by a different tract, climbing high passed dark pinewoods onto the uplands of the Forest, through Cefn Einion, and over the River Unk. After winding down passed the Iron Age fort on Fron Hill, they reached Newcastle where they stayed the night at the Crown Inn:

> We were now on the old coach road from Ludlow into Wales which winds its way at a general level of 1,300 ft above sea level over the southern uplands of the Clun Forest. The Heather and gorse were in full bloom that August day as I rode over this beautiful wild country of rounded hills and wide stretches of moor. Now it was one long prospect of fragrant beauty, and air that would make the old feel young again, and not a soul in sight for miles. Occasionally a dark wood of larch or pine rose up in striking contrast to the colour scheme of green, purple and gold.

A narrow ancient drove road connecting England to Wales runs from Clun for over ten miles across the south Shropshire heights.

The road crosses Offa's Dyke and, following the crest of the ridge, it is impossible not be gladdened by the view of folding hills and distant cloud-capped mountains, the giants of wild Wales – a wonderful panorama. Bettws-y-Crwyn is a remote village close to the border, one of several English villages to have a Welsh language place name. This one translates roughly as 'chapel of the fleeces.' The population of the parish is spread thinly across the hills separating the upper valleys of the Clun and Teme rivers. At the last count in 2011, that was 239 souls. Its church, St Mary's, is the highest in Shropshire at 400m (1,300 feet) above sea level and stands close to the old road. Up here in the churchyard, there is a wonderful outlook over the hills and dales of south Shropshire, which are seen stretching away for many a mile in picturesque stages, with Brown Clee Hill bringing up the rear beyond the dark ridges of Wenlock Edge. 700 years ago, a simple thatch-roofed church stood on this windswept hill, and parts of that remain in the fabric of the existing grey stone building. Like many other isolated churches in the marches, it has an elaborate screen; here it is 16th century but has been much altered during its lifetime. This is indeed a lonely place. Over the centuries, life here for the farmers and cottagers must have been challenging, to say the least. Hard winters, anxious springs, and disappointing harvests may have been all they might have expected.

In addition to being home to a famous breed of sheep, the Kerry Hills are a breeding ground of rivers. Teme, Clun, Ithon, and Mule all rise here. On the neighbouring Pool Hill, a lofty moorland south of the village of Beguildy, the Herefordshire bound Lugg springs to life. After leaving Bettws-y-Crywn in a westerly direction, the air still belongs to Shropshire despite being on the wrong side of the Dyke. The mapmakers have pushed the border out to include the Clun at its source, but not the Ithon nor the Mule, both Welsh rivers aiming to stay in Wales. The princely Teme becomes the southern part of the county 'bulge' as well as the national border, after a short run from its birth on Cilfaesty Hill. Down in the valley by the Newtown road, Kerry, the village, has one area of interest – the church of St Michael and All Angels, with its bulky tower. The 12th century tower was constructed as they were in those far off war-torn times, to include an option as a refuge in case of attack. In 1176, there was a sort of war going on here on holy grounds between the diocese of St David's and that of St Asaph, over which it had parish rights. The ecclesiastical dispute arose before a planned church re-dedication ceremony in which the Bishop of St David's, in whose diocese it belonged, would have expected to perform. At the time, though, the see was vacant, and St Asaph saw a chance to usurp the parish for itself. Enter the formidable Giraldus Cambrensis, Gerald of Wales, then Archdeacon of Brecon and defender of St David's in a Bishop's absence. He took possession of St Michael's, had the bells rung to indicate his authority and warned the Bishop of St Asaph 'not to thrust his sickle into another man's corn'. Then followed an extraordinary battle of excommunications from the church door, ending in the Bishop of St Asaph retreating through an angry gathering of villagers. Gerald claimed the victory, and Kerry remained with St David's for a further 700 years.

Of Lydbury and Bishop's Castle

On the day Magdalene Weale on her trusty pony, Sandy, galloped along the lane leading from the tiny hamlet of Round Oak, the view would have opened out for her somewhere by the crossroads at Red House Bridge:

> There it is! Walcot Hall, a fine brick mansion, built by the hero of Plassey, Robert Clive. It's great hanging woods commemorate the victory won in India, for the name 'PLASSEY' is cut in enormous letters in the trees and can be seen from the road. While I slept at the inn*[34] Sandy spent the night in the stables once owned by the great Robert, and the following morning, we galloped over the soft turf of the park as we made for the road again. Half a mile east of Lydbury a pretty country road rejoicing in the name of Stank Lane goes up to Oakeley Mynd. Here 1,000 feet above sea

---

[34] the Powis Arms is still owned by the Walcot Estate and remains open for business.

level we look down on Bishop's Castle nestling beneath the outlying hills of the Clun Forest, and beyond it the plain of the Onny and Camlad rivers.

Walcot Hall is an elegant Georgian country house once owned by Robert Clive of India. The house we see is not the original house, which was of the Elizabethan period, but the remodelled version by Clive after he purchased the estate in 1763. He was then the Member of Parliament for Shrewsbury. To make the changes to his new home, Clive employed the most sought-after architect of the day, Sir William Chambers, who had already achieved fame for creating the Chinese Pagoda at Kew Gardens. After Clive's death in 1774, Walcot was inherited by his eldest son, Edward, whose first commitment to improving the estate was to plant many trees about the grounds, some of which now form the basis of Walcot's celebrated arboretum. Edward eventually moved on to greater things at Powis Castle, following his marriage to Lord Powis's daughter, Lady Henrietta Herbert in 1784, and within 20 years had been given the revived title of Earl. His new stately pile had also become home for his father's booty from his East India days. After nearly 200 years, Walcot Hall had served its purpose for the Clive family, and was sold in 1933 to Ernest Stevens. He had made a fortune making pots and pans in Cradley Heath in the West Midlands and used much of his wealth to buy property of distinction. Like Clive before him, Walcot was only one of several estates Stevens eventually owned, others being in the Stourbridge area. This family remained at Walcot until 1956. Ironically, the business which had provided the means for their serial purchasing, folded in the 1960s. The present owners of the estate since 1957 are the Parish family, who have joined the long list of estate owners offering exclusive wedding venues as a means of financing their possession. Sir Richard Colt Hoare made the point during a visit to Walcot that he thought Clive's Oakley Park property by the Teme the better for its riverside position.

I entered Lord Clive's park at Walcot, a large brick house and a piece of water before it. Far inferior in point of situation to

Downton Castle or Oakly Park where he and Mr Knight, uniting their properties, might make the most beautiful succession of rides and walks imaginable[35].

The church of St Michael and All Angels in Lydbury North is part 12th century and one of Simon Jenkins's thousand best parish churches. In the north transept is the Roman Catholic Plowden chapel, empty, cold, and lacking in any family memorials or religious art forms, but where mass is still said once a year for the descendants in nearby Plowden Hall. The Plowden estate, within which sits the half-timbered sixteenth century hall, nestles in a nook of the hills above the Onny river, amidst shady woodlands. Henry Timmins described it in *Nooks and Corners of Shropshire*:

> Its broad, somewhat low entrance front is pleasantly quaint and simple, with nothing imposing about it, though the deep browed portico and massive hall door beneath lend a touch of character. A better view is obtained by passing to the back of the house. From this point of view the ancient Manor House rears its weather stained gables, slender chimneys and mossy roofs against the rich dark foliage that clothes the rearward hill, while the close-cropped lawns, the trim yew hedges, and gay coloured parterres of the old fashioned garden in the foreground, form an appropriate setting for this beau-ideal of an English homestead.

This splendid retreat was the home of Edmund Plowden, the great lawyer of the Elizabethan era. Being a Roman Catholic, he was once arrested for attending a mass. During his trial he called on the celebrant of the mass, who had turned witness for the prosecution, to swear to his priesthood. When he refused to do so, Plowden called out his now famous dictum: 'The case is altered. No priest, no mass. No mass, no violation of the law.' In contrast with the Plowden chapel at Lydbury, the Walcot Chapel has been

---

[35] A reference to the OS map shows the Teme flowing through Oakly Park then passed Downton Castle. Somewhere along that stretch of river was the dividing line between the two estates.

reappointed in recent times and has an air of regular use. The coats of arms of Robert Clive's times still hang above the pews. Dividing nave from chancel is the ubiquitous 15th century oak screen and above it appears the Ten Commandments, finely written in old English lettering of 1615. The fine, old, panelled oak nave roof was once hidden by an ugly whitewashed ceiling, but fortunately for us, the offending ceiling was removed some time ago and the view upwards is open for all to see and admire. Outside, the 13th century tower has a rare one-handed clock, installed in 1725. After his ramble around the Plowden estate, Timmins dropped in at St Michael's for some quiet contemplation.

> The interior of the church wears an antiquated air, as of primeval repose, and appears to belong mainly to the twelfth and thirteenth centuries. Many of the high-backed Jacobean pews are rudely adorned with carving as is also the oaken pulpit, while one or two of the former still have the link and staple used in the 'good old times' when the worshippers were accustomed to lock themselves up in their pews, a habit that affords a curious insight into the everyday manners of a bygone generation.

Bishop's Castle, Mary Webb's Mallard's Keep in *House in Dormer Forest,* is one of my favourite towns of Britain. It is a village-town, unpretentious yet completely self-centred. I first came upon it in 1974 while on a holiday tour of the Welsh borders. Though the main street of many shapes and colours running downhill from the castle square is a typical sign of medieval influence, I knew nothing of such things at the time. Neither had I ever seen a brewery building like there Is here st the top of the town before, currently known as the Three Tuns brewery, I remember thinking it resembled a cathedral of beer. Being a townie boy from the industrial north, to see all this was a game-changer for me, a magical introduction to a timeless world and a country community living in the very slow lane. I loved it then and love it still. Enough to keep a second home just two miles away.

The history of this market town began in Saxon times. Edwin Shakehead owned vast estates at Lydbury and gifted some of his land to the then Bishop of Hereford in gratitude for allegedly being cured of the palsy, the cause of his unfortunate name, at St Ethelbert's tomb. Lydbury was not marcher land, but bishops were marcher lords and so a castle had to be built to defend his acquisition. The town of Lydbury Castle began to grow around it, entirely separate from Lydbury village a few miles away. A new name seemed appropriate and necessary, and the Bishop's Castle was the obvious choice. By the mid-12th century, when the town was becoming a target for Welsh attacks, the castle on the motte was still a timber construction so steps were taken to rebuild it in stone. Throughout the early middle ages, border fluctuations meant territory disputes were a regular occurrence, but the castle remained intact until the 17th century when it finally ran out of use. By 1719, the castle buildings had gone and the Castle Hotel now stands proudly at the top of the town, built on part of the vacant site. Sir Richard Colt Hoare didn't think much of the place in the early 19th century:

> The town is a borough commanded by Lord Clive. It is dreary and dull. The ground around it is uncommonly rich and valuable owing probably to the quantity of manure running down on it from the town on all sides. However, the Castle Hotel was good.

Arthur Bradley found himself on the road from Montgomery on the very evening of the town's annual agricultural show of 1903, when the needs of the casual visitor in the Castle – the one hostelry available – had small chance of supply.

> The untimeliness of such an advent dawned upon me slowly and painfully as I encountered trap after trap, raising the dust of a not unusually travelled road, and some of them requiring more of it than their fair share. Then suspicion ripened into certainty as the foremost of these curious processions, only to be seen on such rare occasions hove slowly in sight. I soon found that both the interior and the yard of mine inn exhibited as cheerful a pandemonium as the occasion could possibly demand. It was quite obvious that to discuss bed and board with such distraught functionaries as

laboured within would have been fatuous as well as unkind, so having extracted that the main question of bed presented no difficulties, I deferred the other indefinitely and resigned myself to tobacco and the humours of the scene.

The Three Tuns Brewery was erected on its current site on Salop Street, even as the old castle was being demolished, and it remains the oldest licensed brewery site in Britain. Lucky it is if any small country town has two breweries, but Bishop's Castle has just that. At the bottom of the High Street is The Six Bells pub and brewery, which takes its name from the six bells of the church of St John the Baptist on the opposite side of the road. Previously a farmhouse, the Six Bells was altered in 1750 to become an inn offering lodgings and a secure livestock paddock to drovers moving their sheep along the Clun-Clee Ridgeway that passes beside the inn. Even in the 19th century, Bishop's Castle was a drowsy little market town, yet still an important centre for an extensive agricultural district, and renowned for its great cattle fairs. St John's Church is a Victorian rebuild except for its 13th century tower, but the churchyard has several interesting graves, including two Napoleonic prisoners-of-war and one for a 'Native of Africa' who died here in 1801. A tombstone near the belfry door bears the following inscription: *A la memoire de Louis Paces, Lieut-Colonel de Chevaux legers, chevalier des ordres militaires des deux Siciles et d'Espayne. Mort a Bishop's Castle le 1 Mais 1814, age de 40 ans.* In memory of Louis Paces, Lieutenant Colonel of Light Horses, Knight of the Military Orders of the Two Sicilies and Espaigne.

When a fellow traveller once told Magdalene Weale that he couldn't see the point in having such a place as Bishop's Castle because it leads to nowhere, she responded with short thrift:

If so, then Bishop's Castle will not pass the test, for it is not one of those towns which link the countryside with the great outside world, an outpost of civilization, so to speak. No, it exists to supply the needs of the large agricultural district around it, and its cattle fairs are important institutions. Surely here is enough justification for its existence! It is also the centre of the United Pack, and the kennels are here.

The United Pack of Fox Hounds dates from 1839, when it was created by the uniting of two other private packs from Church Stretton and Craven Arms. Although the United has a continuous existence from that time, its Craven Arms connections go back at least to the 1790s. After initial kennelling at various sites around south Shropshire during the early years, the hunt took possession of newly built kennels just outside Bishop's Castle and has remained in this location ever since. I am told that the pack is today a team of legal trail-hunting horses and hounds, primarily a fund-raising activity when it seeks not only to support itself but to also raise money for its adopted charities. It is a familiar sight along the back roads around Bishop's Castle in the summer and across the surrounding countryside during the autumn and winter hunting season and has become a well-supported part of the south Shropshire rural scene. It is also the basis for Magdalene Weale's connections with the area. At various stages in her book, *Through the Shropshire Hills on Horseback,* she demonstrated her alertness and resilience when confronted by men who showed complete disdain towards her. On one occasion, when attending a meeting of the United Pack hunt, she was approached by the master of the pack outside the Castle Hotel, where she had stabled Sandy for the night. He invited her for a drink in the bar, after which he offered to saddle her pony for her. Knowing full well that her steed wouldn't respond kindly to a stranger, the event developed, thus:

'*No, you mustn't*', she advised him. '*She'll kick you. She doesn't like men.*' The Master looked at the innkeeper who was standing close by and responded contemptuously '*We don't heed their blathering, do we?*' and advanced jauntily into Sandy's box. As MW waited in confidence knowing that her pony would not fail her, back went Sandy's ears and up went her heels in spontaneous defiance. The Master dropped the saddle and turned away in fright. '*Never mind, Sandy,*' MW called out. '*Better luck next time - and you're not what he called you!*'

That event wasn't the only time Sandy had shown a hatred of men, those who had shown some unkindness. It happened again some days later:

> Only once in the whole of my tour was I warned off property, and only once was I refused admission to an inn on the untruthful plea that they were full up. I turned from the door of that inn to shake the dust off my feet, but Sandy registered her disgust at this unwonted hospitality in more emphatic and substantial manner - right on the landlords white cobbled entrance, too! My heart rejoiced; for the second time Sandy had not failed me.

Bishop's Castle once had a railway, known locally as the 'queer little railway'. It was first thought of in 1860 as part of a grander scheme to build a connection from Craven Arms to the Newtown to Oswestry line of the Cambrian Railways. There had been a loud outcry when the town saw itself being left out in the cold, but when the promoters succeeded in getting Parliamentary approval, the *Shrewsbury Chronicle* of the 22nd March sarcastically reported,

> *The oldest inhabitant has not seen such a miserable attempt at rejoicing as was witnessed on Saturday last. Only a few bell ringers could or rather would be found, and the resulting sound was most discordant. The innkeepers were too patriotic and loved their town so well to part with their strong ale without getting paid for it, and after several attempts the rejoicing was given up in despair.*

The formal opening of this short line fell on 24th October 1865, the first train leaving from Strefford Bridge junction on the main Shrewsbury/Hereford line a mile from Craven Arms. At that time, the only station building was at Plowden, then unfinished, and there was nothing at all yet at Bishop's Castle. In the event, the idea of the railway was too ambitious. Only nine miles or so was completed as far as Lydham Heath where there was an awkward two-and-a-quarter mile reversal to Bishop's Castle, and the railway remained unknown to the outside world. In 1927, a traveller tried to book to Bishop's Castle from Monmouth but was met with blank looks from clerks who confessed to never having heard of that town and found no mention of it in any of their timetables. Be that as it may, there was no denying that the line was as pretty as they come, following the Onny river valley beneath the southern slope of the Long Mynd. Soon after leaving Eaton eastwards, railway and river entered a narrow valley between great wooded heights, both running parallel with the A489 road. Even the eventually built little red-brick Gothic stations added to the magic, a view picked up by John Betjeman when compiling his 1951 *Shropshire Shell Guide.*

Stiperstones and The Devil's Mines

The Stiperstones Ridge is a distinctive hilltop formation with a dramatic 8km (5m) skyline, and most western part of the group known as the Shropshire Hills. It's a quartzite ridge, formed some 480 million years ago above the glaciers of the Ice Age. Constant thawing and freezing shattered the quartzite into a mass of jumbled scree and several isolated jagged tors that have become impressive features. At 536m (1,759ft) above sea level, one of these tors, the Manstone Rock, is the second-highest point in Shropshire, surpassed only by the summit of Brown Clee Hill (540m (1,772ft)) on the edge of Corvedale in the east of the county. However, chief among the dramatic outcrops of the Stiperstones is the atmospheric outline of the Devil's Chair, a constant reminder that this sometimes, eerie landscape has for centuries been a breeding ground of legends and myths. According to one legend, the rocks covering the hillside around the Chair were brought there by the Devil himself. It is said he was carrying a load of stones in his apron while travelling across Britain from Ireland, when he fancied a bit of a rest. He was actually planning to use his stones to fill in the Gatten Valley on the other side of the ridge and known as Hell's Gutter. As he arose after his rest on the highest point of the Stiperstones, his apron strings snapped, the rocks tumbled out but instead of picking them up, the Devil left them scattered over the ridge, where they still lie. The legendary rock chair was to hold a profound significance for the local novelist and poet, Mary Webb, in her stories; in particular, her first, *The Golden Arrow,* in which it was both setting and symbol.

In the late 19th century, the area around the Stiperstones was a thriving industrial area, at different times containing one of the largest lead mines in Western Europe, and the largest barytes mine in England. There would have been many more people living and working here in those days, but life would have been hard. The Romans were the first to mine commercially for lead and other minerals in Shropshire. From the 12th century onwards, the tiny hamlet of Shelve became an important lead mining centre, as did the nearby Grit mines and those at Roman Gravels. The principal owners of most of the mines reads like the revered estate masters of Bronte novels – the Earls of Tankerville of Chillingham Castle in Northumberland; the Thynnes of Longleat in Wiltshire; and the Mores of Linley Hall near Bishop's Castle. By 1875, this small area was producing over 10% of the UK's demand for lead ore and 25% of our barytes, a mineral used to create the chemical barium. Coal, too, had been mined on a small scale since the 16th century. During those times, the view from the Stiperstones would have been a very industrial one with up to a dozen engine houses each with a tall chimney belching out smoke. The Devil watching all this from his chair might have felt quite at home. The rural surroundings of Linley Hill now misrepresent the industrial developments made over subsequent centuries to extract zinc, copper, as well as lead and barytes, turning this pleasant countryside into desolate slag heaps. The bubble finally burst in the latter half of the 19th century when cheap imports brought the price down from a high of £20 per ton to barely half that. The smaller mines who couldn't cope closed, and even the larger producers had to turn to mining only barytes to make ends meet. The Huglith Mine survived until 1947 and the largest at Snailbeach closed in 1955. There has been no serious mining since.

This Shropshire landscape can be a lonely one even today. It was certainly so in Victorian and Edwardian times when the population was sparse, when isolated cottages and remote farms and villages were connected by narrow winding lanes and the roughest of tracks. This part of south Shropshire is still connected by a web of narrow lanes barely a tractor wide and perilous to the unwary traveller in the quest to discover the county's many enchanting nooks and corners. Into this shattered landscape came Magdalene Weale in 1932 riding Sandy, her hired pony. She arrived in the heart of a land of dereliction, moorland at its most desolate and ruined mine shafts looking forlorn. Grey mounds and decayed workings dotted the countryside in mournful profusion and dark pools enhanced the gloom of the scene. Not surprisingly, she quickly developed a presumptuous but – happily, as it turned out – an erroneous view of the subsequent landscape of post-industrial Britain:

> If the Welsh coalfields or the great industrial areas of the North ever become forsaken, what an abomination of desolation will ensue! Only a volcanic upheaval will suffice to restore the fair face of Nature. For the industrialism of the nineteenth century was a monstrous growth, consuming the green beauty of the countryside with its corroding breath.

During the mining industry's heydays, families lived in village communities; others preferred smallholdings scattered over the hillsides. They were encouraged by the landowners to squat and make small enclosures, for which they would then be charged a rent. These communities still existed as Magdalene Weale rode around the lanes:

> Half-way up from the Minsterley road, clinging desperately to the steep slopes, the little homes of shepherds lead a precarious existence. Higher up, the ruins of cottages, scarcely discernible amid the heather, show Nature's relentless power. Old Mrs Pugh tells of how she came to her cottage years ago. She had nothing to start with until her husband built, first a hovel with a turf roof and an improvised chimney. Then they kindled the fire and created the smoke which gave them the rights to live there. Then with stones from the hillside her cottage home arose, next a patch of wild moorland was reclaimed, and now two cows graze in their field, fenced against the ever-encroaching heather.

The steep sided short valleys of the Stiperstones are called beaches. They are the result of glacial activity probably caused by large volumes of water during periods of thaw. It wasn't only shepherds and miners who eked out how they could in these difficult terrains; there were other, equally less fortunate beings. Here, in the disused quarry at Snailsbeach, was the headquarters of many of the gypsy tribes which roamed the border country. They lived in mud huts less than four feet high and looking much like the prehistoric pit dwellings on the Clee Hills. At the approach of a stranger, dark skinned children would crawl out of the huts like rabbits from a burrow and summon the adults of the tribe whinberry picking up on the hill.

Near the village of Pontesbury there were stone quarries, and in a little house not far from these quarries, Mary Webb wrote *The Golden Arrow*. Nearby Habberley Hall was an early 17th century manor house, once the home of the romantic Shropshire family, the Myttons. In *Golden Arrow*, Webb referred to it as Bitterley. The huge Huglith Barytes Mine was perched on the wooded slope of Huglith Hill above Habberley, and it would have been fascinating to watch the men loading the glittering metal onto trucks, which were then carried on overhead cables to the factory at Pontesbury where it was crushed. There was, however, some danger involved in working in these mines. Silicosis[36] was a frequent consequence of working in the mine, and hereabouts men of around forty became incapacitated and prematurely aged, victims to the need of earning a living. Pursuing the course of a rippling brook, Henry Timmins followed the road, now the A488, through the Hope Valley:

> A narrow dingle whose sides present an unbroken expanse of greenwood, its verdure looking fresh and bright after the passage of recent rains, while the carol of many a feathered friend enlivens our onward march.

---

[36] A form of occupational lung disease caused by the inhalation of crystalline silica dust, particularly by stone-cutting miners.

It is obvious from his report that Timmins travelled through this valley during late spring or summer when strong sunshine accentuates the narrow woodland surroundings. I have driven many times along the road that descends the valley in wintertime, with little light penetrating the mist and canopy of trees. Then it appeared as a damp and dreary place.

The Shropshire highlands, never very high but almost worthy of the name of mountains through their impressive outlines and dizzy slopes, offer a diversity of scenery that ranges from the almost startling Stretton Hills, Stipperstones, and the first sight of the Breiddens, to the exquisite outline of Corndon Hill. Roads in the district are generally excellent and, where hilly, are skilfully gradiented, but the wilder country of hilltop and deep wood is criss-crossed with a tangle of lanes, cart tracks, and footpaths, that offer perpetual possibilities to the indefatigable pedestrian, or even the cyclist rough rider. On Stiperstones, the steep slopes can be tricky in places where the path has worn to a narrow trough, while elsewhere the way becomes a confusion of large, flat grey stones that lie about the hillside like tombstones with no name. On neighbouring Linley Hill, larch woods reach up wistfully towards the gaunt, unchanging heights and the Devil's Chair.

Below Corndon Hill, the village of Chirbury is a quiet, modestly picturesque affair with a claim to a venerable past. An Augustinian priory was founded here at the end of the 12th century, based around St Michael's church, and seemed to prosper at first, acquiring land outside the parish between Chirbury and Churchstoke. The present farm at Caeprior suggests monastic origins. However, harvest failures and plagues of the early 14th century took their toll on the community, which by 1423 was said to be 'in a state of spiritual and material collapse'. After the dissolution of the monasteries, the priory's land holdings were acquired by the Herberts of Montgomery, and apart from the church, which was returned to the parish, virtually nothing remains of the monastic buildings. Just outside the village, at a spot known as King's Orchard on the Montgomery road, are the outlines of a fortress built in 915 by Aethelflaeda, the 'Lady of the Mercians' and daughter of Alfred the Great, not as a defence against the Welsh, rather against the possibility of a Viking attack because at that time the western frontier of Mercia was under threat from a Danish invasion. Before Montgomery is reached along this road, it is crossed by Offa's Dyke, and most of the section of the Dyke from there south to the A489 Newtown road forms the national border.

On banks of the Camlad Brook is old Heightley Hall – a mere farmhouse now, though in bygone days it was the ancestral home of the Newtons, an ancient family of more than local fame. The first to settle here, in 1501, was Sir Peter Newton, builder of the old Council House in Shrewsbury, and the great philosopher, Sir Isaac Newton, is a descendant of the family who once graced the old hall. The Camlad is the only river to cross from England into Wales and does so twice within sight of Heightley. A mile or so to the south of Chirbury, in an undulating well wooded park where the Camlad squeezes through a deep gorge, stands the ancient timbered mansion of Marrington Hall, 'a very noble and sweet place,' Samuel Pepys once said. Timmins went that way, too, as he descended from the Stiperstones ridge:

> To vary our route, we will return to Chirbury by way of Marrington Dingle. Here the Camlad has carved out for itself a deep, narrow gorge, running in a due northerly direction; a famous place for wildflowers, ferns and mosses, which flourish amain beneath the cool shade of the overarching copses, draping with a mantle of luscious verdure the banks of the winding steam.

Enclosed amidst ancient oaks, under the lee of a range of high heather-clad hills, the Elizabethan Marrington Hall faces out towards the distant highlands of Montgomery, commanding a prospect of rare beauty. Born here in 1878 was a child with as romantic and historic name as any Welsh parent could wish to bestow to Llywelyn Alberic Emilius Price-Davies. In later life, as if to justify his name and background, while serving king and country in the Boer Wars he became a recipient of the Victoria

Cross, the highest and most prestigious award for gallantry in the face of the enemy that can be awarded to any soldier of British and Commonwealth forces. On his gravestone in Sonning, Berkshire, his name is written as L.A.E Price-Davies. Marrington is currently the home (in 2018) of the Honourable Katherine Odeyne de Grey, mother of the 8th Earl of Powis.

Blue Remembered Stretton Hills

Church Stretton lies at the heart of the South Shropshire hills 21km (13 mi) south of Shrewsbury and 24km (15 mi) north of Ludlow, and is the only town within the Shropshire Hills Area of Outstanding Natural Beauty. It is enclosed on its eastern side by the peaks of the Lawley, Caer Caradoc, and Ragleth Hill, combining to form the Stretton Hills, and on the western side by the broad hill expanse known as Long Mynd with its 11km (7 mi) stretch of heath and moorland plateau. The space in between is known locally as the Stretton Gap. The town sits in a spectacular setting, nicknamed Little Switzerland in the late-Victorian and Edwardian period because of the spectacular hilly landscape. Hitherto, it has become a popular base for walkers and cyclists from which to explore the Shropshire Hills, these 'Blue Remembered Hills' lauded in the poetry of A.E. Housman, and more recently by local author Keith Pybus whose book bearing that famed title is alive with tales of places and people of his beloved Shropshire. Arriving by train, you are met and escorted on the walk into town by a stately avenue of limes planted in 1884 following a recommendation by the Reverend Holland Sandford, who saw the town's early development as a tourist attraction and chose to put his own mark on it. He paid for most of them himself and then decided to extend his idea beyond Watling Street, from where he could follow the parade from his rectory. That very route into town now bears his name.

Church Stretton grew, not on this old thoroughfare, but scattered among the folds of the hills away from danger. Today the modern A49 road, which was constructed on its current alignment in the late 1930s, runs along a similar course to the Roman road. Across the main highway and looming over it, the summit of Caer Caradoc at 459m (1,506ft) is crowned by an Iron Age fort, the centre of the legend that this was the site of the final battle of Caractacus against the Roman legions in AD 51 during the conquest of Britain. The evidence has been frequently argued in and out of books for centuries that the Stretton Caer Caradoc is the popular choice – and certainly with the local tourist office. However, it is not the only site attributed to the British chieftain's last stand as I have already mentioned on two occasions in this book, and we will come to yet another possibility in later pages. Some think the hill with the same name, between Clun and Knighton, has a good claim. Others again plump for Coxall Knoll above the Teme at Brampton Bryan. Even Cefn Carnedd, a strongly defended multi-vallate hillfort near Caerswys in Powys, has been suggested elsewhere as a possible site and is close to a Roman settlement, crucial to their conquest plans for central Wales. A writer in a 19th century copy of *Archaeoligia Cambrensis* placed the scene of conflict on Breidden Hill above the River Severn near Welshpool, yet another strong contender because of its closeness to 'a river of uncertain depth flowing passed'. No-one has yet produced convincing proof that any of these sites meet the necessary criteria, so the arguments will continue until someone does.

Thomas Pennant was in no doubt about the hill's credentials:

Notwithstanding this place is styled Caer Caradoc, it certainly was not that which was attacked by Ostorius, and so admirably described by Tacitus. The learned Camden places it at Gaer Ditches,[37] about three miles south of Clun, on the left of the road to Knighton; and gives, as I am informed, a faithful description of the trenches and ramparts. I never saw the place, therefore am uncertain on what river it stood, the fords of which the Roman attackers found so difficult. No such river is to be seen near the post which I ascended; it therefore could not have been the spot on which our hero was defeated: yet it is highly probable that it had

---

[37] Caer Caradoc hilltop fort is by Stow Hill between Clun and Knighton

been a post occupied by him, and that it was named from that circumstance.

Halfway along Sandford Avenue is Stretton Antiques Market, a local institution and Aladdin's Cave covering four floors under one roof where anyone can amble away a few hours rooting through the vast collection of vintage knick-knacks, chipped crockery, second-hand furniture, and lots more of what you don't need. I have 'ambled' the numerous convoluted store rooms on many occasions, following the yellow footprints painted on the floors, although it still would not be impossible to get lost in there, pondering the uselessness of much on view and the wisdom of storing large furniture units, the heaviest displays, on the top floor. Nevertheless, it is a must-visit for followers of the hunt for a bargain.

For most of its history, Church Stretton has been a small rural market town servicing local agriculture, both arable and livestock. Six fairs used to be held each year at which cattle, sheep, and ponies were sold and farm labourers and domestic servants were hired. One such occasion became known as 'Deadman's Fair' held on St Andrew's Day, November 30th, each year, so called due to the regularity of revellers under the influence not surviving the walk home over the Long Mynd. In 1865, the Reverend Donald Carr got very close to adding to the statistics when he became lost in deep snow after trying to return on foot from Rattlinghope on the far side of the mynd. He had been giving a service at the church and seemingly had no thoughts for his own safety as he set out on his return journey, presumably trusting that his guardian angel would see him home. By all accounts, he was a very lucky man. Defying all the odds on survival, he finally made it back to his Rectory at Woolstaston.

The Long Mynd is formed from a series of hills roughly 12km (7mi) long and 5km (3mi) wide. It lies between the Stiperstones range to the west and the Stretton Hills to the east. Its broad-backed lofty ridge, running north and south throws out high precipitous spurs into the vale below. The deep combs are partially clad with fern and gorse and watered by mynd brooks. An ancient trackway, the Port Way, runs across the summit from Plowden at its southern end, becoming a metalled road before its northern drop at Woolstaston. It is likely to have originated as a drove road similar to the Kerry Ridgeway, and possibly an extension of that along which cattle and sheep were moved between Bishop's Castle and Shrewsbury. The Long Mynd's most striking characteristic is its spaciousness. It is a great tableland of rolling moors, wild and lonely, the home of curlew and buzzard, fox and red grouse and once the haunt of the wolf and wild boar. It is more varied, too, with its heights and glens, its open moorland and treacherous bogs, its cascades and eerie mountain pools. These wastes were once the land of Eadric the Wild who – so the legend says – lies entombed with his men in the depths of an old lead mine, and like Arthur and Glyndŵr, await their hour of vengeance. The narrow tree covered valleys were not a convenient way to travel in ancient days, often flooded after heavy rain. Over time, the Port Way became the main highway for travellers avoiding the toll road, Roman Watling Street, through the Stretton Gap. However, these days, the Long Mynd is a playground for walkers, and like our Shropshire Hills pony lady, for horse riders, too. John Hillaby once walked naked across this open expanse, unconcerned of meeting any male or female ramblers of the day. It would not be wise to do so today, unless of course you *are* the naked rambler:

> On top of the great hill the turf was elastic, the wind blew slightly and horses that had been left out to graze galloped way madly from the bat-like shadows of the gliders. I took off my shirt and still felt hot, so I took everything off and still felt fine (Risky!) You can walk on the very top of the Mynd for six or seven miles before reaching a deep canyon where I dressed and went down into the respectability of Church Stretton for supper.

"The Long Mynd is wild country, and more dangerous than the Stiperstones. They are hard but they are straight. The Long Mynd is not so hard but it is treacherous – like a woman!" So said the farmer of Batchcott Heights, when once directing Magdalene Weale:

I was taken aback, but though I repudiate the insinuations against my sex, I know what he meant. There is something almost feminine in the sleek curves of this mountain range in its infinite variety of mood and scene. But it is a very primitive and very capricious femininity, that of some wild creature of the woodland, which one moment will tolerate a caress and the next will greet your approach with a snarl.

The road from Church Stretton over the Mynd is only for the steady driver, the very strenuous cyclist and perhaps the capable equestrian, but will reveal the topography of the Shropshire highlands to the west and north west. The road climbs steeply and mounts to the broad summit ridge where it crosses the Port Way continuing to Ratlinghope (pronounced Ratchup) on the western slopes. On the way down, which is again steep and used to be gated, it is essential to pause now and then to take in the views. Woods sprawl on the hillside against a background of rising moorland, while below are cattle pastures split by the East Onny river. The forward skyline is a strangely irregular series of outcrops that variously resemble castle ruins, or huge fins of a long extinct sea creature, or the teeth of a mastodon, or a cross-cut saw, projecting from the hog's back of the Stiperstones ridge. Once on the other side, and the spring sun climbs passed mid-morning, the lumps and bumps of the western flanks of the Mynd stand out in varicose fashion, its nooks and crannies etching shadowy lines at all angles from the summit plateau to the valley floor.

In St Margaret's churchyard at Ratlinghope is the grave of Richard Munslow, who died in 1906. He was Britain's last sin-eater, one who performed an ancient ritual over a deceased person shortly after death to cleanse the soul of sin, allowing the departed to rest in peace. Traditionally, the sin-eater was a local beggar, but Munslow was a prosperous farmer who volunteered to perform the work for his parish, allegedly as a result of losing three of his children to scarlet fever all within a week. The ritual involved drinking a bowl of ale and eating a crust of bread at the bedside while reciting words of absolution and accepting the sins of the dead into his own soul – a risky move, I would've thought, in view of the power of superstitions, even in Victorian times. In an account of his visit to Ross on Wye in 1818, antiquarian, the Reverend Thomas Fosbroke, wrote of a sin-eater who lived by the Ross highway. He described him as:

> A gaunt, ghastly, lean, miserable, poor rascal, who lived alone in a hovel made of the wreck of a boat near the river where few would approach by day and none dare by night for fear, or at least awe, which all felt of that recluse.

In such surroundings, Arthur Bradley often yearned to exchange walking stick for rod:

> Here by the eager running Onny, while renewing an acquaintance with the trout of Plowden, I found a group of loggers with their white tents busy amount the alders, familiar folk enough to those who haunt the smaller streams of Wales and the border. There would seem some spice of romance about the clogger's trade. He pursues it in the pleasant places of the earth, in sequestered glens where silvery streams dance beneath the shade of the timber on which he makes discriminating and no wanton onslaught.

The clogger was once a common sight by a small river where alders grow thick. He would have lodgings in a nearby village and every day come to the riverbank to work. He would have made a bargain with the land owner for all the standing trees on the river bank, which would be felled, the bark stripped, and the wood, which has to be green as it is easier to cut, sawn into short lengths and then cut into the rough shape of the finished sole. This the clogger would have done for a few months until he had built up a pyramid of shaped blocks and stored them in his tent to dry. When he had built up a handsome pile, the soles would be sent away somewhere for the master clog maker to turn them into the finished article. Making clogs was, and still is, a skilled job though there can't be many nowadays who would tolerate such an uncertain career. I know of a clog maker still plying this trade in Kington, but I have heard of no other, at least in the borders.

Magdalene Weale's holiday in the Shropshire hills was nearing its
end. For over two weeks she had travelled alone in a dangerous
world where women had learnt to be subservient to and often
dependent on their menfolk. Staying in inns that no doubt would
have buzzed with challenging whispers, or even of hopeful
encounters. But now her play was over and it was time to ring
down the curtain, put out the lights and return to London. It had
been a wonderful ride over high moorlands, lonely and free, where
the only signs of life were the sheep and the wild ponies and
curlews crying overhead. For the final time, at 1,200 feet up on the
slopes of Corndon, she dropped down and over the border again
into Shropshire. They were back home in the realm of the titular
deity of the Stiperstones and in the shadow of his dark throne:

> Standing on the highest point of Stapeley Hill and looking out
> over the moor, I realise that man is here an intruder. The hill
> ponies with their foals which gaze at me with curious, distrustful
> eyes, the cattle and sheep which keep at a safe distance, are the
> rightful denizens of this lonely place. Even the little homesteads of
> the shepherds are tolerated, it seems to me, only because they
> minister to the needs of the dumb beasts. Nature is here supreme.

A few more miles brought them to Hogstow Hall, Sandy's home.
And here Magdalene bade farewell to her quadruped travelling
companion, who no doubt was tempered by the knowledge that
she was happy to be home again among her courtyard friends.

Bomere Pool is one of many lakes and pools formed at the end of
the Ice Age that remain in the landscape of north Shropshire. They
are known as kettle-hole meres – shallow, sediment-filled bodies
of water formed by retreating glaciers. Bomere is the 'Sarn Mere'
of Mary Webb's most famous novel, *Precious Bane*. She wrote the
book in 1920 while living at Spring Cottage on Lyth Hill overlooking the pool.

Now the principal focus of a country park within easy reach of
Shrewsbury, the narrow ridge of Lyth Hill provides panoramic views
of the Shropshire Hills and the Stiperstones to the west and the

pimple shape of the Wrekin and the limestone escarpment of Wenlock Edge in the east. Lyth Hill was always a special place for Mary Webb. She often dreamed of living there and achieved that wish in 1917 when she and her husband Henry moved to Spring Cottage, her final home until just before her untimely death in 1927.

Charles George Harper was nothing if not a critic of people's habits, those he saw as being of the lower classes. His often-outspoken vitriol would win him no acclaim in today's popularity stakes. And so it was that as he came within a few miles of Shrewsbury, he could not resist another pop at his least favourite company:

> Groups and single parties of the townsfolk were to be seen walking along the road in the due performance of the Sunday after-dinner walk. It is most surprising, however, to notice how few are they who, in a large town like this, find sufficient energy to carry them even this short distance beyond their thresholds. Do they not know the Sunday of the British lower middle-class? The late rising, the graceless Sunday paper at the eleven o'clock breakfast, the solid one o'clock dinner, the plethoric after-dinner nap, announced to the startled ear by stertorous snores in awful diapason, the choked awakening, with the early tea, and the deadly dull 'constitutional' Evening service, perhaps, if your Briton be not altogether Godless, supper, yawns all round, bed at an early hour, with the consciousness of having spent a dull day, and a very great satisfaction that it is at last done with.

Hidden away in a recess in the low hills to the south of Shrewsbury is one of the most charming of homes. Pitchford Hall is a large Grade I listed Tudor country house built around 1560. Pevsner called this historic E-shaped half-timbered mansion 'the most splendid piece of black-and-white building in Shropshire'. Timmins, too, held the house in high enough regard to commit his pen to paper:

> Sketches completed, we now make for the village and pace on through the quiet, weed grown street, where the martins are nesting under the lee of the old stone tiled roofs, and the still,

sunny air is redolent of lilac and early honeysuckle. Yonder gable-end with its rough yellow plasterwork, venetian shutters, and mantle of purple wisteria, greets the eye with a pleasant scheme of colour, calling up visions of far-away Italy.[38]

Princess (later Queen) Victoria stayed here In 1832 as a guest of the then owner, Charles Jenkinson, 3rd Earl of Liverpool, and wrote in her diary that the house was 'a curious looking but very comfortable, striped black and white, and in the shape of a cottage'. What Jenkinson thought of her unflattering description of his home is not recorded. Despite its overwhelming presence in the surrounding leafy landscape, Pitchford doesn't dominate. In her wandering memoir of her home county, author Edith Pargeter – better known to followers of Brother Cadfael by her pen name, Ellis Peters – described it as 'a meadow house, utterly at ease with its own charms'. In 1992 it was sold unexpectedly by its then owner Caroline Colthurst, but after a period of uncertainty and neglect, was re-united in 2016 with Caroline's daughter Rowena and her husband James Nason.

Between the village of Cound and the Ludlow road is an undulating hinterland through which the Cound Brook meanders in silent mode. The lanes take their cue from the brook and meander in similar fashion from one hamlet to another where there is generally a choice of ways. It is a land of red soils and stone disclosing itself here and there in the sides of sunken lanes and appearing in sturdy church towers. The man of the border soil, Cledwyn Hughes, remembers his home farming days as he passed along these ways:

Near Condover, I pass a hayfield where the second crop is being gathered in: a second cutting from the same field. Sweet border hayfields where the scented vernal grass, timothy grass and meadow foxtail grow. And the other plants of the field hedgerow: great wild valerian, corn gromwell, harebell and common barberry.

---

[38] Italy was a favourite destination for Timmins and is where he died suddenly while visiting in 1908.

Condover village contains a high proportion of listed buildings, and over half of the village has been classified as a conservation area since 1976. The listed structures include some early cruck framed buildings, black and white timbered cottages and half-timbered houses. The Anglo-Saxon manor of Condover was purchased in 1586 by Thomas Owen, a Judge and Member of Parliament for Shrewsbury who began building a new house by the Cound Brook. The result was Condover Hall, an elegant Grade I listed three storey Elizabethan sandstone building described as the grandest manor house in Shropshire. Owen died before the house was completed, but it remained in the hands of the Owen family until the late 1860s when it passed to the Cholmondeleys.

The last of that family to live in the house, Reginald Cholmondeley, was host to the American writer Mark Twain during his visit to England in 1873 and again in 1879. There are some fine monuments of Owens and Cholmoneleys in the church next door, but their erstwhile home suffered for many years through neglect and decay. It took a multi £1,000,000 rescue and refurbishment to revive it, but the result has meant a metamorphic remodeling as a residential activity centre.

So, this is Uriconium!

Since Jove was worshipped under Wrekin's shade
Or Latin phrase was writ in Shropshire stone,
Since Druids chants desponded in this glade
Or Tuscan general called that field his own,
How long ago? How long?

Wilfred Owen

Just across the river plain and beyond the winding waters of the Severn are the remains of the most famous Roman settlement in Britain. The broken walls and scattered foundations are all that can be seen of the most important town between Dover and Chester, excepting London itself, until the latter days of the

Roman occupation. The line of the old city wall and ditch can still be traced sweeping across surrounding fields in a horseshoe shape to enclose an area of some 170 acres. In the middle of this enclosed space, the ruins of basilica and baths, hypocausts and flues are visible. Here, too, is the Forum with the finest Roman colonnade ever unearthed in Britain. Beneath visitors' feet lie the foundations of a city larger than Pompeii. Before the invasion of the soldiers of Rome in the 1st century AD, the local tribe, the Cornovii, had already begun to farm in the river plain below their main settlement atop the Wrekin hill. Originally named as Viriconium by the Romans who built it – first in AD 50 as a military base for their invasion of Wales, then later in AD 90 as an administrative centre for the defeated Cornovii – it then became known as Viriconium Cornoviorum. And after the Romans had left, it was renamed again by the inhabitants as Uriconium. It was the fourth largest civilian settlement in Roman Britain and was certainly big. Only a small part of the site has been excavated. The visible ruins, which include a large section of basilica wall referred to as the Old Work, are impressive but represent just the fortress bath house complex, a fraction of what still lies beneath unexcavated farmland. Uriconium remained occupied until midway through the 7th century when Penda's Anglo-Saxons arrived and discovered it already deserted. Those Romano-Cornovii who had remained after the legions left had moved a short way down Watling Street to settle around St Andrew's Church. The subsequent community that they called Wroxeter, some of it built from recycled Roman masonry, even now is no more than a small village by the Severn but still within the old city boundary. These twins of history, Uriconium and Wroxeter, are just 8.0km (5 miles) south-east of what many historians assume emerged as the new tribal centre of Pengwern that eventually evolved as Shrewsbury.

Charles Harper seemed unclear on the demise of Uriconium, and on describing what he saw, jumped to the incorrect conclusion that the Roman city had been destroyed and its inhabitants massacred, either by invading Picts and Scots from the north, or Welsh tribes. His confusion was compounded by adding, rather dramatically, that when the Saxons arrived, they found it not only a deserted site, but with grass and shrubs already growing in the streets and upon the walls:

> With pestiferous swamps and pools dealing death, agues and fevers, exhaling the most loathsome effluvia, and all aglow at nights with the phosphorescence arising from a soil poisoned and saturated with the wreck and refuse of an ancient and populous place.

A Bloody Field Near Shrewsbury

On the northern outskirts of Shrewsbury are the large impressive ruins of Haughmond Abbey, founded in 1135 for an Augustinian community by the powerful FitzAlans, lords of Oswestry and Clun. That seems to be the official view, but during excavations in 1907 a small chapel was discovered below the floor of the abbey church which suggests there may have been a foundation at Haughmond earlier than that of the FitzAlans. Unlike the Cistercians who were a self-supporting society of monks and led secluded lives, Augustinians were largely an order of canons, ordained priests, who travelled and worked in communities away from their monasteries. Nevertheless, the extent and quality of building work at Haughmond suggests generous backing and a regular supply of donations for a long time. After the dissolution in 1539, the abbot's hall and rooms were converted for private residential use and later as a farm, until the whole site was placed under the care of the Ministry of Works in 1933. The site is now managed by English Heritage. However, in 1903, there was no public admittance to the private site when Fletcher Moss and his travelling companion arrived on the scene:

> The gates were locked and there was no-one about so, we promptly decided to lift our bikes over the gates, take them to some oak trees in the park and there leave them. Climbing a little up a hill amid the ruins we sat down to rest and lunch. Before us for miles

and miles was one of the most lovely English scenes, the fertile fields stretching down to the Severn and rising again to the mountains of Wales; the conical peak of Caradoc and the Long Mynd by Church Stretton, other hills that we knew not, the spires and towers of ancient Shrewsbury hazy in their smoke and farther round the wooded height of the Wrekin. The white-faced Hereford cattle were knee-deep in the grass, the wandering voice of the cuckoo was on the breeze, and all the air was balmy and fragrant with the breath of early June.

Almost within sight of the abbey ruins and set a little distance back from the road as if it must be hidden from view, is the redundant church of St Mary Magdalene. In 1911 Bradley wrote:

> I know of no other building of the kind in England that has quite such a story to tell. It is now a simple parish church, with a congregation which the very nature of its endowment and situation makes a limited one, for it was not built with any view to the needs of its neighbourhood, but simply and solely as a contemporary memorial of the slaughter that took place upon this Hately field five centuries ago.

In 1403, the Battle of Shrewsbury was fought on this land that has become known as Battlefields. On 21 July of that year an army led by the Lancastrian King Henry IV who had usurped the throne from Richard II, believing he had a legitimate hereditary claim to it, clashed with a rebel army led by Harry 'Hotspur' Percy – the son of the 1st Earl of Northumberland, whose favours the King had previously bought, but then reneged. Regretting his earlier agreement to help oust Richard, the bitter Hotspur now wanted to get rid of Henry, in the process probably complicating the royal heritage even further. And so, to this bloody field near Shrewsbury...

According to the owner of the manor of that time, Richard Hussey, the conflict took place in his field of peas. The outcome was short and brutal – victory for King Henry and ignominious defeat for Hotspur, who may have been killed during the early clashes rather than as Shakespeare had him die in the final moments in a hand-to-hand fight with young Prince Hal. Missing from the hostilities, significantly, was the Welsh rebel Owain Glyndŵr, who some thought intended to join the fray. There was doubt before the start as to which side he would eventually support. In the event, he had decided not to engage on either side, but was said to have watched the progress of battle instead from a viewing position in a tree some distance away, so creating the legend of the Shelton Oak. After the battle, the king had Hotspur's body displayed at the High Cross in Shrewsbury (at the top of Pride Hill), impaled on a spear and supported between two millstones. The body was later quartered, and the parts put on display in Chester, London, Bristol, and Newcastle upon Tyne. Hotspur's head was sent to York and impaled on the north gate, looking towards his own lands. Such were the brutal mediaeval consequences of upsetting the monarch.

Within a few years, the church dedicated to St Mary Magdalene was built near the site of the conflict over the mass burial pit where up to 2,000 dead were unceremoniously dumped. Much of the church was restored in the 1860s by the distinguished local architect, Samuel Pountney Smith, creating as good an air of mediaeval authenticity as could be found in any restoration. The hammer beam roof, timber screen, marble reredos and font, are particularly splendid inclusions, and the tiling throughout the nave and chancel is as perfect as I have seen in any parish church. Visiting this historical site could affect some reminded of the slaughter these fields witnessed 700 years ago. Within the churchyard, old headstones lean in all directions as if the graves below them have moved in unstable ground. This is an unused place now and there seems to be little attention to preventing the stones Inclination to fall. The air is of neglect and ruin and there is nothing to halt the imagination taking hold if you are alone. Outside of the surrounding walls and hedges, the fields are still ploughed and farm produce – including peas – continue to be sown and harvested in age-old tradition, with little care of the past or what may emerge unexpectedly from ploughing the soil.

A Fair County Town

High the vanes of Shrewsbury gleam
Islanded in Severn stream;
The bridges from the steepled crest
Cross the water east and west.

The flag of mourn in conqueror's state
Enters at the English gate;
The vanquished eve, as night prevails,
Bleeds upon the road to Wales.

A.E. Housman: The Welsh Marches

The county town of Shrewsbury began its existence in the 7th century as an island settlement perched on a hilltop inside a loop of the River Severn. It was the early capital of the Kingdom of Powis, the seat of the Welsh prince, Brochwel Yscithrog, and the Celtic Britons called the settlement Pengwern. When the Saxons arrived, their name for it was Scrobbesbyrig. This gradually evolved into Sciropscire which became Shropshire, then Sloppesberie which became Salop, an alternative name for both town and county, then finally Schrosberie, or Shrewsbury, if you say it quickly. Later, the Welsh got into the act and gave it their own name, Amwythig. Today, many first-time visitors to the town are unsure whether to call it Shrozebury or Shroosbury. Percy Thoresby Jones, was convinced and went for Shrozebury. The townsfolk of today say Shroosbury. However, one alternative name is never in doubt. Followers of the romantic novelist Mary Webb, born not far away by the Severnand whose stories cover recognisable Shropshire landmarks, will know Shrewsbury as Silverton.

Shrewsbury claims to be England's finest Tudor town. The skyline is of spires and towers, its central streets still retain many black and white buildings, others hide amid old lanes, courtyards and alleyways. There are just two major road bridges over the Severn loop to the centre. The English Bridge built in 1121 was once the way in from the east, while the Welsh Bridge completed in 1160 was the way out to the west. It was over the Welsh bridge that John Leland entered Shrewsbury in 1540:

> It has six great arches of stone, so callid because it is the way out of town into Wales. This bridge standeth on the west side, and hath at one end of it a great gate to enter by into the town, and at the other end towards Wales a mighty strong tower to prohibit enemies from entering onto the bridge.

The Welsh Bridge once had at the town end a fortified gateway with round towers and over the entrance a statue of Richard Duke of York in armour. It is thought that another tower of similar strength formerly stood at the Welsh end. When William Camden arrived in 1610, he wrote:

> Not much lower upon Severn standeth most pleasantly the famousest City of this Shire risen from the ruin of Old Uriconium. It is seated upon an hill of a reddish earth, and Severn, having two very faire Bridges upon it, gathering himself in manner round in form of a circle, so passeth it, that were it not for a small bank of firm land, it might go for an Island.

In 1720 Daniel Defoe thought Shrewsbury beautiful, large, pleasant, populous, and a rich town, full of gentry yet full of trade, too:

> For here too, is a great manufacture, as well as flannel, as also of white broadcloth, which enriches all the country around it. Here is the greatest market, the greatest plenty of good provisions, and the cheapest that is to be met with in all the western part of England.

The Elizabethan poet, Thomas Churchyard, was born near Shrewsbury in 1520 to farming parents. His father had ensured the young Thomas had a good education and a full purse to follow whatever course his life might take. Fortunately for him, it began in the household of Henry Howard, Earl of Surrey – an English nobleman and one of the founders of English Renaissance poetry.

Churchyard remained with the Howards for twenty years during which time he learnt his poetry skills. His most famous piece, *The Worthiness Of Wales,* was published in 1587.

The man who kick-started the town as an important centre for the Norman invaders, was Roger de Montgomerie. Apart from his family connections with Duke William, Roger had contributed heavily to the Conqueror's invasion forces and therefore qualified for something in return for his services. That something was vast amounts of land on the Welsh borders and an earldom of Shrewsbury. He was also given the freedom to acquire more Welsh territory by whatever means he chose and to administer his own laws and taxes. Building work was crucial to establishing a home and a base from which to control his new territory, so though a castle at Shrewsbury came first, a religious house was equally important for a Norman lord after all the recent slaughter and land grab, to keep his hand in with the Almighty. Following that tradition, in 1083 he established the Abbey of St Peter and Paul outside the town wall as a house for Benedictine monks. Sometime in 1094 Earl Roger's health was failing, and so a few days before his death he entered his own monastery as a monk, complete with the ubiquitous shaven head. He was later buried, appropriately, in a prime position near the altar.

Around 1130 the monastery's prior, Robert Tennant, suggested the abbey needed a relic to attract a regular income, so plans were made to acquire the bones of St Winifred of Holywell, believed at that time to be at rest in her churchyard grave at Gwytherin in North Wales. Winifred had been the abbess of a convent there when she died in the year 660 – for the second time, if her murder by the young chieftain Caradoc fifteen years earlier is to be believed. Consequently, in 1137 her remains were brought to Shrewsbury with great pomp to be re-interred in the abbey church. As it transpired, she arrived a little too early to be laid in her shrine which had not then been completed, so was left for a while at St Giles' church outside the walls.

During the time of Abbot Nicholas Stevens (1361-1399) the shrine had to be rebuilt to continue to attract pilgrims and much-needed revenue. There is no record of just how financially

Figure 16 The Wilfred Owen Monument in the grounds of Shrewsbury Abbey

successful the project was, but the dissolution of the monasteries in 1536 brought a 400-year run to an end when both abbey and shrine were destroyed and Winifred's remains scattered. It is claimed that a fragment of the saint's finger bone is kept in a silver reliquary at the Catholic cathedral on the Town Walls, but my inquiries to verify this in the past have been met mostly with blank stares. The bones of Winifred's saintly uncle, Bueno, who allegedly resuscitated his niece after Caradoc's fatal attack, were apparently buried somewhere within the brickwork of the walls of the abbey but the whereabouts have never come to light. However, either may be, Shrewsbury should be proud to have had the remains of *two* saints all to themselves.

Following Henry VIII's Acts of Suppression, attempts were made to have the monastery buildings saved for civic use, but all of them failed and much of the church fabric was reduced and the domestic buildings sold off. Later, to add insult to injury, in 1866

Thomas Telford constructed a new road to the English Bridge through the remains of the cloister building, even isolating the surviving 14th century refectory pulpit which is now on the opposite side of the road to the church, and as Timmins observed, 'merely an obstruction in a coal yard!'

Laid out in the grounds of the abbey church is a strange-looking memorial. It is a sculpture by Paul de Monchaux called 'Symmetry', and represents the makeshift raft on which Wilfred Owen was attempting to cross the Sambre-Oise Canal when he was killed just one week from the end of World War I. The legend on one side of the sculpture proclaims in ironic and unforgettable tones, the first words of Owen's poem, *Strange Meeting*: 'I am the enemy you killed, my friend.' In the circumstances of his death, how can anyone not weep at those sentiments even now, one hundred years on?

When the great Scottish engineer, Thomas Telford, first set foot in Shropshire in 1786, he was given the job of converting Shrewsbury Castle – then a derelict ruin – into a home for the town's MP, Sir William Pulteney. Telford's creation included a panoramic viewing platform and a folly, Laura's Tower, where the original Norman motte and bailey had once stood. The tower was built for Pulteney's daughter and must be one of the most spectacular Wendy Houses ever constructed. Sir William was so impressed by Telford's work on the castle that he convinced the Shropshire County Council to create a new job for the talented engineer – that of Surveyor of Public Works for the county, a post which Telford held until his death in 1834. The remodelled great hall of the castle is now a museum housing the Shropshire Regimental Collection of artifacts and weapons of war dating from the eighteenth century.

During one of his two tours in Wales, Thomas Pennant came to Shrewsbury in 1773 entering through the North Gate below the castle walls. After the castle, the old school would have been the next building in view:

The free school stands near the castle in a broad handsome street. It was founded in 1552 by King Edward VI. The building was

Figure 17 A bronze statue of Charles Darwin outside his old school, now Shrewsbury library

originally of wood, but in 1595 a beautiful and extensive edifice of stone arose in its place which contained the school and library filled with a valuable collection of books and several curiosities, among them three sepulchral stones discovered by ploughing at Wroxeter.

The old schoolhouse is now Shrewsbury library, where I spent many hours researching part of this book. When the construction of the school was finally completed in 1630, these magnificent golden stone walls included classrooms, dormitories, a chapel, and a library, for nearly 300 boys of Protestant parents of Shrewsbury and other Shropshire towns. Charles Darwin was educated here, as was the Elizabethan courtier, Sir Philip Sidney, and George Jeffreys, 1st Baron Jeffreys of Wem, also known infamously as the Hanging Judge. Darwin was born in 1809 in the suburb of Frankwell beyond the Welsh Bridge and gained early attention with his ideas on evolution by natural selection which he published in 1859 with *On the Origin of Species*. After his death in 1882, he was interred alongside Sir Isaac Newton in the north aisle of the nave of Westminster Abbey. Salopians are constantly reminded of Darwin by a life-sized, seated, bronze statue of the man, carved in 1897 by Horace Montford and placed on a polished granite plinth in the centre of the patio besides the main door of the library. He seems to scowl down on any doubting Thomas's who might have poured scorn on his achievements. A few yards away, and facing him, is the bronze bust of *Golden Arrow* author Mary Webb, with the suggestion of a smile on her face. One wonders if it might be in admiration, or contempt.

266

Broadcaster and writer, Stuart Mais, didn't find Shrewsbury as interesting as Chester in its modern settings, but he did discover many more decorated town mansions of great beauty. He saw overhanging, projecting, timbered houses of some antiquity in every court and narrow alleyway. Shrewsbury was, and still is, a pleasant place in which to loiter on fine summer evenings. There was, he wrote, always some fresh surprise waiting around every corner. On its literary merits, he had no doubts:

It is a far cry from Sir Philip Sidney to Charles Darwin, and almost a greater from Darwin to Mary Webb. But there is something about the Shrewsbury atmosphere that makes for the best possible combination of qualities in a writer, generous enthusiasm, vivid imagination and a classical passion for precision. Shrewsbury's standard of intellectual integrity has not, I think, been rivalled.

Samuel Johnson visited Shrewsbury in September 1774 with his *Tour in North Wales* guide, Hester Thrale. He, too, had compared it with Chester, though perhaps unfavourably:

The walls are broken, and narrower than those of Chester. The town is large and has many Gentlemen's houses, but the streets are narrow. I saw Taylor's library. We walked in the Quarry, a very pleasant walk by the river. Our inn was not bad.

Charles Harper was impressed In 1893 with the picturesqueness of old inner Shrewsbury so much that he questions the over-eagerness of the middle classes for the Wye Tour:

Tell me, are you becoming blasé with the restricted circle of the picturesque, in the common acceptation of that misused word? Have you had your fill of glens and gorges, cathedrals, waterfalls and all the other well-worn subjects of the guidebook? Descend then from the contemplation of your castles, from the craggy pinnacles of rugged cliffs, and seek the picturesqueness of the domestic side of life.

When H.V. Morton visited the town in 1926, he waxed lyrical, not about its picturesqueness, but rather the quaint district names:

> There is a charm about a busy, thriving country town like Shrewsbury, quite different from the more obvious charm of a cathedral city. In ancient streets, where houses overhang the pavement, nodding forward in the sun like tired professors of history, the rich stream of English country life flows on unaltered, in the main, since Elizabethan times, and in many essentials, since the days of the Saxon and the Norman. Shrewsbury runs York very close with its street names, although York wins easily with Whipmawhopmagate, but Shoplatch Street is good, as is Dogpole, Wyle Cop, Murivance and Mardol.

Shrewsbury is a town of many churches. In 1788 the tower of one – the huge, red sandstone parish church of St Chad's – collapsed. This great minster church had been around since the 12th century, but time and weather had taken its toll. Sandstone, being porous and vulnerable to water penetration, may have contributed to subsequent disintegration of joints and erosion of the stone's surface, so it seems a disaster was waiting to happen. In his capacity as county surveyor, Thomas Telford was asked by the churchwardens to report on some alarming cracks that had appeared in some of the piers of the central crossing. He started his subsequent report with the words, 'I think, gentlemen, that if you have any other business to discuss, you would be wise to continue your meeting elsewhere, since this church may fall down on your heads at any moment.' That moment arrived just three days later when – it was said – under the strain of the striking of one of its bells, the tower crumbled onto the nave. What was left standing was demolished with the exception of the Lady Chapel, which remains as an inner landmark.

Four years later, a new, very different, St Chad's was built, occupying a prominent position on the southern Shrewsbury skyline and overlooking a riverbank park known as The Quarry. That church is a Grade I listed building, but George Stuart's revolutionary circular design had a mixed reception initially. Stuart's use of iron pillars for internal supports reflected the developments by Shropshire's iron masters of the Severn gorge, but not everyone appreciated his workmanship. In 1774 Rt. Hon. John Byng, 5th Viscount Torrington, so disliked the new church, he decided, 'A building as ugly and as improper would be better suit a Pantheon, or a dancing room!'

An altogether different feature of New St Chad's represents a piece of theatre and appears in the disused graveyard – an old headstone used in the 1984 filming of *A Christmas Carol* with George C. Scott and bearing the name 'Scrooge'.

The hard-to-miss spire of St Mary the Virgin belongs to the church said to have been founded by the Saxon King Edgar around AD 970. St Mary's is a very large church and would grace any town centre as its cathedral. Though rebuilt and extended many times, there is evidence of Saxon foundations beneath the present nave. The spire was the last major alteration to the building when it was added to the west tower in 1477, which at 42m (138ft) is one of the tallest in England. Apart from a partial collapse in 1894, the spire has survived many storms and at least one earthquake. In common with other important churches throughout the marches, St Mary's has a Jesse Window. However, it didn't begin its existence here; it came from... where else but Old St Chad's after the tragic collapse. I confess to being a bit of a font fanatic, having seen many during my walks through Herefordshire some years ago, and St Mary's has a particularly delightful one from the 14th century. Its hollow stem is unusual and the detail on the bowl is rather worn but I haven't seen one like it before, or quite so interesting.

Standing at the highest point, right in the historic heart and founded about the year 900, St Alkmund's Church celebrated its 1100th anniversary in 2012. If the date of foundation is true, it would challenge Old St Chad's as the earliest in the town. Nothing remains of the first St Alkmund's building, and what is seen today is one which is part mediaeval and part Georgian. The tower and spire were built about 1475 and is another notable building that makes the skyline of Shrewsbury so delightful.

It was Thomas Pennant who first mentioned the rise of the business of Shrewsbury's Drapers:

There is in this town no manufacture considerable enough to merit mention; but it draws very great profit from those of Montgomeryshire. This place is the chief mart for them. About 700,000 yards of Welsh webbs, a coarse kind of woollen cloth, are brought here annually, to the Thursday market; and bought up and dressed, that is, the wool is raised on one side, by a set of people called Shearmen. At this time only forty are employed; but in the time of Queen Elizabeth, the trade was so great, that not fewer than six hundred maintained themselves by this occupation.

Overlooking St Mary's Church, the Drapers Guild Hall was built in 1576 with timber, for all the increasing use of stone, where the wealthier drapers saw the chance to show their success with fine carvings and decorations. The first Guild Hall was built in 1485 and was replaced a century later with the present building on the same site. It is now an upmarket restaurant.

With the success of their trading, the leading members of the Draper's Guild used their power and influence to acquire property and establish family dynasties in the town and around the county. Some of their town houses still grace the Shrewsbury centre streets, the finest example being the dual combination on Barker Street of the timber-framed Rowley's House, built by wool merchant, Roger Rowley, towards the end of the 16th century. Attached to it, is the red brick mansion built in 1618 by his son. Henry Timmins was fortunate to gain access into the Drapers' holy temple and left us a brief but shinning description:

> Yonder ancient half-timbered gable overlooking the churchyard is the erstwhile Hall of the Drapers' Guild where, upon passing within, we find ourselves in a spacious, low-ceiled chamber entirely wainscoted with oak and having massive oak tables, benches and lockers coeval with the room. Upon the wall hangs a dark old panel-picture commonly supposed to be the portrait of Degory Watur, the founder, and his lady wife.

Mr Watur (presumably rhymes with Water), though a member of the Guild, was the instigator behind the idea of the almshouses next to St. Mary's in 1444.

In the town square, Shrewsbury has what must be one of the country's best-looking, two storey market houses to have been constructed anywhere. It was built in 1596 of stone to replace a 13th century timber-framed house to store and sell corn under cover. Not surprisingly, the Drapers had their say in how the new market hall would be used by claiming the second floor for wool and cloth sales. The design and construction became one of the most prized works of Shrewsbury's master mason, Walter Hancock, and went up in the astonishingly short time of four months. For sheer size and majesty, his stone edifice is an architectural wonder. At the opposite end of the square but facing the town for which he was elected Mayor in 1762, is the statue of the great Robert Clive of India. In direct contrast to Hancock's masterpiece, the modern shopping mall in the Shoplatch area of the town was opened amid a blaze of publicity and civic celebration in September 1965. Its Victorian predecessor was an Italianate-style marvel of cathedral-like proportions, complete with nave, chancel, even a west transept, all topped by a central 45m (150 ft) tower with steep pyramid roof. However, Nikolaus Pevsner was unimpressed with it, and wasn't alone in his condemnation. But as with so many great architectural achievements of the past, it was just too good for the concrete sixties and was demolished with apparently little ceremony or regret.

The Quarry is the name given to a large, managed, open space south of the centre enclosed within the curve of the Severn loop. The Shrewsbury Carnival is held here every June, as is the Shrewsbury Regatta and Dragon Boat Races during the early summer. Another is the Shrewsbury Flower Show – the longest running flower show in the world – which is held here every year in mid-August.

Cledwyn Hughes recalled being taken to the show when a small boy:

I had to wear a new suit and the trousers rawed the sweating skin on my knees. There was a grasping tie around my throat and solid Brilliantine had been rubbed into my hair. Even in the reaches of the great marquee among the blooms this hair grease smelt persistently above all the fragrances. But what a day, a day to remember! All the smells of all the gardens of the world seemed to be held among the canvas walls. Great blossoms in sloping banks, thrusting their colours stalk upon stalk to the tented sky. Everywhere there was the smell of the trampled grass, all its natural brightness dusted to a dull green. The smell reminded me of home and of haymaking, of days on the stack top and early May mornings when the mowing machines went out with a clatter along the dawn roads to the fields.

But apart from all the official gatherings, the Quarry is the place where the people of Shrewsbury come to chill out at any time of the year. This area of land outside the walls had, since the 14th century, been arable and open. It had been a convenient place for the quarrying of stone and clay for building the old town, hence its name. By the end of the Middle Ages, it had become common land used by the townsfolk for airing and drying, grazing animal pets and digging for building stone. In the early part of the 18th century, the riverbank was starting to be used for leisure walks by the people of Swan Hill – a part of the town immediately east of the Quarry which had become a fashionable place to live. In 1719 a local nurseryman, Thomas Wright, was given the task of planting the river's edge with over four hundred lime trees for newly laid-out walks. A centrepiece to the park is the Dingle, a former quarry within the Quarry, but now a landscaped sunken garden.

Like many visitors before him, Stuart Mais settled in at the Lion Hotel in the Wyle Cop area of the town, mainly – he tells us in his book, *Highways and Byways in the Welsh Marches* – because of its association with Mad Jack Mytton. The Lion has been a popular stopover for many weary travellers to Shrewsbury over five centuries, and a favourite local, too, for Sir Richard Colt Hoare:

I found the Lion Inn much improved since my last visit. Shrewsbury is one of the most irregular built towns I know, so much so it is difficult for a stranger to find his way through it. Its suburbs are very pleasant, particularly the walks on the banks of the river. Some of its churches also bear marks of antiquity and deserve notice.

Not that the Lion was the sole preference for travellers. Another was the Raven Hotel on Castle Street, 'a commodious hostelry whose fame goes back far into the old coaching days'. In its heydays, the Raven had many famous visitors. George Farquhar stayed there while writing his play, *The Recruiting Officer*. Jenny Lind, 'the Swedish Nightingale', was a regular customer. So, too, was William Palmer in 1855, the Rugeley Poisoner, who began to murder his friend and last victim, John Cook, even while they shared a room. Palmer, an English doctor rather overfond of gambling, was found guilty of murder in one of the most notorious cases of the 19th century. Charles Dickens called Palmer 'the greatest villain that ever stood in the Old Bailey'. He was convicted of Cook's murder and hanged the following year. The Raven was demolished in 1960 and replaced with a Woolworths store, itself since replaced as part of the Castle Street and Pride Hill shopping development. But there is one building amongst the hustle and bustle of inner Shrewsbury which has lain hidden for many years yet is so old and precious that the town elders have insisted, quite rightly, it should be preserved behind whatever commercial facade it is found necessary to remain hidden. Henry Timmins saw it in all its ancient glory in 1898, and wrote this:

Finding ourselves once more on Pride Hill, we step across that busy thoroughfare and passing to the rear of Mother Noblett's Toffee Shop, we see before us the pretty Gothic doorway that figures in our sketch. Though much the worse for neglect, and fallen sadly into disrepair, this ancient sandstone structure is clearly the work of at least two periods. The shaft and capital on the left, with the broken archway above it, are of the style known as Early English, while the graceful pointed arch, with its floriated cusps and traces of ball-flower ornamentation are evidently a later insertion and probably date from the later part of the 13th century. A wide stone arch, part of which may be noticed above the passageway, supports the floor within, and a small arched recess near the head of the steps appears to have been used as a holy water stoop. From these indications, it is considered probable the little building before us was at one time the private chapel of Bennett's Hall, the city residence of the Abbot of Haughmond, who according to the custom of those days, had a town house in the capital of the county.

The town's archaeological records show the Gothic style remains of Bennett's Hall as a rare part-survival of a 13th century merchant's town house and is Grade II listed. The building had been partially demolished when Pride Hill was being reconstructed towards the end of the 16th century and lay hidden at the rear of commercial premises until planning permission was sought in 2015 when Pride Hill was being remodernised. The medieval ruins are now incorporated into the new premises of Pret â Manger, opened in 2018. Sadly, the act of preservation has not been a success. So much of the ancient structure has been smothered in plaster, perhaps because the sandstone was in poor health. Similarly, until recently the McDonalds business in the town centre was housed in a medieval building, thought to be the oldest in the world to contain one of its restaurants. When I called in there, I thought at the time that customers seem to have more concept of what they were eating than of their surroundings, not surprisingly. The last Big Mac was served on February 25th, 2017.

Leaving Shrewsbury, Timmins and his touring party of Victorian tourists had one remaining landmark to take in:

We bowl along the dusty highway with homeward bound Salopians, until, some two miles short of our journey's end, we call a halt to take a look at the Shelton Oak, one of the 'lions' of the locality. Yonder it stands, a storm-rent relic of the immemorial past, holding its own bravely yet 'against the tooth of time and oblivion', though bereft of many a stalwart limb by the gales of a thousand winters. This venerable tree still rears aloft its gaunt, grey, wrinkled branches, lifeless now, save for some ragged foliage that yet clings around the lower part of the trunk. The latter has become hollow inside, where a sort of paved chamber affords standing room for perhaps a dozen people.

That 'dusty highway' is now the A458 Welshpool road in the Shrewsbury suburb of Shelton where, long before houses were built and the town exit route was widened, the ancient 'lion' once stood. The Shelton Oak was a tree of considerable age which, by tradition, played a notorious part in the fall of Hotspur at Battlefields. Many sceptics have long doubted the accuracy of Glyndŵr's alleged view towards the violent conflagration at Battlefield. He may certainly have beheld Shrewsbury Castle from here, but the field of battle is far beyond what was possible from this point. The remnants of an old tree which died here in the 1940s and was said to be that of that very oak, were contentiously removed to make way for the new road in the 1950s. After the last worker had left the site, a young oak tree was planted by the side of the modern junction, with a plaque at its base which reads,

Near this site once stood the Shelton Oak from which according to a tradition recorded in the late 18th century Owen Glyndŵr viewed the Battle of Shrewsbury on 31st July 1403.

I'm delighted to report that the Shelton plaque is still in situ at the base of the young oak tree, though that has grown considerably, now standing some 30ft above its companion hedge. Time is yet to tell how long the planting of this oak will be remembered.[39]

While resting on Montford Bridge over the Severn just beyond the outskirts, Charles Harper met a man also resting after walking from Oswestry. Although the man lived in Shrewsbury, there was no work, so he had tried his luck elsewhere. It seems he had been

---

[39] In the 1880s, an acorn said to have been recovered from the original Shelton Oak was planted in the Dingle in The Quarry, in Shrewsbury. Shropshire Council is to plant an acorn from that tree in a new cemetery at the Mytton Oak Remembrance Park, not far from Shelton.

successful in that he had been given a short job unloading coals, for which he had earned enough to pay for his breakfast before returning that morning. Another job was promised to him in five days' time, and he would walk back to secure it. That's thirty-seven miles there and back, and just for the price of a breakfast!

Throughout history, the border district of Shropshire with Powys has seen stubborn fighting between Welsh and Angles, and later between Welsh and Normans, which is why many of the hilltops hereabouts are covered with military camps. But where there was conflict, later came the peace. And here, nestling by a medieval bridge over the Afon Tanat, is a timeless, half-timbered inn where fisherman and travellers alike have found rest and refreshment to drive away the aches and pains of a weary journey or the disappointment of an unsuccessful rod. Cledwyn Hughes is about to end his border journey back at his home farm:

> And now I turn towards Wales and home once more. Home to where patriots wear leeks on March 1st, St David's day. Tradition is that the custom goes back to 640, not long after the time of the saint himself. More likely, the custom reflects the Tudor colours of Henry VII, green and white, and victory at Bosworth. And so, into Llansantffraid again and the summer is yet young. Perhaps today the pike will be on the feed. Perhaps as the car creaks and cools I can go down to the does of the deep Vyrnwy pools and there try my hand against an old enemy.

Part Three

The Northern March

Oswald's Tree

Charles Harper did not like Oswestry. He found it denuded of old buildings and too crowded for a town of its size. The result, he said, was not pretty. Being then on the borders of the Denbighshire coalfield, Oswestry was enjoying a new prosperity from the needs of colliers and collieries – iron and brass foundries and allied machine works. The Cambrian Railway had its engine and carriage works there, and because of all this industrial activity there were a great many hotels and banks. Here, Shropshire once again meets the Welsh county of Powys. Oswestry is the largest market town in the border lands and the influence of the Principality is still felt when you hear the blend of languages. There are many Welsh language street names here. The town's name in Welsh is Croesoswallt, meaning Oswald's Cross, after the assumed martyrdom of the saintly King Oswald in the 7th century. It eventually became known as Oswald's Tree, from which its current English name is derived. Though Oswestry may be seen these days as having been somewhat downgraded and has lost its railway connection even into Wales, it has a rich history. Leland was probably the first to write about it, while compiling his *Itinerary* in the 16th century:

> The site of Oswestry lies in a plain in a valley twelve miles long north west from Shrewsbury, having almost no wood. The distance within between the walls is about one mile. The walls have four gates but no towers beside the gates. The church of St Oswald is a very fair leaded church with a great towered steeple, but it standeth *outside* the New Gate, so that no church is there within the town. This church was once a monastery called White Minster. St Oswald's well is a bow shot from the church in the fields south west. There is a chapel over it of timber and a fountain surrounded by a stone wall.[40]

---

[40] Though the well is contained in a walled surround, there is no chapel now, nor fountain.

The origins of Oswestry began at a battle in 642, in the district known as Maeserfield, between the Anglo-Saxon Penda of Mercia and Oswald of Northumbria, and in which Oswald was killed. According to the legend, Oswald was dismembered and one of his arms was carried by a raven to an ash tree – hence the reference to Oswald's Tree. To add more drama to the legend, the raven is supposed to have let go of the arm, and where it landed emerged a spring that exists today as Oswald's Well. Back in Northumbria before this event, Oswald had been active promoting the Christian faith and had shown generosity in donating land and supporting the introduction of religious houses. Though he might have considered Penda's Mercia ripe for similar conversion, the outcome was disastrous for him. Nevertheless, the posthumous fame as saint and martyr continues today as part of Oswestry's tourism. The town changed hands between the English and the Welsh several times during the Middle Ages, until it was almost totally destroyed by Owain Glyndŵr's forces in 1400. The castle survived a little longer, but during the English Civil War it was reduced to a pile of stones.

The tower of the parish church of St Oswald, King and Martyr, is the tallest and possibly the oldest building in Oswestry – being around 1000 years old. In the north aisle is the tomb of Hugh Yale, an ancestor of Elihu Yale, the founder of the famous US Collegiate School in Connecticut, later to be renamed Yale University. Welsh author and travel writer, Cledwyn Hughes, was born on a farm not far from the town and recalls a time of his youth in weekend relaxation and hopeful girl-watching:

> On Saturday nights in Oswestry the lads from the country farms come into town. Generally, they come neat suited, on bicycles, for with this freedom of transport they could linger after the last bus has gone groaning away, and long after the last train has snaked yellow-lighted along the lowlands of the Severn valley. They come in, hair well-greased and brushed firmly. And they who have worn an opened-neck shirt all the week are now respectable with collar and tie. They stand in nervous groups along the edges of the pavements. Hilarious and laughing self-consciously at half

whispered jokes. Pausing only to watch the smart daughters of the townspeople as they stalk out to the post office or to late shopping.

A short distance to the north of the modern town is the impressive ancient fort known as Old Oswestry. Described by the archaeologist Sir Cyril Fox as 'the outstanding work of early Iron Age type in the Marches', it is a multivallate structure though strangely located on low ground, indicating a confidence of the Cornovii builders that they would have no difficulty defending the site. Such self-assurance seems to have been repeated at a similar site called the Berth near Baschurch, where a double mound of an Iron Age community sits in an area of low-lying wet meadowland. That place has been suggested as eventually becoming the home of the Welsh prince Cynddylan and the legendary British stronghold of Pengwern, an alternative to the origins for Shrewsbury. Significantly, the lower western bank and ditch of Old Oswestry coincides with a section of Wats Dyke – the ancient defensive earthwork stretching through the northern Welsh marches and which some say predates the Dyke of King Offa. Running parallel with each other from Oswestry, Offa's great border barrier runs out of puff before reaching the town of Mold and leaves Wat's earthwork to continue towards the Dee estuary shore. It remains unclear who constructed Wat's Dyke and when, but the argument for dating it earlier than Offa's is its condition. Many stretches of Wat's Dyke have disappeared into the landscape, as have most if not all the ditches, while the best bits are barely recognisable, and only in a few places. By contrast, there are stretches of Offa's Dyke, particularly near Clun, which are still in remarkably good nick after nearly 1,300 years.

A mile or two to the east of Oswestry's old fort is Park Hall estate, where there was one of the finest Tudor mansions in England until, on Boxing Day 1918, it was destroyed by fire – yet another of our great houses disappearing in tragic circumstances. The fatal conflagration happened after Charles Harper's visit, for he saw the Hall as 'a fine specimen of black and white building of the first Queen Elizabeth's time, and with a domestic chapel'. The estate was sandwiched between the main Chester to Shrewsbury railway and the Cambrian line, which carried local trains into Mid Wales after the two lines split at Gobowen. At one time, Park Hall had a station halt on each line.

Leading up to World War 1, the estate's owner was Major Wynne Corrie, and in 1915 he gave Park Hall over to the military to use as their local headquarters. In the spring of that year, a military camp was constructed to train the troops, with the area to the east of the hill fort being used for excavating trenches and testing explosives. Stretches of North Shropshire were chosen, too, for military activities during World War 2. Land between the A5 and A438 roads bordered in the south by the River Severn and in the north by Kinnerley Heath, became a vast unpopulated area used by the Army. It was at one time covered in single bomb storage units, spaced out for obvious reasons, and all connected to a central railway line running east to west across the whole landscape. Known as the Central Ammunition Depot (CAD), it ceased operations in 1959 but was reserved for Army training, mostly with no-live firing. Although some parts of the northern training grounds are now accessible to the public, there is a part of the southern training area ominously called Burning Ground, where ammunition was decommissioned but remains 'active' and out-of-bounds to the public.

The tower of the red sandstone church of St Mary's at Kinnerley has some fine bells. A local story tells the tale of a farmer who was returning from the beast fair at Shrewsbury where he had sold his two cows, Dobbin and Golden. On that day. the bells were being recast and the farmer stopped at the foundry to watch the work being done. He was asked if he might be prepared to contribute to the cost of the bells and in answer donated the money that he had received from the sale of his two cows. Consequently, the two bells are called Dobbin and Golden.

Hidden away in the small north Shropshire village of Woolston is a saint's shrine in the form of a well and chapel. It is claimed to be the location where, in 1138, prior Robert Pennant and a few monks of Shrewsbury Abbey rested overnight with the remains of St Winifred when being moved from Gwytherin in North Wales. It is unclear whether the site was chosen for its existing water source, or if the spring started miraculously, like at Holywell, when some part of Winifred's remains connected with the ground. During my research here, I did not discover any claims of saintly intercessions, unlike Holywell. Away from the village community, the site is a lonely, damp spot surrounded by trees and wild shrubs. A black and white timber-framed well house currently sits over a stone enclosure within which is the emergence of the gentle spring. A narrow, stepped entrance leads into a dark chamber, where there are two more lower bathing areas also constructed of stone. At the back of the chamber is an empty recess, suggesting it once held a statuette. There is a feeling of neglect, for the well at least.

The original building above the well was said to date from the late 15th century and may have been constructed at the prompting of Margaret Beaufort, the mother of Henry VII, who had the buildings around Winifred's shrine at Holywell restored. The well house at Woolston, however, is a rebuild by the current owners, the Landmark Trust, which uses it for holiday lets. It was sold to them in 1987 by the family who had lived in it since 1937 but had decided it needed urgent repairs which they could no longer manage. The rotting woodwork and broken bricks were replaced, restoring it to a previously recognised historical condition. But though a public footpath passes close to the site, access to the well is now restricted, and one wonders how future pilgrims might continue their venerations, if not their bathing.

The village of Llanymynech straddles the border between Powys and Shropshire, Wales and England, that runs for the most part down the centre of the main street, with the eastern half of the village in England and the western half in Wales. The two Saxon Dykes of Offa and Wat also merge here for a while by the Montgomery Canal and then separate to pass either side of the village. Here, too, the meandering River Vyrnwy passes just south of the village before wandering away to its destiny with the Severn at Crewgreen. Looming over the village at its back are the dramatic limestone cliffs created by centuries of quarrying. Llanymynech Hill is riddled with old mines and is possibly Wales' earliest copper mining site. The hills here mark the beginning of the Oswestry uplands, a limestone outcrop that continues into North-East Wales to form the eastern ridge of the Clwydian Hills. In 1804 Sir Richard Colt Hoare saw the rugged formation of the escarpment and its industrial aftermath as an advantage for the area:

> Above the village the whole mountain is limestone. The kilns arranged along its sides appear like many habitations. Since the cut of the canal into this country, many advantages will result. The introduction of lime into Shropshire which before was dear and scarce, the reduction of horses and consequent consumption of oats, and the roads bettered.

A former industrial landscape adjacent to the A483 is designated now as the Llanymynech Heritage Area and is home to one of only three remaining Hoffmann kilns in the British Isles, and the only one with a chimney. The limestone quarry which fed the kiln is now the Shropshire Wildlife Trust's Llanymynech Rocks Nature Reserve. From this point, the national border loops westward to enclose the environs of Oswestry, so keeping them English.

The Pistyll, a Grand Cataract

Wild Wales author George Borrow described the Welsh side of the border as 'Powisland, a once great province of Welsh Princes'. Borrow walked south from Llangollen along established tracks of the Berwyn foothills, and followed a lonely road around Mynydd Mawr to reach Llanrhaedr-ym-Mochnant in the Tanat valley. Here, he took a room in the Wynnstay Arms – more evidence of the influence of Sir Watkin and the Wynnstay clan. Borrow described the inn as large but not very cheerful. During a customary jug of ale, he famously entered conversation with an old local man:

> 'How do you know that I come from South Wales?' said I.
> 'By your English,' said the old fellow, 'anybody may know you are South Welsh by your English; it is so accursedly bad.

But let's hear you speak a little Welsh; then I shall be certain as to who you are.'

I did as he bad me, saying a few words in Welsh.

'There's Welsh,' said the old fellow, 'but who but a South Welshman would talk Welsh in this manner? It's nearly as bad as your English.'

In 1938 Percy Thoresby Jones, thought the most pleasant approach to Llanrhaeadr was by way of Penybont Fawr, a hamlet smelling delightfully of wood smoke on the day, with a homely tavern where a cheerful stranger is welcomed. Llanrhaeadr, with the modest Wynnstay Hotel, is chiefly visited for its proximity to the extraordinary Pistyll Rhaeadr waterfall:

> But is also a good starting point for tramps over the wilder and higher Berwyns. The most spectacular excursion is the trip up the Tanat valley to Llangynog and thence literally upward by the (in places) dangerous road that crosses the Berwyns by the lofty pass of Milltir Cerrig and descends to Llandderfel near Bala.

The 16th century Grade II listed church of St Dogfan in Llanrhaeadr is best known for its former vicar, Dr William Morgan who, around 1580, translated the Bible into Welsh and later became Bishop, first at Llandaff Cathedral and then at St. Asaph. William Worthington, another popular and generous vicar at St Dogfan, set his memory in stone literally, by organising the building of the road from the village to the Pistyll Rhaeadr in 1748. The Pistyll is the spectacular end-game of the Afon Disgynfa falling in three stages, over a 73m (240ft) cliff-face to begin a new life below as the Afon Rhaeadr. It is counted as one of the Seven Wonders of Wales and is a Site of Special Scientific Interest. This popular attraction is not, however, the tallest waterfall in Wales, which will disappoint local tourism. That's because the Pistyll's drop is broken by the natural formation of a rock bridge, leaving the tallest fall stage at about 40m (130ft). There are at least two other waterfalls in Wales with longer single drops, but like many revered visitors to Llanrhaeadr

before him and long after, Borrow was here to see only the
Pistyll's spectacular fall:

> I advanced across the vale till within a furlong of the cataract,
> when I was stopped by a deep hollow into which the waters of the
> cataract tumble. On the side of this hollow I sat down and gazed
> down before me. The water comes spouting over a crag of perhaps
> one hundred feet in altitude between two hills. After reaching the
> bottom of a precipice, the water rushes in a narrow brook down
> the vale in the direction of Llanrhaeadr. What shall I liken it to? I
> scarcely know, unless to an immense skein of silk agitated and
> disturbed by tempestuous blasts, or the long tail of a grey courser
> at furious speed. Through the long silvery threads or hairs, or
> what looked such, I could here and there see the black sides of the
> crag down which the Pistyll precipitated itself with something
> between a boom and a roar. There are many remarkable cataracts
> in Britain and neighbouring isles, even the Celtic Isle of Man has
> its waterfall, but this waterfall, the grand cataract of North Wales,
> far exceeds them all in altitude and beauty. I never saw water
> falling so gracefully as here.

When in Llanrhaeadr, Samuel Johnson and Hester Thale stayed
at the house of William Worthington but declared that the
'entertainment' was poor, though the house by the side of the river
was 'not bad':

> The town is very old and very mean and though we slept the night
> at Dr Worthington's, the warmth of our welcome made some
> amends for the wretchedness of our accommodation. In the
> morning we saw the famous cascade at Pistyll Rhaeadr, where we
> went on borrowed horses and were not disappointed in our
> entertainment. It is a glorious waterfall.

The village of Llangynog lies at the head of the Tanat Valley where
the Afon Eirth and the Afon Tanat converge at the foot of the
Berwyn mountain range. Named after St Cynog – yet another
offspring of King Brychan of Brycheiniog, progenitor of a sizeable

noted family of Celtic saints – in recent times it was a thriving centre for mining and quarrying, and home to over 2,000 people. A hundred years ago it was important enough to have its own railway. Now it is a quiet place aroused only by summer tourists, seasonal walkers, and mountain scramblers. The village is surrounded by mountains creating as dramatic a background as in any Lakeland pass or Scottish glen. Beyond the village to the west, the Milltir Cerrig mountain pass crosses the Berwyns at an altitude of 486m (1594ft) before descending, sometimes sharply, to the head of Llyn Tegid, Bala lake. Thomas Pennant found the valley exceedingly picturesque:

> Enclosed by hills on all sides, except its entrance, and watered by the Tanat river which springs not far off. The upper end is bounded by two vast precipices, down which at times fall two great cataracts.[41]

Two miles along a narrow lane that accompanies the youthful Tanat falling from its source, is an ancient church in the hamlet of Pennant Melangell. It is built on a Bronze Age burial site where human remains

Figure 18 The Pistyll Rhaeadr waterfall, Mid-Wales

---

[41] The Tanat is born 520m (1,706ft) higher up the valley in the Berwyns from the confluence of Nant Cerriggwynion and Nant y Groes-fagl. Although there are several waterfalls tumbling from the upper valleys, there is no evidence – apart from the Pistyll Llanrhaeadr – of a second 'vast precipice and great cataract'. It is likely that he was referring only to the Pistyll which falls in two stages down the same drop.

discovered during the reconstruction of the east end apse were assumed to be as those of the locally venerated St Melangell, after whom the church is dedicated. In the churchyard are two very old yews, estimated to have been planted there 2,000 years ago. It is a typical saintly churchyard scene which will be repeated elsewhere during my tour of North Wales. St Melangell's is one of the loveliest churches in the principality, and one of the most remote. Its great treasure is the saint's impressive shrine installed in the chancel, and the effect is unique not only in Britain but has been described as of pan-European significance, too.

I arrived at the church on a day in early summer 2017 just as a service was about to begin and persuaded the vicar not to start before, I had my photos, after which brazen act, I left. I will never make a greater error. Had I stayed, I may have discovered more about saintly Melangell and her guardians in the hills.

Nestling under a hanging wood, and above some of the finest meadows stretching down to the Tanat river, is Llangedwyn Hall – once the fine old seat of Sir Watkins Williams-Wynn, 10th Baronet, heir to Owain ap Gruffudd, the 12th century King of Gwynedd, and lord of the extensive Wynnstay estates. Sir Watkin lived his final years behind these high hedges and is buried in the churchyard opposite the Hall's gates, along with several other Williams-Wynns who also lived their twilight terms at Llangedwyn. In the early 19th century, the poet Robert Southey was a visitor when it was the home of his friend, Charles Williams-Wynn. Though only secondary to Wynnstay Hall at Ruabon and occupied mostly as an occasional residence, Llangedwyn remained with the Williams-Wynn family until 1988.

Before George Borrow could gain access to Glundŵr's castle at Sycharth, he had to seek permission from the steward of Llandegwyn to which the castle mound then belonged. Sycharth Castle, a motte and bailey like any other, lies forgotten and unnoticed in a rural setting in the Cynllaith river valley. It was Owain Glyndwr's main home from 1369. There, he lived the easy life with his wife Margaret Hanmer and their nine children, until in 1403, it was reduced to charred rubble by the avenging forces of Prince Hal of Monmouth, later Henry V. Having made his way to the castle, Borrow achieved another ambition which he had highlighted in *Wild Wales*:

> On top of this hill in a timber house dwelt the great Welshman with his wife, a comely, kindly woman, and his progeny of stout boys and blooming girls, and there, though cramped for want of rooms, he feasted bards, including Iolo Goch, who required his hospitality with odes difficult to compose and which few bookworms understand. There he dwelt for many years, the virtual if not the nominal King of North Wales, occasionally no doubt, looking down with self-complaisance from the top of his fastness on the parks and fish-ponds of which he had several, his mill, his pigeon tower, his ploughed lands, and the cottages of a thousand retainers huddled round the lower parts of the hill, or strewn about the valley.

Mad, Bad, Squire of Halston Hall

> In the secluded spots of our favoured land time deals gently with our English homes, and dull indeed must be the soul of him who, journeying in our country lanes, could come unmoved to where the lordly castle of the once great family of FitzWarins rises from the flowery waters of the moat in the village street of Whittington.
> (*Fletcher Moss*)

Whittington Castle stands in a clump of trees by the roadside, not on any hilltop, but in the centre of a village. And one comes upon it suddenly, a great fortified gateway of grey stone reflected in the waters of what was once the castle's moat. It is more a fortified family-sized Norman residence, and is the only one in England maintained by the local community. Admission is free, but then there's not much else to look at beyond the gateway. To help with financing the burden, battle re-enactments and occasional weddings take place, following the modern trend for such celebrations to be held against historic backgrounds. Its position by the highway is a puzzle, because there are no natural defence features which would guard against attacks, particularly from Welsh forces. There was once an Iron Age village on the site, so it is likely that there was an earlier Saxon timber fortress here and, as was often the case, was replaced by one of stone after the arrival of the marcher lords. The builder of this replacement, William Peverel, had no male heir, so the castle ended up with his daughter Mellet, who seems to have offered her hand and castle in marriage to the victor of a tournament. That very fortunate man was Warin de Metz of Lorraine, and it was he who started a very long line of resident Warins lasting well into the 15th century. The two imposing gatehouse towers that grab your gaze as you arrive at the village are clearly the main feature of the castle today and built into the north tower is a Grade 1 listed 17th century cottage, currently used as the castle shop.

I arrived at Whittington at an awkward time, for there was great traffic chaos and an inconvenient disruption even disgruntled villagers seemed unprepared for.

> The enemy forces lined up before the great drum towers of the gatehouse, the unsuspecting and angry people pushed back behind the attacking lines, but it seemed nothing would prevent the inevitable surge to the castle walls. Across the breasts of metalled bodies of the advancing army was writ the legend 'Tarmac'. The order was given to close the road while cautious progress was made, so denying the guardians access to their castle and the villagers to their homes. The battle would last only a few hours when the Tarmacians would complete their task then retreat, leaving the Whittingtonians with the steaming remains, a freshly resurfaced road.

At Whittington in 1893, Charles Harper lodged with a cottager, but he, too, was momentarily thrown off-guard by an advancing force – the sight of a traction engine and caravan combination passing through the village. The unconventional traveller, in the eyes of our literary Londoner, suggested to him there might in future be no limit to the ways of tourists:

The variety of methods in touring is surprising. There are those who walk, who drive a four-in-hand, who go a-boating, and others, as we have seen, who take to the open road in a caravan. The democratic cycle has let loose an army of pedallers upon the highways, and the ancient hostelries that decayed with the demise of the coaching era, have taken a new lease of life by reason of them. Ways the most ingenious have been contrived that make for novelty in peripatetic holidays, but no-one has yet bethought him of the steam roller or the traction engine as an entirely novel and unconventional conveyance a-wheel. Look to it, my friends!

Halston Hall, a few miles beyond Whittington, is an architecturally pleasing Grade I listed William and Mary house in secluded parkland, set well back from the Ellesmere road. Halston was the seat of the Mytton family, and Thomas Pennant's maternal ancestry. At this place was born General Thomas Mytton, an English officer in Oliver Cromwell's Parliamentary army during the English Civil War. The scene of his actions was chiefly in North Wales, where his prowess seems to have been subduing most of the castles that were in the hands of Royalists. However, finding later that Cromwell had further designs than the mere defence of Liberty, the cause in which he engaged, Mytton resigned his command and retired to manage his Halston estates.

The house's history stretches back some 700 years and was for a good deal of that time the home of wealthy Shropshire squires. In 1798 the master of the house, John Mytton, died suddenly at the age of thirty and the estate was left to his two-year-old son, also John. By today's values, Halston was worth at that time around £5 million and the annual income from the estate's assets was in excess of £800,000, quite a hefty golden egg for such a young lad. Without a father figure to control his early days, young John grew up a wild boy. Although the family could afford the best education, his schooling was a disaster from the start. He was expelled from Westminster after just one year for fighting with one of the masters, and only managed three terms at Harrow before he was expelled again. Even private tutors failed to hold his attention much, and he was ill-suited for Cambridge

University where he was granted entry purely on financial grounds. It is well documented that John took with him 2,000 bottles of port to sustain himself during his studies. Inevitably, a degree was beyond him, and so he was destined for a career in the army. He joined the 7th Hussars, ending up in post-Napoleon France as part of a force of occupation, but even there he spent his time drinking and gambling until he resigned his commission. In 1817 Mytton reached 21 years of age and finally came into his inheritance. He married the following year but his wife died two years later. He married again soon after, but she couldn't bear his constant appalling behaviour towards her, so she ran away.

The abundance of wealth led him into a life of many indulgences, gambling being high on his list of enjoyment. He bought a horse which was already a proven consistent winner of races, and promptly won the Gold Cup at Lichfield. Much of his time was spent at the Oswestry racecourse, where he gambled and drank recklessly. He hunted regularly with his own pack, whatever the weather, reputedly keeping as many as 2,000 hounds and feeding his favourites on steak and champagne. Though he owned a vast wardrobe, he sometimes dressed carelessly for the chase in winter and was known to have ridden naked through snow drifts and swollen rivers in full spate. It seemed at times that Mytton had a disregard for his own safety, or that of his passengers when travelling dangerously on the estate in his gig. His wild and irresponsible ways had by now earned him the title of Mad Jack. He was also now drinking eight bottles of port each day. Formal dinners in the Hall were no longer on his agenda; rather he sustained himself on cobnuts when in season or imposing himself on his tenant farmers eating their food and drinking their ale.

After fifteen years, the inheritance was almost gone, but Mad Jack had no concerns for the consequences of debt and insolvency. He wanted to spend every penny there was. His adviser had calculated that if he reduced his expenditure to £6,000 per year for six years, Halston might not have to be sold. Mytton's response was typical. 'I wouldn't give a damn to live on £6,000 a year!' He made a couple of attempts to enter Parliament, buying votes on the first occasion to successfully represent Shrewsbury as their

Tory MP. True to form, his time in the House of Commons was short-lived, attending for barely thirty minutes before getting bored and leaving. He didn't contest his seat at the following election, but his dislike for parliamentary procedures didn't stop him trying again in 1831. This time as a Whig candidate, he came last in the polls. He was not around for the elections of the following year because by then he had gone into exile in France to escape his creditors. Unable to pay his debts, he finally returned to England to face the music and was confined to the King's Bench Prison in Southwark. Worn out by too much recklessness, bloated by drink and looking older than his 38 years, Mad Jack Mytton died in 1834 while still incarcerated.

Fletcher Moss wrote in 1903 that his father's elder brother knew John Mytton and told wonderful tales about him:

> As Mad Jack grew up his great delight was in fighting or playing at highway robbery. He disguised himself and robbed his own butler, who had been sent to Oswestry for money and boasted no one could take it off him. When riding about the country he would take his horse into the inn or farmhouse to warm it by the fire and give it ale or beef as he had himself.

Opposite the entrance to Attingham Park near Shrewsbury and standing on the banks of the Severn, is a handsome Grade II building smart enough to be the home of a wealthy country gentleman but is in fact the Mytton and Mermaid Hotel. I'm not sure who the Mermaid might have been, but the Mytton name recalls the night after his death when his body lay there while being transported for burial at Halston. He was finely laid to rest in the family vault of a timber-framed chapel in the grounds of the Hall, surrounded by ancient yews and guarded by a herd of fine-looking Herefords. Despite his restless nature, Mytton fathered several children with his second wife, Caroline Gifford, and his eldest daughter, Barbara, married into the Somerset family. Had he lived, Mad Jack would probably have rubbed shoulders with Dukes of Beaufort and ridden with grandchildren through the grounds of their new home at Badminton Hall:

Alas! The Squire of Halston has no fellows now. The squire as a class is as extinct as the Iguanodon. Poor Squire! Have you not some happy hunting ground in the Beyond; were Port is still the favoured drink, where jolly purpled-faced fellows ride to hounds and halloo lustily when the fox breaks cover? There should be no heeltaps in that shadowy country, and ghostly toasts to the First Gentleman in Europe (King George IV) should still be honoured, with the breaking of airy glasses. (*Charles Harper*)

Today, Halston Hall remains a house of substantial size and quality and belongs now to the Harvey family. In the manner of many other estate owners these days, they let their magnificent home for weddings and formal assemblies and the vast grounds and lakes for syndicate duck and pheasant shoots – a pastime Mad Jack would no doubt have taken part in on a regular basis. In September 2017, on a breezy day of sunshine and high clouds, I was shown around the park and the black and white timber chapel where the Myttons lie in their vault and the Herefords keep a wary eye out for their restless spirits. Once in the gloomy chapel nave, surrounded by darkened pews, it was explained to me who lay beneath our feet. One was Mad Jack, of course, but exactly which one was kept a secret. The Harveys rarely have official open days for the chapel but tell me they do their best to show the chapel to visitors when requested. Wedding blessings, family christenings, and occasional family services, as well as a carol service at Christmas for locals and friends, ensure the Myttons at rest below the floor do not have the place entirely to themselves. It was a privilege to be as close as anyone gets to a civil war General and an eccentric Regency rake.

Meres, and the Shame of Moreton Say

Thomas Pennant once chose the wrong day for travelling through north Shropshire. The roads would have been bad enough in the late 18th century, but the journey from his home in north Wales across the Dee plains on that day proved one with mixed feelings:

The greatest part of the way to Ellesmere is flat, dirty, and unpleasing. On the approach to the town, the way becomes more agreeable, and about it breaks into beautiful risings, fertile and finely wooded. The bottoms are destitute of rivers, but frequently filled with little lakes called here meres, elegantly bordered by the cultivated hills. The town is seated on a lake of a hundred and one acres in dimension, and well stocked with fish. The Duke of Bridgwater owns this fine water.

Ellesmere is Shropshire's most northerly town, being just 5km (3 mi) from the County Borough of Wrexham and therefore close to the national boundary. The town started life as a Norman motte in 1086 when Roger de Montgomerie decided he needed a defensive outpost here. His eastern view from his motte was, and would be now, the great glacial lake still called the Mere, these days a tourist attraction for fishing and boating. The Mere is the largest of many other meres in this area. In fact, there are 25 all told, though some are small and classed simply as pools. Together they make up what is often referred to as the North Shropshire Lake District. They were all formed by the melting of the ice shelf at the end of the Ice Age, the deeper kettle basins becoming meres and the shallower ones filling with plant matter would form mosses. None are fed by river water as the Cumbrian lakes are from its mountains, but sustained instead by evaporation, rainfall, and accumulating groundwater in the case of meres and evaporation in that of the mosses.

The plain between Overton and Ellesmere once formed the bed of one giant lake. Geologists called it Lapworth Lake after Charles Lapworth, who first suggested in 1898 that it had existed. The theory is based on the fact that the Severn once flowed northwards from its source In Mid Wales to join the Dee estuary at Chester, but a huge barrier of ice blocked the river's path turning the whole area into Lapworth's lake. Eventually, this water overflowed to the south beyond the line of Wenlock Edge and formed a deep gorge where Ironbridge is now, and the Severn began to drain north Shropshire, having found a new way to the sea at Chepstow in the south.

Figure 19 Colemere. One of many stretches of water in North Shropshire which once formed the giant Lapworth lake

The market town of Whitchurch is also close to the Welsh border, just 3km (2mi) from Wrexham's eastern county line. Whitchurch began as a Roman military base built around AD 52, 'a day's march from Deva (Chester) or Uriconium (Wroxeter)'. They called it Mediolanum, meaning Middle of the Plain, but it is not the Mediolanum of classical geographer Claudius Ptolemy – as William Camden believed – which he had placed at Caersws in Powys:

That Mediolanum, a town of the Ordovices, which both Antonine the Emperor, and Ptolome speak of, stood in this shire, I am in a manner persuaded upon probability. The footings whereof, I have sought after with all diligence, but little or nothing have I found of it.

Whitchurch's birth in Roman times makes it the oldest continuously inhabited town in Shropshire, and time has been a significant industry in the town since the 17th century in the shape of J.B. Joyce and Company, the oldest clock makers in the world.

Not far from Whitchurch, in the rural village of Moreton Say, the externally insignificant red brick church of St Margaret of Antioch hides the remains of Robert Clive of India. The man was justifiably celebrated with a statue in the square in Shrewsbury, but here was ignominiously dumped beneath a corner of the nave in 1774 after allegedly committing suicide. Presumably, the Clive family who lived at nearby Styche Hall where Robert was born were very much aware of his hidden presence under the church's floor, but although there were other family tombs in the churchyard it would appear, they did nothing for their most famous son. Church law of the times forbade proper burial for self-inflicted deaths. Clive was reported to have practised years of drug abuse to relieve a history of pains and discomforts, finally apparently running out of tolerance. The only evidence that he lies here is a modest brass plaque over the priest's doorway in the chancel. According to church records, workmen found his bones beneath the floorboards which they were replacing during a refurbishment. A report from the Board for Social Responsibility in 1959 noted that most people now believed that anyone who attempted suicide must have been experiencing a degree of mental distress and deserved special sympathy and understanding (*Church Times, July 2017*). The report has led to the introduction of Canon B58 which calls for sympathy and consideration when interring suicides and unbaptised deceased. When might there now be forgiveness for this great man?

At the very time I arrived outside the church, the local schoolchildren were leaving by the curate's door after their visit. I wonder what they learnt from the experience. Also, in the chancel is an elaborate tomb of former husbands of a local landowner, Lady Jane Grosvenor, of whom not many have any knowledge – least of all, I would have thought, today's children of Moreton Say. Did they question the teacher on the lack of a tomb for someone they did know from their history books?

Four miles south-east of Wrexham, in the ancient district of English Maelor, is the site of the first Celtic Christian monastery, founded there – we are told – around AD 560 and said to have housed at one time up to three thousand monks. Since the departure of the Romans, Britain had become a target for European expansion, and the Angles and Saxons were already creating instability and chaos. Territory grabbing was the name of the game and one, Aethelfrith, was gaining more than most for his northern border kingdom of Bernicia. In 613, he had reached the plains of Cheshire and Bangor Is-y-Coed, Bangor on Dee, where the Celtic monastic community lay in his way. They were easy meat and were slaughtered with unreliable sources telling of 1,200 monks killed. In contrast, but perhaps more believable, the Anglo-Saxon Chronicles later recorded that barely 200 monks were slain. However, there are no remains of any kind, either of monastic buildings or burials, to support the historical story, and there is a serious lack of evidence to gauge what is factual and what is myth. Most of what we know comes from the writings of Bede, but without any verification even the words of the venerable Northumbrian monk can only be speculative. Though the presence of a Celtic religious community of some kind at Bangor has not been challenged, it would be highly unusual for a gathering of such high numbers in one place at that time. The monks would have needed an even larger number of lay helpers to supply food and other basic support services, and there is no record of any significant numbers being on hand where Bangor is now. Although Camden gives it a mention, it is barely in passing and unqualified:

> But, Dee which seemeth to rush rather than to run out of Wales, no sooner is entered into Cheshire but he passeth more mildly with a slower stream by Bovium, a City that had been of great name in that age, and afterward a famous monastery. It was called by the Britons *Bonchor, or Banchor*,[42] of the ancient English.

Pennant doesn't say anything about Celtic monks here, instead preferring a proven body of men whose transport, though changed, has not declined since his day:

> The ancient British boats, the coracles, are much in use on the Dee at Bangor for purpose of salmon fishing. They have now lost the cause of their name, being no longer covered in *coria* or hides, but with strong pitched canvas. They hold only a single person who uses a paddle with great dexterity.

A few miles south of Bangor is the attractive village of Overton, where a grove of ancient yew trees surrounding St Mary's Church

---

[42] Banchor became Bangor, but Camden's identification is wrong here. Roman Bovium was their name for Holt, 11km (7 miles) further north.

are listed as another of the Severn Wonders of Wales and are commemorated in an anonymously written rhyme,

Pistyll Rhaeadr and Wrexham steeple,
Snowdon's mountain without its people,
Overton yew trees, St Winefride wells,
Llangollen bridge, and Gresford bells.

The oldest tree, protected behind iron railings, is thought to be 2,000 years old. Yews are poisonous to animals and humans and have become a Christian symbol of death, which may explain their regularity in churchyards.

Chirk, and the Nightingale of Ceiriog

Towards the end of the 19th century, Charles Harper and his travelling companion had moved quickly along a new section of Telford's road towards Holyhead:

> If settlements upon this road of recent make were insignificant, the country was lovely. The Welsh hills bounded the view, and the lands between were obviously rich, even to the unpractised eyes of us Londoners. Great parks, beautifully wooded and coated with the most luxuriant turf, every now and again bordered the highway, and noble mansions peeped grandly from woodland drives.

The border town of Chirk (Y Waun) was founded by the Normans more than a thousand years ago and stands above the confluence of the rivers Ceiriog and Dee. Castell Y Waun, a motte and bailey construction on the southern edges of the town, was the first castle to guard the Ceriog Valley. In modern times, Chirk was a coal mining community, with coal being worked locally since the 17th century at Black Park and Brynkinallt. The Brynkinallt estates had belonged to the ancient Welsh tribe of the Trevors since the 10th century. The Duke of Wellington's grandmother, Lady Dungannon, was a Trevor and lived for a time at Brynkinallt Hall. The future conqueror of Napoleon spent much of his youthful holidays there when a student at Eton. It was where the young Wellesley experienced the most serious defeat of his memorable career when falling into a quarrel with a farmer's son over a game of marbles. He was on the point of hoisting the flag of victory, when the farmer boy's sister appeared upon the scene brandishing a wetted towel and began to thrash her brother's opponent. According to all accounts, the later defeat of the French was no more crushing than the utter discomfit of the young future hero of Europe on this occasion. The heroine of this affair lived to see her victim crowned with his fullest honours, and she became quite a person of distinction in her locality on the strength of the punishment she had administered in the days of their youth.

The largest coal deposits around Chirk were on the other side of the Dee valley at Ruabon, and in 1845 the Scottish railway engineer, Henry Robertson, succeeded in obtaining Parliamentary approval to extend the North Wales Mineral Railway from Chester to Shrewsbury. The intention was to open up the valuable coalfields of Ruabon and Wrexham to markets in Shropshire towns. That would require providing the means for crossing two deep river valleys either side of Chirk. Telford had already built his Llangollen Canal to do just that, with aqueduacts over the Ceiriog at Chirk and the Dee at Pontcyllyste. Robertson appointed Thomas Brassey to first build a lengthy railway viaduct across the Dee connecting Ruabon with Chirk, which he duly completed in 1848, followed closely by another, shorter one, running alongside Telford's Ceiriog aqueduct. Both bridges cross the England/Wales border.

Figure 20 George Henry Borrow

In 1801, Sir Richard Colt Hoare saw the Ceiriog conduit still only partly constructed while on his way to his retreat at Bala:

> In the valley below Chirk on the road from Oswestry, an aqueduct is now being constructed to convey the water of the canal across the valley. From the level of the canal which is now nearly brought to this spot the arches of the aqueduct must be of very considerable height and I doubt if two rows of them have yet been erected. When it is finished it will have the most grand and picturesque appearance, the background being finely wooded and the foreground also; from the winding of the road downhill the sudden and unexpected view of the aqueduct forms a fine subject for a picture.

On another, later journey to Bala, Colt Hoare left us a poignant record of the progress of Telford's great aqueduct building to carry the Llangollen canal over the Ceiriog and the Dee:

> I found the canal much advanced and the fine aqueduct of ten arches which traverses the vale beneath Chirk nearly finished. When time has given the stone a few mellow tints it will be a most picturesque object. The other fine aqueduct over the Dee and which will be a still grander object (Pontcysyllte) has not advanced much but the canal has been brought to it; there are seventeen piers erected to bear the arches.

At the beginning of the 14th century, a marcher fortress was constructed above Chirk at Crogen Hill by a close relative of Roger Mortimer, 1st Earl of March, on the orders of Edward I. It was to replace the Norman motte to better control the Ceiriog Valley. That was at a time prior to the whole area in the vicinity of the castle becoming heavily wooded with oaks and elms, blocking the view up the valley. Eventually Chirk Castle on Crogen Hill became the seat of the Myddleton family when it was bought by Sir Thomas Myddelton in 1593 for £5,000 (approx £14million in 2017). Offa's Dyke passes close to the castle walls on its way north through the park. The castle stands on a height at some distance from the village and occupies a site which has been fortified as far back as history goes. In ancient times it was known as Castell Crogen and celebrated as the place where Henry II met with one of his numerous defeats at the hands of the Welsh. From the terrace, thirteen counties are supposed to be visible. Harper cast doubt on this, and of course boundaries have changed several times since his day:

> Certainly, when the fates are kind and the weeping skies of this mountainous land have cleared, a vast track of country lies spread out beneath this hill; but thirteen counties is too long a list for belief, except to the most credulous of tourists.

The parish church of St Mary's in Chirk seems at some stage to have been converted into the mortuary chapel of the Myddletons, so large and numerous are the monuments of that family. The largest, of white marble with life-size statues, is dedicated to Sir Richard Myddleton, Bart., and his son Sir William. Sir Richard, we are told by the epitaph, was '*Heir to the Virtues as well as the Estate of the Illustrious House of Chirk Castle*'. That of his son can hardly be acclaimed for its modesty: '*Sir William survived his Father just long enough to tell the world Whose Son and Successor he was: being a Gentleman of such Singular Rectitude of Manners, such strict Probity, unaffected Meekness, disinterested Charity, and exalted Piety, as qualified him early for this Place, whither he hastened to receive the rewards of his Virtues.*' This apparent self-aggrandisement seems to have followed an unfulfilled life, for even though Sir William succeeded, the baronetcy became extinct on his early death in 1718 and unmarried, two years after his father.

From Chirk, the B4500 threads its way westwards through the Ceiriog valley below the high ridge on which Chirk Castle stands. At Pontfadog, the north bank of the Afon Ceiriog is deeply wooded and was more so when Henry II brought his army in search of Owen Gwynedd, Prince of North Wales, in 1165. In spite of being outnumbered, Owen's men knew well the lie of the land and they were skilled in the tactic of raid and ambush. The two armies finally met where Offa's Dyke crosses the valley, but Henry's frustrated and ill-prepared forces suffered heavy losses and retreated. Satisfied that he had done adequate damage to the English advance, Owen withdrew to the safety of the Berwyn mountains. The heaps of slain are said to have been buried in the trenches of the Dyke, and this place is known even today as 'the Pass of Graves'. In 1923, another battle was fought between the English and the Welsh in this valley. Warrington Borough Council sought a Parliamentary Bill to flood the Ceiriog Valley to create two reservoirs. Had it succeeded, three villages, 127 homes, and a beautiful Welsh valley that David Lloyd George once described as 'a little bit of heaven on earth' would have been destroyed. Very fortunately for the population then, and local tourism since, the proposal was defeated, and once again the English withdrew.

Until April 2013, there stood by Cilcochwyn Farm above the village of Pontfadog, a very old oak tree – old enough maybe to have taken an arrow or two in King Henry's battle. But after 1,200 years, it has become a victim of storm and climate change. I have seen a sad photograph of the oak's remains lying in a heap by the farm gate. In 1898 Arthur Bradley considered Pontfadog, located in a remote part of the valley within sight of the Berwyn mountains, stunningly beautiful:

> It is quite a noteworthy physical feature, the fashion in which this deep vale of Ceiriog drives through the high bordering hills into the heart of Wales. Shoulder behind shoulder comes tumbling down a thousand feet or more to the narrow riband of meadows, through which the joyous little river, hidden behind screens of alders and willows, makes merry music.

The 17th century Welsh poet Huw Morus, a favourite of George Borrow, was born at Pandy, one of the villages in the valley. He took the Bardic name Eos Ceiriog, the Nightingale of Ceiriog, and became the most famous poet in Wales. There is a memorial to him at the pony trekking stables in Pandy, and in a back room of the Glyn Ceiriog Memorial Institute, a window is dedicated to George Borrow commemorating the author's trek from Llangollen to find the Nightingale's place of birth. It is likely Borrow took the track where there is now a modern road which ascends steeply from Llangollen through Gwernant Wood to the ridge road overlooking the Ceiriog valley:

The morning was lowering, and before we had got to the top it started to rain. In a little time, we entered the valley of the Ceiriog. The valley is very narrow, huge hills overhanging it on both sides, those on the east side lumpy and bare, those on the west precipitous, and partially clad with wood. Just above the mill there is a meeting of streams, the Tarw from the west rolls down a dark valley into the Ceiriog. After I had looked at the place (Pandy) for some time with considerable interest we proceeded towards the south, and in about twenty minutes reached a neat kind of house, on our right hand, which John Jones told me stood on the ground of Huw Morus!

Beautiful though it is today, the valley was once industrial with extensive slate quarries, some of which can still be traced on the hillsides. Slate mining here dates back at least as far as the Tudor era, but the heyday started in the 19th century with the opening of mines at Glynceiriog. The Glyn Valley Tramway was built in 1873 to take the slate to a wharf on the Shropshire Union Canal, running alongside the road as far as Chirk Bank then later to sidings on the Great Western Railway line at Chirk station.

Pennant would not have known Telford's road, but took the high lane from the castle gates passed New Hall, where the later owner of the Ceiriog Mines, Sir Edward Wynne, would live, then over Cefn Uchaf and descended to Llangollen by Pengwern Vale:

On leaving Chirk castle, I ascend the front of the nearby heights amidst the magnificent and flourishing plantations that arise under the direction of the present owner. This lofty hill extends towards Llangollen and affords a prospect uncommonly great. The distant view is boundless. One side impends over a most beautiful valley, watered by the Dee, diversified with groves, and bounded towards the end by barren and naked rocks, tier above tier.

In a different time, Arthur Bradley did have the benefit of the Scottish engineer's great road, still hardly out of its youth:

But we must travel to Llangollen by the Holyhead Road, and resisting all temptations to loiter among the bowery gardens of the Bloody Hand Hotel, we will mount our iron steeds and head for that still more famous hostelry of the same name which stands in the narrow streets of Llangollen. It is a fine highway this, as good as any in the kingdom, and as we swing round the high shoulder below Pen y Craig, where in similar fashion as the Ceiriog but on an infinitely grander scale, the Dee valley, broad and beautiful, seems to open out Wales in very truth indeed. We have fairly set our faces westward and are bowling up the valley, whose wild and fantastic hills fill the sky but three or four miles beyond us. Dear to the hearts of the drivers of the Holyhead mail was these three miles of gentle downward slope over a perfect road, with fresh horses waiting at the foot of it in the yard of the Bloody Hand[43] at Llangollen

Williams-Wynns, Princes in Wales

Emerging from Chirk and reaching a point high above the Dee valley, our distinguished travellers would turn their backs for a moment from the fascination of the wild grouping of mountains in the distance on their westward path. For it would never do to pass by in this part of the world without some word of recognition to a famous family seat at Wynnstay Hall, spreading its woods and parklands over the low ridges above Ruabon and within easy sight. The Williams-Wynn dynasty can be traced to Gywdir Castle further west in the Conwy valley, where Sir John Wynn, 1st Baronet, is recorded as living in the mid-16th century. Sir John was a direct male descendant of Owain ap Gruffudd, also known as Owain Gwynedd, the 12th century pretender to the title of Prince of Wales. They were at the time one of Wales' oldest and wealthiest families. The present ageing 11th Baronet, Sir David Watkin Williams-Wynn, lives in practical seclusion on one of the remaining Williams-Wynns' estates near St Asaph. His son Charles, the future 12th Baronet, seems to have adopted a similar isolated existence.

Wynnstay Hall was started in the 17th century when the 5th Baronet married into the family who owned the estate and has

---

[43] The name 'Bloody Hand' derives from the red hand on the coat of arms of the Myddleton family. Renamed Hand Hotel, the hostelries remain in business in Chirk and Llangollen.

been the family seat ever since. Before then, the estate was known as Watstay, on account of Wat's Dyke running through the park to the rear of the house. Parts of the grounds were landscaped by Capability Brown, and the park was regarded as one of the largest and most important in Wales. The powerful Williams-Wynn family vied regularly with the Myddletons of Chirk Castle for parliamentary control of the Wrexham constituency. Disastrously, on the night of March 6th, 1858, Wynnstay Hall was destroyed by fire and several valuable Welsh manuscripts were lost, along with family portraits and the greater part of a fine library. It was rebuilt in the French Renaissance style with a high mansard roof, which became the iconic view of the Hall, especially from Telford's road. With the growth of the industrial revolution, Wynnstay ended up on the verge of an industrial desert of collieries, ironworks, terracotta and brick factories. But over the scarred and grimy hillside of Cefn Mawr, the Williams-Wynns saw all that they possessed and commanded. When in 1893 Charles Harper reached the outskirts of Ruabon and saw the great mansion seated on a knoll in the park that stretched for five miles between Cefn and Ruabon, nothing looked more princely:

> The late Baronet was the last of his line who commanded so greatly the reverence of the Welsh people and grown into a jealousy of the great wealth and traditions of the Wynns. The days are passed when these baronets were received in their progresses through the principality with almost royal honours. They were all-powerful, and this old verse records the sort of way in which the peasantry regarded them,

> > *If God Almighty were to die,*
> > *Who'd be God Almighty then?*
> > *To this the Welshman made reply*
> > *'Sir Watkins Williams Wynn!'*

In the end, heavy death duties caught them out and the Williams-Wynns moved from Wynnstay to nearby Plas Belan, a smaller house in the estate grounds. In 1948, they left the area completely, severing a link with Ruabon of over two centuries. Much of the estate was put up for sale and Wynnstay Hall became a private school. The school itself closed in 1994 and the house was converted into luxury apartments.

Cefn Mawr is a village on a hill beside the Dee, which here makes a great bend in a deep valley and doubles back again on itself. The collieries, ironworks, and brick manufactories once filled the valley and a ridge on which it was built, and great perpendicular scars show curiously against the hillside where stone quarries once worked. It would have been a busy scene, where hammers and anvils clanged and reverberated around the hillsides. George Borrow passed this way on his *Wild Wales* tour and must have been horrified with what he saw:

> I ascended a hill, from the top of which I looked down into a smoky valley. I descended, passing by a great many collieries, in which I observed grimy men working amidst smoke and flame. A ridge to the east particularly struck my attention; it was covered with dusky edifices, from which proceeded thundering sounds, and puffs of smoke.

But that was then, when the residents of Wynnstay watched and wondered how much more they could take out of the landscape. The brickworks of J.C. Edwards at the Penybont works closed in 1960, and the clay pits are now a landfill site. So, too, the factories at Trefynant, Acrefair, and Rhosllannerchrugog. The huge works which I knew as Monsanto Chemicals, then became the Flexsys company, still American-owned, closed in 2010 and left a great hole in Cefn Mawr, physically and spiritually. The long association between the chemical industry and Cefn Mawr had started in 1867 when Robert Graesser, an industrial chemist from the Saxony region of Germany, established a chemical works which Monsanto later acquired. Though all the factory buildings have been demolished, concerns have been expressed that there may be contamination for years to come. The community may never recover, at least not for a few generations. In recent years, on an adjacent headland where there was once a coal mine, a large community estate was built to house the families of redundant workers. Plas Madoc is an ugly, desperate place that would win no prizes for architecture, and where dreams may take forever to come true. Ironically, and in great contrast, the neighboring town of Ruabon, which grew outside the gates of Wynnstay Park, is a delight in comparison. There is an abundance of shops, the streets are busy, and there is an air of comfortable prosperity. The 1925 guide claimed that *'Ruabon is usually associated, in the minds of the travelling public, with coal mines and the manufacture of bricks. But, although the village is deservedly noted for the high quality of its terra-cotta, it ought to be better known for the beauty of its surroundings, and as a delightful holiday resort.'* The 14th century St Mary's Church is particularly significant in that the building is shared by the town's Anglican and Roman Catholic communities. This sharing agreement was inaugurated in 1980 and arose because of the apparent poor state of the existing Roman Catholic Church, which required a substantial donation from somewhere to repair it. It seems a wiser and more generous approach was decided by the opposing bishops, who are now brought together in an ecumenical alliance fostering Christian unity under one roof. In the chancel is a marble Wynnstay memorial which Thomas Pennant described as:

> A great monument of Henry Wynn, tenth son of old Sir John Wynn of Gwydir, who died in 1671. His attitude is that of a fanatical preacher; and his dress a most unhappy subject for the sculptor ... on one side kneels Sir John of Wynnstay and on the other Jane, his wife.

To be fair with the folks at Cefn, Ruabon has had its bad moments, too, as Charles Harper wrote:

> It is a stony, coaly place, thriving from the wealth underground, and frankly utilitarian. Miners with safety lamps, and faces black like the devils of childish imaginations, passed us on their way home from work, and coal grit took the place of the flour-like dust of

other highways. All the way between Ruabon and Wrexham, collieries alternate with brick and tile works, and the productiveness of this coalfield of nearly fifty square miles is immense.

Substantial remains of Offa's Dyke can be seen on the western outskirts of Ruabon, and traces of the earlier Wat's Dyke can be seen on the eastern side of the town; ironically, they are both now well behind the national border in Wales.

Llangollen

Passing the (Chirk) station there is a pretty glimpse of the canal with its wooded banks. Passenger boats, drawn briskly by horses, ply upon it between here and Llangollen, crossing the wonderful aqueduct, built a century ago (now two centuries ago), over the Dee valley by Telford, a performance greatly calculated to upset the equanimity of the timid or the uninitiated. For the boat entirely fills the channel, and thus hovers in mid-air for many hundred yards at a dizzy height above the world below, which hereabouts is a dream of beauty. *(Bradley)*

On July 25th, 1795, Richard Myddelton of Chirk Castle laid the foundation stone to the Pontcysyllte (Pont-ker-suth-tay) aqueduct – one of Thomas Telford's greatest achievements, which he completed in 1805 with the advice and guidance from canal engineer William Jessop. At 307 metres long and 39 metres high with nineteen slender piers carrying a cast iron trough filled with one-and-a-half million litres of water, it is the longest and highest aqueduct in Britain, a Grade I listed structure, Schedule Ancient Monument and a World Heritage site. Following the opening of the canal-in-the-sky, a large warehouse was built by the wharf in the Trevor Basin to handle narrowboat cargoes, and tramways linked the canal basin with the iron foundries and chemical plants at Acrefair and Ruabon. The distinguished Victorian scientist Michael Faraday described the aqueduct from the valley below as looking 'as light as a cloud', and Sir Walter Scott called it the most impressive work of art he had ever seen. Originally called the Ellesmere Canal and the Shropshire Union Canal, the Llangollen Canal was built to connect the River Severn at Shrewsbury to the River Mersey at Ellesmere Port. The intention was to run the canal due north from the Pontcysyllte aqueduct, climbing by locks towards John Wilkinson's flourishing ironworks at Brymbo and tapping into the Wrexham coal traffic before descending by the Allyn valley to Chester. The Napoleonic War brought an end to any of those plans, and the outcome was the somewhat less commercial diversion to Llangollen. The guru of narrow boat riders, L.T.C. Rolt, labelled it 'the Welsh Canal' when, in May 1949, he made his move to achieve his ambition to take his beloved boat *Cressy* over Telford's aqueduct:

> As we approached the basin at Fron Cysyllte we could see away to our right the tall stone piers of the (Pontcysyllte) aqueduct that carries the canal across the Dee. The canal widens into a small basin at this point for it was once its temporary terminus while the great aqueduct was still being built.

Rolt claimed *Cressy* to be the first leisure boat to cross the Pontcysyllte since before the war years, and always regretted that there hadn't been anybody there with a camera to record the event:

> I remember one warm and still summer night of such beauty that, reluctant to close our cabin doors and go to bed, I decided on an impulse to take my rubber dinghy and paddle it alone on to the great aqueduct. When I reached the middle, I shipped my paddle and sat quietly, one hand keeping the dinghy motionless by grasping the edge of the iron trough. It was after midnight and few lights pricked the darkness of the valley slopes. There was not a breath of wind and the only sound was the soothing and ceaseless whispering and chuckling of the river as it rippled over its boulder-strewn bed far below.

In 2016 we stayed for a few days in a cottage a short walk from the aqueduct, which is approached by the canal and towpath along an embankment, itself a unique feat of engineering being no less than 30m (97ft) high. Except for the prehistoric Silbury Hill in Wiltshire, no greater earthwork has ever been constructed in Britain, so far as I know. Its slopes are now thickly clothed with trees, concealing its height and closing off the view to the valley below. I don't usually take risks with my comfort zone, being generally terrified of heights, but the Pontcysyllte was a walk I had to do. The towpath on the east side is bordered with an elegant iron railing but on the west, there is only the rim of the iron trough standing about six inches above the water level. I had an uninterrupted view up the Vale of Llangollen towards the ancient Welsh fortress of Castell Dinas Bran that guards the town. The panorama was breathtaking and despite my discomfort on a par with Archdeacon William Coxe's own terror on the Skirrid mountain during his tour of Monmouthshire, it really was an experience worthy of the moment.

In his book, *Narrowboat Nomads*, Steve Heywood points out the traffic difficulties that can occur on the Pontcysyllte Aqueduct:

> As for canal boats crossing the aqueduct there is only enough room for one boat at a time. There are no hard and fast rules governing right of way, which often leads to some strange behaviour and bewildering impasses mid-stream, particularly during busy holiday periods when, in addition to local working boats and tourers, there is a prevalence of hire boats.

I've never been much of a boating enthusiast on any kind of water, but if for a moment the pain of coping with such situations, and with locks and ill-trained novices is left aside, there's something about narrow boating that grabs the imagination.

Seven miles north-west of Chirk, along the A5 and squeezed between the shoulders of the Berwyns and Eglwyseg mountains with the Afon Dyfrdwy (River Dee) gurgling by at its side, the town of Llangollen is the only river crossing point for miles. It is not a pretty town, but it has been the base for thousands of seasonal visitors for over 200 years. But in 1784, Henry Wyndham viewed it as 'a miserable town, though in respect of romantic scenery, it is scarcely to be equalled by any situation in Wales'. Thomas Pennant wrote:

> It is a small and poor town, seated in a most romantic spot, near a pretty common watered by the Dee, which, emblematic of its country, runs with great passion through the valley. I know no place in North Wales where the refined lover of picturesque scenes, the sentimental, or the romantic, can give a fuller indulgence to his inclination. No place abounds more with various rides or solemn walks. From this central spot, he may (as I have done) visit the seat of Owain Glyndwr and the fine valleys of the Dee, to its source beyond the great Llyn Tegid (Bala Lake); or pass over the mountains to the fertile vale of Clwyd.

The Dee Bridge in the centre of Llangollen was built in 1345 and is a scheduled ancient monument, though it was widened in the 1960s to accommodate modern traffic. Llangollen was already a popular place for tourists by the 1840s. Travel up to this point had been by horse-drawn carriage, but by then the Shrewsbury to Chester railway line had been completed, allowing passengers to alight at Llangollen Road-by-Chirk (later known as Whitehurst Halt) and then take a horse-drawn coach towards Holyhead.

Llangollen's biggest attraction happens every year during the second week of July. The International Eisteddfod brings together singers and dancers from around the world to perform to audiences of more than 100,000 over the six days of the event. The Eisteddfod's founder was a local Welshman called Harold Tudor, who had a vision towards the end of World War 2 to unite all warring nations. Having explained his plans at first to the organisers of the National Eisteddfod of Wales – the official Welsh language celebration – and told they didn't like his idea, he had better responses from like-minded friends in and around the town, and preparations were set in progress to go ahead with Harold's conception. The first event was held in 1947, but poor old Harold fell out with the festival committee over future venues and hence forward had to pay to watch like everyone else. Star performers over the years have included Luciano Pavarotti, who first competed in 1955 with his father and a choir from their home town of Modena, the Russian Red Army Ensemble, and the South African group, Ladysmith Black Mambazo. The 70th anniversary of the Eisteddfod occurred on July 3rd, 2017. That was when I made my first ever visit, which extended into a two-day affair to take in everything that was on offer in the arena and on the various field platforms. The main events take place in a purpose-built pavilion, beginning in the morning with competitions in music and dance by contestants of all ages from around the world, and ending each evening with a concert by guest artistes of renown in front of an audience of several thousand. That year, it was the turn of Welsh opera singer, Sir Bryn Terfel, American jazz/soul singer Gregory Porter, and Cardiff rock band, Manic Street Preachers. Very different entertainments and none of it done on the cheap, but the experience for those attending will have been priceless.

Feudal fragments on hill tops are common enough in Wales, as elsewhere in Britain, but surely few others stand-alone amid the clouds in such grim and uncompromising defiance as those splintered walls of Castell Dinas Bran. For immediately above Llangollen, an isolated cone-shaped hill springs sharply upward to a height of nearly 245 m (800 feet). Visible on its narrow crown and seemingly bidding eternal resistance to time and storms, savage fang-like remains of prehistoric masonry stand poised in a fashion which recalls the robber's castle of a child's dream. Bradley, too, pondered on ancient lives and mysteries that remain locked on these scattered stones:

> What generations of men have fought and fallen within easy sight of the watchers from the aerial parapet? What sights these old walls have seen. What tales they could tell if these rude stones could speak. The fifteenth century bard, Gutyn Owen, lived in Llangollen and wrote of unrequited love for Myfanwy Trevor, known by her rare beauty breaking many hearts in Powysland,

> > *My song shall tell the world how bright*
> > *Is she who robs my soul of rest,*
> > *As fair her face, all smiles and light,*
> > *As snow new fallen on Aran's crest.*

In scarlet robes, with queenly gait.
Thou comest, and all before thee kneel.
I see thee, and I curse my fate;
New torments and new love I feel.

Yet little care by thee is shown
For lays that others prize as dear;
By all besides my fame is known,
All others flock my harp to hear.

Ah, bid me sing, as well I can,
Nor scorn my melody as vain,
Or 'neath the walls of Dinas Bran
Behold me perish in my pain.

In 1804. Sir Richard Colt Hoare and his travelling companion Richard Fenton climbed to the rocky foundations of Dinas Bran and discovered the remains trifling, built of thin slate stones, but fortified strongly to the north by nature and to the south by a deep foss cut into the rock:

> There appears a heap of rubbish and cinders with many of the stones almost vitrified, proving beyond doubt that it had been part destroyed by fire. At the western extremity there are fragments of a rich canopy of freestone round a window looking out to the curious rocks of Glywseg over a narrow vale at the base of the mountain, clearly belonging to some small oratory or lady's private apartment. Hence perhaps Myfanwy might have looked out to expect her amorous bard.

George Borrow arrived in Llangollen in 1854 with his wife and daughter for the start of his *Wild Wales* and took lodgings in a cottage that was to be their base for his North Wales adventure. During the 19th century, the Dee valley around Llangollen was an important textile producing district, and the mills there, as at Newtown in Powys, rivalled those in Yorkshire and Lancashire. Many of the workmen at these 'flannel factories' were dissenters

Figure 21 The ancient Castle of Dinas Bran above Llangollen

from the Church of England, Protestant separatists about whom Borrow tended to show prejudiced views, even as he got here. The episode of the 'poor black cat' was typical of his zealous attitude. The feline belonged to a previous vicar of Llangollen and had been left behind when the vicar moved on. His successor brought with him his own cat and decided the late vicar's pet no longer had any business at the vicarage and persuaded it out to seek another home by driving it out. Unfortunately, it could not find one:

> Almost all the people of the suburb were dissenters, as indeed were the generality of the people of Llangollen, and knowing the cat to be a church cat, not only would not harbour it, but did all they could to make it miserable; while the few who were not dissenters, would not receive it into their houses, so that the cat had no home and was dreadfully persecuted by nine-tenths of the suburb. Oh, there never was a cat so persecuted as that Church of England animal, and solely on account of the opinions which it was supposed to have imbibed in the house of its late master, for I never could learn that the dissenters of the suburb, nor indeed of Llangollen in general, were in the habit of

persecuting other cats; the cat was a Church of England cat, and that was enough!

Borrow's religious bigotry didn't stop at dissenting Welsh men, either. His feelings towards the nuns of Old Pengwern Hall on the outskirts of Llangollen were voiced strongly in conversation with John Jones, his local guide:

> 'You seem to admire that old building,' said Jones. 'I was not admiring it,' said Borrows, 'I was thinking of the present and former state. Formerly it was a place devoted to gorgeous idolatry and obscene lust. Now it is a quiet old barn in which hay and straw is placed, and a few broken old tumbrels stowed away.'

There is more to Old Pengwern Hall than that. Before it became a nunnery, it was the home of ancestors of the wealthy Mostyn family, and they still owned this property at the time of Borrow's argument.

On 3rd October, Borrow returned to the cottage at Llangollen after a day's walk to Ruabon. Two weeks before, in the Crimea, a battle had been fought and won against the Russian army near to the River Almar. It was the first skirmish of the infamous war in which the combined French and British forces would see action at Balaclava, ending in a long siege of the Russian port of Sevastopol. The British army, with a strong Welsh contingent, was under the control of Fitzroy Somerset, 1st Baron Raglan, and news had reached Llangollen that the Allies, and in particular Welsh fusiliers, had not just secured an initial victory but had already won the war. It seems that street celebrations were well advanced by the time Borrow returned from his ramble. The clerk of the old church was standing at his door. 'Ah,' said the old gentleman, 'Let us congratulate each other,' he added, shaking Borrow's hand. 'Sebastopol taken, and in so short a time. How fortunate.' Forced to listen while the old man told the story of battle, Borrow knew well that news from afar in those heady days of Empire development might not be as it first appeared, and so history records in this case. However, he knew that the reward for loan of his patient ear would be more welcome than a hearty handshake.

'I have heard you are fond of good ale, and I intend to fetch you a pint of such ale as I am sure you never drank in your life.'

Towards the end of October, Borrow's wife and daughter left Llangollen to return to Norfolk, while he prepared to continue his walk around Wales. Some 40 years later, Arthur Bradley appeared in Llangollen to prepare his own book on North Wales:

> I have read most of the books written by travellers in Wales, from the days of the invaluable Pennant till the beginning of the railroad period, and can only at this moment remember the names of three or four of them; but the eccentric East Anglian genius is with me at all times. I look for him in the snug corner of wayside inn parlours, criticising his mug of ale, and astonishing a rustic audience with quotations in Suffolk Welsh from Dafydd ap Gwilym or Huw Morus, or Twm o'r Nant. I see him trudging over the moorland roads before me swinging his umbrella and spouting his own translations of Iolo Goch, or pulling up at some lonely cottage and paralysing its simple inmates with his knowledge of their tongue and folk-lore.

In writing of Wales and the borders, it is impossible to escape the companionship of the incomparable George Borrow. He was equipped for his exploration of the Principality by a knowledge of the Welsh language of which he was not a little proud, justifiably. During his many attempts to air his accomplishments, he had frequent opportunities of conversing with various characters of the peasantry in the border counties but was often at a loss whether to address chance acquaintances in Welsh or English.

In the 19th century, Llangollen was little more than a large village. The demand for accommodation was intermittent but for a few days at Easter and Whitsuntide, the Northern and Midland towns' folk burst into the vale, and the inhabitants of the town slept on the floors of their own homes or walked about all night to make room for them. In the August holidays, the fearsome char-à-bancs invaded the leafy lanes, while down at the railway station trains heavily congested with perspiring people went labouring slowly towards Barmouth and the west coast. From that time, Llangollen was, and still is, called upon to cater for every traveller who aims their vehicle in the direction of North Wales. One of the targets for the Victorian elite was Plas Newydd, one-time home of the 'Ladies of Llangollen', Sarah Ponsonby and Eleanor Butler. Their extraordinary friendship began in 1778 at a boarding school in Kilkenny in Ireland and lasted for the rest of their lives. At first, there was no suspicions as to how strong the friendship was, until they each refused marriages arranged by their wealthy parents and ran away together, escaping after several attempts to England. The couple finally arrived in Llangollen and decided to settle there. They bought a plain old farmhouse called Pen-y-Maes, and even though they were penn-y-less, gradually turned it into an exotic, pretentious residence decorated in the Gothic style mainly with donated bits and pieces, and gave it a new name, Plas Newydd. William Wordsworth, one of many frequent callers, described it as 'a low roofed cot' while George Borrow's view was as 'a small gloomy mansion'. The black and white battens which now cover the exterior of the house were not the idea of the ladies, but General John Yorke who had lived at Erdigg as a child and bought Plas Newydd after their deaths.

The ladies adopted the oddest of manners, dressed in men's black clothing and wore top hats. Their reputation for eccentricity and quirkiness spread beyond the border, and national personalities of the day and the wealthy travellers along Telford's London to Holyhead road that passed through the town at the bottom of their lane, couldn't resist visiting them. Samuel Johnson and Hester Thrale came for tea on their tour of North Wales, as did the occasional Duke and Duchess. At a time when lesbianism was only a subject for speculation and gossip, the 'Ladies' attracted much of that around the town and surrounding areas. It was quite astonishing how a couple of non-conformist cranks could attract the high and mighty of the land into their odd little world. The 19th century dandy. Hermann Prince Pukler-Muskau, called them 'the most celebrated virgins in Europe'.

World's End

From Llangollen, a back-lane climbs behind the Festival Ground and winds its way around Dibren Wood towards the Creigiau Eglwyseg limestone escarpment. This is the old road along which George Borrow set out to walk to Wrexham. Then, it was not much more than a little used track, and enquiries by cyclist Fletcher Moss for the whereabouts of World's End proved difficult until an ostler at their inn suggested it was seven miles uphill, hard to find, and reachable only by donkey. The bicycles were replaced by a young horse with a dogcart and a driver who knew the way.

> The road becomes more like a track, and as the giant hills close around us, with white rock cliffs rising to the sky, a change comes o'er the spirit of our dreams. We feel this must be World's End. A ghostly old black-and-white house, faded and mellowed with age, nestling snugly at the base of the encircling mountains, sheltered with ancient trees, firs, and yews, with masses of hoary lichens on its stone roof, their colours brightened with the wild geraniums and flowers which grow even in the crannies and on the roughness of the big chimney. Its glamour steals over us as the daylight dies. The diamond paned windows are deeply set, the trees above cast greyish flickering shadows on the walls while the giant hills look down on all. It is indeed a ghostly place.

What they had discovered at the very end of the narrow Eglwyseg Glen below the Eglwyseg Rocks was the remote Elizabethan Manor House of Plas Uchaf. The present timber-framed and stone building dates from the 16th century but is thought to stand on the site of a hunting lodge belonging to Owain ap Cadwgan, a prince of Powys. If it is to be believed, he brought the beautiful Welsh princess Nest, wife of the Norman lord Gerald de Windsor, to Plas Uchaf when he abducted her and her children in 1109. Plas Uchaf was later the home of Colonel John Jones, a prominent Republican, brother-in-law of Oliver Cromwell, and one of the regicides of Charles I. Curiously, since then the house has mainly been owned or at least lived in by various Joneses, though not necessarily related. During the war years, it was the venue for top secret talks between Winston Churchill and the German Foreign Minister, Joachim Von Ribbentrop. Today, it is hidden behind a barrier of trees and shrubs, and the lane which passed in front of the house has been diverted to improve privacy.

When George Borrow set out from Llangollen to walk to Wrexham via World's End, the weather that day was not in his favour, it was misty and it rained. At Plas Uchaf he was given directions but continued still unassured. After he had walked a little way farther and reached the Moor, his way became further indistinct. A well-defined path led to the east while northward, the direction in which he wanted to go, there appeared scarcely any path at all. He turned east and by so doing went wrong, as he soon found, and chose his next move in his normal Borrow-like fashion:

> I mounted the side of a hill covered with moss-like grass, and here and there heather. By the time I arrived at the top of the hill the sun shone out, and I saw Ruabon and Cefn Mawr before me in the distance. 'I am going wrong,' said I, 'I should have kept on due north. However, I will not go back, but will steeplechase it across country to Wrexham which must be towards the north-east.'

When compiling the Wrexham addition for the *Real* series of books for Seren, author Grahame Davies wrote:

> What is not in doubt, is that the view eastwards is one of the most stunning in Wales, and there's no other place where the contrast between Welsh highlands and the English plain is so stark. The one side open, flat, orderly, sunlit; its roads straight and broad, its horizon stretching to infinite distances and possibilities; the other side secretive, mountainous, unruly, shadowed; its paths narrow and twisting, its horizons bounded closely by the next dark hill.

In the valley bottom, the remains of the Abbey Valle Crucis, Abbey of the Vale of the Cross, are about two miles out of

Llangollen. Founded in 1201 by Prince Madog ap Gruffydd, it was the only Cistercian monastery to be built in Welsh Maelor and the last by a Welsh ruler. It was named after the nearby pillar, or cross of Eliseg, which stands on a mound by the side of the road to the Horshoe Pass. After the 16th century dissolution, the site fell into disrepair and in the late 18th century some of the buildings that remained were used as a farm. In 1803, Sir Richard Colt Hoare found time for a spot of sketching, and considered that the ruins:

> Though not so well preserved as their beautiful architecture should have merited, still merit the attention of every traveller who will view them as an artist or antiquarian. To the former they will afford much employment for his pencil. The ruins are surrounded by fine old ash trees whose delicate taper corresponds well with the elegant light Gothic architecture of the building, but I wish one or two of them removed to admit a more perfect view of the fine western front.

As later visitors discovered, access to the abbey ruins was at the convenience of a guardian, and when Fletcher Moss and his companion arrived carrying their camera equipment, there was no-one in attendance. They climbed the walls to gain entrance to take their photos, then presumably had to climb out, no doubt leaving their sixpence fee by the guardian's door! In 1936 Thomas Roscoe approached Llangollen from the north, through the wild mountain region around Denbigh, Ruthin, and Llandegla. On seeing the Cross of Eliseg, he recalled to mind the 17th century antiquary and scholar, Edward Lhuyd – the first in those days to transcribe the inscription on the pillar — though not before the Cromwellians had knocked it from its pedestal:

> This column was raised as a memorial of the dead, a rude improvement on the ruder monuments of Druidical times. It was covered with inscriptions and raised on a tumulus, according to the customs of ancient times, when pillars were placed under every green tree.

The column, originally a round-shafted cross, stands on a knoll beside the A452 road up to the Horseshoe Pass. The inscription, now illegible, was transcribed by Lhuyd in 1696 and shows that the cross was erected by Cyngen ap Cadell, a 9th century ruler of Powys, to honour his great grandfather, Elisedd ap Gwylog, for his victory over a Mercian force a century before. Not long after Elisedd's exploits, the Mercian King Offa started building his Dyke to pass through this district, probably below the Cregiau Eglwyseg cliffs.

The Horseshoe

As often as I have seen the lovely region around Llangollen, it now showed itself in bolder lights and shadows, as different as they were surprising. I had left my night lodgings in Llangollen early, and the autumnal morning had started brightly enough, displaying the surrounding scenery under the warmest colours. The sky was cloudless and the air clear, yet in less than an hour produced a change, almost instantaneously yielding a scene on entering the valley as different as it was wild and impressive. It contrasted strikingly with the appearance I had just described. The sky grew dark and threatening, the mist came sweeping in on both sides from the Berwyn and Bryneglwys heights stretching above and before me. All features of the Deeside landscape became lost in the dim light embracing hillsides and river valley. Ahead, where the curving of the vale stretched along the side of the converging Denbighshire hills, the clouds came driving in, changing the prospect until all became veiled in a blanket fog. I was driving, part blind, up the Horseshoe Pass, and after a hair-raising slow climb in second gear, I arrived at the summit where the blanket lifted as suddenly as it had engulfed me in the valley below. The Berwyn mountains are still some distance to the west at this point, but it was possible for Sir Richard Colt Hoare and Richard Fenton to see beyond them:

> The pass was prodigiously steep but then we come to a mountain tract and open an extensive view. We see the Arenig Fawr, an old acquaintance, and have a clear view of Snowdon.

The November day had now turned bright again, and as I stood with my back to the Ponderosa Café the old waste tips of Llantysilio Mountain blocked my view westwards. The Moel-y-Faen slate quarry had been operating since the 17th century and had kept going until 1940. At the end, the waste covered the whole of the northern end of the mountain, so in the early travelling days of Colt Hoare and Fenton, their view would not have been so restricted. Among the quarried stones, a very deep clear azure blue lake had formed at the bottom of a spectacular crater. It is known locally as the Blue Lagoon and is a popular spot for some wild swimming and diving, with participants travelling from all parts of the UK to reach the site, particularly on bank holiday weekends. Much to their disappointment, I'm sure, there is a plan to drain and cover it in as part of a major project to return the carved-up mountain to heath and heather moorland. This is a huge project, we are told, and will take until 2032.

During the hot dry summerof 2018 the mountain caught fire and burned for 40 days, closing the road to all traffic. The fire spread alarmingly, turning the landscape black and the air thick with grey smoke. When the fire was finally extinguished, half the mountain had been burnt and the peatland areas were particularly badly affected, with wildlife habitats destroyed and sheep grazing areas unusable. The moors here were a favourite walking area for George Alexander Graber, a.k.a Alexander Cordell, a prolific Welsh novelist whose books reflected the grim realities of the lives of Welsh ironworkers and miners in the nineteenth century. He spent his final years at Rhosddu in Wrexham and died on the 13th November 1997 at the age of 83, though it seems in unusual circumstances. Two local farmers discovered his body on the mountainside overlooking the Horseshoe Pass, allegedly in a kneeling position, forehead to the ground, as if in prayer. It was reported, too, that he had with him a bottle of brandy and anti-depressant tablets, and the implications of intended suicide added to the mystery. A postmortem, however, found that the cause of death was heart failure, perhaps brought on by exhaustion while climbing these very high hills.

Back in Llangollen, Bradley had vacated his room in the Hand Hotel and was on Telford's road again:

> The railroad indeed flinches altogether from this wooded spur of Moel-y-Geraint and burrows through it in a long tunnel; the river making a most remarkable horse-shoe circuit of five miles, and a most enchanting circuit it is, in its efforts to get around it. Telford, however, chose to face the hill and has left us, as a legacy of his decision, a mile or more of steady collar work, the bane of westward bound cyclists and joy of those returning to the English border counties.[44]

Rebellion

The village of Glyndyfrdwy is halfway between Llangollen and Corwen. At first glance, it is nothing other than plain, perhaps even dull, but Glyndyfrdwy has a place in Welsh history of which all Cymry will be aware. It was the birthplace of their true Prince of Wales, Owain Glyndŵr (Camden seems to have been unsure of the origin of the man's name and referred to him throughout *Brittannia* as Owen Glendowerdwy). Glyndŵr was born Owain ap Gruffudd Fychan in a motte castle on the banks of the river in 1359. By a fortuitous act of breeding, Owain was a descendant of the Princes of Powys through his father's line, and of the lords of Deheubarth in South Wales on his mother's. His father died when Owain was ten years old, and in an unusual break with Welsh tradition, rather than the son-of-the-father nomenclature, he took as his surname the Glyn of the place of his birth and Dŵr for the water of the Dee. During the early years of his life, he led a quiet existence looking after his estates at Glyndyfrdwy and Sycharth. In 1383, he married Margaret, the daughter of Sir David Hanmer, a marcher judge, but in the following year he was called to join a military campaign in

---

[44] The hill Bradley called Moel-y-Geraint, or Barber's Hill, rises on the left immediately as the A5 leaves Llangollen, and is not the hill and spur with the railway tunnel, which is just beyond the village of Berwyn and the Horseshoe Falls.

Scotland fighting for the English king, Richard II. Owain witnessed Richard's dethronement in 1399 and the seizure of the throne by Henry Bolingbroke, lord of the House of Lancaster. In the following year he became embroiled in a land dispute with his neighbour and close friend of the new King Henry IV, Lord Reynold Grey of Ruthin. Though Owain called on the King to resolve the issue, his plea was refused. This was the spark that ignited Glyndŵr's revolt against English rule. From September 1400 onwards, he set out to take back all Wales from the English, starting with Lord Grey's castle at Ruthin, which he destroyed in his first attack. It was the incentive for a group of local supporters to proclaim him Prince of Wales, and for the next dozen years he pillaged and burned wherever he discovered continuing English influence on Welsh soil.

The year 2004 was a very important one in Wales; it was the 600th anniversary of the establishment of Glyndŵr's Parliament at Machynlleth in Montgomeryshire, as well as the 600th anniversary of his crowning ceremony as Prince of Wales. As an important part of the commemoration and celebrations of 1404-2004, Llysgenhadaeth Glyndŵr – a group which promotes the heritage of the Welsh prince – presented the people of Machynlleth with Cleddyf y Genedl, the Sword of the Nation, a magnificent hand-made weapon that had been commissioned especially for the occasion. The same group in 2007 presented a replica silver and gold-plated crown to the people of Wales. Both are now housed in Machynlleth's Council Offices.

Rebirth of a Railway

Being a Victorian traveller, Arthur Bradley made use of the numerous trains available wherever he wanted to go in Wales or England, and it is not surprising that he would often praise their virtuous timetables:

Corwen possesses quite a busy little station; for the Great Western, on its road to Dolgellau and Barmouth is here met by a branch of the London and North Western coming from Rhyl, Chester and

Denbigh down the Vale of Clwyd. All parts, therefore, of the country north of the Dee valley are in touch with one another, this central route being linked to the seacoast, not only by the Clwyd railway, but by a line connecting Bala with Festiniog and Conway.

The former station house at Corwen is now the offices of the town's main employer (2016), Ifor Williams Trailers, started 60 years ago by a farmer looking to transport sheep to local markets. The Llangollen train to Corwen is running again now, but only as far as a basic platform on the outskirts at what is encouragingly named as Corwen East. The line runs alongside the Dee below the northern flanks of the Berwyns. Forming part of the Cambrian Mountains, the Berwyns are an impressive barrier between the modern counties of Powys and Gwynedd but are a gaunt, troublesome range of mountains. The streams of the north-western slopes empty into Bala Lake, and from the southern slopes the River Tanat wanders down through its valley towards the border. Lake Vyrnwy, the reservoir for Liverpool, is also fed from draining brooks of the Berwyns. Nevertheless, they presented an attractive proposition to Bradley.

> I wish I had time to scramble up one of the many streams that come leaping down the hill-sides towards the Dee, and look out from these high ledges over the wild, heather-clad wilderness that rolls southward far into Montgomery, where for miles and miles, a great solitude and silence reign, which are only broken by the plaintive piping of the curlews, the crow of cock grouse, and the plashing of peaty streams towards the infant Ceiriog.

In the heady days of rail travel, Llangollen was on the Ruabon to Barmouth route, transporting passengers through one of the most beautiful landscapes in Britain. In 1955, this Great Western line of the British Railways Company carried a twelve-year-old boy, his parents and siblings, along that glorious line from Manchester to their seaside holiday on the west Wales coast. I had never seen mountains so high or so close before, but when the mass of Cader Idris filled my view as we steamed by Bala lake and drew near to

Dolgellau, I felt the first yearnings for wild adventures of long rambles in the countryside and hikes over high mountains that would become a large part of my growing years. Ten years later, Dr Richard Beeching, then chairman of British Railways, decided this beautiful line was unworthy of further expenditure and closed it to passengers. The section as far as the Llangollen goods yard remained open for freight traffic until April 1968, but when that small relief ended, the track was removed with unseemly haste from the whole line to Barmouth. In 1972, the Llangollen Railway Trust formed to buy the station buildings with high hopes of reintroducing an ex-GWR steam locomotive or two and operate as a volunteer-run heritage railway. After receiving a generous donation from the Shell Oil company, they started with a small section of exit track which has now been extended as far as Corwen East – a creaking, jolting, da-da-de-da distance of ten miles alongside the babbling waters of the Dee.

On the outskirts of Corwen, Rhug (pronounced Reeg) Hall is the Denbighshire home of Robert Vaughan Wynn, 8th Baron Newborough. His ancestors were the great Salusbury family of Lleweni near Denbigh. The seat of this branch of the Wynn family is Peplow Hall on the eastern fringes of Shropshire, Rhug is where his lordship spends much of his time running his organic farming business. The estate covers 12,500 acres extending from Gwyddelwern to the north, Carrog the east, Cynwyd the south, and Maerdy to the west. The 6,700-acre farm in Denbighshire is the geographical core of the estate, along with the Hall. The Bison Grill bistro opposite the main drive is a popular eating house, often for his Lordship, and a local landmark where his organic food is sold in large quantities. Sir Richard Colt Hoare visited Rhug in 1801, where Captain Salusbury was building a new house near the site of the old one:

> It is built of a yellow grit stone brought from Ruabon. The front has a handsome Ionic portico, large enough to permit a carriage to drive up to the door. The front rooms will command a good view of the Vale of Dee when the old house and some trees are removed. Much remains to be done. The old house is in part pulled down.

Near the old house is an ancient tumulus which I understand is not to be removed.

Shapely Hills of Clwyd

From the descent of the hill as you enter the Vale of Clwyd you have a most charming and extensive view of the whole Vale from its narrow beginning to its most expanded reach exhibiting a most rich and finely wooded prospect, but tame and not picturesque. Hence by a charming road finely shaded with hedgerows, to Ruthin. Here we dined but could not stay to see it, and in the evening after a most delightful ride, to Denbigh. (*Richard Fenton*)

The shapely hills of the Clwydian range are now in sight, and we are dropping down the long slope of Bryn Saith Marchog. This area once belonged to the house of Powys Fadog, Lower Powys, and ruled in the late 13th century by Gruffudd Fychan II, Lord of Glyndyfrdwy, Owain Glyndŵr's father. In these rolling fields, Glyndŵr came to blows with Lord Grey of Ruthin at the outset of rebellion and took him prisoner. Seen from a moderate distance, the town of Ruthin is picturesque while retaining a medieval air. It is recognised today as one of the most sought-after places in North Wales in which to live and is an attractive town to explore. A fine collection of ancient houses, many disguised now by shop fronts, cluster around the square and in the central streets where red brick is the prevailing colour there is a wealth of black and white, like Nantclwyd y Dre, built in 1425, claimed to be the oldest timber-frame house in the whole of Wales. It would have been part of the rebuilding work after Glyndŵr's willful destruction. A Dutch-style building built in 1647 with seven dormer windows and known as the 'Seven eyes of Ruthin', for a long time an inn but now a restaurant, is the most photographed of all the central attractions. George Borrow described Ruthin as a dull town and made no mention of the eccentric architecture. Near the castle gate, an enclosed passage leading to a raised walk that skirts the ancient walls looks down to where a mediaeval mill once stood beside the

Clwyd river. Adjoining the Victorian Gothic Castle Hotel are the meagre remains of the ancient bastion of Lord Reginald Grey', Glyndŵr's detested foe. My first ever visit to Ruthin in 2016 was a pleasant surprise. The towns of North Wales have not had a great time of it since the end of coal mining and as a result can't help the drab underinvested way some of them now look, but Ruthin has beauty and charm. Ludlow in Shropshire, it has an irresistible power which, like many before me, will draw me back time and again. Wyndham, too, saw Ruthin in a different light:

> Ruthin is a large and well inhabited town on the river Clwyd, and I shall here observe in general, that the towns in North Wales are much superior in beauty of buildings, and in the space of their streets, to those of South Wales.

The Clwydian Hills are a chain of striking and varied heights that look like mountains, especially when seen from across the level vale, though their culminating point, Moel Fammau, is under 610m (2000ft) high. The chain is broken by two main gaps. Through one, runs the A541 linking Denbigh with Mold; the other by the A494 Mold to Ruthin highway. Moel Fenlli, the hill immediately above Ruthin, is crowned by a substantial Iron Age fort and at 511m (1,677ft) is the second highest peak of the whole range. From up there, the vale floor appears as a chess board of browns and greens, daubed with spreading woods, the spacious parks of its numerous country houses and dotted with frequent villages. Beyond the Vale are the colourful ridges of the mysterious Hiraethog district, an area of sparsely populated moorland which extends unbroken to the Conwy Valley, as Camden described:

> The Vale itself, with its green meadows, yellow cornfields, villages, and fair houses standing thick, and many beautiful churches, giveth wonderful great contentment to such as behold it from above.

The main A525 route continues through the Clwydian Vale towards the Dee estuary and the waters of Liverpool Bay. Along the way, it passes through the county town of Denbighshire.

Denbigh is a market town eight miles to the north west of Ruthin that grew around a glove-making industry which has now gone, leaving the twice weekly markets to provide for the sprawling community developments in the outskirts. The ruined hilltop castle, with its spectacular gatehouse, dominates the town and surrounding countryside. Denbigh was founded in the late 13th century as an English town that was contained within its walls while the resentful Welsh were kept outside. The remains of St Hilary's 'chapel within the walls' was built around 1300 while the town continued to grow outside the castle grounds. Another church, the parish church of St Marcella's over a mile away, was used for burials because St Hilary's, like the castle, was built on rock.

Throughout the castle's declining years, poorly built housing appeared against it walls. The cottage in which the great explorer, Sir Henry Morton Stanley, was born stood by the gatehouse. He started life illegitimately as John Rowlands in 1841 and emigrated to America when 18 years of age. At some stage, he seems to have created a new identity for himself, either out of a chance meeting with a wealthy trader whose name was Henry Hope Stanley, or from having heard the man's name in conversation. Whichever was true, he adopted a variation of that name as his own, and from then on history lay on the horizon. For years Stanley roamed aimlessly, occasionally filling in time as a soldier serving on both sides in the American Civil War, a seaman on merchant ships, and a journalist in the early days of frontier expansion. In 1869, he was commissioned by the *New York Herald* to go to Africa and search for the Scottish missionary and explorer, David Livingstone, of whom little had been heard since he had set out to discover the source of the Nile three years before. When he did eventually find him, his claimed greeting, 'Dr. Livingstone, I presume?', was henceforward etched in folklore. A bronze statue of Stanley with hand outstretched in greeting, was unveiled outside Denbigh market hall in 2011, but the memorial was not without opposition and controversy, not least because once he had left for the US he never reappeared in Wales.

Towards the end of the English Civil War, Denbigh was the last Royalist stronghold to fall. Its last defender was Sir William Salusbury who, in the eventual realization of defeat, haggled for days with the Parliamentary leader, General Thomas Mytton, over the terms of surrender. He then ended his defiance by throwing the keys from the top of the Goblin tower on the town walls, shouting to his adversary, 'The world is yours, make it your dunghill!'

A short distance from the castle, but still within the walls, is a building commissioned in 1579 by Robert Dudley, the Earl of Leicester and favourite of Elizabeth I. It was intended to be a church, but he ran out of money and it was never completed. At the time, Dudley was also Baron Denbigh and owned much of the land hereabouts that also included the cathedral city of St Asaph. His strong Puritan beliefs led him to pursue the idea of a large preaching house for the Puritan movement in opposition to St Hilary's Catholic chapel in Denbigh and the Protestant centre at St Asaph. Although still in an unfinished state, Dudley appointed as his first vicar William Morgan of Llanrhaeadr-ym-Mochnant, the eventual translator of the Bible into Welsh. By 1584, the church was still not completed and progress ground to a halt. Four years later, Dudley was dead and the building finally abandoned. The crumbling roofless walls still survive, now behind the gates of a small private compound. Nearby St Hilary's within the walls continued to be used until in 1874, when it became too small for the growing town and it too was abandoned. All but the tower was demolished in 1923. On one of his last visits to North Wales, Sir Richard Colt Hoare found Denbigh had a very picturesque appearance seen from the St Asaph road.

> Immediately after my arrival I walked out in search of the most advantageous points of view and encircled the castle. I fixed my point at last from the limestone quarries on the road leading to St Asaph. Here the town appears to very great advantage: the ruins of a fine castle at the summit and by its side the church in ruins, a fine rich country terminated in mountains at a distance with a very good and broken foreground, and the town covering the declivities of a steep hill, well blended with trees. The whole forms a rich

picturesque scene, worthy of the pencil of a Poussin, and similar in many respects to those he chose for his pencil.

Arthur Bradley saw Denbigh as a great deal more than a pleasant country town:

> For when you have climbed up its long steep street to the marketplace, there is yet another pull, if you would see its full beauties, to the old castle which crowns the summit of all. And in reaching this you pass beneath a massive gateway that marks the entrance to the old Norman town, now consisting of but a few ancient cottages and scattered buildings of a later date. On the wide castle green stands the shell of the long-abandoned parish church. On the highest point of all, nearly five hundred feet above the vale below, rise the stately ruins of the great Norman fortress with the battered effigy above its gateway of its founder and grantee, Henry de Lacy, Earl of Lincoln.

Known locally as Eglwys-wen, the white church, the parish church of St Marcella's stands on raised ground away from the town centre and has a stunning, uninterrupted backdrop of Moel Arthur and the whole Clwydian range. The fabric of the church is mostly late 16th century, but its recorded history goes way back to the times of the Dark Ages. Following the destruction of the Celtic monastery at Bangor on Dee by Aethelfrith in 613, the community there had all but ceased to exist. All that is, as the tale is told, except for brothers Deifyr and Tyrnog and their sister Marchell, who escaped beyond the mountains to the west into the valley of the Clwyd. Having chosen to go separate ways, Marchell found this spot on a small mound by a well overlooking the Clwydian Vale and built a shelter of willow and thatch. She is said to have spent the rest of her days in prayer and meditation, giving assistance to weary travellers and, as so often happened in those circumstances, became recognised as a saint, even in life. After her death, her followers replaced her shelter with a chapel of wattle and mud that in time became a church of bricks and mortar before someone decided the walls should be covered in whitewash. It's a good story, and St Marcella's is a simple but very fine church in what is undoubtedly a spectacular landscape. Its Grade I listing is a bit of a surprise, for although the church has a splendid 15th century hammer beam roof and a colourful 16th century alabaster altar tomb of Sir John and Dame Joan Salusbury of Llewenni gracing the south chapel there is no rood screen or Jesse window, and the modern seating makes the interior of the church look architecturally plain. However, within the busy churchyard is the tomb of Twm o'r Nant, real name Thomas Edwards – the Welsh poet and self-styled dramatist who died in 1810. Could his presence have added credence to the grading?

On the west side of Denbigh, set deep in the Denbighshire countryside, is the rambling 18th century Gwaenynog Hall, a house that has literary connections from two different centuries. A branch of the Myddelton family settled here in the 16th century and became leading lights in Denbighshire circles. In the mid-18th century, the house was remodelled by Colonel John Myddleton, and both Thomas Pennant and man of letters, Samuel Johnson, stayed at Gwaenynog as guests of the Colonel. Johnson came here in 1774 with Hester Thrale, and to commemorate this visit, Myddleton erected a monument to Johnson by the River Ystrad which runs through the estate. In the late 19th century, Gwaenynog Hall was owned by Frederick Burton, the uncle of the English Lake District's most recognised resident author, Beatrix Potter. She visited North Wales thirteen times between 1895 and 1913 and fell in love with the house and its gardens. She used the kitchen garden as the setting for *The Tale of the Flopsy Bunnies*, and sketches of the garden feature in her book.

Today, the old hall remains in the hands of the Burtons, with Mrs Janie Smith, Beatrix's great niece. In September 2017, I was shown around the reconstructed flower beds with which Potter was so familiar. Janie had rebuilt the kitchen garden to the original design In 1988, with the help of her daughter, Frances, and Mr McGregor's the old garden cottage remains in situ, much to the enjoyment of Flopsy readers. However, I was there to learn less about rabbits and more about the visits of Dr Johnson and Hester Thrale, who came to dinner with Colonel Myddleton. Johnson was unimpressed with the house and would rank it at best only as second rate:

> The rooms were low and the passage above the stairs gloomy, but the furniture was good. The table was well supplied except the fruit was bad. It was truly the dinner of a country gentleman. Two tables were filled with company not inelegant. After dinner the talk was about preserving the Welsh language.

Hester, too, had reservations, but more with the company they kept:

> Here I first saw a group of genuine Welsh folks and cannot boast the elegant of the society. The women were vastly below the men in proportion, their manners were gross, and their language more contracted. However, the men were not drunk, nor the women inclined to disgrace themselves.

In letters to friends, Hester often referred to Johnson's eating habits while touring Wales. She once wrote that, 'a leg of pork, boiled till it dropped from the bone, a veal pie with plums and sugar, or the outside cut of a salt buttock of beef were his favourite dainties'. On another occasion, she referred to a dish of young peas they had been served at table as 'charming', to which Johnson replied, 'Perhaps they would be so – to a pig!'

Figure 22 Dr Samuel Johnson

In the 16th century, Sir John Salusbury built a house on the outskirts of Denbigh that would become the head house for one of the most influential families of Wales and the courts of English monarchs. Lleweni Hall developed into an enormous Elizabethan pile and a leading seat of Welsh culture during the life of Hester Thrale, whose maiden name was Hester Lynch Salusbury. She spent part of her childhood on the estate and explored many of the Hall's 200 rooms. On a later visit in 1774 with Dr Johnson, she wrote:

> Superfluous space seems to be a source of satisfaction in a large house, and here is a hall and gallery which never seem intended for use but merely stateliness of appearance.

Like many great houses of the 16th and 17th centuries, renowned players of the arts and literary world were welcome visitors, and as Meurig Owen mentions in his own *Grand Tour of North Wales*, 'William Shakespeare stayed at Lleweni in isolation to escape a time of plague.' Hester Thrale, herself a highly literate person and aware of the Shakespeare connection with Lleweni, would have seen the significance of bringing a Shakespearean authority in Samuel Johnson into her ancestral home:

> Today we rode on to my parish church at Tremeirchion where many of my progenitors, including my father, lie buried. The church is in a dismal condition, the seats all tumbling about, the altar rail falling, the vessels for the consecrated elements only pewter, the cloth upon the table in a thousand holes, and the floor strewn with rushes. Of the seats, however, wretched as they are, my family possess fourteen, and these the best.

In the early years of the 19th century, the great house of the Salusbury's became too costly to maintain and was sold. The new owner, William Hughes, a copper mining magnate, used large parts of Lleweni to build his own pile at Kinmel Hall near Abegele which he did not live to see completed, and was finished by his descendants in 1871. What was left of Lleweni was later used as a farm.

The first red brick house to be built on a palatial scale anywhere in Wales was constructed in 1567 by Sir Richard Clough of Denbigh[45]

---

[45] Clough's knighthood was created as a result of a visit to the Holy Land, where he became a Knight of the Holy Sepulchre. Queen Elizabeth I did not approve.

Figure 23 Hester Lynch Thrale

who had become extremely rich as a drapery merchant in Amsterdam. Set below wooded hillside between Denbigh and St Aasaph, Bach y Graig's architectural style owed much to Clough's Dutch associations, with a steeply sloping pyramidical roof, tall chimney stacks, a collection of dormer windows, and the whole crowned with a spectacular cupola. To continue the Dutch theme, Clough used bricks and even labour from Holland to complete his mansion. Sir Richard Colt Hoare's friend, Richard Fenton, questioned the need for importing building materials, as the vale near the house 'afforded the very best for making bricks.'. In addition to the main house, Clough built a separate two storey west block which included an arched entrance to the courtyard. He intended this to be used as a warehouse for a commercial trading centre. The River Clwyd is only a quarter of a mile from the house, and Clough had an even more extraordinary idea to canalise five miles of the river from Rhuddlan and use that stretch to transport goods to and from his warehouses at Bach y Graig. Unfortunately for Clough, he died while in Hamburg in 1570 before he could put this idea into practice.

By the time Hester Thrale, who had by then inherited Bach y Graig, visited the house in 1774, it was in a very poor state, without floors and the windows blocked up, and she was none too pleased. It had 'three excellent rooms over which there seemed little else but pigeon-holes in a manner peeping out of the roof, and at the top of it a ridiculous lantern with a ladder to get up to it'. However, she liked where the house was sited, particularly the surrounding woods:

The gatehouse, however, placed straight before the front door impedes all possibility of view, and the warehouses on the side,

336

however useful, are far from being ornaments to the whole. I really think if the top was taken off and a story of decent rooms built in their stead, the house might yet be convenient and fit for a family. We rode over a part of the estate which is said to be good, and I think it really seems so. The corn fields are surrounded with deep hedge rows planted with oak, which are said to stretch their shade so as to hinder the approach of the sun and prevent the growth of grain. There is a great deal more wood than I thought when I first saw it.

Her ideas came to nothing, even though she had cut down some of the woods to raise cash for the improvement. Hester's second husband, Gabriele Pozzi, thought it more of a mausoleum and wanted it demolished and replaced with a more convenient mansion, Brynbella, a few miles up the road. The main house was pulled down in 1817 and Bach y Graig was left as a farmhouse, now a Grade II listed building, and the rest remained as farm buildings.

It seems Hester must have agreed with her husband's determination to pull down Clough's old house, as it was by all accounts unfit to inhabit, but she foresaw the possibility of remodeling the farmhouse, perhaps to resell or reuse to accommodate visitors to Brynbella. And that is exactly what happened. Located at the end of a long private driveway, the farmhouse is impressively set in 200 acres of fertile farmland, which includes a trail through 40 acres of woodland. The owners for the last 200 years or so have been the Roberts family, who currently keep 210 head of cattle and run a bed and breakfast business. In 2017, I booked a few nights' stay there, from where I could tour the local estates of the Myddletons and Salusburys, the ancient landed gentry of Denbigh. I stayed a second time in 2018, when I met to my great surprise and satisfaction Mr Tim Clough – a descendant of the builder of Bach y Graig. He and his wife had arrived from their home in the mid-western US state of Wisconsin to learn more of his ancestor's life in north Wales, and so together we enjoyed a few days learning what we could.

Thomas Pennant will have known of Bach y Graig, but his home at Downing wasn't far away and his writings record only his awareness of the section of Clwydian landscape nearby:

> I must not pass unnoticed the strong British Post (Moel y Gaer) which soars above the road. It lies on the summit of a hill and is surrounded with a great foss and dyke of a circular form, with an entrance as usual to such places. This seems to have been an outpost of the Ordovices in order to defend their country against the Roman invaders.

Hester Thrale died in 1821 and is buried in the family vault of Corpus Christi church at Tremeirchion near her home at Brynbella. The vault that includes her second husband was originally placed outside the church but is now covered by the north transept. A wall tablet in the chapel records her as 'Doctor Johnson's Mrs Thrale'. Poor Mr Prozzi doesn't get a mention. Writing to her daughter Queeney in September 1803, Mrs Prozzi said of the church (Corpus Christi):

> It was a place like a stable, you know; and we have made a vault for ourselves and my poor Salusbury ancestors whose bones we found by digging under the altar.

The Vale of Clwyd at Ruthin is 5km (3 mi) wide. At its mouth, between Rhyl and St Asaph, it is perhaps twice that width. The Clwydian Hills sharply define its eastern wall, and though these are devoid of naked crags with which the more sombre sides of the Berwyns are regularly marked, they nevertheless leap up and down in bold fashion as they edge towards the sea. On the summit of Moel Famau, the highest point, are the remains of a building which at first glance looks like a military defence platform, but is in fact all that is left of an Egyptian three tiered tower built in 1810 to commemorate the golden jubilee of George III. It was designed by Thomas Harrison of Chester but when funds ran short it was never finished. Part of the incomplete tower was brought down in a storm in 1862, and for safety the rest of the upper section was demolished, leaving just the base. Not far away, Thomas Roscoe was aiming for the tops, when:

> At Llannerch, the Wanderer paused to admire the delicious view of the vale, with the majestic boundary between the Clwyd and Flintshire. On ascending the ridge, the entire valley breaks upon the eye, with the far western boundaries and the tracts of the lofty Snowdon beyond. Midway from end to end, the prospect is enriched with towns and castles; and towering above the rest frowns the rock of Denbigh, the shattered fragments of its castle crowning the summit of its isolated hill.

When Camden reached St Asaph, he did not see it at its best:

> Beneath Bodvari, in the vale glideth the Clwyd, and the *Elwy*, a little river conjoyneth with it, where there is a Bishops See. This place the Britons call *LlanElwy*, Englishmen Saint *Asaph* and the Historiographers, *Asaphensis*. Neither is the town of any beauty, nor the church building memorable: yet something would be said of it, in regard of antiquity.

Britain's second smallest city is sandwiched between the Clwyd and Elwy rivers. St Asaph has been a city twice, only recently since 2012, having had its original status terminated at the end of the 20th century following a reappraisal of the automatic entitlement rule for cathedral-possessing communities. As Cledwyn Hughes travelled through sometime in 1947:

> A lamplighter was cycling through the streets of the city with his long touch pole slung over one shoulder. He was racing from lamp to lamp, halting, and then prodding his pole into the darkness of the inside of the gas lamp. A moment of flicker and then the curved reflector at the back of the lamp caught the glare of the mantel in a great dazzle of light.

A statue of Welsh Bible translator, Bishop William Morgan, stands in the cathedral yard. Although Queen Elizabeth

I officially recognised Morgan's work, the English gentry did not. Even the Welsh-born gentry had abandoned their native tongue, and there was no expectation that the established church in Wales would experience any opposition to the English Bible from their congregations. The fact is that the Welsh church in the 16th century was administered by the English clergy to audiences who neither spoke nor understood the English language – a deliberate act and part of the planned Anglicising of the Welsh nation. Dr Morgan's Bible had put the brakes on that. In 1804, Richard Fenton almost pulled no punches in his description, but I'm disappointed that Georgian etiquette prevented clearer details:

> I am sorry to say that the churchyard is kept very slovenly, nettles of great height suffered to grow in a grove under the walls of the church; and there is an awkward excrescence on the north side to the east of the north transept and joining it, which is an adit to a vault belonging to the Bodelwyddan family. It has a most disgraceful external, being covered with nettles.

Black Gold and Cannon Fodder

The town of Mold (Yr Wyddgrug) sits by the River Alyn and, surprisingly to some maybe, is the county town of Flintshire. It was the county town of Clwyd from 1974 to 1996, since when Clwyd has lost its county council status. The 18th century landscape painter Richard Wilson, a co-founder of the Royal Academy, died here in 1782 and is buried in St Mary's churchyard. In the church, a stained-glass window commemorates him, the town's most famous son. In 1833, while quarrying for stone in a small mound near to where the present-day Rugby club house stands, workmen discovered a stone-lined grave with a crushed gold cape around the fragmentary remains of a skeleton. The Mold Gold Cape now forms one of the great treasures of the British Museum in London. In 1937, Stuart Mais was blissfully unaware of this find, sure only of the next bus out of town:

Mold came as a pleasant surprise. I was glad to find another bus going on immediately, but after Buckley it was the very Heaven. It's one Main Street is wide and dignified, and as soon as we left it behind, we climbed quickly and steeply up a hill of limestone rock, always a concomitant of beauty.

This part of North Wales was once known as Welsh Maelor or Maelor Gymraeg, the name given to a medieval land area of the ancient Welsh Kingdom of Powys prior to being split in two by the construction of Offa's Dyke in the 8th century. Welsh Maelor ended up with most of Flintshire and the territory west of the River Dee to the Clwyd hills. The separated section in England became known as English Maelor, Maelor Saesneg, and covered the area where the national border bulges eastwards around Wrexham almost to Whitchurch. In 1996 a local government reorganisation placed much of both Maelors in the new Welsh county borough of Wrexham. The subsequent town of Wrexham has grown to become the largest in North Wales, and the fourth largest urban area in the whole of Wales.

Prior to the Roman conquest, the tribal area within which Wrexham evolved was that of the Cornovii people, who held the lowland forests of Cheshire, Shropshire, and northern parts of Herefordshire. After the Norman Conquest, the marcher lordship of Bromfield and Yale in north-eastern Wales included Wrexham. The rich seams of iron ore, coal, and lead below ground meant the town's rapid development and growth above it was inevitable. This took place in the suburbs to the south-west, along the valley of the River Clywedog. Offa's Dyke dissects the valley between the site of John Wilkinson's great ironworks at Bersham and the lead mines below the northern flanks of Minera Mountain. Unlike most major towns and cities throughout Britain, Wrexham did not start life beside a castle. However, there was one not far away at Erddig. The castle there was a late 11th century earthwork motte and bailey fortress, most likely founded by Hugh d'Avranches, the Norman Earl of Chester. In 1774, Henry Wyndham saw wealth and prosperity in the suburbs and surrounding countryside:

The large and handsome town of Wrexham is delightfully situated in a fruitful country, which may be considered as part of the Vale Royal of Cheshire, being only divided from it at a little distance by the river Dee. The beauty of this country has induced many families to fix their residence in its neighbourhood, and most of the gentle swells and elevations are crowned with good houses. Among these the best and most conspicuous is the seat of Mr Yorke at Erddig.

The estate of Acton Hall, north of the inhabited town, was the birthplace of Judge George Jeffreys, 'the hanging judge', in 1647. The estate was purchased in the late 18th century by Sir Foster Cunliffe, one of the founders of the Society of British Bowmen. The Four Dogs gateway to the estate, representing the greyhound crest on the Cunliffe arms, was his idea. Then in 1920, the diamond king Sir Bernard Oppenheimer, who had bought Acton Park from the Cunliffes, opened a polishing factory staffed by disabled ex-service men of World War 1. By the end of World War 2, the old hall was in a sorry state and was demolished in 1954, and the park is now a civil amenity for the people of Wrexham.

But there is no getting away from the fact that Wrexham, the town, grew on coal mining, iron foundries, steelworks, smoke, steam, fire, dirt, dust, sweat, poverty, and early deaths. Wealth came nowhere near the working inhabitants. Cledwyn Hughes saw Wrexham how everybody else did:

As a dreary Industrial town, a grey town with grey people. It lacks a public hall and has none of the elegance and charm of Chester or the healthy agricultural air of Oswestry. In the quiet back street, a tired-faced miner, the early evening clap of clogs, black with coal dust. The cap is grey and pulled down low over one ear where the wrinkles are black, the hurried pit-head bath and only the reaches of the body washed clean. A black ridge, too, under the worried eyes. The miner walks on, his clogs beating time into the distance. I go back to my room and draw the evening curtains. The fire light dances bright on brass rings and in each curved metal there is a reflection of the gay fire in my room, the gay pictures on the wall. Outside, more clogs are coming, other feet tramping home.

Elsewhere in North Wales ironworking started around 1640 at Bersham – a small wooded hamlet by the River Clywedog – initially to make cannons for use in the English Civil War. It was when Isaac Wilkinson took over the works in 1753 that further usage for iron in armoury production was developed. Up to that time the process for boring cannon had been difficult, until Isaac's son John created a machine in 1774 that enabled them to make smooth bore cannons. Having succeeded his father at Bersham, John Wilkinson began to gain notoriety as an arms supplier to warring governments around the world, but as each returned to peace, the market for cannons dried up. By now Bersham had outgrown its early usefulness, so Wilkinson bought land at nearby Brymbo on what would eventually become Brymbo Steel Works. Brymbo Hall, one of Britain's lost manor houses, had been built on open moorland, partly to the designs of Inigo Jones. After Wilkinson bought the house, he discovered that the area nearby was rich in coal and ironstone deposits. Several small coal pits had existed there even before Wilkinson purchased the estate, but it was here, near his home, where Wilkinson constructed his ironworks in 1796 and erected the first blast furnace, with almost 900 tons of iron being produced in this first year. In 1967, Brymbo Steel was nationalised, along with the rest of the steel industry, becoming a division of the British Steel Corporation. Steel production lasted until 1990, when the steelworks was closed and 1,100 workers lost their jobs. Apart from Wilkinson's blast furnace and casting house, all the steel processing buildings have gone, leaving a vast empty area which will eventually be filled with houses. Brymbo Hall was demolished in 1973.

The Wrexham area has been the centre of coal mining since the 17th century. Mines were still operating into the 1950s at Minera, Brymbo, Cefn Mawr, and Ruabon. The last colliery to work the Ruabon coalfield was Bersham Colliery at Rhostyllen, which closed in December 1986. One of the deepest mines was at Gresford. In 1934, 2,200 miners were employed at the colliery, 1,850 of them underground workers. A shaft known as the Dennis shaft, after the Dennis industrialist family of Ruabon, and the pit owners, reached depths of almost 700m (2,300 feet). That same year one of the worst disasters in the history of coal mining occurred on 22nd September, when an explosion killed 254 men and boys, initially.[46]

An immediate rescue bid resulted in further deaths from the fatal effects of poisonous air, so it was decided that further rescue attempts were too dangerous and the shaft into the Dennis section was capped. However, explosions continued underground and three days after the initial blast, a rescuer named George Brown became the final victim when he was killed by flying debris after the cap blew off. The Dennis shaft was never reopened and the bodies of the 254 victims were left in their sealed tomb. In spite of the loudly voiced condemnation of failures in safety procedures and poor mine management, a cause was never established. Gresford Colliery finally closed in November 1973 and the site redeveloped as an industrial estate. A memorial to the victims of the disaster, constructed using a wheel from the old pit-head winding gear, was erected for all to see by the nearby junction of the A483 with B5445.

The 15th century All Saints Church at Gresford has been described as the finest parish church in Wales, along with that of St Giles in Wrexham. It is said to have the most surviving medieval stained glass of any Welsh church. All Saints is remarkable for its size, beauty, and interior monuments. It was designated a Grade I listed building on June 7th, 1963, as 'an exceptional example of a late-medieval church with fine medieval glass and furnishings'. The community was richly supported by the immensely wealthy and powerful Thomas Stanley, 1st Earl of Derby, who paid for the large central east window. The earl's second wife, Lady Margaret Beaufort, had also been married before, to Edmund Tudor, and their son would become Henry VII, the first Tudor monarch, following victory in the battle at Bosworth. The presence of several memorials to the local Trevalyn Hall branch of the powerful Trevor (Trefor) family might add further credence to why the church is so large and so well endowed with stained glass. In the churchyard is

---

[46] The worst-ever mining disaster was at Senghenydd in 1913, with 439 deaths.

one of the largest collections of yew trees in Wales, one of which is claimed to be over 1,600 years old.

George Borrow made his way from Chester along 'a broad and excellent road', passing through Pulford and crossing the River Alyn by Marford Mill. At Hosley Bank, near Gresford, he got his first sight of a distant Wrexham. There were no quarries or gravel pits to fill his view, no bustling industrial estates or dual carriageways, but a fair variety of woods, green meads and arable fields:

> The town is reckoned to be a Welsh town, but its appearance is not Welsh. Its inhabitants have neither the look or language of Welshmen, and its name shows it was founded by some Saxon adventurer, Wrexham being a Saxon compound, signifying the home of a Rex, and identical, or nearly so, with the Wrexham of East Anglia. It is a stirring, bustling place of much traffic and of several thousand inhabitants. Its most remarkable object is the church which stands on the south western side, and to this church, after wandering for some time about the streets, I repaired.

Sir Richard Colt Hoare wrote in 1797, 'St Giles's church at Wrexham is the handsomest I have seen in Wales. It is rich in ornamented Gothic architecture.' Previously, Leland saw it as 'one of the fairest in all north Wales'. More recently, the author Simon Jenkins described it as 'the glory of the marches'. St Giles is Wrexham's most prominent landmark, the largest parish church in Wales, and Grade I listed. The great tower built in 1506 is a remarkable piece of decorative architecture and the sole surviving monument of Tudor Wrexham. In the churchyard lies Elihu Yale, founder of the USA's famed college at New Haven in Connecticut, after whom it is named. Yale was born in Boston, Massachusetts in 1649, but came from Welsh ancestry – the family seat being at Plas yn Lal near Llandegla in Denbighshire. He died in England in 1721, and his tomb in the churchyard was restored in 1874 with the help of Yale College funds. The inscription on it runs: -

Born in America, Europe bred,
In Afric travell'd and in Asia wed,
Where long he liv'd and thriv'd, in London dead.
Much good, some ill he did; so, hope all's even
And that his soul thro' mercy's gone to Heaven.
You that survive and read this tale take care,
For this most certain exit to prepare;
Where blest in peace, the actions of the just
Smell sweet and blossom in the silent dust.

Yale once 'liv'd and thriv'd' in Asia as Governor of Fort St George in Madras. The 'some ill' includes the murder of his groom, whom he had hanged for taking his horse without permission. Whether it was an accident of inheritance or the appeal of the natural beauty of the area that brought wealthy families to the Wrexham area, their presence here was a major factor in the social life of the community. The Yales of Llandegla, Yorkes of Erddig, Jeffreys followed by Cunliffes of Acton Hall, Palmers of Cefn Park, and the family seat at Ruabon of the Williams-Wynns, Wynnstay Hall, that became known as the home of 'the Princes in Wales'. Mindful of the rise in new housing to cater for the growth in population, the roads to satisfy insatiable traffic demands, and the establishment of new employment opportunities to replace the lost industries of coal and steel, Wrexham and Gresford's magnificent centres for Christian worship must be highly gratifying to the feelings and self-esteem of once-suffering communities. To have two churches of such quality practically within sight of each other is a rare blessing. In truth, though I lost my perseverance for religion by the time I reached my thirties, visiting so many fine churches throughout the whole of my tour of the borders, has given me immense pleasure.

As we near Chester, expensive-looking houses in the village of Eccleston by the Dee indicates we are in the territory of the Duke of Westminster. At Aldford, too, on the east bank of the river, most of the building stock was constructed as a designed village in the middle of the 19th century by Sir Richard Grosvenor, 2nd Marquis of Westminster. In his book, *England Revisited*, writer, broadcaster, and environmentalist, John Seymour thought there was something sterile and antiseptic about the way Aldford was filled with houses of the same period and all the same design. Everything appeared too neat and too tidy. According to Pennant some 150 years earlier:

> The most extensive prospect is from a bench on Eccleston hill, on the roadside, which takes in the vast environs of Wales, Cheshire and part of Shropshire, forming an admirable composition of rich cultivation, bounded by hills of various forms.

Across the river from Aldford is Eaton Hall, the great seat of the ancient family of the Grosvenors. They are descended from Gilbert le Gros Veneur, nephew of Hugh 'Lupus' d'Avranches, 1st Earl of Chester, himself the nephew of William the Conqueror. Through good marriages, fortuitous circumstances, and even highly successful international business developments, the family's landowning and wealth over eight centuries has gradually increased to its present extraordinary level. Arguably, they have become more influential in Britain than the monarch. The Grosvenors eventually rose to the ranks of nobility in 1874 when Hugh Lupus Grosvenor became the 1st Duke of Westminster.

The Eaton estate covers an area of about 4,400 ha (10,872 acres) but that is just 13% of the Duke's total land and estate ownership. He owns far more of Britain than the Queen herself. We are told that, due to the family's vast wealth, their movements have to be kept a secret. A helicopter is used for their transport, and the children are closely guarded to deter kidnappers. The first substantial house at Eaton was designed by architect William Samwell and built for Sir Thomas Grosvenor, 3rd Baronet, who inherited the estate in 1664 at the age of 19. However, the fabric of the present house is only about fifty years old and the French château casing even less so. It is at least the fifth building on the site since the original house went up in the 15th century. Either the Grosvenors chose bad builders each time, or they were very unlucky, or they just couldn't make up their minds what style of house they wanted. Being so wealthy, it is hard to believe that such trivia would bother them much.

Next to the Hall is Eaton Chapel with its extraordinary clock tower. Designed by Alfred Waterhouse at the same time as the 1870 rebuild of the Hall, the clock tower has outlasted it. It has also been given a Grade I listing, the only associated listed building that I am aware of where the parent house is not listed at all. The Hall and chapel are strictly private as befits the richest family in England, but at least the formal gardens can be visited on three days during the year in support of charity. There is still more to tell about the Grosvenors and their vast estates, but more doesn't suit the theme of this book.

And so, to Deva

> The approach to Chester is over a very narrow and dangerous bridge of seven irregular arches, till of late rendered more inconvenient by the ancient gateways at each end, formerly necessary enough to prevent the inroads of my Welsh countrymen, who often carried fire and sword to these suburbs which were so frequently burnt as to be called the Briton's Tre-boeth, or burnt town. (*Thos. Pennant*)

Deva Victrix is the name the Romans gave their walled city on the River Dee, close to the northern border between England and Wales. It is one of the best-preserved walled cities in Britain, and the only one with a complete circuit. The first settlement here was a major Roman military base in AD 75. Under the governorship of Julius Agricola, it was initially built for the launch of an offensive against the Deceangli tribe of North Wales, and another to eliminate the druids of Ynys Mon, the Isle of Angelsey. Like Isca Caerleon in South Wales, Deva contained barracks, granaries, military baths and administrative buildings. Its position on the border and the large harbour made it one of the most militarily effective Roman bases in Britain. The size of the fortress – larger than any other built during their campaign – suggests that it may have been constructed with the intention to become the capital of a unified British Isles under Rome. The civilian settlement which grew up outside the walls and remained after the Romans departed, became the city of Chester.

Three years or so following the Norman Conquest, Duke William's army arrived at Chester and built their motte-and-bailey castle outside the Roman walls in an elevated position overlooking the river. William appointed Hugh d'Avranches as Earl of Chester[47] as his commander-in-charge of the northern march territory. Fifty years later, they re-strengthened the crumbling walls and extended them southwards to the river, which even then was changing course and silting up on the west side of the city where previously the Romans had their port.

From that time and throughout the Middle Ages, the walls provided a haven for the townsfolk and in due course a trading area where guilds, civic officials, and the urban elite would run the city to suit their interests. By the 18th century, the walls had been adapted for leisurely walks that enhanced the attractions for visitors. This new use for a 2000-year- old unique facility has increased the need for regular maintenance, and even today unfortunate but necessary diversions appear regularly which interrupt wall walkers and direct traffic through broken gates. In addition, Roman remains continue to be discovered, creating more disruptions and additional pressure on the city's purse.

Post-Conquest Norman castles developed as timber forts and, provided they survived early vulnerability, were then upgraded to more defendable stone bastions, usually by the start of the 12th century. Chester was no exception, but unlike the classic marvels of Chepstow, Chirk, or Conwy, there is little here that would interest either a student of medieval architecture or a castle bagger for long. There are few remains of the original stone building. The structure known as Agricola's Tower, marking the gateway to the inner bailey, still exists and a short section of curtain wall that includes the Flag Tower, itself the replacement for the original keep. The rest of the castle complex visible today was rebuilt

---

[47] He became the 2nd Earl, replacing the 1st Earl, Gerbod the Fleming, who was being held captive after the Battle of Cassel in Flanders

between 1788 and 1822 in neo-classical styles designed by architect and bridge builder, Thomas Harrison. Nikolaus Pevsner applauded Harrison's work and wrote the outcome constituted 'one of the most powerful monuments of the Greek Revival in the whole of England'. Parts of the neo-classical buildings are now used as Crown Courts and as a military museum.

Chester's cathedral was not the first one in the city; that status was given to the Norman church of St John's in 1075. There is a tradition that an earlier church was erected on the site of the later Cathedral by King Ethelred in 689 and that its founder was directed by a vision to build a grand edifice on the spot which should be marked out for him by the appearance of a white hind. The building which is now the Cathedral of St Werburgh is thought to have started life as a Roman temple of Apollo. That was followed by a Saxon church dedicated to Saints Peter and Paul. St Werburgh died in 699 and was buried first at Hanbury in Staffordshire, where her brother, Coenred was King of Mercia at that time and decided to move his sister's remains to a more conspicuous place within the church there. When the tomb was opened, her body was found to be intact and the preservation was taken as a sign of divine favour. Her subsequent shrine remained at Hanbury until the increasing Danish threat forced another move, this time to the Saxon church at Chester. Her temporary resting place there became permanent when the Mercian Queen Aethelflaed turned the church into a monastery dedicated to Werburgh. Then in 1092 Earl Hugh d'Avranches replaced Aethelflaed's building with a larger Benedictine abbey containing St Werburgh's shrine. After Henry VIII's dissolution in 1540, the King allowed the abbey buildings to be used as a church for the diocese of Chester.

The present cathedral building is constructed of red sandstone – in this case, Keuper sandstone from a quarry in the Cheshire basin. Though the stone lends itself to detailed carving, it is easily eroded by rain and wind, and has poor resistance to pollution. Not surprisingly, Chester is one of the most heavily restored of England's cathedrals, and includes much refacing and many new details. Hester Thrale did not consider it in the first rank:

The perimeter wall is a wonderful work, I think, but it is wholly useless, it is so totally neglected and forgotten. Of the Cathedral, she said 'A mean edifice adorned in the Gothic taste, but its appearance so fresh that it seemed more like imitation than reality. The altar piece tapestry only gives poverty of look to the whole, and it is altogether the poorest cathedral I have yet seen.

Author and local historian, Adrian Bristow, described the tapestry as once bright with glowing colours depicting the confrontation between St Paul and Elymas, the Cyprus sorcerer, before the Roman Governor. Some eleven feet high and fifteen feet wide, it was woven under the guardianship of the Archbishop of Canterbury's Manor at Mortlake from a copy of a Raphael cartoon for the Sistine Chapel and was presented to Chester Cathedral in 1660. It was hung around the high altar until 1843, when it was moved to the north transept to make way for a mosaic of the Last Supper. It was moved again, this time to the refectory when new organ pipes were needed in the transept, and where it still hangs above the servery, faded and out of sight. In

Figure 24 A meeting of the Rows in the centre of Chester

the cloisters, visitors are surrounded by stained glass windows, one of which bears these words: *To remember two valiant men of Cheshire, George Leigh Malory and Andrew Comyn Irvine, who among the snows of Mount Everest adventured their lives even unto death -June 8th, 1924.*

Without doubt, the uniqueness of the city of Chester has much to do with its medieval Rows – the covered walkways raised above the centre streets. They were created as long ago as the 13th century when erecting new homes and businesses where ground levels along the city streets had become uneven over centuries, partly by debris from the destruction of Roman buildings. The effect of this was to place new frontages above street level, with storage cellars below. Shops appeared at first floor level, and as opportunities arose, the cellars also became shops, so todays visitors have two tiers of choices. In general, the buildings containing the Rows are black and white, all are listed, and some are recorded in the English Heritage Archive. Such is the weight of desire to preserve these magnificent buildings, that in July 2010 they were rightly considered as an applicant for the new United Kingdom Tentative List for World Heritage status. Quite a contrasting situation when in 1720, Daniel Defoe saw the Rows as a disagreeable addition to the city's architecture:

> The buildings of Chester are very old; nor do the Rows as they call them, add anything, in my opinion, to the beauty of the city; but just to the contrary, they serve to make the city look both old and ugly. The great church here is a very magnificent building, but 'tis built of a red, sandy, ill looking stone, which takes much from the beauty of it, and which yielding to the weather, seems to crumble, and suffer by time, which defaces the building.

Chester is a city of secrets and commemorative plaques, forty-five in all, and 14th century stone townhouses hidden behind modern facades. It is a city of mediaeval churches, nine of those, 17th century almshouses, six remaining of those. Ancient inns like the Red Lion and the Coach and Horses on Northgate Street, the Old King's Head on Lower Bridge Street, and the Bear and Billet, an outstanding timber building originally the townhouse of the Earls of Shrewsbury. Dated 1664, the 'Bear' replaced the earlier house destroyed during the civil war and has been an inn since the 18th century. Chester has been a city frequented by many famous people. The likes of Arthur Wellesley, Duke of Wellington, who stayed at Forest House on Love Street as guest of the city's High Sheriff in 1817, Charles Kingsley, historian and novelist (he wrote *The Water Babies* – a favourite of mine as a child), and was also a priest of the Church of England, and Canon of Chester Cathedral from 1870-1873. Charles Dickens performed at the Chester Music Hall in 1867. Group Captain Leonard Cheshire, the highly decorated Royal Airforce pilot of World War 2 and recipient of the Victoria Cross, the highest award for gallantry, was born in Chester, as was Tom Rolt, the narrowboat traveller.

George Borrow began his walk in *Wild Wales* at Chester in 1854. On the first night, he booked a room at the Coach and Horses in Northgate Street, a 17th century inn opposite the town hall, and with great expectations of delights to come, ordered as his first meal cheese and a pint of ale:

> Cheshire cheese has always been reckoned excellent, and now that I am in the capital of the cheese country, of course I shall have some of the very prime. Neither the cheese nor the ale sets the standard for his stay in Chester, and both sample mouthfuls were ejected through an open window into the street. Well, if I have been deceived in the cheese, I have not at any rate been deceived in the ale, which I expected to find execrable!

The inn is now called the Coach House and fully modernised to cater for Chester's 21st century tourists. Northgate Street, however, has seen better days but has been highlighted recently as a hotspot in the national crime statistics. Chester's Racecourse, known as the Roodee after the cross, or rood standing in the centre of the course, has evolved on the site of the Roman harbour. A section of the city's wall, alongside which ships used to moor until the river silted up, forms one side of the course where spectators can watch races for free. The first recorded race was held on February 9th, 1539, and in 2008 the restaurant '1539' opened beside the course as a reminder of that event. When I first saw the legend over the restaurant's entrance, I was completely at a loss as to the motive behind it, as I'm sure is everyone else who sees it for the first time. The Roodee is thought to be the oldest racecourse in England but is also the smallest at 1.8km (1 mile and 1 furlong) long. However, it is a very popular venue and is usually well attended when races are held, due probably to the ease of access by road and rail and the proximity of hotels and bars.

Before the 19th century, the small township of Saltney was 2,000 acres of marshland subject to floods at every tide. Whilst the marsh was not entirely uninhabited or without pathways, it appears to have been a dreary and dangerous place. At the eastern extremity of Saltney, the land rises suddenly to become Chester, but was in pre-Roman days the western boundary of Cornovii territory. During the 18th century, a paved way – a forerunner of today's A5104 Chester Road – and later a canal, were constructed side by side across the Saltney marshes. This was Sir John Glynne's coal route to the River Dee intended as a commercial venture from the Bretton end. However, the canal appears to have been filled in around 1775. The English-Welsh border runs down the centre of Boundary Lane in the Lache district of Saltney town, creating, as at Llanymynech, a community living in both countries. Houses on the west side of the street are in the Flintshire County Council area, while those on the east side are in the Cheshire West and Chester Unitary Authority area. One might wonder how the two police forces of this split might cope with any social unrest. Nearby, at Broughton, is the massive Airbus UK plant employing 7,000 people and is understood to be the largest manufacturing plant in the UK. The company makes the wings here for the Airbus A380 double-decked, wide-body, four-engine jet airliner, manufactured by the European manufacturer based in Toulouse. These huge wings must then be shipped to France. There are daily flights of a Beluga transport aircraft for the 380 components, but the wings themselves are too large to be transported by air and require multi-modular transport using Flintshire's roads, the River Dee, and the Port of Mostyn.

Hawarden (pronounced Harden) is a neat little village whose most famous resident was the 19th century Prime Minister, William Gladstone, and has two castles. Its church of St Deiniol, another of Gilbert Scott's recreations, is rich in William Morris and Edward Burne-Jones stained glass. Although named in 2014 on The Sunday Times' Best Places to Live list, the town is a rather sad place and wanting in appearances of ease and comfort which one usually expects to find situated outside an ancestral park and within the realms of a landed family. However, W.G did his best to attract the masses by donating his substantial library of 30,000 books in 1889 to what was the village grammar school. Gladstone died nine years later, and a new library building designed by Chester's John Douglas was opened in his honour, followed later by the addition of a residential wing. Many believe the result is the finest library in Britain, is Grade 1 listed, and now houses 150,000 volumes. On a quiet day, I was shown around a silent impressively furnished reading room, where the next day they would be holding their annual festival of books, which they proudly call, if tongue-in-cheek, the 'Gladfest'. Through poor timing and worse organisation, I was going to miss this unique event this year.

Rising above the library lawns is the great man's huge bronze statue on a base of Portland stone. Designed in 1925 by the Irish sculptor, John Hughes, it was intended originally for the city of Dublin as the Irish National Memorial but was declined by the city council there and erected here instead. The Victorian visitor to Hawarden was presented with many reminders of the local hero. Photographs of him, full-length or half-length and in every conceivable posture, were for sale at every turn. As were walking sticks with the grand old head carved upon the handles. Even a pat of butter bearing the old man's countenance could be bought, as well as a bar of Gladstone soap. You can only wonder if the Hawarden people ever found a way of persuading their hens to lay Gladstone eggs! Charles Harper, though, being an enthusiastic critic of personality whenever the moment suited him, did not miss the opportunity on this occasion:

It is a singular irony which has made a demagogue of the owner of so beautiful a demesne as Hawarden Park. You who chance to pass through the lodge gates and adventure upon the lovely lawns and deep delightful dells of this woodland estate cannot but feel surprise at the mental and political attitudes of a country gentleman and rural squire who damns privilege and has thumped metaphorical tubs any time, and all the time, during the last fifty years in anathema of class and glorification of that superlatively virtuous noun - the People.

A quarter of a mile out along the Chester road are the ruins of Ewloe Castle, standing on the edge of a deep wooded dingle. It is a small fortress consisting of the remains of two towers, once overgrown with ivy and commanding the view of deep wooded glens. In the woods near this place, part of the flower of the army despatched by Henry II from his camp on Saltney marsh in 1157 were surprised and defeated by Dafydd and his brother, Conan, the sons of Owen ap Gruffudd. They forced the King's men into the depth of the narrow valley until they became entangled in the undergrowth of the wood. The attack was sudden, and fierce, and unexpected, the slaughter dreadful, and the pursuit carried even to Henry's Saltney encampment where the King suffered a second defeat. This was the incentive for a Welsh rebel surge towards Chester. Later, the Llywelyns chose Ewloe Castle as their starting point for a major assault on Chester, but in 1247 they agreed terms with Henry III which allowed them to retain lands west of the River Conwy.

Where Welsh River meets Irish Sea

Out from Chester I go along the north-west road which runs by the Dee estuary. Here there is an industrial belt with a range of factories making animal products, metal stampings etc. The towns along the edge of the estuary are Connah's Quay, Flint, Bagillt and Mostyn. Dreary and rather depressing they are after the cleanliness and well-kept orderliness in the agricultural areas of the Marches.

There was a mist, a fog from the sea, salty and hiding the ugliness of this part of my journey. (*Cledwyn Hughes*)

Until the 18th century, the area where Connah's Quay now stands was nothing more than fields. There were more sea birds here than people. The original name of New Quay was changed sometime after 1860 when it was discovered there were too many other New Quays. The new name is a mystery which no-one has yet solved, but who was Connah and why was that name chosen? It was not until the silting of the Dee ended Chester's port activities that anyone took notice of the river bank here. New docks were built and when, in the 19th century, the emerging railways arrived as well, Connah's Quay became a vital source of trade and finance for the greater Flintshire area. At the beginning of the 20th century, the John Summers Steel Company moved from Stalybridge near Manchester to Shotton and became the biggest employer in the area. The business became part of the British Steel Corporation in 1967, which now, for the time being at least, has become Tata Steel. Yet the people here still call it John Summers!

Charles Harper ended his tour here and must have viewed the landscape with a huge sense of disappointment:

> The last day of our tour, and we had reached the sands of Dee, now spanned by the great girders of the Hawarden Bridge, built to carry the Wrexham, Mold, and Connah's Quay railway across to Wirral and to its junction with the other lines to Liverpool. Another railway runs along the estuary from Chester to Flint and the seacoast, and the coal mines of Buckley and chemical works of Flint town smirch the sky, viewed from Connah's Quay, with thick trails of black smoke.

A mile further west along the river, the huge gas fuelled power station belching steam on the south bank is the second to be built here within fifty years. The first was coal powered and by all accounts incapable in the end of supplying the needs of North Wales. The present station built by GEC Alsthom and completed in March 1996 at a cost of £580m, was initially owned by Powergen. In 2004 they became EON

UK and in 2015 a German energy company called UNIPER – the name being a portmanteau of 'unique' and 'performance'. Something to live up to, clearly. Local man, Thomas Pennant would have been familiar with very different scenery.

> I took the lower road by the shore blackened with the smoke and soot of smelting houses and in the more flourishing times of the collieries with vast stacks of coal. After crossing a small brook, I entered the town of Flint, a place laid out with great regularity but the streets far from completed. I cannot assign any derivation of the word (Flint), our country is totally destitute of the fossil usually so called. I can only remark that the name is purely Saxon. The channel of the Dee at present is at some distance from the walls, but formerly flowed beneath them. There are still some rings to which ships were moored.

King Edward I started to build Flint Castle, the first of his 'Iron Ring' of North Wales, in 1277 as part of the campaign to make the last Prince Llywelyn bow to English rule. He would not have been pleased to know it would take ten years to complete, and then immediately besieged by Llywelyn's forces to prevent Edward from gaining any further ground. By 1294 the castle was already partially destroyed and had to be rebuilt long after Edward's campaign had failed in Its purpose. Later, the gay Edward II welcomed his favourite, Piers Gaveston, here on his return from exile. Here, too, the unfortunate Richard II was handed over to the Duke of Lancaster, the envoy of would-be usurper, Henry Bolingbroke, in 1399. By the castle entrance is a steel sculpture of King Richard and his much-loved greyhound, Mathe. The story goes that Mathe was so attached to Richard that he would greet him each time by putting his paws on the King's shoulders. After Richard's detention, Bolingbroke went to see him and on entering the room Mathe greeted Henry by putting his paws on his shoulders. Richard is said then to have known that the greyhound greets the monarch not the master, and Henry would be king.

At the time of its construction, Flint Castle was beside the river and surrounded by a moat so that ships could moor right next to it. It was only one day's march from Chester and supplies could be brought along the Dee. Now the river has retreated several hundred yards and the ruins are high and dry, as is the moat. In the 2011 census, 57.1% of the townsfolk of Flint stated they were Welsh and many claim to have some knowledge of the Welsh language, but Scouse English seems to be spoken more often these days. I spoke briefly to a man who said his surname was Thomas. Certainly Welsh that, but I assumed from his accent that he must have connections with Liverpool, a clear indication of the influence and nearness of the Merseyside city. To the contrary he told me he had been born nearby in Wales and had lived all his life in these parts. The bigger surprise is the large contingent of Polish speakers in Flint since the relaxation of trade and immigration laws within the European Union. Many shops in the centre have English and Polish information displayed, and some specialise in Polish products. In 1836 Roscoe recorded that the town had all the appearance of a fallen and deserted capital:

> Presenting evidences of its former extent and importance in long lines of half dilapidated edifices and broken streets. In its decline it seems to have partaken the fate of its once towering and lordly fortress whose time-dismantled ruins threw its broad shadow in the clear moonlight upon the sands, like the reflection of those vanished scenes, assorted well with the travellers mood, as he resumed his onward path along the river's edge. He listened to the growing swell of those eternal surges which came sweeping over the sands, when the bulwarks were in their glory, as now they hasten their decay; and the moon shed a fitful light on the bleak prospect and far spreading shores of the Dee, as he pursued the lonely path along the banks towards the ancient abbey of Basingwerk.

In early medieval times, the town of Bagillt was part of the Kingdom of Gwynedd. In the 12th century, Llewellyn the Great used Castell Hen Blas, a motte and bailey fortress above the town, as a forward base near the boundary of Gwynedd and Mercia. Hen Blas was the birthplace of Dafydd ap Llywelyn, to Llewelyn the Great and Joan, the Illegitimate daughter of King John, in 1212. Dafydd's birth was commemorated on July 25th, 2010 by the unveiling of a plaque on the wall of the Upper Shippe Inn in the centre of the town, 770 years after the issue of the earliest surviving charter of Dafydd appointing himself as Prince of North Wales in 1240.

By the late 18th century, Bagillt had become a centre of mineral extraction and manufacturing and hundreds of men laboured in eleven collieries that surrounded the village. There was also a factory and works that produced and refined zinc, lead and iron – hardly a recipe for a healthy life to be had anywhere here. Bagillt already had several quays on the banks of the Dee where fishing boats had moored for centuries, but by the early 19th century, the quays had developed into docks where cargo destined for the factories and foundries of England were loaded.

Between the town of Mold and the coastal roads, Halkyn Mountain is a vast wild open common space rising 244m (800ft) above sea level, sandwiched between the A541 Mold to Denbigh road and the A55 North Wales Expressway, and designated a Special Area of Conservation (SAC). Access from the Mold road was described in Tweddel's 1890 *Handy Guide to Mold and the Neighborhood* as,

"A *quiet little village, on the confines of Halkyn mountain, forming a remarkably pleasant excursion from Mold, from which it is about four miles distant. The highway branches off to the right, along a narrow lane that will prove attractive to the botanist, and the lover of wild flowers, for here nature displays her varied chorus, according to the season of the year, primroses, hyacinths, cowslips, wild roses, honeysuckle, ferns, foxgloves, and innumerable other wayside flowers gladden the sight, and give the air the redolence of their perfume.*"

But Halkyn has been the scene of industrial activity for centuries. 2000 years of lead mining and limestone quarrying, and all of it the property of the Grosvenors of Eaton by virtue of a grant given to Sir Richard Grosvenor by Charles I in 1634. Two large quarries, at Hendre and Pant-y-pwll-dŵr, continue to take chunks out of the mountain for road building over the border in north-west England. Catch it in the wrong light and indifferent weather, and the Halkyn landscape may appear scrubby and not visually pleasing, but on a bright clear day the wildness can grow on you, and the views looking northwards over the Dee estuary and the Clwyd Hills to the south make it worth the while being there.

The local wealthy Mostyn family lineage originated at Pengwern Hall not far from Llangollen but following the marriage of Ieuan Fychan of Pengwern and Angharad, the daughter and heiress of Hywel ap Tudur ab Ithel Fychan of Mostyn Hall on the banks of the Dee estuary, Mostyn became the family's chief residence and power base. It was Hywel ap Tudur who started building land ownership in the 14th century. He was one of the greatest estate builders of his time, and between 1328 and 1355, managed to acquire substantial areas of land around Mostyn and Whitford. His purchases on such a large scale were unprecedented, laying the foundation for the Mostyn estate in Flintshire. Mostyn Estates Ltd still possesses much of what Hywel procured, making it – except for the Crown Estates – the oldest landholding institution in Wales.

By the early 15th century, the Mostyn empire began to spread across North Wales. In 1540 Thomas ap Richard ap Hywel became the first member of the family to inherit all five family estates after the death of his father, and he formerly adopted Mostyn as his family's name, becoming Thomas Mostyn. As another happenstance of their marriage, the ap Tudur's had joined up with the descendants of the Penmynydd Tudur's of Angelsey, who eventually produced Henry Tudor, who as Henry VII became the first Welsh King of England. The Mostyn wealth level went even higher in the 16th century when they discovered coal beneath their land. Coal was first discovered in the township as early as the 13th century, but in 1616 the Mostyn Colliery had three active pits that by 1619 had produced up to 10,000 tons. However, by the start of the 18th century these same pits were struggling to survive, partly from the rise of coal production in Cumbria, but more from the movement of the channel in the Dee estuary which at the beginning of business, flowed close enough to the shore for ships of 200 tons to dock. After 200 years, the Mostyn Colliery closed in 1884 with its neighbour at Point of Ayr becoming one of the last deep mines in Wales until that closed in 1996.

The Enclosure Act of 1843 enabled the Mostyns to extend their land ownership further along the North Wales coastline, taking in a little-known remote village of Llandudno. Initially, to the Mostyns it looked a good site to build a harbour for crossings to Ireland, but a fashionable seaside resort also appealed to them. The clincher came when developer Owen Williams claimed Llandudno would make a perfect place for a resort, and so Edward Mostyn gave instructions to proceed with the work of bringing the Victorian recreation town into existence. The street and road names of Llandudno survive as a permanent reminder of the Mostyn family's influence on the development of the town. Almost all the names represent their family roots.

The Port of Mostyn is still owned by the Mostyn family, and nowadays services the offshore wind farms and ships the wings for the Airbus A380 manufactured at Broughton to France. It is one of the oldest ports in the country and has a long history of handling cargoes, including steel, timber and wood pulp, bulk cargoes of coal, iron and sulphur for the region's heavy industries of the time. Until 2004 Mostyn served as a port from which ferries sailed to Dublin.

In the 18th century Thomas Pennant was a regular visitor to Mostyn Hall:

> The great gloomy hall is of very old date, furnished with the high Dais, or elevated upper end, and its long table for the lord and his jovial companions; and another on the side, the seat of the inferior partakers of the good cheer. The walls are adorned in a suitable manner with ancient militia guns, swords, and pikes; with helmets and breast plates; with funereal achievements, and with a variety of spoils of the chase. A falcon is nailed against the upper end of the room, with two bells hung to each foot.

In the higher part of the township, located in a field barely a couple of miles from Mostyn Hall, stands the curious 10th century wheel cross called Maen Achwynfan, or the stone of lamentation. The pillar is probably the tallest wheel cross in the whole of Wales at 3.4m (11ft) high and covered with intricate knot work patterns carved on its surface. From its position close to a five-way junction of lanes, it might have been intended as a marker for trackways of

Figure 25 Thomas Pennant

some significance. A more likely explanation is that it was erected to commemorate an important person, or event associated with this spot. The artwork, said to be of Viking origin, seems too elaborate for a signpost. What is sadly obvious is that there is no permitted access into the field where the pillar stands and convenient parking is practically non-existent. Pennant probably had no such restrictions in his day and living in the locality[48] he would have been as familiar with the stone as anyone:

---

[48] Downing Hall was built in 1627 by the Pennant family and was later Thomas's home. It was partially destroyed in a fire in the early 20th century and afterwards left derelict until it was demolished in 1953.

I do not presume to attempt a guess at the age, but shall observe that it must have been previous to the reign of gross superstition among the Welsh, otherwise the sculptor would have employed his chisel in striking out legendary stories, instead of the elegant knots and interlaced work that cover the stone.

Rhuddlan Castle is another addition to Edward I's building frenzy, and a strong looking bastion at that. This one had a three-sided moat, with the sea-borne Clwyd river protecting its fourth side. Samuel Johnson wrote that the castle:

> Is still a very noble ruin. All the walls remain so that a complete platform and elevations not very imperfect may be taken. It encloses a square of about thirty yards. The middle space was always open. The wall is, I believe, about thirty feet high very thick, flanked with six round towers each about eighteen feet or less in diameter. Only one tower had a chimney, so that here was commodity of living. It was only a place of strength.

During the castle's construction, the river's course was cleverly straightened and dredged to allow ships to sail inland as far as the castle to allow provisions and troops to reach it in the event of a siege. Within shouting distance of Edward's castle is a Norman-built motte and bailey fort which was thrown up in 1073 by Robert of Rhuddlan, a henchman of Hugh d'Avranches. This was Gerald of Wales's most northerly stop on his crusading campaign and we are told that Team Baldwin succeeded with more conversions before moving the short distance back south to St Asaph Cathedral to meet with his former adversary, Bishop Adam.

St Winifred and Holywell

One cannot imagine the atmosphere between Gerald and Adam after their spat twelve years earlier over parish suzerainty in the Kerry hills of Shropshire. The surprise is that Gerald may not have seen fit to visit Winifred's Well at Holywell. He was not a supporter of such places and doubted their authenticity and thought the monks at Basingwerk were behind an invention to create revenue for the abbey. According to Thomas Pennant, the town of Holywell was very inconsiderable till the beginning of the 18th century, the houses were few, the streets unpaved, and there was no market. Nowadays, Holywell is classed as a market town. It sits close to the Dee estuary and takes its name from the Holy Well, the legendary scene of the martyr of St Winifred in the 7th century, and now one of the Seven Wonders of Wales. North Wales has numerous springs and wells, some of them celebrated by having saintly sources, and there is none more famous of than this one. Often referred to as 'The Lourdes of Wales' St Winifred's renowned shrine has been a major place of Catholic pilgrimage for almost 14 centuries. It claims to be the oldest continually visited pilgrimage site in Great Britain with uninterrupted healing activities. Today, the site is administered by the Vocationist Fathers, a Roman Catholic congregation of priests and lay brothers founded in Italy in 1920, but there doesn't appear to be any previous connection by this group either with St Winifred herself or the town.

The story of Winifred's murder by Caradog and her subsequent restoration back to life by her uncle Bueno is well documented. The virgin Gwenfrewi – that is her Welsh name – when propositioned by the expectant youth, rejected his approach and was beheaded on the spot for her refusal. When her guardian replaced the head on Gwenfrewi's shoulders, life returned. Meanwhile, the spring which appeared where her head had temporarily rested, became the great symbol of a miraculous cure. There have been many doubters since the event. Henry Penruddocke Wyndham was one of many and said so in his 1774 writings. He even cited Gerald of Wales as being silent on the issue in 1188:

> It is here needless to attempt to refute the preposterous fable of St Winifred, or to fatigue the patience of my reader with its absurdities. It will be enough to say that the whole legend is a modern invention, and that though its fictitious date is so early as the 7th century, it was even unknown in the later time of Giraldus.

He, who never neglected an opportunity of recording and cele-
brating miracles, is entirely silent on this topic, and yet he lodged
one night at the abbey of Basingwerk, within a mile of Holywell.

In 1720 Daniel Defoe described the Well dedicated to the holy
virgin, but he was skeptical that any cures were miraculous:

> Many pilgrims resort to it, with no less devotion than ignorance;
> under this chapel the water gushes out in a great stream, and
> the place where it breaks out is formed like a basin or cistern in
> which they bath. The water is intensely cold, and indeed there
> is no great miracle in that point, considering the rocks it flows
> from, where it is impregnated by divers minerals, the virtue of
> which, and not of the saint, I suppose, work the greatest part
> of the cures.

The spring rises in a central basin which has steps for access by
the sick. In 1712 it was Celia Fiennes' sense of propriety which
prevented her stepping into the Well:

> It's a cold water and clear and runs off very quick so that it would
> be a pleasant refreshment in summer to wash oneself in, but
> I think I could not have been persuaded to have gone in unless it
> might have had curtains to have drawn about some part of it to
> have sheltered from the street, for wet garments are no covering to
> the body.

Dr Samuel Johnson later agreed with Miss Fiennes. 'The bath is
completely and indecently open. A woman bathed while we all
looked on.' But then sheepishly added:

> The well water is very clear, but so copious that it yields one
> hundred tuns of water in a minute. It is all at once a very great
> stream which within perhaps thirty yards of its eruption turns a
> mill and in a course of two miles eighteen mills more. In descent
> down the valley it is very quick and then falls into the sea.

The Well has been housed in a unique, late 15th century building set into a hillside, and is covered by three circular arches supported by pillars, above which is a chapel. The waters have been flowing through this structure with unfinished force ever since and there have been thousands of visitors from around the world every year, especially from Ireland. Despite notices which state that the water is for drinking only and bathing is strictly forbidden, when I was there in 2017 there were no stewards around to prevent hordes of Irish children using the Well as a swimming pool – and who could guess what else? – while parents looked on unconcerned. Alongside the Catholic chapel is the Protestant Parish Church of St James, originally of the 14th century but rebuilt in 1770. The rededication of the later church to Protestantism may have been made to disassociate it from the Catholic practices next door.

As a Justice of the Peace during the reign of Elizabeth I, Sir Thomas Mostyn was expected to enforce the religious changes of the time and to secure the transformation from a Catholic to a Protestant state. Here in Holywell, St Winifred's watery shrine, the most prominent focus for Catholic resistance in the whole of Wales and north-west England, was a persistent problem. Religious bigotry had its effect on both sides, and during the Reformation period, the Catholic shrine suffered considerably, as Hester Thrale mentioned when she accompanied Dr Johnson:

> On this day we were carried to Holywell, where we saw the devastation committed by Puritanism, which in its zeal had battered poor St Winifred and displaced her statue, broken three of the columns surrounding the Well which had any effigies upon them, and left nothing but the stone at the bottom of the water which bears any mark of ancient superstition and is spotted with red in two or three places, and Roman Catholics believe from their hearts that it was stained from the blood of that favourite virgin martyr.

Six hundred years ago, the warrior king, Henry V, undertook a pilgrimage on foot six months after routing French forces at the Battle of Agincourt on October 25th, 1415. The King's pilgrimage began at Shrewsbury Abbey, where the relics of St Winifred were then enshrined, and ended at the Well. Henry would have arrived at the abbey, in the words of the Reverend Paul Firmin, a recent vicar of the abbey, 'in the panoply of kingly estate but from thence walked as a penitent'. The King suspended his official activities to undertake his act of devotion in a personal capacity, but his sacrifice was recorded by Adam of Usk in his Chronicle of 1421.

So much has been written and acclaimed about the miracle of Holywell but less of Winifred's 'second' life and death and eventual internment at Gwytherin, about which prior Robert Pennant tells us in his '*Vita et translatio S. Wenefredae*' (*Life and Transfer of St Winifred*) and author Ellis Peters included in her *Brother Cadfael Chronicles*. Neither leaves us with a true-life description of the later events any more than the saint's earlier murder and recapitation. However, the possibilities of realism at the isolated hamlet of Gwytherin are strengthened by historical facts about the supposed site of Winifred's final resting place and the absence of any attempts, particularly by the Catholic Church, to gain extra notoriety and capital in support of their activities at Holywell.

Gwytherin lies within the ancient landscape of Hiraethog, an area long been known for its remains of burial and ceremonial features from periods stretching back thousands of years. Times when the hillsides were used for summer grazing their domestic herds by Neolithic and Bronze Age people, and later by Iron Age settlers making their first attempts at cultivating the land. Next to the churchyard at Gwytherin, a grassy mound being used as grazing land may hide evidence of Bronze Age burials where a later Celtic community built their own settlement for Christian worship. It was to this place that Winifred is thought to have come to join a mixed monastic group headed by a Scottish nobleman with a Latin name, Elerius – known to have studied at St Asaph – and his mother, both of whom had escaped the purges of Edwin of Northumbria. By then, Winifred's earlier treatment at the hands of Caradog was known by her new family, who perhaps even accepted her previous death and revival, but at Gwytherin there was no Holy Well, nor pilgrims seeking cures, or saintly blessings.

At Gwytherin, she would be protected and allowed to follow her destiny in whichever way she chose. Eventually, we are told, she became an abbess and died there, finally, in AD 660. Her remains were interred in a reliquary box and kept in their church until Prior Robert called in 1138 to collect her bones for a new monastic shrine in Shrewsbury Abbey. It was the final irony. Now at Gwytherin, the grass grows over the rounded hill in the meadow while around the church the ancient yews and ceremonial standing stones await new dawns. No-one attends services anymore, nor lights any candles or prays for Gwenfrewi's wandering spirit. St Winifred's Church has long been deconsecrated, the village pub has closed and Gwytherin is left to renew its long state of idleness.

Back in Holywell in 1804, Sir Richard Colt Hoare and Richard Fenton left their rooms at the White Horse Inn to continue their tour:

> After breakfast we made our first visit to Basingwerk Abbey. It stands on a gentle eminence above and on the borders of a great marsh which extends towards the Cheshire coast. Its ruins are extensive, the architecture a mixture of Saxon and Gothic and not elegant in its structure. Though almost surrounded by the busy clang of manufactories, copper works, cotton mills etc, etc, it has not yet quite lost its solitary and sequestered appearance. Its mouldering walls are sheltered by some fine trees.

After a near disastrous battle at Ewloe in 1157, Henry II donated funds for the building of the abbey at Basingwerk in gratitude for the preservation of his life. The abbey's founder, Ranulf II, Earl of Chester, had already temporary settled monks from the fashionable Cistercian monastery of Savigny in Normandy at Hen Blâs – the Norman fortification near Bagillt – but they wanted their own place and had chosen a wild coastal site at Greenfield. During the 12th and 13th centuries, the Basingwerk monks received patronage, including land, both from Welsh princes and the English crown. In 1240, Llywelyn the Great's son Dafydd granted them St James's Church and St Winifred's pilgrimage shrine at Holywell. This generosity did not protect the abbey from the 1276 and 1283 campaigns of Edward I against the Welsh princes, despite guarantees by both sides. In 1481, the abbot was a certain Thomas Pennant, an ancestor of the 18th century traveller and writer from Downing. During Pennant's abbacy, the community declined to barely a few monks making the eventual surrender at the dissolution a simple matter.

At the point where the stream flows out of Winifred's Well and down a deep wooded glen, the industrial revolution began in North Wales. Greenfield is the area between Holywell and the Dee estuary, and is best known for its history of paper making which began when the first mill was built in 1770. The site was ideal with the constant water flow from the Well stream. In addition to the paper mill, there was a copper mill, a flannel mill, a cotton mill, three corn mills, two snuff mills, a battery works, and a Courtauld's rayon factory that, along with another at Flint, was at the centre of the rayon industry in the UK, employing thousands of local people. Both factoriess closed in 1985, despite Prime Minister Margaret Thatcher's intervention to avoid a huge unemployment worry. A drinks and bottling plant, run by W. Hall & Sons at Greenfield, closed only recently after 140 years.

At the start of the 19th century, Holywell had an air of prosperity. The valley had a line of working mills from Winifred's Well to the Greenfield dock. There had been a continuous growth of workers from the surrounding areas and those who weren't employed in the mills were at home picking and preparing cotton for them. In 1798, Rev Richard Warner observed:

> The works are kept in such excellent order that one of the first emotions occurring to the mind is that of wonder at so much work carried on with so much cleanliness.

So, St Winifred might have created another miracle. But towards the end of the 18th century, times they were a-changing. War was brewing in Europe. Napoleon was on the move and trade in England was affected as material sources were either redirected for military needs or were running out altogether. The Parys Mine on Yns Môn (Anglesey) that supplied the Greenfield factories with much of the cheap ore was being exhausted and the company's rolling mill and copper forge had to be sold off. And in the valley, the mills were showing their age, some desperately in need of repair. More serious were the changes in the estuary channels, making it difficult for ships to use the Greenfield wharf. Although in 1830 Holywell was still a major brass making centre, competition was strengthening in Birmingham and Merseyside, where new owners had transferred production to St Helens. Towards the end of the 19th century, heavy US import tariffs terminally affected Holywell copper, and production ceased. The decline of the cotton industry, together with the loss of markets to the Lancashire mills, was another factor in Holywell's continuing isolation. When the Welsh Flannel Company was formed in 1874 to rescue the two woollen mills in the valley, there were just 200 employees.

Even with the arrival of the railways in 1869, the valley never regained the prosperity of the 1780s. The shifting channels in the estuary meant that smaller vessels now had to be used to transfer imported raw materials and exported finished goods to ocean-going ships at Liverpool. The people of Holywell prayed again to Gwenfrewi, but this time she didn't hear them.

Three years, eight months and twenty-two days after leaving Sudbrook on the banks of the Severn estuary, I stood finally on the very end of the wharf were the Holywell stream enters the estuary of the Dee, and Wat's Dyke falls away from the land. Beside me stood an estuary cockle picker, dressed in heavy-duty bib and brace oilskin trousers, cockle bag and rake tucked under his arm. The date was the 2nd July, the opening day of the season, and he was awaiting his lift out to cockle beds on the mid-estuary banks to follow his sport. He told me he has one of only 53 full licences issued this year, based on how many cockles can be sustainably harvested. The beds are managed by Natural Resources Wales, which issues licences only to those eligible to harvest the edible marine bivalve molluscs to ensure a continuous and stable income for professional cocklers.

On the seafront at Prestatyn, a strange shaft-like sculpture dubbed the 'Polo Mint' is the culmination of years of pressure by various walking groups who wanted to see something to commemorate the 177-mile long Offa's Dyke path either here or on Sedbury Cliffs by the Severn. It's siting here has not been a great success, partly because the monument had to be closed shortly after it was erected amid health and safety fears. The stainless-steel ring on legs surrounded by box shaped stone blocks has been described perhaps over-enthusiastically as stunning, but how does it represent an 8th century Mercian defence barrier, of which the path is but a mirror? There's nothing about it that reminds me of the Dyke's massive construction not far off 200 miles in length, the reasons for its existence, nor the human sacrifices made in its building. And what of Wat's Dyke? Of that there is nothing.

Figure 26 The Offa's Dyke Monument 'Beginning and End' on the sea front at Prestatyn in North Wales

Part Four

Ending Days: The Wye Tour

Ross to Monmouth

Not until the mid-18th century did anyone take much interest in scenery. Dr John Egerton, who was Rector of Ross on Wye from 1745-81, started the whole thing off by taking his guests down the river by boat. Thomas Dudley Fosbroke, a curate at Walford near Ross from 1810, wasn't a contemporary of Egerton though knew of him, understood his motives and followed his ideas, enjoying time on the river whenever time allowed:

> The poet, the artist, and the lover of nature are alike charmed with the diversified and enchanting scenes that pass before them in panoramic succession as they glide along this stately, meandering stream. Nothing should tempt the tourist to give up the water for the land. Parties arriving by rail or steamboat at Chepstow who desire to see the river, should proceed by land to Ross and go down with the stream. The current being very strong in places, it is very toilsome and tedious to make the voyage up from Chepstow.

The Reverend William Gilpin already understood the potential of the River Wye as a tourist attraction. He was known as one of the originators of the idea of the picturesque, along with contemporaries Richard Payne Knight and Sir Uvedale Price. Gilpin published his first book, *Essay on Prints,* in 1768 in which he explained the principles of 'picturesque' as he saw them in landscape paintings. During the late 1760s and 1770s, Gilpin travelled extensively and applied these principles to the landscapes he saw, committing his thoughts and sketches in his notebooks. He started *Observations on the River Wye* in 1770 and illustrated his tour with appropriate descriptions of the countryside that he passed through. However, by the time they were published, they were ten years out of date. Not only that, his sketches were not topographically accurate. This allowed him to comment critically and apply greater emphasis on his way of looking at the scenery and landscapes in picturesque terms:

After sailing four miles from Ross, we came to Goodrich castle where a very grand view presented itself and we rested on our oars to examine it. A reach of the river forming a noble bay is spread before the eye. The bank on the right is steep and covered with wood, beyond which a bold promontory shoots out crowned with the castle rising among the trees. This view, which is one of the grandest on the river, I should not scruple to call correctly picturesque, which is seldom the character of a purely natural scene.

Fosbroke's tour of the Wye in 1818 included a visit to Goodrich Court, built by Samuel Rush Meyrick for his private collection of military armour. The collection was available for public viewing every day and must have been high on the tourists' list for visiting. The Gothic-styled Court was by all accounts an awesome sight from the river, even more so was the ruined medieval castle on the adjoining headland. In his own account of his tour, Fosbroke wrote:

Crowning the summit of a bold promontory with a hanging wood beneath reaching to the water's edge and backed by Coppet Wood and other hills, it offers a most tempting subject to the pencil; nor are the other fronts of the Court less attractive.

At Monmouth, the Tudor antiquarian, John Leland, found it enclosed by a wall where it was not defended by the Wye or the Monnow:

But now, through age, the wall is broken and much of the defence is down. Nevertheless, extensive ruins remain along with a deep ditch. In the wall are four gates: Monk's Gate, East Gate, Wye Gate and Monnow Gate which is above the bridge crossing the Monnow.... And outside Monk's Gate is Archenfield.

It is generally accepted that a Roman military fort was established at Monmouth around AD 55 during the first advances against the Silures, making it the earliest Roman fort in Wales. Few remains have been found, but recent excavations suggest the fort was built close to the town centre. Evidence of iron workings dating from the Roman period have been discovered, suggesting they were drawing on sources from the local forests of iron ore and charcoal for smelting. Iron was still being produced and worked here in the 18th and 19th centuries.

The castle, originally an earth and timber ringwork fortress, was built by William FitzOsbern shortly after constructing his lordship base at Chepstow. Sited high above the confluence of the Monnow with the Wye, it also linked the Forest of Dean to the east, Celtic Gwent to the south and west and Saxon Archenfield to the north. The town developed primarily as a market town and an agricultural centre, rather than as a centre of industry. The wool industry was important in its early growth, and from the 15th century the town was a centre for the production of the very popular knitted and felted caps. These were eventually given the generic title of the Monmouth Cap and the district of Over Monnow where they were made was called Capper's Town.

Your majesty says very true: if your majesty is remembered of it, the Welshmen did good service in a garden where leeks did grow, wearing leeks in their Monmouth caps; which, your majesty knows, to this hour is an honourable badge of the service; and I do believe your majesty takes no scorn to wear the leek upon Saint Davy's day. (Fluellen, Shakespeare's *Henry V*)

However, Monmouth Caps did not exist at Agincourt. Shakespeare was stretching poetic licence by one hundred and fifty years or so. Much later, there were iron and tinplate works at Monmouth, together with paper and corn mills, and the town had become an important river port with warehouses and wharves along the River Wye. All these were eventually removed for the building of the A40 relief road.

When Henry Wyndham sallied into Monmouth in 1774, he was relieved to discover the town not yet overburdened with poverty:

Monmouth is a very large and handsome town; its streets are spacious and decently built; they are frequently adorned with good houses which are inhabited by families of fortune.

By the time of Charles Harper's arrival in 1893, boundary confusion agitated his desire for national fairness:

> This is the capital town of Monmouthshire, geographically and ethnologically a Welsh county but politically included in England. Yet, in the usual haphazard and erratic ordinances of the legislature, Monmouth is for some purposes English and for others Welsh. Judicially, it comes within an English assize circuit, but is included in the scope of the Welsh Intermediate Education Act; yet it is excluded from the operation of the Act for Sunday Closing in Wales. The county is thoroughly Welsh in religious sentiment and religious feeling, and in many districts, Welsh is the preferred language.

In the 20th century, Monmouth, like many other large towns of its day, was becoming overwhelmed by the motor car. John Hillaby, at one point saw the irony of the crowded town centre when he was here in 1968:

> In the cobbled Agincourt Square a host of little cars hooted and squealed as they tried to get out. All this takes place under a commemorative statue to that maker of almost silent engines, Charles Stewart Rolls,[49] who with his head on one side, seems to be wincing at the noise.

High above the statue of Rolls, standing in a niche of the Shire Hall, is Monmouth's noblest son, Henry V, the victor of Agincourt who was born in the castle and brought a fine set of French bells back to his birthplace. The story is that when he set sail for England after the siege of Calais, the citizens there celebrated his departure somewhat prematurely by a mighty peal of bells. On the deck of his galleon, the impetuous Hotspur heard the noise, turned back, and removed the bells which now hang in the tower of St Mary's priory church. At an unusual trial at the Shire Hall in

---

[49] In 1904, Rolls established a new car-making business with Henry Royce, but six years later he was killed in an aeroplane crash at the age of thirty-two.

November 1839, John Frost, Zephaniah Williams, and William Jones – all leaders of the Chartist movement – became the last men in Britain to be sentenced to be hanged, drawn, and quartered, after being found guilty of treason following riots in Newport that led to 20 deaths. Fortunately for the accused, the authorities decided such barbaric sentences deserved to be left in the past, and so they were condemned instead to transportation to Tasmania.

Within the site of the castle walls, Great Castle House is a handsome edifice of red sandstone built partly from the castle foundations. Once described as 'striking and a house of splendid swagger outside and in', it was constructed in 1673 for Henry Somerset, the 3rd Marquis of Worcester, who was at the time Lord President of the Council of Wales and the Marches. At the end of the 18th century, William Coxe recorded the house as being:

Occupied by Mrs. Elisabeth Tudor, mistress of the most respectable school for young ladies in this part of England. The apartments are commodious and well proportioned, and several stuccoed Ceilings, richly ornamented with wreaths and festoons of flowers, are not unworthy of notice.

Since the mid-19th century, it has been the Headquarters of Royal Monmouthshire Royal Engineers, and contains the Regimental Museum.

Hard by Leland's Monk's Gate was a Benedictine priory founded in 1075. Parts of the medieval monastic buildings remain, including an exceptional oriel window. Alongside these, St Mary's still serves as the parish and civic church for the town. Its tower of red sandstone dates from the 14th century, but the building deteriorated after the dissolution of the monasteries in 1536, and by the start of the 18th century was described as ruinous and decayed. Significant rebuilding was undertaken and a new spire, rising to a height of 60m (200ft), added later. But by the late 19th century, the church had to be completely rebuilt. At the eastern end of the churchyard is the gravestone of John Renie, an obscure local house painter who died in 1832 at the age of 33. It comprises a rectangular carved 285-letter acrostic puzzle that from the capital H on the centre square, the sentence 'Here lies John Renie' may be read in any direction, and it is claimed that the sentence may be read a total of 46,000 different ways. It is likely that Renie carved the stone himself, and it may well be that his intention was to confuse the Devil, so ensuring his passage to heaven. The gravestone was Grade II listed on October 8th, 2005, but in fact Renie's remains lie elsewhere. Also alleged to be buried here with a listed gravestone, is Charles Heath (1761-1831), a printer and writer who became a leading radical in Monmouth and was twice elected Mayor. The gruesome facts are that sometime during the mid-19th century, decaying parts of bodies were appearing above ground in the churchyard, so Monmouth Council decided to close it for burials and open a new cemetery on Osbaston Road, making it likely that the remains of John Renie and Charles Heath were moved there.

The name Geoffrey of Monmouth has for centuries been associated with the town. He was born around the beginning of the 12th century in the Welsh Marches, most probably in the Monmouth area, and he may have served as a monk for a while in the Benedictine priory, but most of his adult life appears to have been spent outside Wales. In his writings, always in Latin, he refers to himself as Galfridus Monemutensis, for the same reason as Gerald of Wales called himself Giraldus Cambrensis. It was then an accepted way of identifying with a place of birth or heritage. Geoffrey was thought to be a Welsh cleric, but there is doubt now as to this authenticity. Early scholars assumed that he was Welsh, or at least spoke Welsh, but there is no real evidence that he was either of Welsh or Norman descent, unlike Gerald who was born in Pembrokeshire of mixed Welsh and Norman parentage. It is likely that Geoffrey's parents were among the many Bretons who took part in the Norman Conquest and settled in the south-east of Wales. Monmouth had initially been held by a Breton lord, Gwethenoc, and it was under his lordship that the priory and church of St Mary were founded. It is accepted, however, that Geoffrey did become a major figure in the development of British historiography and the popularity of tales of King Arthur. He is best known for his chronicle *Historia Regum Britanniae, the History of the Kings of Britain*, widely popular in its day and translated into various other languages from its original Latin. Nowadays, although Geoffrey's work may be considered historically unreliable, his creations of the Merlin and Arthurian myths gained a popularity that lasts to this day. William Coxe recognised the weaknesses in Geoffrey's stories and may have had proof that they were indeed myths:

> We have, however, no need of any other argument than the confession of Geoffrey himself, who acknowledges that the *Historia* was not wholly a translation of the Welsh manuscript. He vows that he added several parts, particularly Merlin's prophecies and inserted some circumstances which he had heard from that most learned historian, Walter, Archdeacon of Oxford.

The first large building that meets the eye as you arrive at the junction of the A466 Wye Valley road with the A40 dual carriageway is the renowned Monmouth School. It is an independent boys' boarding and day school, founded in 1614 with a bequest from William Jones, a successful London haberdasher. The school is still run as a trust by the Worshipful Company of Haberdashers. Jones was brought up in Monmouth and his motivation for his generosity appears philanthropic but also evangelical. He demonstrated his desire to realign the religious doctrines of an area in the marches that was still strongly Roman Catholic. He also intended it to be a free school for local Monmouth boys, but the school's governing body was often embroiled in controversy as succeeding headmasters pursued a course towards fee-paying boarders. Today, the school provides boarding and day places as well as preparatory departments, but in a single-sex environment. However, in 1892, the Haberdashers' Monmouth School for Girls was opened on the Hereford road. Both schools are entirely fee-paying.

In 1937, the journalist and broadcaster, Stuart Mais, travelled to Monmouth from London by bus – continuing the method of transport he always favoured:

> When I made my first exploration of the Wye Valley, I went, unwisely, by a night bus from London to Monmouth. It was unwise

because the bus was full of Welsh unemployed miners, who sang 'All through the Night' all through the night. It was a memorable night in other ways. I saw the first streaks of dawn over the Cotswolds and I saw miners on their bicycles going on the shift in the Forest of Dean. The queer medley of woods and mines. It was just half past six when my fellow passengers roused the quiet Monnow Street of Monmouth with 'Land of My Fathers'. I was the only one to alight. I stood on the pavement hardly able to believe my ears, and I felt a pang of loneliness as I heard their voices gradually fade away under the Monnow Gate. Monmouth possesses a host of medieval inns where you will overhear the raciest story in the most vivid idiom. It's Hotel, the Beaufort Arms, is outstanding in comfort, in service, in good food and in cheapness.

While we are here, something should be said about inns. Many a traveller of old days, before say the late 18th century, had to put up with appalling accommodation compared to the high expectations of today. The cleanliness of rooms left much to be desired. In a visit to the town of Montgomery in 1784, the Rt. Hon. John Byng wrote in his Torrington Diaries:

> Here began a specimen of Welsh dirt; for my blankets stank so intolerably that I was obliged to use a quarter of brandy to sweeten them.

It would have been a common experience to stay in a room with dirt and dust covering the floors and furniture, the bed a haven for fleas, and the all-pervading scent of urine and excrement from poor or non-existent sanitation. Thin, wooden partitions, which often served as bedroom walls, were no defence against the noises of the house, adjoining properties, and surrounding streets. Bawling children and barking dogs would add to the general hustle and bustle. The standards of the day were as much as an inn owner was prepared to offer. Usually, that depended on his or her own ways of care and tidiness. There were no laws or consumer rights to which they could refer, no health and safety protecting authorities, no ombudsman services to complain to. Just take-it-or-leave-it basic fare. Some large, well established inns were good, certainly, for those with wealth or power, but mostly they were bad and ugly. For a period of about two hundred years from the mid-17th century, coaching inns served as a place of lodging for coach travellers. Inns began to cater for richer clients in the mid-18th century, and one of the first to offer much improved services in a modern sense was opened in Exeter in 1768.

Close to the bridge outside the Monnow gate is the little church of St Thomas the Martyr, which contains some Saxon stonework and a fine Norman arch. The Thomas in the dedication is Becket, murdered at Canterbury in 1170. It is known that this church was in use by 1186, but fifty years later it was seriously damaged by fire during a battle for Monmouth between supporters of King Henry III and baronial troops led by Richard Marshal, Earl of Pembroke. The following year, in a moment of royal pique, Henry ordered the constable of St Briavels to donate thirteen oak trees from the Royal Forest of Dean towards the repair of the church. By then, it had lost its importance and had become a satellite to St Mary's Priory Church. In 1543, Leland wrote:

> Beyond the Monnow Gate is a suburb in the diocese of Llandaff where once stood the parish church of St Thomas, but now is only a little chapel dedicated to the saint.

When Coxe visited St Thomas's at the end of the 18th century, he saw desolation and neglect. Major restoration work was carried out in 1830 by the prolific architect Thomas Wyatt on behalf of the Duke of Beaufort. He installed new pews and galleries made from oaks grown on the Beaufort estates, and rebuilt the west front in brick. Since then, there have been further restorations, including Wyatt's brick front replaced with one of red sandstone to match the rest of the building. It is hard to visualize how the original Norman construction would have looked, inside or out. Apart from the wonderful Norman chancel arch, there can be little left. The visual effect of this church is worth more now than its surviving original parts.

While Coxe was enjoying his stay in Monmouth, he wrote in praise of the open fields between the town and the Wye:

> The walks in the vicinity of Monmouth are extremely pleasant, particularly Chippenham meadow, which is a general rendezvous for company at the close of summer evenings. It is a flat oval plain, enclosed between the Wye, the Monnow, and the south side of town. At the south-eastern extremity, the Monnow falls into the Wye beneath a group of elms, which rise near the banks of the River Trothy. The meadow is skirted by gentle eminences feathered with underwood or clothed with hanging groves of oak and elm. These are surmounted by higher ridges of hills and mountains, all mantled with wood.

The Monmouth Races were an activity which all classes enjoyed. According to Keith Kissack in his book *Monmouth, The Making of a County Town,* from 1718 meetings were held on Chippenham Meadow and were accompanied by balls and assemblies in the presence of the Somersets. It is not clear when the racing moved to Vauxhall Fields on the other side of town, but by 1902 Monmouth Races had placed the town at the centre of the National Hunt Racing calendar until they stopped altogether in 1933, ending almost two hundred years of racing history here.[50]

Monmouth remained a relatively sedate and quiet small town for most of the 20th century. Although its passenger rail services ended in 1959, its road connections greatly improved following construction of the new A40 bypass that connected the town to the M4 motorway at Newport and M50 at Ross. These improved communications contributed to the development of the town, with suburbs extending beyond the rivers Wye and Monnow to the south-east, the west, and north of the old town centre.

---

[50] Chippenham Meadow is now a public park, registered by CADW as site of historic interest in Wales.

Monmouth to Tintern

On the eastern side of the river from Monmouth rises a significant hill known as the Kymin. On the summit, about 244m (800ft) above sea level, are two neo-classical monuments, the Roundhouse and the Naval Temple, built between 1794 and 1800. The Roundhouse was built by a group of principal gentlemen of Monmouth who called themselves the Monmouth Picnic Club, later renamed the Kymin Club. It was led by the town's Sheriff, Philip Meakins Hardwick, 'for the purpose of dining together and spending the day in a social and friendly manner'. The subscription list for funding was headed by the local landowner, the Duke of Beaufort, and eight Members of Parliament. The building was sited to take advantage of the views, and local antiquarian and publisher, Charles Heath, boasted that ten counties could be seen from the spot. The Naval Temple was constructed near to hand by the Kymin Club to commemorate the second anniversary of the British naval victory at the Battle of the Nile in 1798, and in recognition of sixteen of the British Royal Navy's Admirals who had delivered significant victories in other major sea battles around the world up to that date. It was dedicated by the Duchess of Beaufort. She was the daughter of Admiral Boscawen, one of those commemorated in the new building. William Coxe and Sir Richard Colt Hoare took advantage of being in Monmouth in 1798 to visit the summit:

> We ascended the Kymin, a high hill above Monmouth commanding an extensive view, where a Naval Temple (in very bad taste) has been erected to the memory of our naval heroes. Retired and shady walks affording some good views of the adjacent country have been cut in the woods adjoining. Parties of pleasure resort to this spot in summer where a house is opened to supply them with refreshment.

The sun had set before Gilpin's party arrived from Ross, so they made a new arrangement with their boatman and embarked again the next morning for Chepstow. In his writing, he continued the picturesque theme:

Pasturage not only presents an agreeable surface, but the cattle which graze it add great variety and animation to the scene. The meadows below Monmouth which run shelving from the hills to the waterside were particularly beautiful and well inhabited. Flocks of sheep were everywhere and herds of cattle occupying the lower ground. We often sailed passed groups of them leaving their sides in the water or retiring from the heat under sheltered banks.

Homely inns with honest country fare are the rule once the rambler leaves the deceptive fringe of the Wye below Monmouth, and anglers may be the only company one meets at these places. But there is no common ground between the angler and the pedestrian. The one spends a contemplative day with sophisticated devices for the due ensnaring of trout or grayling, and so home when evening falls to the 'Angler's Rest', or 'Fisherman's Retreat', whichever stands by the banks of his stream. The other is consumed with a raging thirst for many a mile, and none so pleased as when, after an exhausting itinerary of some twenty or thirty miles, he drops, all dusty and grimed, into the most comfortable chair of some village inn, where he may become the most grateful stranger. He may be Stuart Mais gazing through the open Inn door at the sylvan scenery beyond:

> The road, railway and river run side by side to the sea. Tree covered hills rise steeply on both sides of the winding Wye. There were many anglers wading in the wide waters, presumably in search of the famous Wye salmon. It was rather fun trying to guess round which of the many bends Tintern Abbey was going to appear. When it did, I was struck by its size, it's colour and the fact that it needed only a roof to be perfect. It is unsafe to leave buses till they put you down as far as they go. It is queer, in view of its size, to recall that the abbey was described as one of the poorest of all the abbeys in the fifteenth century and exercised no temporal or ecclesiastical power.

Five miles south of Monmouth, the ancient townlet of Trellech slumbers on a plateau above the west bank of the Wye. It's a small place in modern terms, but during the 13th century it was thought to be the third largest town in Gwent. The town's origins are hazy, but it is known that by the end of the 13th century there were 378 burgage plots recorded in, which would have made it bigger than Cardiff or Chepstow at the time. Then a disastrous raid In 1291 based on a frivolous disagreement by two local clan leaders left the town in ruins from which it never recovered. The Black Death struck in 1340 and again in 1350, and the ravages of Owain Glyndŵr and his men in the early 15th century further reduced any chances of recovery in the town's importance. Archaeological investigations to discover the medieval town commenced first In the early 1990s by the South Wales Centre for Historical and Interdisciplinary Research at the University of Wales in Newport. Then in 2005 a young archaeology graduate Stuart Wilson bought a field on what is now farmland, in which he was convinced were remains of the lost town. Wilson's subsequent excavations have indeed unearthed medieval walls which appear to be the remains he was searching for. The site along a minor road is some distance beyond where it was originally thought to be and would have been a surprise to the University team. In another field on the road to Tintern are three large stone monoliths – known locally as Harold's Stones – and an ancient water source that locals call the Virtuous Well continue to add flavour to the mystery and speculation about its secret past. During research for his *Southern Marches*, H.J. Massingham discovered that many of the stone structures had been cut from breccia quarries in the neighbourhood.

It is decidedly stone conscious, for the dry walling there is the best I saw out of Radnorshire, the farmhouses and bartons are very massive and the stones of the Virtuous Well of great age. But the real point about it is its fine church with a spire and an impressive Early English nave. There is a preaching cross of great antiquity in the churchyard, a floriated one within, a three-decker pulpit, some good tombs and 17th century altar rails with barley-sugar legs and a richly carved and embossed chest. But to me the choicest prize is the sundial erected by Lady Magdalene Probert in 1689. It stands on a double pedestal and its panels other than the dial face have carvings of the parish tumulus, the three monoliths and the Virtuous Well - a delightful example of parochial piety.

Below the plateau is the riverside village of Llandogo, where elevated woods cover the hillside above a bend in the river. Here, the Cleddon Brook falls 215 m (700 ft) down to the Wye. The waters of the brook, renamed locally as the Shoots, descend almost perpendicular from a grove of giant beeches, then down a rocky chasm through woodlands, carpeted in spring with primroses and windflowers among clouds of cherry blossom, and emerging at the bottom by a group of dark yews. Llandogo is a place of great age, being founded – according to the Book of Llandaff – by St Oudoceus, himself the Bishop of Llandaff in the 6th century, the village name being a reform of Llan Oudocei. The good bishop lived here in retirement by the Cleddon brook, and it was once thought that Gildas the historian was also living here on an island in the river. If it was true, Gildas' island would have been a dangerous place to be, as the river here is narrow and tidal. In winter, I have seen the high waters rushing down from Monmouth towards the sea carrying fallen trees and all manner of storm detritus. More likely that his island was Flat Holm in the Bristol Channel, some distance from the mouth of the Wye. Thomas Fosbroke wrote that Llandogo stands at the foot of a lofty hill, whose indented side is mantled with deep woods with cottages intermingled:

> In winter a cascade falls from the abrupt eminence. From hence the Wye becomes a tidal river and the result is that the translucent stream which has hitherto alternately reflected, as in a mirror, the awful projection of the rocks and the soft verdure of the banks, is affected by the influence of the tide and rendered turbid and unpleasing to the eye.

Until the 19th century, Llandogo was a river port and boat yard where flat bottom boats called Trows were built for trading up and down the Wye and the Severn and across the channel to Bristol. Wye quarries and brickyards required these barges to carry heavyweight freight to Avonmouth and Newport. The ironworks at Tintern also needed the Chepstow port for importing iron ore from Lancashire and exporting finished goods to foreign countries, as well as Bristol for the home market. The historic Llandoger Trow public house by the harbour in the centre of Bristol takes its name from these craft.

The philosopher, mathematician, and political activist Bertrand Russell was born in 1872 at Cleddon Hall in the heights above Llandogo. Russell was a prominent anti-war campaigner, and when war broke out in 1914 ended up in prison for engaging in pacifist activities. He famously wrote of his experience in his autobiography:

> I found prison in many ways quite agreeable. I had no engagements, no difficult decisions to make, no fear of callers, no interruptions to my work. I read enormously; I wrote a book, *Introduction to Mathematical Philosophy*... and began the work for *Analysis of Mind*.

Russell went to prison again in 1918 for publicly arguing against the US entering the war. Later in his life, he became an outspoken protagonist of nuclear disarmament and in September 1961, at the age of 89, Russell was jailed yet again for seven days in Brixton Prison for breach of the peace after taking part in an anti-nuclear demonstration in London. The magistrate offered to exempt him from jail if he pledged himself to good behaviour, to which Russell replied: "No, I won't." If he was unlucky to be interred for being an outspoken critic in less tolerant times, in October 1948 he was very lucky indeed, for an entirely unrelated reason. While en route to a lecture in Trondheim, Russell was one of twenty-four survivors of a plane crash. He said at the time that he owed his life to smoking, since the people who died were in the non-smoking part of the aircraft! Following his death on February 2nd, 1970, at his home in Penrhyndeudraeth in North Wales, in accordance with his will there was no religious ceremony, and after cremation his ashes were scattered over a Welsh mountain.

As far as I'm aware, no historian or media travel correspondent that has ever written of their experiences of Gwent/

Monmouthshire has missed the opportunity to include a visit to the great abbey ruins at Tintern. Maintained these days by CADW, the Welsh Government's environment service, the abbey has become the jewel in their crown. Grand though the view is of those ancient Cistercian stones, the site has become one of the great attractions for coach tours, day trippers, photography enthusiasts, and selfie addicts. But casual callers be warned. I recall an experience years ago when walking in the Yorkshire Dales and arriving at a similar tourist spot at Bolton Abbey on a bank holiday weekend, I have rarely seen so many people assembled in a place which wasn't a football ground. That day, a few young men had taken the opportunity to show off their expensive looking motor vehicles and their high-powered sound systems. The resulting cacophony echoing around the site was unbearable, and the attending stewards seemed powerless to stop it. Not that anything like that has happened at Tintern yet, but time will tell whether this grand historic site can cope with increasing demands of people and traffic.

Tintern Abbey was founded by Walter de Clare, the Lord of Chepstow, in 1131. It was only the second Cistercian foundation in Britain and the first in Wales. The monks who de Clare chose to settle at Tintern came from L'Aumône Abbey, at Citeaux in eastern France. They followed the strict Rules of St Benedict: obedience, poverty, chastity, silence, prayer, and, if that wasn't enough, hard work. The last monks left at the dissolution of the monasteries in 1536, at which time the roofs were taken down and the rest of the buildings left to decay and fall in time. In the 17th and 18th centuries, the ruins became inhabited by workers in the local wire works, and as more families moved into the area seeking employment, they built shelters within the ruins and lean-tos against the walls, both inside and out. When it became fashionable for tourists to discover the beauty of the Wye Valley, and particularly the picturesque ivy-clad abbey, there were bound to be conflicts of interest. Coxe recorded that his first appearance of the celebrated remains of the abbey church, did not meet his expectations as they were half concealed by other buildings, and the triangular shape of the gable ends had a too formal appearance:

After passing a miserable row of cottages, and forcing our way through a crowd of importunate beggars, we stopped to examine the rich architecture of the west front; but the door being suddenly opened, the inside perspective of the church called forth an instantaneous burst of admiration, and filled me with delight, such as I scarcely ever before experienced on a similar occasion.

Gilpin's view was stranger still. He decided the ruins weren't picturesque enough:

The eye is pleased with the tufting so of a tree if it rests with delight on the shattered arches of a Gothic ruin. Such objects, independent of composition, are beautiful in themselves, but the rock, bleak, naked and unadorned, seems scarcely to deserve a place among them. Tint it with mosses and lychens of varying hues and you give it degree of beauty. Adorn it with shrubs and hanging herbage, and you will make it more picturesque. Connect with wood and water and broken ground, and you make it in the highest degree interesting.

While Sir Richard Colt Hoare was employed in sketching the north-western side of the abbey building, Coxe crossed the river via the ferry and walked down the east bank for about half a mile along what is now the old railway bed. From this point the ruins assume a different character, and he saw them on a gentler eminence, standing above the river without the intervention of a single hovel to obstruct his view. The grand east window, then wholly covered with shrubs and half mantled with ivy, rose like the portal of a majestic edifice clothed in foliage. Through the opening and

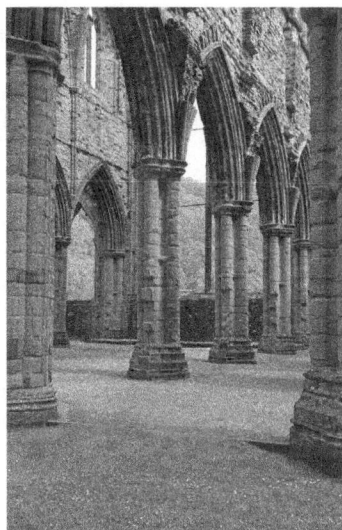

Figure 27 Ruined nave of Tintern Abbey

391

along the length of the church, the clusters of ivy twined around the pillars, or hung suspended from the arches, resembled clusters of small trees, while the thick mantle of greenery seen through the tracery of the west window appeared like an unending forest:

> The abbey looks well from the opposite side of the river. The building is here less covered in ivy, but its form is rather too straight and uniform and the beauty of the architecture not sufficiently discernible. But nothing can possibly exceed the beauty and elegance of the interior part of the building. The old ferryman remembers when the ivy was constantly cut and carried away for people to burn or feed to cattle in winter. He said that the clearing of the rubbish from the building cost the Duke of Beaufort £150. I wish he had still completed the improvement by removing the cottages and orchards round the building.

The Rt. Hon. John Byng also suggested in 1734 that the Somerset Beauforts should remove the cottages blocking the entrance to leave the abbey to stand backed by woods and open to the water, adding an improvement of his own:

> The way to enjoy Tintern Abbey properly, and at leisure, is to bring wines and cold meats, with corn for the horses. Spread your table in the ruins, and possibly procure a Welsh harper from Chepstow.

In 1842 William Makepeace Thackeray visualised *and* heard some natural additions to the holy scene:

> A number of choristers clothed in black are still to be found in the abbey church who exercise their throats all day long - a colony of jackdaws may be seen whistling round the abbey pinnacles and heard chattering always, their very noise somehow adding to the agreeable silence as you stand within and in a sort of happy wonder upon the ruins.

There is no question in my mind that any view of Tintern Abbey, whichever position one sees it for the first time, will remain forever in the memory. Whatever the atmospheric conditions, it is a stunning prospect. Massingham called it as it was, and as it is still:

> Can anything match the majesty of Tintern Abbey? Standing on its meadow within its screen of woods, it remains the most perfect symbol in stone of the triune hierarchy between God, man and nature anywhere in the marches.

In the 16th century, Britain was importing its needs for wire, especially for carding combs used for preparing raw wool for spinning. In 1566 a wire works was established at Tintern by William Humphrey, who until then had been at the Royal Mint in London. His decision bore fruit, as well as high levels of wire production, and within thirty years demand became so great that a second works was built further up the valley at Whitebrook. Iron for the wire was bought initially from Richard Hanbury's forges at Pontypool, but eventually the Tintern company recognised that they could produce all the charcoal they needed for smelting on their own doorstep, and so decided to build their own forge close to the wire works. By the middle of the 18th century, Tintern had become a smoky, heavy industrial centre, stretching two miles up the side valley of the Angidy river from its junction with the Wye. This surge in industrial activity at Tintern and elsewhere in Gwent increased the pressure on the county's roads, which were described towards the end of the 18th century as nothing better than wide ditches. They were ill-suited for heavy loads of coal and iron on horse-drawn vehicles. Charcoal was being used intensely the whole time, and the local forests were being devastated to a point that concerned Admiral Nelson, who needed oaks for his ships. He found it necessary to visit the Wye Valley to see for himself what could be done to maintain his supply.

Apart from the occasional howl of wood-cutting saws, the Wye Valley is probably more peaceful today than it has been for almost two hundred years. Until the end of the 19th century, there used to be iron works here, pouring out smoke, and many barges on the river carrying cider to the Severn and coal upstream. Local records tell of gangs of up to thirty men who pulled the heavy river craft up through the rapids, harnessed to ropes by chest-bands. To make any progress against the spring floods would have taken considerable effort and they were often obliged to crawl on all fours.

In 1971, one hundred and twenty-five square miles of the Wye Valley from Chepstow to north of Ross on Wye was designated an AONB, Area of Outstanding Natural Beauty. Nowhere along this stretch can be seen now at leisure from a railway carriage, in spite of there being at one time three branch lines merging at Monmouth. Then, trains from Ross and Monmouth followed the Wye through the same picturesque riverside scenery as Victorian boat tours until, emerging from the Tidenham tunnel above Chepstow, rail passengers would be suddenly presented with the breathtaking view of the broad Severn estuary. The old station and signal box at Tintern survive, having been faithfully restored as an exhibition centre and picnic site.[51]

As Charles Harper discovered towards the end of the 19th century, Monmouthshire trains rarely ran to the tourist tune, and a day trip to Raglan and return to Tintern in time for dinner was nigh impossible:

> There was, then, nothing for it but to walk the ten miles or so early in the morning and return by the afternoon train. The way across country from Tintern by way of Old Furnace, an almost entirely deserted hamlet that was once a busy settlement of wiredrawers and tin-plate workers. The road winds up the hillside with oozy moors and dark pine coppices on either hand, and a mountain stream splashes picturesquely among the lichen-covered rocks that crop up here and there from above the spongy turf, spangled with wildflowers and the nodding stems of tall foxglove. Here and there one comes upon ruined engine-houses and dilapidated ovens, overgrown and green with waving ferns, and banked-up reservoirs of water choked with duckweed and

---

[51] The Wye Valley line closed for passenger traffic on January 5th, 1959 and the iron bridge was dismantled. The old Tintern station building near the site of the bridge has been preserved as a refreshment and tourist centre.

populous with all manner of amphibious creatures. 'Tis many a long year since the waterpower of Old Furnace was in request and the hatches of the mill leets are rotting way with neglect.

The poet William Wordsworth visited the Wye Valley with his sister Dorothy in 1798 and took a boat down the river from Monmouth to Tintern, and such was the impression the scenery made on him, he penned one of his most remembered works, *Lines Composed A Few Miles from Tintern Abbey.* Cycling down the valley from Monmouth, Fletcher Moss and companion thought it lacked the great variety of hop yards and orchards of Herefordshire in which the last few days had quickly sped away. During their pilgrimages to old homes[52] they had sought out those where their predecessors lived and died and which the 'destroying hand of man or time' had spared:

> Where crowds of tourists go, we have shunned, but sometimes we erred. At Tintern we met with fashionable folk, the air resounded with jarring noises, irritating to our ears. Incongruous tourists unconsciously vex other senses, and we felt annoyed that we could not see Tintern's grey ruin in the peace and quiet of its wondrous beauty.

In his book, *Coming Down the Wye,* Robert Gibbings wrote:

> It was evening when I stepped ashore by the old Anchor Inn at Tintern, the evening of the harvest moon. On that night, in less prosaic times, lovers came from far and near to whisper promises to each other while, from the west end of the abbey, they watched the full moon fill the great empty circle in the head of the eastern window. The building was glowing in the evening light, warm as the rose-tinted walls of Petra. After sunset a shimmering veil of mist filled the valley, through which the church appeared tenuous and unsubstantial.

---

[52] *Pilgrimages to Old Homes* by Fletcher Moss was published in 1903

Tintern to Chepstow

Sandwiched between Chepstow Racecourse and the Wye flowing passed the Lancaut peninsular, is the Grade 1 registered Historic Park of the Piercefield Estate, one of the most outstanding examples of 18th century picturesque landscapes in Britain. In *Observations on the River Wye,* William Gilpin wrote in 1770:

> The situation of Piercefield Park is noble, and little indeed was left for improvement but to open walks and views through the woods, to the various objects around them. All this the ingenious proprietor hath done with great judgement, and hath shown his rocks, his woods and his precipices under various forms, and to great advantage. Sometimes a broad face of rock is presented, stretching along a vast space, like the walls of a citadel. Sometimes it is broken by intervening trees. In other parts the rocks rise above the woods; a little further they sink below them. Sometimes they are seen through them, and sometimes one series of rocks appears rising above another, and though many of these objects are repeatedly seen, yet seen with new accompaniments, they appear new. The winding of the precipice is the magical secret, by which all these enchanting scenes are produced.

In 1836, Thomas Roscoe described Piercefield as a beautiful example of landscape gardening, a ramble along the three-mile walk of Piercefield Terrace far less gratifying than the same distance would prove through a wild greenwood, or over breezy hills:

> But the way it gently undulates on one side and on the other descends precipitately into a deep vale, the thick majestic woods which encompass some portions of it give Piercefield a charm which makes it the Elan of Monmouthshire.

Piercefield House, or the remains of it, was previously a farmhouse before being bought in 1736 by Valentine Morris, who had made his fortune in the Caribbean from his sugar plantations. He commissioned Sir John Soane, an English architect who specialised in the Neo-Classical style, to build a new house on the site. But it was Morris's son, also named Valentine, who later had the grounds landscaped with additional viewpoints for the new tourists on the Wye Tour. Whatever improvements Valentine Junior had to make, the estate's profitability failed and he was forced to sell it. The purchaser, George Smith, a joint owner of the Monmouthshire Bank[53] didn't have any better luck. The bank failed in 1793 and Smith was ruined. Even before that drastic event, the Rt. Hon. John Byng wrote about the situation at Piercefield in 1774:

> I know not Mr Smith's income, but it is not a station of retirement, or for a man of small fortune being forever on an exhibition and in a glare, and so famed that an owner and his servants become showmen.

In 1802, the estate was bought by Nathaniel Wells, a man of mixed race and yet another beneficiary of the proceeds from Caribbean sugar. He became a well-respected figure around the county and in 1818 was appointed Sheriff of Monmouthshire. In 1861 Piercefield came into the ownership of Henry Clay, another banker who also owned a brewery in Burton-on-Trent, and the estate stayed with the Clay family until 1926. It was at that time that the Chepstow Racecourse Company became the new owners, since when the house has been left to deteriorate. It is now just a shell, much to the frustrations and anger of Chepstonians.

It is possible to cross Piercefield estate via a couple of footpaths which are rights of way, allowing access to Valentine Morris's picturesque walks and viewpoints along the route popular with the Victorian Wye tourists. William Thackeray was here in 1842 and afterwards recorded:

> At the foot of the Wyndcliff rock is a pretty little toy of a cottage, containing a huge walnut tree slab, being the section of an ancient tree that stood a few years back in the Chepstow castle moat and was blown down in a storm. The little rooms, seats, nay chandeliers, of this cottage are all gayly covered in moss, and the

---

[53] The other joint owner was John Curre of Itton Court near Chepstow.

cottage is hidden from the road in a thicket of laurels. Here parties may picnic at their leisure and passing it on the next day we heard issuing from the thicket the sound of a Welsh harp, a very old, feeble and unsatisfactory instrument that performed for a considerable period. This is Moss Cottage[54] that was built by the Duke of Beaufort as a picturesque feature.

In July 1875 the diarist Francis Kilvert travelled by train on a rare visit to the Wye Valley, but he thought it not a great success. Apart from his stop at Tintern Abbey, which he enjoyed, the weather turned foul, and having taken the coach from Tintern towards Chepstow, he disliked being enclosed and wished he had walked in the open:

> I was disappointed in the famous view from the Wynd Cliff. The weather was certainly not favourable for distant views, not a gleam of sunshine, a misty horizon, and rain driving up the Channel with the rising tide. The view may be fine and wide on a clear day but any view would be spoilt by the filthy ditch which they call the Wye in the foreground,[55] a ditch full of muddy water at the best of times, namely high water, but now a scene of ugly foreshore and wastes of hideous mud banks with a sluggish brown stream winding low in the bottom between. I thought the vast height of the Wynd Cliff itself with its grey crags peeping from amongst the thick foliage more imposing than the outlook from its top. I came down by its steps and was disgusted by the trick of the Moss Cottage in which, judging by the stench of the place, the inmates seem to be keeping a polecat or badger.

Above the site of Moss Cottage, at the top of the 365 steps to the crest of the Wyncliff rocks, is a viewing platform known as the Eagle's Nest, a vantage point to exceed all others. It was named by Victorian tourists who compared this popular spot to an eyrie. From it can be seen the river below on its way towards Chepstow,

---

[54] Demolished in 1952

[55] When the Wye tide is at its lowest, the river in places upstream becomes very shallow and may well resemble a muddy ditch. It looks as though Kilvert was unfortunate to catch it at such a time.

the estuary, and the two great motorway crossings. The clearer the day, the further the view which may stretch to the Cotswold Hills. The words of local author, Charles Heath, who described what he saw from here on a visit in 1801, have been reproduced on a public information board on display:

> Here let me pause as the eye surveys this terrestrial paradise, the winding of the river, the farm on the peninsular, the waving woods contrasted with the bare and ragged rocks, the town, the castle and the bridge of Chepstow, the splendid course of the Severn and the hills of Gloucestershire and Somerset.

Kilvert was unlucky, but I and others know what he missed. There is no longer a Moss Cottage, so we don't know what he saw there – or worse, what he smelled – but records show it would surely have been a case for the Health and Safety inspectors had they been around then.

His Wye tour over, Henry Wyndham chose to leave the Welsh shore by the Old Passage route:

> We completed our tour at Chepstow, and after reviewing with new pleasures the castle, the cliffs of the Wye, and the elegant remains of Tintern Abbey, we proceeded to the ferry house at Beachley; from whence the boat, with strong wind, wafted us across the Severn to Aust within the short space of nine minutes.

Thomas Roscoe caught a steam vessel for Bristol, with the intention of continuing his tour by taking the packet from thence to Tenby in South Wales the following morning:

> Proceeding steadily down the Wye, it was observable that the fair and clear mountain stream had changed to a broad and stately river. Picturesque cliffs flank her course on the left, displaying a curiously varied stratification and crowned with overhanging woods. Gliding smoothly on in the golden light of an autumn afternoon (for my wanderings had now extended from spring to the first month of that rich season of the year) I soon found the

river widening rapidly, and recognizing the Aust cliffs and the little ruined shrine of St Tecla on its island rock, I knew that the Wye here mingled her waves with those of her sister stream, the Severn.

On returning to Chepstow, the Rt. Hon. John Byng saw the quay stacked with immense piles of bark for exportation to Ireland and other merchandise for the continent:

> Incredible numbers of iron water pipes like cannon each nine feet long and weighing eight hundredweight which are going to France but whether for the Paris aqueducts or the Kings water works is not known.

As for the *Wild Wales* rambler, George Borrow, he went to the Beaufort Hotel, booked a private room, and ordered the best dinner which they could provide:

> Then leaving my satchel behind me I went to the castle, amongst the ruins of which I groped and wandered for nearly an hour, occasionally repeating verses of Scott's *The Norman Horseshoe*. I then went down to the Wye and drank the waters at its mouth, even as sometime before I had drunk of the waters at its source. Then returning to the inn, I got my dinner, after which I called for a bottle of port, and placing my feet against the side of the grate I passed my time drinking wine and singing Welsh songs till ten o'clock at night, when I paid my reckoning, amounting to something considerable. Then shouldering my satchel I proceeded to the railway station where I purchased a first class ticket, and ensconcing myself in a comfortable carriage was soon on the way to London, where I arrived at about four o'clock in the morning, having had during the whole of my journey a most uproarious set of neighbours a few carriages behind me, namely some one hundred and fifty of Napier's tars returning from their expedition to the Baltic.

At the end of his tour, rather than endure another crossing of the Severn by ferry, Sir Richard Colt Hoare decided to return via Gloucester and travel across country to his home at Stourhead.

Index

Page numbers in italics refer to illustrations. Those with the suffix 'n.' refer to information in the notes.

Where names are given in both English and Welsh, the English variation has been indexed. Churches, inns and hotels are indexed under their place name.

Personal names: nobility are indexed by title, names containing 'ap' or 'ferch' are indexed by first name.

All other names are entered by the last element. Kings and Queens refer to England unless otherwise stated.

www.ingramcontent.com/pod-product-compliance
Lightning Source LLC
Chambersburg PA
CBHW031938080426
42735CB00007B/172